HIGHLIGHTS *of the* *Catholic* FAITH

HIGHLIGHTS *of the* *Catholic* FAITH

REV. PETER V. ARMENIO

Midwest Theological Forum
Downers Grove, Illinois

Published in the United States of America by

MIDWEST THEOLOGICAL FORUM
4340 Cross Street, Suite 1
Downers Grove, IL 60515 USA
Tel: 630-541-8519 • Fax: 331-777-5819
www.theologicalforum.org

First Edition

ISBN 978-1-948139-84-7

Author: Rev. Peter V. Armenio
Managing Editor: Stephen J. Chojnicki
Contributing Editors: Renee Mota-Martinez; Constance J. Nielsen, PhD
Cover design: Jesus Cardenas

Acknowledgments

English translation of the *Catechism of the Catholic Church* for the United States of America copyright ©1994, United States Catholic Conference, Inc.—Libreria Editrice Vaticana. English translation of the *Catechism of the Catholic Church: Modifications from the Editio Typica* copyright ©1997, United States Catholic Conference, Inc.—Libreria Editrice Vaticana.

Scripture quotations are from the *Catholic Edition of the Revised Standard Version* of the Bible, copyright ©1965, 1966, National Council of the Churches of Christ in the United States of America. Used by permission. All rights reserved.

Disclaimer: The editor of this book has attempted to give proper credit to all sources used in the text and illustrations. Any miscredit or lack of credit is unintended and will be corrected in the next edition.

Nihil Obstat

Reverend John Balluff, S.T.D.
Censor Deputatus
September 21, 2022

Permission to Publish

Most Reverend Ronald A. Hicks
Bishop, Diocese of Joliet
September 23, 2022

The *Nihil Obstat* and *Permission to Publish* are official declarations that a book is free of doctrinal and moral error. No implication is contained therein that those who have granted the *Nihil Obstat* and *Permission to Publish* agree with the content, opinions, or statements expressed. Nor do they assume any legal responsibilitv associated with publication.

Contents

vii Abbreviations Used for the Books of the Bible

viii Abbreviations Used for Documents of the Magisterium

ix Preface

xi Introduction

1 Chapter 1:
God Reveals Himself

15 Chapter 2:
One God in Three Divine Persons

35 Chapter 3:
Creation and the Fall

49 Chapter 4:
Freedom and Happiness

63 Chapter 5:
The Moral Act

85 Chapter 6:
And the Word Was Made Flesh

105 Chapter 7:
The Paschal Mystery

129 Chapter 8:
The Holy Spirit

139 Chapter 9:
The Church of Christ

157 Chapter 10:
Christianity and the Common Good

203 Chapter 11:
Sacramental Contact with Christ

219 Chapter 12:
Baptism: New Life in Christ

239 Chapter 13:
Confirmation: Anointed in the Holy Spirit

253 Chapter 14:
The Holy Eucharist, God's Greatest Gift

285 Chapter 15:
Reconciliation and Renewal

307 Chapter 16:
The Anointing of the Sick

327 Chapter 17:
Marriage and Spousal Love

365 Chapter 18:
Marriage and Family

387 Chapter 19:
Holy Orders

409 Chapter 20:
Conversation with God

437 Chapter 21:
Conclusion

443 Suggested Reading

445 Thematic Index

449 Topical Index

Abbreviations Used for the Books of the Bible

Old Testament

Gn	Genesis
Ex	Exodus
Lv	Leviticus
Nm	Numbers
Dt	Deuteronomy
Jos	Joshua
Jgs	Judges
Ru	Ruth
1 Sm	1 Samuel
2 Sm	2 Samuel
1 Kgs	1 Kings
2 Kgs	2 Kings
1 Chr	1 Chronicles
2 Chr	2 Chronicles
Ezr	Ezra
Neh	Nehemiah
Tb	Tobit
Jdt	Judith
Est	Esther
Jb	Job
Ps	Psalms
Prv	Proverbs
Eccl	Ecclesiastes
Sg	Song of Songs
Wis	Wisdom
Sir	Sirach
Is	Isaiah
Jer	Jeremiah
Lam	Lamentations
Bar	Baruch
Ez	Ezekiel
Dn	Daniel
Hos	Hosea
Jl	Joel
Am	Amos
Ob	Obadiah
Jon	Jonah
Mi	Micah
Na	Nahum
Hb	Habakkuk
Zep	Zephaniah
Hg	Haggai
Zec	Zechariah
Mal	Malachi
1 Mc	1 Maccabees
2 Mc	2 Maccabees

New Testament

Mt	Matthew
Mk	Mark
Lk	Luke
Jn	John
Acts	Acts of the Apostles
Rom	Romans
1 Cor	1 Corinthians
2 Cor	2 Corinthians
Gal	Galatians
Eph	Ephesians
Phil	Philippians
Col	Colossians
1 Thes	1 Thessalonians
2 Thes	2 Thessalonians
1 Tm	1 Timothy
2 Tm	2 Timothy
Ti	Titus
Phlm	Philemon
Heb	Hebrews
Jas	James
1 Pt	1 Peter
2 Pt	2 Peter
1 Jn	1 John
2 Jn	2 John
3 Jn	3 John
Jude	Jude
Rev	Revelation

Abbreviations Used for Documents of the Magisterium

ANF *Ante-Nicene Fathers*. Buffalo, NY: Christian Literature Publishing Co., 1885.

CA St. John Paul II, Encyclical Letter on the Hundredth Anniversary of *Rerum Novarum, Centesimus Annus*. May 1, 1991.

CCC *Catechism of the Catholic Church* for the United States of America. Washington, DC: United States Catholic Conference, Inc., 1994; *Catechism of the Catholic Church: Modifications from the Editio Typica*. Washington, DC: United States Catholic Conference, Inc., 1997.

CIC *Code of Canon Law, Latin/English Edition* for the United States of America. Washington, DC: Canon Law Society of America, 1983.

CiV Pope Benedict XVI, Encyclical Letter on Integral Human Development in Charity and Truth *Caritas in Veritate*. June 29, 2009.

CoG St. Augustine of Hippo, *The City of God*. Edited by Marcus Dodds. 2014.

CSA St. Augustine of Hippo, *The Confessions of Saint Augustine*. Translated by E. B. Pusey (Edward Bouverie). 2013.

CPB St. Josemaria Escriva, *Christ Is Passing By*. Princeton, NJ: Scepter Publishers, 1974.

CPIG St. John Paul II, *General Audience* "By the Communion of Persons Man Becomes the Image of God." November 14, 1979.

DSFK St. Faustina Kowalska, *Diary of Saint Maria Faustina Kowalska: Divine Mercy in My Soul*. Stockbridge, MA: Marian Press, 2005.

EG Pope Francis, Apostolic Exhortation on the Proclamation of the Gospel in Today's World *Evangelii Gaudium*. November 24, 2013.

FT Pope Francis, Encyclical Letter on Fraternity and Social Friendship *Fratelli Tutti*. October 3, 2020.

GS Second Ecumenical Council of the Vatican, Pastoral Constitution on the Church in the Modern World *Gaudium et Spes*. December 7, 1965.

HBP James Socias, ed.. *Handbook of Prayers*, 8th American Edition. Downers Grove, IL: Midwest Theological Forum, 2019.

ID Bl. Pius IX, Apostolic Constitution on the Immaculate Conception *Ineffabilis Deus*. December 8, 1854.

LG Second Ecumenical Council of the Vatican, Dogmatic Constitution on the Church *Lumen Gentium*. November 21, 1964.

LS Pope Francis, Encyclical Letter on Care for Our Common Home *Laudato Si'*. May 24, 2015.

MD St. John Paul II, Apostolic Letter on the Dignity and Vocation of Women *Mulieris Dignitatem*. August 15, 1988.

NNFA Pope Francis, *Address to the National Numerous Family Association*. December 28, 2014.

OBap *The Order of Baptism of Children*. Washington, DC: United States Conference of Catholic Bishops, 2020.

OCM *The Order of Celebrating Matrimony within Mass* (Washington, DC: United States Conference of Catholic Bishops, 2016.

OCon *The Order of Confirmation*. Washington, DC: United States Conference of Catholic Bishops, 2016.

PH Sacred Congregation for the Doctrine of the Faith, Declaration on Certain Questions Concerning Sexual Ethics *Persona Humana*. December 29, 1975.

RMiss *Roman Missal*, Third Edition. Downers Grove, IL: Midwest Theological Forum, 2010.

RN Pope Leo XIII, Encyclical Letter on Capital and Labor *Rerum Novarum*. May 15, 1891.

SC Second Ecumenical Council of the Vatican, Constitution on the Sacred Liturgy *Sacrosanctum Concilium*. December 4, 1963.

STh St. Thomas Aquinas, *Summa Theologiæ*.

ThAv St. Teresa of Avila, *The Collected Works of St. Teresa of Avila*. Washington, DC: ICS Publications, 2011.

VS St. John Paul II, Encyclical Letter on Some Fundamental Questions of the Church's Moral Teaching *Veritatis Splendor*. August 6, 1993.

Preface

Upon reading the title of this book, an understandable first reaction might be to ask: "Why another book on the Catholic faith?" More than enough religion books of all stripes exist. If this book were written to simply cover the contents of the Church's dogmatic and moral teaching, of course, it would be superfluous. So, why this book?

I would answer by offering the two main aims of this book. The primary purpose of the *Highlights of the Catholic Faith* is to clearly present Jesus Christ as the absolute center of our Catholic faith. The reader will see, from the beginning, that the life of Christ is brimming with inexhaustible riches, ready for the taking. This book is not simply an intellectual exercise in what the Church teaches; it is a guide to the full life of discipleship based on the model of Christ and fueled by the graces of the Sacraments.

In contemplating Christ's life, there is no separation between belief, faith, and action. His divinity, teachings, and life of charity all form the unified Revelation of the incarnate Word of God. Some books will focus solely on one area such as the Trinity or moral teaching. The *Catechism of the Catholic Church,* on which the current book is based, is more comprehensive but orders the teaching of the Church according to three distinct areas—the Creed, the Ten Commandments, and the Sacraments. *Highlights of the Catholic Faith* seeks to integrate the dogmatic, moral, and sacramental teachings of the Church into a vision of a life lived in Christ that ultimately brings us happiness and teaches us how to love, leading to our eternal salvation. The various fields are not isolated as if the moral life were separate from faith in God or the sacramental life of the Church. The basic applications of the Ten Commandments are integrated into the appropriate tenets of Catholic doctrines and the Sacraments; thereby, they are better understood as the necessary conditions for authentic, deep discipleship.

Second, this work is meant to serve as a tool for bringing others to Christ through example and persuasive explanations—to provide both younger and older lay Christians with enough knowledge of the Catholic faith to evangelize family and friends. Many Catholics of good faith lack sufficient understanding of Church teaching to engage in discussions or answer questions about their faith. Most people may, regrettably, be unaware of basic principles: that Jesus Christ is our God and Savior, that he is truly present in the Eucharist, and that the goal of the Christian life is perfection in charity. Even more difficult, many do not understand how the moral teachings of the Church are not a limit on freedom but rather a blueprint for how to preserve and defend the dignity of the human person and how to authentically love. To spread this message requires education. A resource that provides a clear understanding of the meaning of the Gospel will enable the modern Catholic to implement Pope Francis's evangelical teaching on attraction, encounter, and accompaniment. In addition to attracting people to Christ by giving witness to his love, the Christian disciple should be ready to give cogent explanations of the Catholic faith's teachings.

The origin of this initiative to produce a book based on the *Catechism* was spawned by widespread clamor, especially among the young, for a complete overview of Catholic teaching. In my pastoral work over the years, I have frequently noticed an ardent desire for spiritual renewal manifested in Eucharistic Adoration and the recitation of the Rosary. This phenomenon implicitly reveals a hunger to know and understand the basic components of Catholic belief. This quest for deeper spiritual life must go "hand and glove" with a substantial knowledge of the contents of the *Catechism*. Knowledge of doctrine closely linked with spiritual piety will ensure that Catholic identity will sink deep roots into the heart of the disciple of Christ. It certainly is my hope that this commentary on the *Catechism* will draw readers to a greater friendship with Christ through love of the Word of God coupled with reception of the Sacraments.

This book is ideally meant to implement those powerful words of the first Pope, St. Peter, when he said: "Always be prepared to make a defense to any one who calls you to account for the hope that is in you."[1] Perhaps, in its own small way, this work will function as a loudspeaker in proclaiming the Good News of Jesus—that God loves each one of us, has a plan for our happiness, and "has purchased for us the rewards of everlasting life."[2]

Rev. Peter V. Armenio, PhD

1. 1 Pt 3:15.
2. "Litany of the Blessed Virgin Mary," in HBP, 421.

Introduction

As the title indicates, this book is meant to highlight the main tenets of Catholic teaching so wonderfully expressed in the *Catechism of the Catholic Church*. The contents of theology contained in this unique resource, which was literally a project of the entire Church, has the clear stamp of divine intervention. First, this handbook of Catholic thought transmits the basics of Catholic teaching spanning more than two millennia. Second, during the time of its production, the *Catechism* pooled input from theological insights, pastoral suggestions, points of emphasis, and cultural considerations from the Church around the globe. Virtually all the bishops of the Catholic Church, from diverse nationalities and cultures, contributed to this monumental project whose purpose is to make more accessible the whole body of Catholic teachings in the spirit of the Second Vatican Council. The *Catechism* represents both the mind and the will of the entire Church. In short, the message of the *Catechism* is universal, embracing every age and culture.

Given the way the *Catechism* was composed, it can be confidently argued that the Holy Spirit had a major hand in its composition. Any statement coming from the Church through its bishops and Pope enjoys special enlightenment and assistance from the Holy Spirit. If someone desires to know the Church's position on any issue or topic regarding faith or morals, the *Catechism* is the most reliable resource. If someone determines to read it cover to cover, he or she is struck by its marvelous unity and thoroughness despite so much varying and diverse input that reflect particular cultural needs. The whole work beautifully hangs together as if there were just one author.

While the *Catechism* is a most impressive compilation of Sacred Scripture, the writings of the Early Church Fathers, and the best of pastoral and mystical theology, it certainly is not a mere collection of two-thousand-year-old facts. It is a well-developed game plan leading to conversion and transformation in Christ. It is a learning tool that should lead to the formation of both a mindset and a lifestyle. If these teachings are learned and lived, the result is holiness that will mirror the face of Christ.

The "elephant in the room," though, is the huge chasm between the fine-tuned instruction in the official *Catechism* and the average

Catholic's actual knowledge. For a variety of reasons, there is a general lack of familiarity with the basic tenets of the Catholic Church despite the colossal effort to write and distribute the *Catechism*. Without any ill intent but due to insufficient doctrinal exposure, many professed Catholics are unaware that Jesus Christ is God and the ultimate meaning of human life. Many Christians regard Christ the way a historian might esteem a great political leader or a pianist revere Mozart. Weak education in the Catholic faith deprives many of the "too good to be true" knowledge that Christ heals and renews anyone who seeks his mercy in the Sacrament of Penance and Reconciliation or that he is fully and truly present in the Eucharist, and that through the Sacraments he wishes to bring us happiness, joy, and peace.

This knowledge is life-changing. Once, a young man who was being gently corrected for not genuflecting in front of the tabernacle in a chapel retorted that there was no ostensible reason to genuflect. When asked what he understood about the Eucharist, he replied that it was a mere symbol of gathering people together. He was instructed to study the theology of the Holy Eucharist, and he dutifully did. After diligent reading, he was discovered kneeling in front of the tabernacle. When kindly asked why he was on his knees, he explained his amazing discovery that Christ was truly present in the tabernacle, and silent adoration is the appropriate response. This sort of reaction is not infrequent after a fresh discovery of some fascinating truth of the Catholic faith. It is tragic that this treasure trove of rich truths, meant to impact daily life and promise true happiness, remains unknown to so many people of good will.

This oblivion to Catholic truths is also reflected in widespread misunderstanding of the Church's moral teaching. Knowledge of objective moral laws and how to practically apply them to human behavior are absolutely crucial to leading a dignified, fulfilled life. Embracing the Ten Commandments, for instance, leads to self-control and freedom—conversely, violating and rejecting the moral law leads to disillusionment and enslavement. Many people carry emotional and psychological wounds caused by sin, which is often the result of ignorance of the moral law. A greater knowledge and understanding of moral principles interpreted by the Church ultimately leads to wholeness and interior peace. Ancient philosophers, such as Plato and Aristotle, introduced the idea that virtue leads to happiness and fulfillment. In this vein, these ancient thinkers accord with the Old Testament by asserting that a truly fulfilled life depends directly on consistent moral behavior, inspired by objective moral standards. In significant part, the *Catechism* explains moral laws required by human nature that were known long before the dawn of Christianity.

Philosophy built on reason, and even the wisdom of the Old Testament, does not come close to the beauty of what Christ revealed or the redemption that he has won for us. Another important incentive for studying the *Catechism* is its profound penetration of the life and words of Jesus Christ, who promised his Apostles and their successors divine guidance for the instruction of all people until the end of time. In formulating the *Catechism* under the guidance of the Holy Spirit, the Church has designed this work to attract people to Christ through a greater understanding of his teaching.

Learning the Catholic faith should never be viewed as a mere academic exercise to accumulate theological facts or simply to get "the straight scoop" on official Catholic doctrine. Jesus Christ, the Savior of the world, did not come to communicate interesting religious facts and original insights; rather, he calls every disciple to conversion and holiness. Christ's teaching, interpreted and transmitted through the Catholic Church, has as its aim the replication of Jesus' life in the order of love. The goodness, kindness, and mercy of Christ will be reflected in the life of the Christian to the degree that he or she will act on the grace that he or she has been given by putting into practice the rich variety of truths put forth by the *Catechism*. Theological knowledge, regardless of its intrinsic value and profundity, does not make someone a better person unless it influences his or her attitude and behavior. A Catholic education, if it does not serve the purpose of instilling virtue, becomes a stagnant body of knowledge that has as much relevance to personal life as a calculus course. Everything contained in the *Catechism* must be "incarnated" into dispositions, sentiments, and action that reflect the life of Christ.

For the dogmatic, sacramental, and moral teaching of the Catholic Church to have bearing on a person's personal life, it must first be learned. A bit of popular wisdom derived from classical philosophy—that one cannot love what one does not know—applies in spades to the teachings of the *Catechism*. A good Christian, thus, can become immersed in God and replete with charity by following the road map of the *Catechism*. In the process of attaining personal union with Jesus Christ through an established theological roadmap, the individual can embrace personal fulfillment and true joy. It is no accident that the very first description of Jesus Christ at his Birth was "good news of a great joy."[1] It is vital that the teachings of the *Catechism* be seen as a body of truths that ultimately describe the Good News of Christ. St. Jerome, the great father of the Church who first translated the Bible into Latin—the vernacular language of his day—wrote that ignorance of Scripture is ignorance of Christ. By extension, that same ignorance can be applied to gaps in the knowledge of the basic truths of Church teaching.

The *Catechism* elaborates thoroughly (though not exhaustively) on every facet of Catholic teaching; for many people, however, this rich assortment of truths remains "buried in the ground." Even the essentials of the *Catechism* are missing from the intellectual repertoire of most modern Christians. Given the inestimable value of the contents of the Church's teachings, the norm should be that most lay Catholics are well acquainted with it. If they readily know the names of athletes and actors and are familiar with trendy songs, movies, and TV programs, which are of only passing value, it should make sense that people would be more conversant with immutable truths that lead to eternal life. This book, therefore, is meant to be a "user-friendly tool" to make the Catholic faith more accessible and widely known.

The Catholic faith, in too many instances, is one of the best kept secrets; this book aims to let as many as possible in on the secret. I hope that it can serve as a convincing invitation for the reader to appreciate the Catholic faith, which is meant to have a positive impact in all aspects of human life, through a better understanding and appreciation of the inexhaustible riches of Jesus Christ.

Highlights of the Catholic Faith is not another *Compendium* or replication of the *Catechism*, nor does it strictly follow the *Catechism* in its organization. The *Catechism* proceeds systematically through three sections on the Creed, the Sacraments, and the Ten Commandments. This book presents the material in a less linear way, illustrating how these three areas of Catholic teaching work together in an

1. Lk 2:10.

integrated Christian life. Though this book will discuss the doctrinal, sacramental, and moral aspects of the Catholic faith, the unifying thread is the love of the one true God incarnate in Jesus Christ, the Son of God. Analogous to the saying that "all roads lead to Rome," all truths of the *Catechism* ultimately lead to God the Father through Jesus Christ by the power of the Holy Spirit. The Catholic faith, thus, must not be seen as a series of dogmas as much as truths pointing to the divine life of the Blessed Trinity through Jesus Christ.

The first part opens with the tenets of the Creed that involve the act of faith in the existence of God as a Trinity of Persons. From this starting point, the discussion turns immediately to the human person, who was created by God for happiness but tragically wounded by the effects of the Fall and Original Sin. The story of human existence continues with the loving intervention of God, who sent his only Son to liberate fallen humanity from sin and death with the offer of redemption through the life, Death, Resurrection, and Ascension of Christ. This section culminates in the institution of Christ's Church on earth and her mission to transform the entire world according to the plan of God.

The work of transforming the world is no easy task, and it is not God's ultimate plan. The final purpose of the redemption that Christ won for us is that every person be saved and live in eternity with God. To achieve this purpose, Christ instituted the Sacraments to impart his grace, strengthen us in this life, and make us holy. The second section covers the Seven Sacraments, highlighting the special grace that each one offers to arm us against sin and self-destruction, to embolden us to live a life of charity in service to others, and to prepare us to be with God in heaven by making it possible for us to love as Christ loved.

My hope is that this presentation, in addition to offering a summary of the teachings of the *Catechism*, will aid people in understanding that the dogmatic and theological teachings of the Catholic Church, which are the teachings of Christ, are not simply academic and theological hair-splitting. These truths have a profound impact on how we live, which in turn pave the way to a more humane, just society. The answers to the big questions—Where do we come from? What is our purpose? Where will we go in the end?—form and shape who we are and how we live. The answers can only be found in the love of God, revealed in Jesus Christ, his Son.

I further hope that, having been informed, the reader will be inspired to evangelize. For this reason, this book is aimed at lay Catholics because they are presently called to carry the lion's share of teaching the Gospel message to others. Amid a general loss of Christian culture and ethos, it is urgent that the lay faithful are doctrinally prepared to effectively contribute to a broader knowledge of the Catholic faith starting with family, friends, and colleagues. Just as in the primitive Church, when lay Christians bore a big part of the burden of evangelizing a hostile and pagan world, today's lay Catholics are once again called to give an encore of what their first-century Christian brothers and sisters accomplished.

The lay Catholic—in a workplace or schoolyard, on a sports field, at home, or at a party—might be the only contact someone has with Catholicism, so he or she needs to be "on top of their game" regarding Catholic teaching. These fraternal exchanges cannot be reduced to quick responses; rather, they should be the fruit of diligent study of doctrinal truths that are especially pertinent to the circumstances of modern culture. In many instances, a friend or colleague will be the only vehicle through which the contents of Catholic faith will be communicated. Given the general absence of doctrinal and moral knowledge of Church teaching forged by centuries of wisdom and reflection on the Gospel, lay people need to pick up the baton and spread the faith.

Too many opportunities are missed because the nurse, the hairdresser, the teacher, the accountant, the mom, or the dad were not able to give convincing answers to why Jesus Christ is the meaning of human life and therefore the exclusive source of everlasting happiness. The usual setting to teach the contents of the *Catechism* should be amid the hustle and bustle of the workplace and family life.

A certain barber who took time to learn his faith has had scores of opportunities to enlighten his customers on the Christian faith while cutting their hair. In the course of his work and relationships, he has helped people give serious consideration to the Catholic faith due to both his witness and fine explanations of different areas of Catholic theology. In another case, a college undergraduate explained some of the basic points of the *Catechism* to his non-Christian roommate, who converted and later entered the Catholic

Church. These special anecdotes should not be the occasional exception but a common occurrence.

This book also draws from sources outside of the *Catechism*. There is a focus on current problems facing Christians who are determined to live a moral life in Christ; its goal is to bring the teaching "down to earth" and to show its practical value for daily life. This book also draws from the broader wealth of Catholic teaching, especially from St. John Paul II's emphasis on the dignity of the human person and on the self-giving example of Jesus Christ. As he was the Pope who spearheaded the mission to create the *Catechism*, this book incorporates the immense treasure of the teaching of St. John Paul the Great. Besides being Pope, no other modern theologian has done more to explain the Gospel to the modern world and unpack the teachings of Vatican II for the New Evangelization. Other modern holy men and women are explored as witnesses to a life lived in Christ, including St. Josemaria Escriva, St. Maria Goretti, Bl. Carlo Acutis, and St. Giuseppe Moscati. This book will be an obvious success if its description of the rudiments of the Catholic faith prompts the reader to explore more assiduously the inexhaustible and rich teachings of Jesus Christ, beginning with a study of the *Catechism* itself.

This book will also have accomplished its purpose if the reader becomes enamored of Catholic teaching and experiences life-changing results. In the spirit of the writings of the recent Popes, it is highly recommended to implore assistance from the Holy Spirit for both a love and understanding of the Deposit of Faith, which traces back to Christ himself. For anyone genuinely interested in living and teaching the Catholic faith, serious study—though vital—is insufficient. There must be a firm commitment to developing a spiritual life in addition to the intellectual endeavor of learning the contents of the *Catechism*. Spiritualizing one's study of the faith will involve mulling over all the doctrinal points in the presence of God and at the same time clamoring for enlightenment from the Holy Spirit. May the contents of the *Catechism* explained by this work bring about a deeper love for the Gospel and a sense of urgency to attract as many souls as possible to the saving power of the Catholic faith.

CHAPTER 1

GOD REVEALS HIMSELF

The overarching reason why theology is a science of unlimited scope rests on the reality that the infinite God is self-revealing. He desires to reveal himself to those he has lovingly created. By forming a people from which would come the divine Redeemer, God, amazingly, also created a means to communicate through the medium of human language—whether through his prophets or his own Son-made-man. Yet, throughout a major part of the history of humankind, divine self-disclosure has been consigned to the vast wonders of the created world.

God first reveals himself by leaving telltale signs of his presence in the grandeur of the universe. The created world serves as an information center about the attributes of God since the work performed communicates much about the worker. In this sense the created world presents a quest for God whereby human beings find signs of truth, goodness, and beauty, ultimately leading to an incomprehensible supreme being. The beauty, immensity, and rich variety of the universe have easily led many to the realization that God exists and that he created and governs the universe with care. Creation can be likened to a magnificent work of art that points to the presence of a loving, powerful God.

All of creation is stamped, as it were, with the signature of infinite intelligence. The well-choreographed ecosystems, with their intricate growth cycles and complex interdependence, point to a divine event planner. Such organization suggests an overarching intelligence that manifests itself through sophisticated, fine-tuned engineering laced with high-level mathematical logic. The harmonious order (on both an astronomical and subatomic level) reveals that there must be an infinite, all-perfect being responsible for everything that exists. Such order does not merely form out of chaos.

The fact that scientists can carry out highly specialized experiments and make stunning discoveries with logical explanations depends upon a universe run by predictable laws. This realization enables the human intellect to spontaneously perceive the virtual presence of an intelligent being behind it all. Everyone who engages in any type of learning—whether the artificial intelligence of computer science or a simple study of gardening—is reminded that God has left a mark of his presence that is easily "picked up" by human reason.

The order and vast wonder of the universe coupled with the world's beauty speak of an intelligence who arranged all things and presented them as a gift suited to the human person. The human person marvels at nature's beauty and realizes that it must come from somewhere. The breathtaking splendor of snow-capped mountains complemented by a blanket of shimmering evergreens under a bright sun bespeaks a magnificently powerful divine artist. Considering both the beauty and the order of the universe—from the orbiting stars of a galaxy to the function of a single cell—the world can be likened to an elaborate, extensive symphony orchestra that plays exquisite music and requires a single conductor.

Based on the instinctive connection between the order, harmony, and beauty of the universe and the idea of divine intervention, the human person can rationally deduce God's existence. Both ancient and Christian philosophers have come up with proofs of the existence of God through rational demonstration. It is in the realm of observation and common knowledge that every being finds the reason, or cause, of its existence in something else that already exists. For something to come into existence, there must be something else that precedes it that causes the existence of a new entity. A tomato plant exists because a previous tomato plant produced the tomato seeds. The string of causes cannot go back to an infinite number of causes because we would never get to the present being in question. It would be intellectually dishonest to simply refuse to try to rationally explain how things came into existence in the first place. The existence of the universe finds its ultimate explanation in a transcendent cause, or first mover, that enjoys infinite perfection. This infinite perfection must include an eternal existence, not caused by another, and limitless power, not gained from another. Both Aristotle and St. Thomas Aquinas concluded that there must be a "prime mover" or an "uncaused cause," a creator that is not himself created, whom we call God. As St. Paul wrote of the Gentiles, who did not know God's self-Revelation to the Jewish people, "What can be known about God is plain to them, because God has shown it to them. Ever since the creation of the world his invisible nature, namely, his eternal power and deity, has been clearly perceived in the things that have been made."[1]

God's existence can be proven not only in terms of cosmological phenomenon but also through the discovery of an objective moral law spiritually written on the human mind and heart. (The heart represents the innermost part of the human person.) St. Paul also wrote of the Gentiles that "what the law requires is written on their hearts" and that "their conscience also bears witness."[2] The awareness of innate moral standards expressed in clear internal criteria points to a divine Lawgiver. It is of universal acceptance that it is wrong to kill, steal, lie, insult, etc. Love for family and friends and just, truthful dealing with others form part of the moral law that is written on the tablet of the human heart. If someone so much as accidentally steps on someone else's toe, he or she is inspired to apologize. Done on purpose with no apology, it would cause a reaction, perhaps a violent or even a legal one. What causes such apologies, or defensive responses? Why do we all seek to make amends or feel justified to demand them? Why do we seek justice in the world for ourselves and for others? It is because every human person carries, within the recesses of his or her heart, objective standards of morality independent of nationality, age, or culture. St. Augustine states that this intuition of what is morally right and wrong proves the existence of God since that ability for moral discernment did not just appear out of nowhere. These interior, shared moral standards point to a divine legislator who universally issues the same principles of morality for everyone; therefore, the contents of the moral law found in the recesses of the human heart form part of God's self-disclosure.

A study of the created world can lead to not only God's *existence* but also some of his *attributes*, including God's love for humanity. Even without the explicit communication that marks Sacred Scripture, God reveals that he infinitely loves the human person. In the process of learning about the intricacies of one's surroundings—the attraction of the world in its beauty; the power that the human person has to understand, dominate, and make use of the things of the earth; the special place of the human person within the world—a person begins to realize that the world was ordered for the well-being of humankind. The question that creation prompts

1. Rom 1:19–20.
2. Rom 2:15.

us to raise is, "How did all this happen?" These amenities did not appear spontaneously but have been provided by a divine and loving owner. God's love can be discerned if one compares the world to a home left for a visitor who happens to find food in the cupboard and refrigerator, comfortable furniture, a nice bed, and a pleasant temperature. God arranged the world for the enjoyment and thriving of all people, who receive it as a pure gift.

This is not to reject the scientific theory of evolution or any other theory of how, historically speaking, such aspects of this glorious world came to be. Natural processes are always open to scientific inquiry. It is only to acknowledge that—however the world has historically been shaped over time—God is the source of being and the divine Planner. A theory of evolution that insists on random events sprung from chaos as the only explanation for this remarkably ordered universe may be incompatible with the existence of a divine Creator, but there is no reason why faith in God as the Architect must reject a scientific study of how things came to be. This has particular bearing on the dignity of the human person. As Pope Benedict XVI explained, "We are not some casual and meaningless product of evolution. Each of us is the result of a thought of God. Each of us is willed, each of us is loved, each of us is necessary."[3]

There is also evidence of God's existence in the fact that the human person is naturally a religious being. Throughout human history virtually every culture, whether intellectually sophisticated or not, has exhibited strong religious sentiments. In part, this is the result of the human response to the marvels of the natural world. It was common among ancient groups of people to worship created things such as the sun, earth, and water since the emergence and the sustenance of life was intimately linked to these elements. By reflecting on its own thought process and capacity to choose and love, the human mind also grows to understand that existence is not only limited to the material world but also embraces the mysterious world of the spirit. Though often born of much ignorance, and sometimes including outright immoral practices, ancient pagan religions demonstrate an acknowledgment of the need to be grateful for the goods of the earth, and they regard a world of the spirit as its source. In nearly every culture, religious ceremonies and customs accompany special times in a person's life such as birth, marriage, and death.

3. Pope Benedict XVI, *Homily*, Mass to Inaugurate His Pontificate (April 24, 2005).

Spiritual practices are in many instances aimed to ward off evil and obtain blessings and protection. Even though most people of the ancient world engaged in idolatrous cults across many centuries, this still universally attests to the fact that an inherent part of the human condition is the exercise of some form of religion.

It is only in recent times that individual people have opted for an atheistic view regarding their origin and that of the world. They deny the existence of God, in many cases with a certain alacrity, as if this denial were itself a religious truth. In some academic circles a person might well be denigrated for associating God with any scientific finding. Once, in a lab where biological research was taking place, one of the scientists declared that the beauty of their fascinating discoveries pointed to the existence of God. Unfortunately, a colleague reacted by stating that any kind of religious comment or metaphysical conclusion had absolutely no place in that laboratory. It makes no reasonable sense to reject a priori the logical conclusion of divine intervention for the simple reason that the intervention is divine. It would certainly be within the realm of scientific integrity that knowledge of the scientific world would lead to an openness to the possibility of an intelligent creator.

Possible reasons for atheism in the face of cogent, compelling evidence for proof of the existence of God are complex and various. The presence of evil and its consequent tragic suffering cause some to reject explanations that include a benevolent God. How could an all-powerful and all-loving God allow such tragedies to occur? Though the reality of so much evil and human suffering will never be totally understood, the free will to reject God and his life-giving laws certainly plays a major role in producing so much anxiety and strife. The universe in its beauty *was* created by a loving God in an orderly way for the good of humanity, but since God has gifted the human person with the *freedom* to love him and obey his laws, there exists also the prospect of abusing that freedom through the rejection of God and his laws.

Another common reason given for atheism and agnosticism is the inordinate indulgence of sensual desires. A carnal life, focused entirely on physical pleasure, severely dulls the mind and heart's capacity for a spiritual life and the proper exercise of conscience. The human mind tends to rationalize and excuse personal wrongdoing by disagreeing with the tenets of the natural law or professing that God does not even exist as a way of justifying an immoral or self-indulgent act or lifestyle. When the moral law loses its validity and force in one's personal conduct, God is often simply taken out of the equation. It is hard to accept the objective moral standards of the Ten Commandments—let alone that they are revealed by God—if a person feels that he or she can create a morality tailored to the passions. With so many violations of conscience, which is meant to be inspired by the natural law, it is not uncommon that God is considered totally irrelevant or, worse, his existence is called into question. Simply put, sinfulness without repentance calls for a self-rationalization that demands liberation from a guilty conscience, which ultimately leads to categorically denying God's existence.

God, however, never ceases to reach out to his people, to communicate his plan for a loving relationship with his children ordered toward their happiness and fulfillment.

Divine Revelation

God reveals himself through the grandeur, beauty, and goodness of both the material world and the richness of the human spirit. This divine presence—whether seen from the vantage point of material creation, human experience, or the discovery of the moral law—is the fruit of natural reason. Natural reason, though, can only go so far in knowing about the inner life of God and his plan for humankind. A finite mind cannot find its own way up to the infinite; the infinite must come down to it. God in his infinite goodness and wisdom chose to reveal himself and his will directly through verbal communication. The contents of these Revelations span millennia, and they include truths both accessible to and beyond the capacity of human reason.

Much of the moral content of Divine Revelation can be discovered through the light of reason. For this reason, most cultures have devised similar codes of law and morality; however, the human mind and will are handicapped due to the effects of Original Sin. Human beings can, as noted above, perceive a common moral law, but sin clouds human judgment and hinders the ability to perceive what is good. For this reason, most cultures are also marked by gross violations of human dignity. Considering the inherent weakness of the human condition, God has spoken through his prophets and in a spectacular way through his Son to ensure that there be no ambiguity regarding his will for humanity.

More than just the moral law or his very existence, God wanted to communicate his divine life with the intention of adopting every person as a child of God. In human relationships, one person comes to truly know another only by communicating and thereby revealing his or her own inner life. Through Divine Revelation God gives every human person knowledge of himself and the possibility for a personal relationship that goes beyond his or her natural capacity.

This work of supernatural self-communication was done gradually and in stages. God first made himself known when he created man and woman. He conveyed to them his will and blessed them with special graces and gifts. Though our first parents disobeyed God, by which sin was brought into the world, God continued to reveal himself through a series of covenants that would become more elaborate. God promised his blessings and protection for those who would stay faithful to his mandates. Some of the highlights of God's Revelation include his covenants with Noah, Abraham, and Moses. He spared Noah and his family in the great Flood by commanding him to construct an Ark. After that catastrophe, God promised never to punish the world again in that sort of way on account of sin. Some years later God communicated with Abraham, choosing him to be the father of a chosen people. If they would remain faithful to God's will, God would make them a great nation. Once the chosen people were a significant population, Revelation in the Old Testament reached a high-water mark when God revealed the Ten Commandments to Moses on Mount Sinai. Again, blessings would be bestowed on the chosen people if they would abide by the Mosaic Law, which is nothing more than the natural law inscribed in human nature. Divine Revelation reached its pinnacle when God the Father sent his own divine Son, speaking through the Word-made-flesh.

Sacred Scripture

Promised and predicted by the prophets and Psalms, Jesus Christ's life and teachings summarize the whole scope of Divine Revelation. Among the chosen people, God illuminated the minds of divinely selected people called to transmit truths and messages coming from God himself. God's Revelation in the Old Testament not only involved his plan for the chosen people of Israel but also was a preparation for his ultimate plan for the salvation of all people in Christ. Because of this, the mystery of Christ makes itself present in prophecy, imagery, and *prototype* throughout the Old Testament. Revelation up to the time of Christ was mediated through the history and prophets of Israel, and it reached a dramatic and spectacular climax when God the Father spoke directly through his divine Son, who took on a human nature. Since Jesus Christ is God, all of Scripture is centered on him and his teachings.

As the true Son of the one God, Jesus is not a mere prophet or holy teacher. He is not merely a historical figure we can study and in whom we can take an interest. Jesus' teachings are meant for all people in every time because he is God. The absolute center of attention in the New Testament are the words, actions, and instruction of Jesus Christ, with special treatment given to his Passion, Death, Resurrection, and Ascension as well as the beginning of the Church. The four Gospels form the nucleus of the New Testament since they center on Jesus Christ, the visible Revelation of the love of the Father by means of the Incarnation (literally, the taking on of flesh) of the Son of God. The whole purpose of Sacred Scripture is to reveal Jesus Christ and nourish his disciples with his truths.

The three stages in the formation of the Gospels consist of the following: first, the earthly life and teaching of Jesus Christ; then the oral tradition transmitted to the first disciples of Christ; and last, the written account of the life of Christ and his instructions. The initial teaching task of spreading the Gospel was entrusted to his Apostles. Those who had lived closely with Jesus and heard his words were commissioned to spread the Good News of salvation. The oral tradition consists in the spoken word of the Apostles through preaching, their example and lifestyle, and the institutions they formed. In time, writers connected to the Apostles wrote about Jesus' life and teachings under the inspiration of the Holy Spirit. Sacred Tradition begins with the teachings of the Apostles based on Christ's words together with their interpretation through the guidance of the Holy Spirit, some of which also forms the writings of the New Testament. It was through careful study of the Tradition dating back to the Apostles that the Church determined which of the writings were inspired by God. The complete list of inspired texts is called the "canon" of Scripture. This canon forms the authoritative written words of Jesus and the teachings of the Apostles, the "Good News" that would be entrusted to their successors, the bishops, to teach and preserve until the end of time.

Though written through the agency of divinely chosen writers, every word in the Bible, both the Old Testament and New, is inspired by God; therefore, the entire body of writing is called the Word of God. God is the ultimate Author of Sacred Scripture, who uses the Sacred Authors' respective styles, cultures, and personalities to transcribe what he wanted written; they are also true Authors of Scripture. God chose these writers, enlightened their minds, and moved their wills to write what he wanted—and only what he wanted. Under the promptings and inspiration of the Holy Spirit and confirmed by the Church as inspired, Sacred Scripture transmits infallible truth ordered to our salvation. The infallibility of Scripture does not extend to empirical matters of science or history. God's purpose was not to reveal the laws of nature or the order of the material universe but his own self. Sacred Scripture is infallible in matters pertaining to faith and morals, not a scientific understanding of the universe. Thus, it is unsurprising that the authors write according to their limited understanding of scientific or historical matters, but this in no way impairs their ability to infallibly relate what God wanted to be revealed about himself and his plan for humanity.

This interplay between God's ultimate, true authorship and the Sacred Authors' true, inspired authorship put his Revelation into writing, which requires a certain approach to reading Scripture. The Scriptures are written in human language by human beings, so the reader must try to understand what the writer truly wanted to convey. This means that modes of expression, figures of speech, and cultural mindsets must be taken into consideration for a full understanding of the meaning of the text. This does not mean, however, that Sacred Scripture is just an antiquated text written in days gone by that no longer speaks to modern people. As divinely inspired, the Scriptures are a living Word that speaks personally to every person in all circumstances with the guidance of the Holy Spirit. The Scriptures are meant as a means of salvation for *everyone*.

The reading of Sacred Scripture, however, should not become *individualistic*. The Second Ecumenical Council of the Vatican, or Vatican II, was held in the 1960s. An Ecumenical Council is a meeting of all the bishops of the Catholic Church in union with the Pope as the head. When the whole Church is gathered in this way, dogmatic pronouncements approved by the Pope are judged to be infallible. Vatican II also produced many "pastoral" documents, which are not presented as morally binding teaching but rather seek to apply the teaching of the Church to specific situations. Vatican II's Dogmatic Constitution on Divine Revelation *Dei Verbum* gives some guidance on how to interpret Scripture.

First, Scripture should be read while taking into account the content and unity of the entire body of Scripture, which is centered on Jesus Christ and his message. Any individual passage must be understood in light of the whole. Second, Sacred Scripture must be read according to the interpretation of the living Tradition of the Church. The Gospel message was entrusted to the Apostles and to their successors, the bishops. United with the bishops, we are united to the Apostles, through whose teaching we are united to Christ; therefore, under the guidance of the Holy Spirit, it is up to the Church to give the proper interpretation of the inspired text. Finally, the meaning given to the words of Sacred Scripture must agree with the whole body of Catholic teaching and Christ's plan of salvation, never contradicting it. This is called the *analogy of faith*. When a person is reading Scripture, he or she is not only hearing the Word of God but also participating in the lived faith of the Church in communion with all God's people.

The Church's authority over the interpretation of Scripture is not a limitation on the Word of God. Divinely inspired, the words of Scripture are layered with meaning. St. Augustine, who initially despised Scripture for the "lowliness of its style," eventually praised the Bible: "While it lay open to all to read, it reserved the majesty of its mysteries within its profounder meaning."[4] How does one get to the "profounder meaning" of Sacred Scripture? According to the ancient tradition of the Church, there are two general interpretations of the Word of God: the literal sense and spiritual sense. The *literal sense* is the meaning the author wanted to convey through the literary style and figurative language of the time period in which it was written. It relates the actions and events described by the written word, and on their own they are instructive. The *spiritual sense*, building on the literal sense, consists of the interpretation of those actions and events. God speaks not so much *in* the description of events but *with* the events themselves. As the *Catechism* teaches,

4. CSA, Book VI.

"Thanks to the unity of God's plan, not only the text of Scripture but also the realities and events about which it speaks can be signs.[5]" This layer of meaning is not intended by the Sacred Author but by the Holy Spirit. In turn, the spiritual sense can be classified in three senses: the allegorical, moral, and anagogical sense. The *allegorical sense* goes beyond the immediate meaning of the words and prefigures future events connected to salvation or some aspect of Jesus' life and teachings. The *moral sense* serves as a vehicle of instruction on behavior and conduct specified by God. Finally, the *anagogical sense* interprets events and teachings as signs of the eternal life to come.

Since both the Old and New Testaments come directly from God through his inspiration, they should be accepted wholeheartedly as the most certain of truths regarding the contents of the faith and as guidelines for moral conduct. On a natural level, the inspired Word enjoys credibility on several counts. First, there is a marvelous unity centered on Christ in both the New and Old Testaments, which is especially evident in the writings of the prophets and the wisdom literature. Written many centuries before Jesus' Birth, scores of prophecies reveal fascinating details about the Messiah; hundreds of prophecies concerning his Birth, life, and Death all came true. The Psalms, some of which date to perhaps a millennium before Christ, include a surprising number of details about Christ's Passion. About 800 years before Christ, the Book of Isaiah prophesied so much about Christ—especially his Passion and Death—that some have called it the "fifth Gospel." Virtually the entire life of Christ can be found in Old Testament prophecies.

Perhaps the most persuasive reason for credibility is that the contents of the New Testament bring out what is best in the human spirit. The words of Christ and the rest of the New Testament reveal the greatness and potential excellence of the human person. While glimmers of truth can be found in countless writings throughout the world, the ideals of virtue and nobility of life found in Christ's teachings and Sacred Scripture have no parallel in any other body of literature.

Sacred Tradition

The transmission of the teachings of the Apostles through the development of doctrine, expressions of worship with respect to the

5. CCC 117.

Sacraments, and spiritual disciplines all form what is called Sacred Tradition, which is intimately linked to Sacred Scripture. Scripture itself is a product of this Tradition, as the first preaching of the Good News of Jesus was oral rather than written. It was the teaching authority of the Church, with its Apostolic Tradition, that determined which books were inspired and, therefore, were included in the canon of Scripture. The source of both Sacred Scripture and Sacred Tradition is Christ and the teachings of his Apostles under the enlightenment and guidance of the Holy Spirit. Directed by the Holy Spirit, the Apostles, who both knew and penetrated the profound teachings of Christ, passed along their knowledge to their successors, the bishops, who in turn preserved, proclaimed, and handed on the same living tradition.

Since the inspired, written Word of God forms only a part of Sacred Tradition, explanations and right applications of the Scriptures is essential. An important part of Sacred Tradition is based on the writings of the Fathers of the Church, who lived within a few centuries of the Apostles. A Father of the Church is a Christian who lived during the early historical period of the Church (typically prior to AD 800) who is notable in his theological contributions, sound in his teaching, and characterized by his holy life. These ancient writers clarify and interpret Sacred Scripture through theological and philosophical elaborations. Their writings give a real sense of how the ancient Church interpreted and applied the teachings of Christ to their culture and daily life. Their clear, early interpretations of the Gospel makes it easier to trust that we correctly understand how Christ wanted his instructions to be put into practice.

For example, though the words of Our Lord are clear regarding his Real Presence in the Eucharist, many still question and debate whether Jesus is truly present in the Blessed Sacrament. The Early Church Fathers, however, confirmed Christ's Real Presence in the Eucharist, which underscores Christ's intentions, as they lived so close in time to him and his Apostles. With the aid of the Holy Spirit, the Apostles and their successors have wonderfully reinforced the doctrine of the Real Presence, and through Tradition we have beautiful applications of how to both venerate and capitalize on this gift, from tabernacles to Eucharistic chapels to the practice of Eucharistic Adoration and a Holy Hour before the Blessed Sacrament. It is interesting to note that the essential teachings and applications of Christian traditions have basically remained the same, albeit with different emphases and theological development, over the years. The Church is ever old and ever new.

The contents of both Sacred Scripture and Sacred Tradition are entrusted to the Church in what is called the Deposit of Faith. Through her Magisterium—her teaching authority, vested in the bishops under the Roman Pontiff—the Church has the task to interpret, apply, and teach the Word of God; the Magisterium is not the *source* of Divine Revelation. Anything included in the Deposit of Faith is there precisely by virtue of its being determined to be from God and not of human origin. The Church is *at the service of* the Deposit of Faith, and the Magisterium is entrusted with its *preservation*. For the Church to *change* or *invent* a teaching would be to depart from Christ. "Jesus Christ is the same yesterday and today and for ever,"[6] but his teaching can be interpreted and applied in limitless ways. The Church has the authority to proclaim the interpretations of certain teachings as articles of faith called "dogmas" that must be wholeheartedly accepted by the faithful.

Not only can the Church proclaim articles of faith that must be accepted, the Magisterium can also reject interpretations that are judged to not authentically communicate the Gospel of Christ. Throughout the ages the Church makes binding statements regarding matters of belief when certain doctrinal errors are significantly transmitted, certain prevalent behavior is incompatible with the moral law, or when particular cultural trends are incompatible with the Gospel message. This can be in a matter of faith, for example, when some early Christians denied the full divinity of Jesus. This can also be in matters of morals, for example, when some modern Christians go astray in a culture that accepts same-sex romantic relationships as normal. Such difficulties always further the development of Church teaching. In the first case, the Church refined her explanation of the one God in three divine Persons; in the second case, the issues surrounding human sexuality have resulted in a more developed anthropology based on the reality of being made in the image and likeness of God. The teachings of the Church will always provide sure guidance for integrating the Deposit of Faith, which originates in Christ's teaching, to contemporary circumstances and daily life.

---

6. Heb 13:8.

Chapter 2

One God in Three Divine Persons

One of the chief notable beliefs of the Jewish religion, as seen in the Old Testament, is a belief in one God who completely transcends the material world as opposed to the other nations and tribes, who worshiped multiple gods by way of idols wrought by human hands. Virtually everyone, barring the tribes of Israel, practiced some form of polytheism. In an unprecedented, dramatic way, God explicitly revealed himself to the chosen people as the one and only God. In a certain sense, the history of God's chosen people consists of events, permitted or willed by God, designed to pull them away from pagan religious cults and bring them back to fidelity to the one true God.

This obligation to worship and love the one true God was especially apparent after Moses received the Ten Commandments on Mount Sinai. When God first formed his covenant with Abraham, he did not explicitly reveal that he alone was God. He first prepared his chosen people by asking them simply to worship him and him alone. In the Ten Commandments, given through Moses, God more fully revealed himself as the *only* God.

The Ten Commandments are an elaboration of the Two Great Commandments that Jesus so strongly emphasized in his public life: that we must love God above all things and love our neighbor as ourselves. The last seven Commandments pertain to the treatment of one's neighbor, whereas the first three focus on our relationship with God.

The First Commandment appears in both the Books of Exodus and Deuteronomy in the Old Testament. This Commandment conveys the supreme importance of God in every person's life: "Hear, O Israel: The Lord our God is one Lord; and you shall love the Lord your God with all your heart, and with all your soul, and with all your might."[1] It also stresses the duty to adhere to the one true God and shun every form of idolatry: "You shall have no other gods

1. Dt 6:4–5.

before me."[2] So important was the divine mandate to monotheistic fidelity that God considered annihilating his people when they fabricated a golden calf as the new object of their religious veneration. The temptation was to turn away from the invisible God first revealed to Abraham, replacing him with something tangible in imitation of the pagan nations. Time and again, God would call his people back from the ignorance of pagan idolatry to the truth of his supreme divinity.

Like the rest of the Ten Commandments, the first is not completely unavailable to human reason. Neither was the notion of one God exclusive to the Jewish people, nor was it a total novelty among the pagans. Greek thinkers, as discussed in the previous chapter, arrived at the conclusion of an all-powerful being through philosophical analysis of the created world. To explain the world, with its limitless and rich variety of entities, the metaphysical response was to infer the existence of a single source that had no source toward which all things were moving. No matter how profound their insights were, however, these ancient sages never came close to discovering that this supreme being was a *personal* God with a *personal* bond to every human being. One God, who is both the Creator and a loving Father, was an alien idea to the Greeks. This God revealed himself to his chosen people.

It was a spectacular event whereby God first revealed himself as a personal God and not merely the "Unmoved Mover" of Aristotle. The famous episode occurred at the scene of the burning bush. The Book of Exodus relates how Moses noticed a bush that was burning but inexplicably not being consumed by the fire. As he approached the strange phenomenon, a voice emanated from the bush, informing Moses that he must remove his shoes for he was standing on hallowed ground. This voice belonged to God, who communicated to Moses as he had never done before when he introduced himself and revealed his name: "I AM WHO I AM"[3] (in Hebrew: *YHWH*, or *Yahweh*).

This disclosure of God's name opened a new era in the history of the Hebrew people. In the Old Testament a name clearly expresses one's identity and specific mission. Even in ordinary interactions, the exchange of names initiates a new relationship. The revelation of a

2. Ex 20:3; Dt 5:7.

3. Ex 3:14.

person's name serves as a necessary, and at times significant, first step in going beyond the anonymity of a bystander to the beginning of a potential friendship with a unique person. God presents himself at this theophany of the burning bush as much more than a detached Creator or unmoved mover. He now reveals himself as a loving Father who wants to be involved in the welfare and salvation of his people and ultimately of the entire human race.

Not only did the first Revelation of God's name to Moses initiate a personal relationship between God and his chosen people, but also the name itself reveals something about who God is. This profound, unusual phrase—"I AM WHO I AM"—names God as transcendent to all creation and endowed with the fullness of perfection. God reveals himself to Moses not as simply a "supreme being" among other lesser beings but as existence itself. "I am the One who is." This self-description indicates that God is the fullness of being by which there is absolutely no limit to his goodness, love, and power. Every possible perfection is implied in the richly charged phrase, "I AM WHO I AM." This pronouncement signifies that God has no beginning or end but is eternally present, transcending time and place. God's infinite perfection means that he is the fullness of truth, goodness, and love. He does not *possess* those transcendental qualities—*he is* those very perfections. Again, in the act of revealing his name, the Source of All initiates an intimate and loving relationship with his people.

The second of the Ten Commandments is a reminder to the chosen people that God's name—remarkably and generously revealed to them—is sacred: "You shall not take the name of the LORD your God in vain."[4] An important aspect of recognizing any person's dignity is respectfully addressing him or her by name. Out of a special deference to that person, one will always refer to his or her name with courtesy. While this holds true in all human relations, this manner of respecting a person's name pertains especially to God. "*Yahweh*" was so sacred a name that the Israelites would not even utter it in casual speech; instead, they referred to God with the title "Lord": *Adonai* in Hebrew, and *Kyrios* in Greek. In the Old Testament blasphemy was punished by death. The Book of Leviticus narrates how a son of an Egyptian and an Israelite was put to death because he "blaspheme[d] the name of the LORD."[5]

4. Ex 20:7.
5. Lv 24:16.

In our culture respect for God's name is sadly often ignored. Though the punishments of the ancient world seem archaic and distant, the obligation to honor God's name is no less a present requirement of the praise owed to God in justice. The Second Commandment forbids irreverent use of God's name and other acts of blasphemy. The Tradition of the Church has always underlined the gravity of blasphemy—speaking contemptuously of God or of his perfections—by classifying it as an intrinsically evil act. The *Catechism* outlines the diverse forms that blasphemy might take, including utterances of hatred, reproach, or defiance toward God; misusing God's name; and blaspheming the name of Jesus. This prohibition extends to language against Christ's Church, the saints, and sacred things.[6] It also extends to the use of God's name in oaths. Taking an oath in the name of God and then committing perjury is a grave insult to God and his name. In all times the one God deserves the respect due to his name.

St. Paul emphasized the importance and power of God's name in the Person of Jesus Christ. In a clear affirmation of Christ's divinity, St. Paul wrote: "Therefore God has highly exalted him and bestowed on him the name which is above every name, that at the name of Jesus every knee should bow, in heaven and on earth and under the earth, and every tongue confess that Jesus Christ is Lord, to the glory of God the Father."[7] The name of Jesus, far from being a word for cursing or complaint, should be respected in the same way as "the Lord's name" and not be taken in vain.

In the Revelation of his name—I AM WHO I AM—God initiated a more intimate relationship with his chosen people. Throughout the history of Israel, God gradually revealed more of himself and his loving plan for the salvation of all. This plan would only be fully revealed in Christ, and through Christ, the Son of God made man, a fuller Revelation of who God is would come.

God Is One Nature in Three Divine Persons

Following the direction of Jesus, every Christian is baptized "in the name of the Father and of the Son and of the Holy Spirit."[8] It is

6. Cf. CCC 2148.
7. Phil 2:9–11.
8. Mt 28:19; cf. OBap, no. 97.

interesting to note that Jesus spoke the word "name" in the *singular* despite the plurality of Father, Son, and Holy Spirit. This emphasizes the oneness of God, who is in three divine Persons. This truth, that God is Trinity, constitutes the central mystery of the Christian faith. All Catholic teaching is derived from the Trinitarian life of God. The ultimate aim of every Christian is to have an intimate relationship with the Father, Son, and Holy Spirit. This revealed truth concerning the three divine Persons strikes at the very heart of Christian life.

It is understandable that the human mind may shy away from this dizzying mystery of faith. We have seen that the light of reason can prove God's existence and enable a person to come to a knowledge of God's perfections through contemplating his creation. Without the light of faith, however, the human person cannot possibly perceive, let alone prove, that God is a Trinity of Persons. The infinite God will always remain beyond the capacity of finite, human reason. This is a good thing. If we could "fit" God into our finite minds, then he would be no bigger than we are! Since God has revealed this mystery, it *is* possible and recommendable to strive to penetrate the reality of the Trinity. Even though this mystery of faith will remain beyond our scope, it is nevertheless possible to understand it better—just not fully—when using reason to contemplate it.

Though the triune nature of God was only first revealed by Christ, once revealed, the presence of the Trinity can be found in the Old Testament. Throughout the Old Testament there are clues hinting at God being three Persons in one divine being. The first hint is found at the very beginning, in the Book of Genesis, when God refers to himself in the first person plural regarding the creation of the first man. "God said, 'Let *us* make man in *our* image, after *our* likeness.'"[9] At the very opening of Scripture, God refers to himself as "us." The Father, Son, and Holy Spirit are revealed in shadows, preparing for the light of Christ's full Revelation.

God also presents himself to the chosen people as their "Father" who, though just and exacting, lavishes mercy and compassion on his people. Referring to God as Father does not imply that he is essentially male. In Sacred Scripture God's constant love for his children is likened to both the love of a father and a mother. Still, in calling God *Father* there are important connotations. First, he is the

9. Gn 1:26.

origin of the whole created world; second, he transcends all of creation; moreover and quite significantly, "Father" implies relationship.

The relational quality of God's Fatherhood is not only relevant in relation to his creatures. The Old Testament use of the term "Father" also prefigures the Revelation of Jesus that God *is Father* in his very being, apart from creation. The verse, "You are my son, / today I have begotten you,"[10] refers in an immediate sense to Israel, but it ultimately points to God the Son, the Second Person of the Trinity. By nature, therefore, God the Father is eternally Father of God the Son. "No one knows the Son except the Father, and no one knows the Father except the Son and any one to whom the Son chooses to reveal him."[11] This speaks to the intimate relationship between the Son and the Father, which Jesus fully affirms when he declares, "I and the Father are one."[12] Jesus, therefore, reveals that God the Father and God the Son are of the same nature. The Creed that is prayed every Sunday in every Catholic Church, formulated by the First Ecumenical Council of Nicæa (AD 325), declares that Jesus Christ, according to his divinity, is "consubstantial with the Father."[13] Drawing from both the First Ecumenical Council of Nicæa and the First Ecumenical Council of Constantinople (AD 381), the same Creed confesses that Jesus is "the Only Begotten Son of God, / born of the Father before all ages. / God from God, Light from Light, / true God from true God, / begotten, not made."[14] God is Father because from all eternity he is begetting God the Son.

The Old Testament also makes several references that, in light of Christ's teachings, refer to the Holy Spirit, the Third Person of the Blessed Trinity. The Holy Spirit is associated with creation and renewal even before Jesus Christ revealed the Spirit's role in sanctification and evangelization. At the point of creation, "the Spirit of God was moving over the face of the waters."[15] The Psalmist also prays to God "take not thy holy Spirit from me."[16]

These references to the Spirit in the Old Testament are intimations of what would be the full, revealed teaching of Christ. Before

10. Ps 2:7.
11. Mt 11:27.
12. Jn 10:30.
13. RMiss, The Order of Mass, no. 18.
14. Ibid.
15. Gn 1:2.
16. Ps 51:11.

his Passion and Death on the Cross, at the Last Supper Jesus Christ explicitly announced another divine Advocate that he and the Father would send to the Apostles and their disciples.[17] After Jesus had ascended into heaven, just as Jesus promised, the Holy Spirit descended upon the Apostles at Pentecost and emboldened them to give witness to the life of Christ and proclaim his teachings. It is God the Father and God the Son who sent the Holy Spirit upon the Apostles. Belief in the Holy Spirit was solemnly declared by the First Ecumenical Council of Constantinople (AD 381): "I believe in the Holy Spirit, the Lord, the giver of life, / who proceeds from the Father."[18] This affirmation that the Holy Spirit is also "Lord" attests to the full divinity of the Third Person of the Trinity.

In the New Testament each divine Person of the Blessed Trinity is revealed in certain major episodes in the life of Christ. The Annunciation to Mary that she was chosen to be the Mother of our God and Savior highlights the presence of Trinity: "The Holy Spirit will come upon you, / and the power of the Most High will overshadow you; / therefore the child to be born will be called holy, / the Son of God."[19] The announcement of the Archangel Gabriel refers to the future child as "the Son of God," with explicit mention to both the Holy Spirit and God the Father as "the power of the Most High." In another episode, when Jesus was baptized, "he saw the Spirit of God descending like a dove, and alighting on him; and lo, a voice from heaven, saying, 'This is my beloved Son, with whom I am well pleased.'"[20] The voice from heaven, the hovering dove, and the baptized Christ reveal simultaneously God as a Trinity of Persons. As Jesus Christ commanded his Apostles and the Church to baptize "in the name of the Father and of the Son and of the Holy Spirit,"[21] this then becomes the new "name" of God, known as three Persons in one divine Being.

Philosophical Explanation of the Trinitarian Life

The truth of God's being a Trinity of Persons is explicitly stated in the teachings of Jesus Christ and was embraced in faith by the

17. Cf. Jn 14:16.
18. RMiss, The Order of Mass, no. 18.
19. Lk 1:35.
20. Mt 3:16–17.
21. Mt 28:19; cf. OBap, no. 97.

Apostles, but it would take centuries to articulate this mystery in clear, cogent theological and philosophical terms. To explain the dogma of the Trinity revealed by Christ and recorded in Scripture, the Church borrowed terminology used in Greek philosophy. The terms "substance," "person," "nature," and "relations" would serve as indispensable philosophical tools to define the Trinitarian mystery faithfully corresponding to the contents of Sacred Scripture. The Church uses the term "substance" or "nature" to describe God's unity and oneness. The word "person" is used to articulate the distinct relations between the divine Persons. The question, "*What* is God?" is answered by stating that God is one divine substance. The answer to the question, "*Who* is God?" is that God is three divine Persons in one substance. Each person—Father, Son, and Holy Spirit—is totally and equally divine. They are, however, not three gods but one God. The distinction between the divine Persons lies strictly in their relationship to each other and no more. The one God *is* three Persons.

Though it is impossible to fully comprehend this profound mystery, an analogy to the human person may shed some light. The human person is made in the image and likeness of God, which means that everyone has a spiritual soul with faculties of an intellect and will. Every man or woman, by virtue of his or her capacity to know and love, reflects the Blessed Trinity. If God were not a Trinity of divine Persons in an infinite relationship with one another, then God would be eternally "isolated" and "alone." Thus, to be made in the image and likeness of God, human persons are not isolated individuals for whom relationships are an extraneous, optional choice. As it is, even the pagan philosophers concluded that human beings are social by nature. This means that the God in whose image we are made must be relational *in himself*. Every human person, with his or her bonds of love, image the Father, Son, and Holy Spirit. Because of this likeness, Revelation about God reveals the truth about the human person, which in turn can teach us more about God.

In addition to the relational aspect of God—revealed in Father, Son, and Holy Spirit—the first few verses of St. John's Gospel tell us something else radically new: "In the beginning was the Word, and the Word was with God and the Word was God."[22] There exists from all eternity the divine Word. What makes this term so unique

22. Jn 1:1.

and charged with an air of mystery is that the "Word" is not only associated with God but *totally identified* with him. "The Word *was* God"—this verse almost seems to suggest that there is another god besides the one God, but with proper study and discernment it affirms the unity of the Father and the Son. In the beginning the Word was "with" God, *and* he "was" God. With the Revelation of the divine Word, the existence of a Second Person was explicitly announced. St. John's Gospel makes it eminently clear that the Word is eternal and a Creator no less than is God the Father.

Referring to God as "Word" is itself revelatory. The human condition can again help lead us to a deeper understanding. The human intellect generates ideas about different entities that are observed and perceived. A word is the verbal expression of a concept or idea through conventional symbolic sounds called language. Words are mediums—audible sounds through which people speak and communicate ideas. A word is not a mere sound but a sound *that signifies* a concept or a truth based on some aspect of reality. Following this relationship between word and idea, the divine Word is intimately connected to a divine idea.

On the human level, ideas are never perfect. Though in many instances they are accurately connected to what is true, they do not possess the full reality of the thing being expressed. They are only symbols. The divine Word, however, which is an expressed divine idea, is truly God. The divine idea is so perfect that it is nothing less than God himself. How can this consideration be shown as reasonable rather than as a theological truth that must be accepted on blind faith? Let us imagine that before the creation of the universe, only God existed and there was nothing else but the Trinitarian life. Amid this inner life of the Trinity before creation, God the Father eternally would be reflecting on himself, generating an idea of himself. This idea is so accurate and complete, as it were, that it is the mirror image of God the Father himself. This perfect reflection that God the Father has of himself is a true divine Person. This divine Person, which is generated through a divine idea, is God the Son. Taken from the Gospel of St. John, the Nicene Creed states, "Through him all things were made."[23] These words make it abundantly clear that the Word is directly responsible for the creation of the universe. The Divine Word "speaks" God the Father in the first

23. RMiss, The Order of Mass, no. 18; cf. Jn 1:3.

place through the created world, which mirrors in a finite way God the Son's beauty, truth, and goodness. In the fullness of time, "the Word became flesh and dwelt among us."[24] The Incarnation gave a special insider's view of God the Father's mercy and compassion.

For a cogent consideration of the existence of the Third Person of the Trinity, the Holy Spirit, we can consider the human soul in its capacity for loving. Within the human condition love follows knowledge since one can only love what is known. Friendship is forged as a consequence of mutual knowledge. One usually makes a new friend after knowing the person by means of words that express one's inner self. The dynamic of human love, by analogy, can bring us to a partial understanding of the Holy Spirit, who is explicitly revealed in connection to the divine Word.

Put in limited human terminology, God the Father conceives such a perfect idea or mental word of himself that he is actually a Person. This Person is called God the Son because the Father generates a personified image, or Word, of himself. God the Father and his Son contemplate each other, forming a bond of love. This bond of love between God the Father and God the Son is itself so perfect that it is *also* a person, called God the Holy Spirit. Notice that the Holy Spirit is not generated by the Father *or* the Son but rather proceeds from both the Father *and* the Son through love. When two people love each other, they form a shared bond of love. In the case of God the Father and God the Son, this bond proceeds from their loving knowledge of each other. The traditional word to express the procession of the Holy Spirit is to "breathe" love for each other. This personification of love beautifully corresponds to the well-known scriptural definition of God that he is Love.[25]

Though all divine intervention involves all three Persons of the Blessed Trinity, nevertheless, particular tasks or works are appropriated to a particular Person of the Trinity. The work of creation is equally the work of all three divine Persons, though it is attributed to God the Father since he is the eternal origin of the generation of God the Son and the procession of God the Holy Spirit. Creation begins with an idea implemented by an effective love to accomplish it, and so it is attributed to the Father.

---

24. Jn 1:14.
25. 1 Jn 4:8.

As will be discussed in the next chapter, creation was damaged through sin, so it would correspond to God the Son to restore it through the redemption. Given that all things were made through the Son, it is fitting that the remaking of creation through the redemption corresponds to God the Son. The actual *implementation* of the plan of creation—originated in the mind of God the Father through God the Son—corresponds to God the Holy Spirit. The work of purification and sanctification, which is an application of Christ's redemption to individual souls, is thus also attributed to the Holy Spirit.

What adds to the mystery of God's Trinitarian life is the reality of perfect oneness. There is absolutely no greater unity than the unity of the three divine Persons. Divine Revelation and Church teachings on the three distinct Persons of the Trinity do not in any way contradict God's unity of being. Although a complete understanding of God being three and one at the same time is impossible regardless of human intellectual gifts, the reflection of the human spirit shows no rational incompatibility in a Trinity of divine Persons in one divine substance.

Since God is pure spirit, no human mind can fully grasp this truth. Though human beings, too, have a spiritual aspect, our minds think in terms of material things—and *material* human imagination offers no direct example for the intellect to fully understand this mystery. The Trinity can only be truly known through a spiritual relationship with God. In her *Spiritual Testimonies*, the great mystic St. Teresa of Avila speaks of her experience of the indwelling of the three Persons of the Trinity. In her struggle to understand, Our Lord told her to stop trying to think about matters of the soul through comparison to corporeal things. He told her, "Don't try to hold Me within yourself but try to hold yourself within Me."[26]

A Trinitarian Spirituality

Each divine Person has a special role to play in a soul's union with the Blessed Trinity. The truth that God is three divine Persons in one God is meant to play a key part of the spiritual life. God has revealed that he is Father, Son, and Holy Spirit so that we can truly have a personal relationship with each divine Person.

26. "Spiritual Testimonies," in ThAv, vol. I, no. 14

Through Baptism a Christian is given the status of a son or daughter of God the Father. As adopted children of God, their spiritual life should include interacting with God as a perfectly loving, merciful father. Having a Father who is infinitely powerful should also give every Christian a deep sense of security and confidence in his constant care. Prayer should prompt us to entrust our daily worries and concerns into the hands of God, our doting Father. This relationship can be difficult depending upon how loving, merciful, and dependable our human fathers have been—but God is a perfect Father who infinitely surpasses even the best vision of human fatherhood we could conceive.

The point of entry into the life of God is Jesus Christ, God the Son made man. Hence, in the liturgy, many prayers end in the phrase, "through Christ Our Lord." We contemplate the Father's love for us through the humanity of Christ. Only through union with God the Son made man, can we grow in the sense and realization that God is our Father. The role of God the Holy Spirit, then, is to unite each of us to God the Father through Jesus Christ.

The Holy Spirit, who is the personification of divine love, grafts us into the life of Jesus Christ in a mystical way. This rebirth in Christ through the work of the Holy Spirit brings about a child-to-Father relationship with God the Father.

In the face of difficulties, we must always recall that God is our Father who loves us infinitely and ardently desires our perfect happiness. One should never see God as a taskmaster who will not tolerate our mistakes or sins. He revels in forgiving us and leading us to true happiness. A major part of prayer should include contemplating the life of Jesus, who in his divinity is the perfect image of God the Father. What is God like? What is God's attitude toward us? What is God's will for me? These questions are answered by looking meditatively at Jesus' life.

The great saints were adept at contemplating the life of Christ. We should also invoke the Holy Spirit to penetrate the life of Christ, be transformed into his image, and live his very life. Given the richness of this mystery, a lifetime is too short to sufficiently penetrate God's inner life revealed for our salvation, sanctification, happiness, and peace.

I Am the Lord Your God; There Is No Other

Since the First Commandment reminds us explicitly of our duty to love God above all things, it directly follows that we try to give him proper worship. A significant part of giving glory to God in response to his exalted and transcendent dignity and infinite love for us involves generous prayer. Through prayer a human person encounters God and enters into communion with each Person of the Blessed Trinity. Consequently, that person receives God's grace, enabling him or her to live a moral life and to love God and neighbor as Christ intended, which brings joy. A person's relationship with God, founded on a life of prayer, is the very basis for living a Christian life. For this reason, we are called, both as individuals and as a faith community, to "pray constantly."[27]

The subject of prayer will be treated more fully in Chapter 20, but here we can touch on the duty to offer God praise, honor, and atonement, which in justice he deserves. This stems from the First Commandment, much illuminated by Christ, and falls under the virtue of religion. The *Catechism* outlines certain sins against the virtue of religion that are violations of the First Commandment to worship the one true God. Appeals for divine intervention must include an appreciation and respect for God's infinite dignity and power. Proper worship and prayer must always recognize the one true God as the only source of supernatural life. Any action that seeks supernatural assistance or guidance apart from God is a great offense against the one true God and constitutes a sin against the virtue of religion.

Such actions can take many forms that can sadly go unrecognized. One example would be superstition: using a trinket, mantra, or action designed to secure a supernatural effect or to avoid bad luck. Another example is believing that a certain number of prayers to a particular saint will automatically guarantee good health. The use of superstitious devices or actions indicates a belief that these objects have hidden powers apart from God. Seeking supernatural assistance through external rituals without recourse to God's infinite goodness goes against the proper worship of God.

A more serious act against the virtue of religion is recourse to forms of divination or occult powers to attempt to predict the future

---

27. 1 Thes 5:17.

or obtain information, for example, through mediums, seances, an Ouija board, or astrology charts. Only God can know the future and the mysteries of the world, both material and spiritual; it is up to God to reveal the future or provide knowledge in a preternatural way if he so wills. Any attempt to learn about the future or gain knowledge unobtainable through natural means without reference to God or his Revelation is sinful. If God is not involved for supernatural assistance, then dangerous demonic powers are likely at work.

The *Catechism* teaches about magic, which involves seeking occult forces through rituals or formulas to obtain either a good or evil effect. Witchcraft is probably its most common manifestation and is a present spiritual danger in the growing practice of Wicca. While Wicca may appear to be a harmless communing with nature, it promises power through ritualized behavior divorced from God's Providence and plan. Today, some New Age philosophies that promise self-fulfillment and physical well-being through actions or beliefs that release hidden "energies" would also fall under the category of magic. Most dreadful and destructive are the practices of satanic worship, which, though frequently made light of, are still present within our culture.

Another common sin against the virtue of religion is irreligion, which consists of disrespect and, in many instances, mockery of God's goodness and sacred dignity. Such offenses against the sacredness of religion include sacrilege: showing serious disrespect, insensitivity, desecration, or malicious action toward the Sacraments, sacred persons, places, or objects. The reception of Holy Communion while in the state of mortal sin is one example of sacrilege.

Probably the most common sin against the virtue of religion is idolatry, which involves dealing with or addressing a finite being as if it were divine. A person might not think of idolatry as common occurrence in the modern world. The term usually conjures images from the Old Testament of the People of God worshiping a golden calf or pagans worshiping Zeus and Apollo. The modern person cannot imagine falling prey to such ignorance; nevertheless, there are contemporary versions of idolatry that could take the form of an obsession with professional work, wealth, power, celebrity, achievement, sports, or even obsession with another person. Whenever a person gives primary allegiance to anyone or anything other than God, he or she falls into idolatry.

Catholics are sometimes falsely accused of idolatry, or even superstition, on account of the practice of honoring the saints or Mary, the Mother of God, through actions of love directed toward images or objects that represent them. The veneration of statues and painted renderings of God, Jesus, Mary, or the saints in Catholic tradition is not idolatry. These images are meant to lead us to a deeper relationship with Christ. We honor the person represented, but our worship is directed to God alone. Likewise, when a Catholic prays "to a saint," he or she seeks a particular intercession based on that saint's close relationship with Christ—not as a being with power apart from God.

In the Old Testament God himself, through his Revelation to Moses, outlined the norms that people should follow in worshiping him precisely to protect them from falling into idolatry or other unworthy forms of false religion. God gave them a plan to follow so they would know how to give proper worship and not fall into sin. A very detailed set of laws was established, which included the institution of a priesthood, construction of the Temple, principal feasts, practices of worship, and above all the celebration of the Sabbath. The Third Commandment rounds out the teaching on the love owed to God by obligating a regular and ritualized day of worship: "Remember the sabbath day, to keep it holy."[28] God set the seventh day apart to be devoted to worship, which includes a rest from earthly labor. From Mosaic times, the Sabbath included rest and the obligation of sacrifice. Both requirements showed the recognition of the power of God over his entire creation and all people.

The importance of Holy Mass as the re-presentation of Jesus' redemptive Sacrifice on the Cross will be discussed in Chapter 14. Here we note that the obligation for Catholics to attend Mass on Sundays and Holy Days of Obligation is the fulfillment of the Third Commandment, which requires us to keep the Sabbath holy. Though the Sabbath of Israel was on the seventh day, when God "rested" from his "work" of creation, the Resurrection of Jesus on the *first day* of the week heralded a "new creation" and introduced notable changes in the practice of divine worship. Granted, this did not happen immediately; the first Christians still practiced the Jewish form of worship in the Temple or the synagogue and then celebrated the liturgy of the Eucharist elsewhere. In Scripture we read that Sts. Peter

28. Ex 20:8; cf. CCC, Part Three, Section Two: "Remember to keep holy the LORD's Day."

and John went up to the Temple at the customary hour of prayer and then celebrated the Eucharist in their homes,[29] but it was "on the *first day of the week,* when we were gathered together to break bread."[30] At the beginning of the second century, St. Ignatius, Bishop of Antioch, spoke of Sunday as the day of Christian worship. The change of the day of worship from the Sabbath also brought about a change of name: the "Lord's Day."

In her maternal care for the faithful, the Church makes attendance at Sunday Mass obligatory because of the tremendous spiritual benefits derived for those who participate. By worshiping on Sunday, we celebrate the completion of the *first* creation and our redemption in the *new* creation in Christ signified by the Resurrection of Jesus, which occurred on a Sunday. The most perfect act of adoration that can be given to God is the offering of the Most Holy Sacrifice of the Mass. The Mass is, therefore, the most perfect prayer that can be offered to God.

Attending Mass on Sunday is a grave obligation. In the case of someone fully cognizant of the serious obligation to attend Sunday Mass, skipping Mass might well be a mortal sin. Obviously, certain circumstances such as sickness or the immediate need to help someone in an emergency would dispense a person from attending Mass or a Holy Day of Obligation. The Christian, though, should not be quick to seek out exceptions and should keep in mind that throughout history Christians have suffered martyrdom to attend Mass. Any time a Catholic misses Sunday Mass due to negligence, he or she should seek the Sacrament of Penance and Reconciliation (cf. Chapter 15) and return to regular Sunday worship.

By virtue of the natural law, the closer the relationship, the greater the duty to love. God, who is the source of our being, established his relationship with us by his creative act of love. We show that love in return by setting aside proper time to worship and give thanks to God. In this way, the requirement to designate a regular time or day dedicated to God, like the other of the Commandments, finds its origin in the natural law. This means that choosing a periodic day or time to give a greater focus on God applies to every person. Keeping the Lord's Day holy enables us to show in a concrete way his importance in our lives, and worshiping God on Sunday is

29. Cf. Acts 2:4–6.

30. Acts 20:7.

a sign of our love for him as well as an example to others in a world that needs the witness of believers.

Faith, Hope, and Love

Despite the challenge to natural reason posed by the oneness of the Trinity, the baptized are empowered by sanctifying grace. The theological virtues of faith, hope, and charity are lovingly given at Baptism. Through these virtues, the believer is enabled to know, trust, and love God beyond natural powers.

Faith is a gratuitous gift, and it is by faith that a person enters a personal relationship with God. God offers the gift of faith to all, and it is up to each person to freely accept this gift. Faith requires a *willing* acceptance of Divine Revelation. This can sometimes be difficult. Divine Revelation often transcends human logic and understanding, but as a person becomes more receptive by God's grace, faith supernaturally enlightens the mind and moves the will beyond its natural capacities. Through the work of the Holy Spirit, as the spiritual relationship with God grows, the intellect is given a supernatural light to know that the contents of Divine Revelation are true. At the same time the will is moved to embrace these truths and live by them. As a person's life grows into the life of Christ, he or she finds a peace and joy that prompts a greater faith in God.

Given the fact that salvation consists of believing in Christ and following the path marked out by his teachings, faith is necessary for salvation. The Church teaches that salvation in Christ is mysteriously available even to those who are not Christian or who may have never heard of Christ. Our Lord, in some fashion, offers the possibility to know him even within the limitations and boundaries of culture, religion, and formation. This still rests on the redemptive work of Christ and the necessity of faith, but as the *Catechism* teaches: "Every man who is ignorant of the Gospel of Christ and of his Church but seeks the truth and does the will of God in accordance with his understanding of it, can be saved. It may be supposed that such persons would have *desired Baptism explicitly* if they had known its necessity" (CCC 1260). If, through no fault of his or her own, a person never had the chance to accept the Gospel message, then God—who knows the truth in his or her heart—offers a path to salvation.

Once accepted, however, we put our faith wholly in Christ, which also means faith in the teachings of the Church he established. When Catholics come against some point of doctrine that they have trouble believing, they are obligated to put their faith in the authority of the Church, humbly submit to all that the Church teaches, and work to educate themselves about the truth regarding why the Church teaches as she does. A person often has trouble believing a point of doctrine because he or she does not understand it. When a Christian who struggles with a point of doctrine submits in faith to the truth of the Church's teachings, this obedience can help the Christian grow in faith until the teaching becomes more understandable and finally embraced. A Christian who is experiencing doubt but desires to remain faithful should make every effort to understand the faith more thoroughly through diligent prayer and study of Catholic teaching.

Though faith is essentially a gratuitous gift from God, human freedom, as always, has a role. As people respond to God's call in their lives, they grow in faith. As God revealed himself to his chosen people gradually over time, so, too, does he work in our lives one step at a time. While reason can never fully grasp the mysteries of faith, it certainly can penetrate those teachings and consequently become more enamored by the riches of Divine Revelation. A greater understanding of the faith fosters a deeper faith in what God has revealed. As these truths come across as compatible with reason, faith is further stimulated. We should always pray for the gift of faith.

While faith is the beginning of a relationship with God, the virtue of hope instills in a person the capacity to trust in God's mercy. Specifically, the person who lives by hope will enjoy a deep confidence that God will give him or her all the graces necessary to reach salvation and reach full union with Jesus Christ. The opposite of hope is despair. Despair involves the loss of trust in God's mercy and love. Our past sins, personal weaknesses, sense of unworthiness, or current sinfulness can all tempt us to lose hope and fall into despair. The virtue of hope resists this rejection of God's mercy, trusting in the promises of Jesus. On the other hand, there is the sin of presumption, which occurs when a person takes God's mercy for granted without any attempt to avoid sin and remain faithful to a Christian life or when a person believes he or she can be saved by personal effort alone without God's grace. Presumption, like despair, is a rejection of God's mercy in the form of not realizing the need everyone has for forgiveness. Hope helps us to put our trust in God and the salvation he offers through Christ without falling into despair or presumption.

Charity "is the theological virtue by which we love God above all things for his own sake, and our neighbor as ourselves for the love of God" (CCC 1822). The theological virtue of charity challenges the Christian to love as Jesus Christ loves his Father and every human being. As so movingly stated in the Gospel, Christ loved to the point of laying down his life for his friends.[31] Though we can never begin to repay God for his bountiful love for us, every individual should in justice strive to love him above all things.

Which love should be given priority—love of God or love of neighbor? The First Commandment clearly commands that everyone love God more than anyone else and above all else; however, a genuine love of God, since he is the source of love itself, necessarily leads to a love of neighbor. St. John made this abundantly clear when he revealed, "If any one says, 'I love God,' and hates his brother, he is a liar."[32] Since love for God automatically extends to love of neighbor, love for others will always serve as a measuring rod for love of God. Charity is the mark of Christ's disciples, as Jesus himself said: "A new commandment I give to you, that you love one another; even as I have loved you, that you also love one another. By this all men will know that you are my disciples, if you have love for one another."[33] For this reason, St. Paul wrote of the theological virtues that "faith, hope, love abide, these three; but the greatest of these is love."[34] As the Church describes, the "holiness of the Church is... expressed in many ways in individuals, who in their walk of life, tend toward the perfection of charity [love]."[35]

31. Cf. Jn 15:13.
32. 1 Jn 4:20.
33. Jn 13:34–35.
34. 1 Cor 13:13.
35. Cf. LG, no. 39.

CHAPTER 3

CREATION AND THE FALL

God's love and goodness are the ultimate explanation for bringing the universe into existence. God needs absolutely nothing to enhance his glory or happiness. He could have remained in perfect happiness without creating a world to be enjoyed by human beings. In his infinite mercy he chose to share his everlasting life with certain creatures endowed with a mind and a will. Sadly, the first man and woman would eventually betray and reject their divine Creator. Out of a divine extravagance of love, God would recreate the human person's capacity for everlasting life by becoming human and offering himself for our salvation. The beginning of the Book of Genesis is like an overture of this "history of salvation."

To understand the richness of meaning in the Bible, it is necessary to learn about its modes of communication. As mentioned earlier, Sacred Scripture is infallible in matters pertaining to faith and morals. It is not a science manual, and often its meaning is communicated in poetic rather than historical language—though much of the Bible is still history. To review what was stated in Chapter 1, Scripture can be read according to two senses: the literal and the spiritual. The literal sense is what the words literally state as well as the actions, dialogue, and events that are related. The spiritual sense is the meaning conveyed not by the words but by the actions, dialogue, and events that are related in the literal. Thus, the creation accounts in Genesis do not need to be *true* in the sense of historical accuracy on the literal level for it to communicate *truth* in the spiritual sense. While one may believe that the events of creation as told in Genesis *are* true on the literal level, it is not *necessary* to believe this to be confident that the story communicates something true about God and his creation according to the spiritual sense. The question for faith and morals is, "What do the events, actions, and utterances of the creation accounts tell us about God and ourselves?" In this way, Scripture offers many layers of meaning and is endlessly fruitful in what it can teach. The only limit to the spiritual interpretation of Scripture is that it can never *contradict* what is said in the literal sense. The literal sense prevents us from "reading into" Scripture our ideas that are not present in the text.

"In the beginning God created the heavens and the earth."[1] The Bible opens with the First Creation Account by strongly emphasizing that God is the all-powerful, prolific Creator. This point is conveyed by several related ideas. The first is that the eternal God gave a distinct starting point—"in the beginning"—to a creation outside of his inner life. Second, God alone creates. The Hebrew word *bara* means "create." In Genesis and throughout Scripture, this verb exclusively has God as the subject. Thirdly, all of creation—signified by the phrase "the heavens and the earth"—depends on God alone. Additionally, God only needs to will something, and it is. "God *said*, 'let there be light'; *and there was* light."[2] Whether God *literally in history uttered the words*, "Let there be light," is irrelevant. The study of Scripture aims to discover the answer to this question: "What does the relating of this action communicate about God?"

What especially interests us here is that God created everything from nothing. Many brilliant people, though awed by the breathtaking beauty and the mind-boggling intelligence reflected in the world, fail to ask the metaphysical question of what caused all this to happen. Why is there anything rather than nothing? Why does anything exist? Many scientists—whether they are studying the organelles of a cell, the subatomic world of a proton, or millions of galaxies that populate the universe—seem to prefer the comfort of avoiding this subject. Dazzling technological advances occur because complex, specialized mathematical applications are applied to a hardware derived ultimately from natural resources that result in state-of-the-art computers. How did this staggering intelligence get inside an electron? Why are these laws rational and stable? The intelligent complexity of the universe that has inspired countless doctoral dissertations—not to mention millions of articles written by countless intellectual superstars—points to a creator.

The study of creation enjoys a special relevance today given the ongoing debates about the origin of the universe and, more precisely, the specific genesis of the human person. There are many theories bandied about to explain the existence of the world. Among scientists it is not uncommon to argue that the universe, with both its animate and inanimate beings, is the consequence of random collisions of molecules over billions of years. As the speculation goes, the virtually limitless combinations of substances could result in the

1. Gn 1:1.
2. Gn 1:3.

complex world as we find it now. How can such order come from chaos? It takes a huge "leap of faith" to believe that the complexity of the human eye, let alone the brain, is the result of the random chance of the right chemicals lining up. The more natural conclusion is that a rational intelligence is behind it all.

By contrast, the first believers proclaimed under no uncertain terms that God is Creator of heaven and earth, just as we affirm in the Nicene Creed "all things visible and invisible."[3] The Fourth Ecumenical Council of the Lateran (AD 1215) confirms this fact again by asserting that both the spiritual and physical world were created out of nothing. What this assertion also tells us is that the visible material world is not *all* that exists. There is a spiritual existence that is distinct from the material, though it is no less real and no less the product of God's creative act.

The First Creation Account in the Book of Genesis indicates that God performed his work of creation within a metaphorical timespan of six days. Clearly, it cannot be taken as our twenty-four-hour solar day since the sun was not even created until "day" three. God may very well have created the universe in six installments—each one lasting billions of years—but what this "six-day" period signifies is a creative order among the array of entities comprising the world. What we find in the First Creation Account in Genesis 1 is a hierarchy among the creatures that corresponds to the six-day period. With each succeeding day the perfection of created things increases until creation culminates in the creation of man and woman: first earth and water; then vegetation, birds, and fish; next mammals; and finally the man and woman in God's own image and likeness. Creation is guided by order and hierarchy.

The progressive complexity of the six-day narrative also underscores how the beings that make up the created world manifest an interdependence on each other. God created the world in such a way that the rain, sun, foliage, and wildlife are interrelated for their existence and preservation. Given the diversity and gradation of perfection among created things, no being is self-sufficient but rather depends on other beings. Nothing, therefore, is superfluous—everything acts a certain way to fulfill a particular purpose for its own perfection and the common good of the world. The interdependence

3. RMiss, The Order of Mass, no. 18.

among creatures drives home that nothing except God possesses the fullness of perfection. Nothing in creation is self-sufficient.

God's Providence continues to oversee and direct the created world, but this is primarily through his secondary causes. That is, God does not directly create rain every time it rains; rather, this happens through other causes (secondary causes) that ultimately are derived from God's creative work. Oceans, rivers, and lakes evaporate into clouds, which in turn condense to produce rain. Rain provides growth for all plant and tree life rather than God directly causing the growth without water. The fruits and vegetables serve as nourishment for the animal kingdom. Everything is sustained by the will of God, who works *through* the things he has created. This is why, as stated in Chapter 1, there can never be contradiction between scientific discovery and God's Revelation. Nature itself is a product of God's divine plan and follows the laws of God.

One of the most significant emphases in the First Creation Account in Genesis is the inherent goodness of the material world. At the end of each day in the seven-day creation narrative, the sacred text states that God looked on what he had made and "God saw that it was good."[4] Every created thing reflects a hint of God's infinite wisdom; from inanimate objects to animals with their sophisticated set of instincts and highly developed sensory organs to the vast ecosystems of the oceans or the forest floor, everything reflects the goodness of God. But nothing in the material world can reflect God's goodness more than the man and the woman created in his image and likeness. Only on the sixth day, after the creation of the human person, did God see that "it was *very* good."[5]

Made in the Image of God

The human person was created last in the First Creation Account because that singular creature straddles both the physical and spiritual world. In symbolic language in the Second Creation Account in Genesis, "God formed man [Adam] of dust from the ground, and breathed into his nostrils the breath of life."[6] This "life" can be taken for the soul. Since man and woman are composed of both body and spirit, every person is a microcosm of the whole created world of

4. Gn 1:10; cf. 1:4, 12, 18, 21, 25, 31.

5. Gn 1:31.

6. Gn 2:7.

spirit and matter. The human body enjoys an exalted dignity because it is animated by a soul. Once the soul is elevated by grace, it is meant to be a temple of the Holy Spirit. As spiritual beings destined for God, the man and the woman possess a created perfection that surpasses the rest of the material order. Though human nature consists of a *union* of body and spirit, even the human body, with its material elements, is meant to be subservient to the soul. Possessing an immortal soul, the human person has a dignity greater than any other material thing.

Another way of looking at human dignity based on Genesis is that the man and the woman are not a means to an end but an end in themselves. The man and the woman were made solely to love God; all the rest of material creation was made for them. All of creation is a gift meant to serve the needs of the human being, who can pick a fruit off a tree or arrange certain elements in such a way to construct a computer. Creation praises God through its service to the human person and by providing the raw material for human work. The human person was made only to love God and be loved in return. This status is expressed when God speaks, "Let them have dominion over the fish of the sea, and over the birds of the air, and over the cattle, and over all the earth, and over every creeping thing that creeps upon the earth."[7] This dominion of the man and the woman is not a matter of power such that we can do whatever we like with God's good creation. It is rather a question of dignity. The man and the woman were made to love God; all other things were made to serve them. Such dignity comes not only from their possessing an immortal soul but also on account of their affinity with God himself: "God created man in his own image, in the image of God he created him; male and female he created them."[8] Human dignity rests not on our being more powerful than the rest of creation but on our being set apart from all of creation.

This truth revealed about the human person in Genesis applies to every human being. God creates each soul individually and immediately at the moment of conception. Though the parents are directly responsible for the physical component of the new person, they are not the cause of the soul, or animating principle. Using the language from above, there are no secondary causes responsible for the soul coming into being. God uniquely wills each human soul, and the

7. Gn 1:26.

8. Gn 1:27.

human soul is ultimately destined for God. It is immortal, and at the moment of death the soul separates from the body and lives a separate existence. Created, however, as a union of body and soul, at the resurrection on the last day, a person's soul will reunite with his or her body.

Being made in God's image and likeness also sets the human person apart from the rest of material creation since we are the only visible creatures who can actually know and love their Creator; this is because we have intellect and free will. The idea that the human being is distinguished from other animals as being rational and free is a premise as old as Socrates (fifth century BC). It is succinctly demonstrated in Genesis in the well-known prohibition from God that Adam and Eve should not eat from the Tree of the Knowledge of Good and Evil.[9] This prohibition demonstrates that the human person, unlike the beasts, has the freedom to *choose* the good rather than being forcibly compelled. It also means that the human person must learn from instruction rather than simply following natural instincts. Both properties are necessary for any being to be able to authentically love: the power to know the good and the freedom to choose the good. God created us to know him and to love him, and this requires an intellect and the freedom necessary to love. Knowledge and love are strictly spiritual powers derived from a spiritual soul. Though the human intellect relies on the senses to draw concepts and ideas, the actual intellectual process falls within the spiritual realm.

Through knowledge and love every man and woman can enter into the life of God and participate in his everlasting life. Being made in the image of God, the human being enjoys the dignity of personhood. A person is never a "what" or a "something" but a "who" or a "someone." The human person is a being capable of self-knowledge; self-ownership; self-possession; and, consequently, total self-giving. Human beings, besides angels, are the only created beings who can worship and honor God through their capacity to know and to love. This ability makes the human person singular and unique among the creatures of the material created world.

The creation accounts of Genesis also reveal God's involvement in the ongoing life and growth of his creation. Each being, whether rational or nonrational, tends toward its own perfection or fulfill-

9. Cf. Gn 2:17.

ment, and God guides each entity toward perfection. Whether it is a subatomic particle or an enormous planet, God exercises constant oversight over what is tiniest and biggest. As opposed to what the Deists claim, God is not like an indifferent watchmaker who created at one point in the past and then removes himself completely from the workings of his creation. Rather, his Providence guides and sustains absolutely everything. With the human person, however, who is made in God's own image and likeness, he exercises a fatherly care. Jesus Christ reveals the care God lavishes on us:

> Are not five sparrows sold for two pennies? And not one of them is forgotten before God. Why, even the hairs of your head are all numbered. Fear not; you are of more value than many sparrows.[10]

Male and Female He Created Them

The seven-day process in the First Creation Account, told in the form of a Hebrew poem, reveals a great deal about God, creation, and the human person. This narrative has the man and the woman created together on the sixth day, both in the image and likeness of God. In the Second Creation Account in Genesis 2, we learn that the human person is by nature a social being made to live not only in communion with God but also with each other. In this version, told in more of a narrative style, Adam is made first on his own until "God said, 'It is not good that the man should be alone; I will make him a helper fit for him.'"[11] The significant word is "fit": God would make Adam a *fit* partner. As St. John Paul II explained, this fit partner was not a servant or even "a 'helper' in activity. . . . Certainly it is a matter of a life's companion."[12] The narrative goes on to reveal that, after naming all the birds and animals, Adam was unsatisfied because "for the man there was not found a helper *fit* for him."[13] Adam realized that, as a human person, he was alone in material creation since he could not have reciprocal knowledge and love with beings of the animal world; he was not only radically different from but also transcended all of material creation. When he discovered Eve, his fit partner, he joyfully realized that she shared in the same nature as he and exclaimed: "This at last is bone of my bones / and

10. Lk 12:6–7.
11. Gn 2:18.
12. MD, no. 6.
13. Gn 1:20.

flesh of my flesh."[14] Adam's solitary life had been "not good." He, like every human person, is fulfilled through relationships with others, and only Eve, another human person, was a "fit" partner. Like the First Creation Account, the Second Creation Account highlights the equality of Adam and Eve in their identity as persons created in God's image and likeness.

The story also, however, highlights that the human person is made for relationship. The entire social nature of the human race, with all our various cultures and communities, begins with this unique union of the first man and the first woman. Though man and woman are equal in nature and dignity, both being made in God's image, they are distinct and complement one another. Because of Adam and Eve's equality—and their distinct complementarity—they can form an intimate spiritual, emotional, and physical unity with each other. Upon creating Eve from Adam, God mandated that they form a union of "one flesh"[15] that is designed to last for life. In becoming one flesh, their physical union could result in a personification of their love expressed in a new life. In this specific way they cooperate in God's work of creation by the reproduction of new life. As from the union of a man and a woman comes a family, and from the family comes society, so the social nature of the human person is inscribed in our very nature.

The Fall and the Effects of Sin

Our first parents, from the moment of their creation, were in close friendship with God, enjoying a deep happiness and sense of fulfillment in the Garden of Eden. Part of the reason for their perpetual joy was a perfect harmony between their mind, will, and passions. Perfect self-control was the order of the day. Adam and Eve were created without sin, which gave them a close relationship and intimacy with God. This union and habitual conformity with God's will resulted in an ongoing happiness and total control of the intellect and will over their appetites and passions. They lived in communion with God, with one another, and in harmony with the natural world.

Part of this exalted existence of the first man and woman was their complete dominion over creation. They were subject to God,

14. Gn 2:23.

15. Gn 2:24.

and the rest of creation, in turn, was subject to them. Creation was quite user-friendly for the first human beings. There was no danger of contracting malaria or being killed by a tornado. This harmony was closely linked to the man and the woman's self-mastery and their harmony with God the Creator.

Our first parents' perfect dominion over the passions was a gift we call "original holiness." The harmony between our first parents and all of creation is called "original justice." Woman and man were immune to disordered passions of the senses. Greed for possessions, vanity, anger, and intemperance were inclinations that were completely foreign to them. Given this original condition, Adam and Eve were never in ill humor, prone to laziness, or tempted to lust over each other. So perfect was their self-mastery that "mastery" is not even the word for it since there was no inner rebellion. Perfectly inclined to the will of God, by grace their passions were aimed at the good in accord with what they knew to be good. Original holiness also meant that the man and woman were neither destined to die nor to become ill or suffer. It is hard to imagine that deterioration of health, old age, and death were not part of human existence.

This ideal situation that gratified our first parents would come to an end. Because Adam and Eve could know and love, they were free in their choices and decisions—and thus God was able to issue a directive. God clearly commanded, "Of the tree of the knowledge of good and evil you shall not eat, for in the day that you eat of it you shall die."[16] If they would eat of this tree, they would lose their life of intimacy with God. They both realized that adherence to God's command was the right thing to do. Whether this directive literally involved a forbidden fruit or not is unimportant; what is at issue is that our first parents were asked to abide by a specific Commandment. For a while they trusted that God, who is infinitely good, commanded them to refrain from the forbidden fruit for their own good. They were free to either obey or disregard this divine mandate. Unfortunately, at the provocation of the Devil, Adam and Eve disobeyed the only Commandment given to them.

The Devil, then, in the form of a serpent, approached Eve and urged her to eat of the forbidden fruit. He deceived her by saying that eating this would give her knowledge, "and you will be like

16. Gn 2:17.

God, knowing good and evil."[17] Here, as always, the Devil tempts by speaking in half-truths. Eve *would* gain knowledge in that she would come to see and experience things she had not yet known, but what she ultimately learned was that disobedience to God would rob her of both freedom and dignity. Eve succumbed to the seductive promises of the Devil because she saw the *apparent* good without considering the evil it would entail:

> When the woman saw that the tree was good for food, and that it was a delight to the eyes, and that the tree was to be desired to make one wise, she took of its fruit and ate; and she also gave some to her husband, and he ate.[18]

Once that happened, humanity and the world would suffer a tragic wound. This sin is called Original Sin since it was the first sin and the template for all others. With Original Sin, evil officially entered the world, bringing all its sad, tragic consequences. The original state of holiness and justice dramatically ended.

Adam and Eve wanted to be like God, but it would consist in the choice of being alienated from God. They lost their original holiness and became fearful of God. The narrative in Genesis reveals that, after they had eaten the forbidden fruit, they covered their nakedness and hid in the garden. Lovingly, God came looking: "Where are you?"[19] God, of course, knew, but the Sacred Author movingly depicts the loss of communion between God and his beloved creation. "I was afraid," answered Adam, "and I hid myself."[20] Disobedience caused shame and a fearful instinct to hide from God. Adam and Eve lost their special relationship with God. Their minds would be clouded, and their wills would be weakened regarding the fulfillment of God's will.

Alienation from God also broke Adam and Eve's communion with one another. From now on the relationship between man and woman would be severely compromised since the man would be driven by lust and a desire to dominate the woman. "Your desire shall be for your husband, / and he shall rule over you";[21] this describes the rupture of the mutual gift of love originally planned by God. The relationship between a man and a woman, discussed in

17. Gn 3:5.
18. Gn 3:6.
19. Gn 3:9.
20. Gn 3:10.
21. Gn 3:16.

more detail in the chapters on marriage, would now be characterized by tension and strife. Since the family is the origin of society, all human relations would now be marked by conflict.

Creation, too, would rebel against the rule of the human person: "Cursed is the ground because of you; / in toil you shall eat of it all the days of your life."[22] Visible creation would become hostile to Adam and Eve and their successive generations. They would now be subject to toil in their work; the threat of natural disasters; sickness; and eventually the suffering, fear, and anguish of death. That over which they once had dominion would now rebel against their rule.

Before long, the world would drown in sin, as demonstrated almost immediately by Cain's murder of his brother Abel. Sin would proliferate at an alarming rate for the rest of history. With the loss of original holiness, human nature no longer carries with it the inner integrity and sanctifying grace that allows complete control of the physical passions by the intellect and will. From the moment of that Original Sin to the end of time, passion for pleasure and inclination toward pride and anger marks the human condition.

As a result, Original Sin is passed on to every human being, all of whom are descended from Adam and Eve: "He has transmitted to us a sin with which we are all born afflicted."[23] This means that every person conceived is deprived of the original holiness and justice enjoyed by our first parents. All of human nature is thus wounded; inclined to sin; and susceptible to sickness, toil, hardship in work, and the decline of the body, which ultimately results in death. It is common personal experience that there is an internal struggle in a person's inclinations, attitudes, feelings, and emotions. The wounded nature caused by Original Sin consists of limitations of the intellect in discerning good and evil. It also shows itself in a weak—and sometimes malicious—will that fails to control selfish passions like lust and anger; it is also inclined to inflict harm on others through gossip, insults, resentment, hatred, violence, and exploitation. Except for Jesus (whose human nature is in union with his divine nature) and his Mother Mary, no human being would ever again enjoy the benefits of original holiness and justice. (The salvation of the Blessed Virgin Mary will be explained in Chapter 14.)

---

22. Gn 3:17.
23. CCC 403.

It was the man and the woman's abuse of their freedom that brought this sad situation, and all subsequent sin at some level consists of the same disobedience to God's Commandments together with a lack of trust that God's Laws lead to happiness. In this first sin Adam and Eve preferred their own prideful ambition over God's will. They were dissatisfied with their creaturely status and felt they could rival God in excellence. They gave in to the deception that they could be happier in contradiction to God's will, that they too could "be like God."[24] Every temptation to sin is a lie like the first, promising happiness when in fact it destroys happiness, as Adam and Eve placed what *appeared* to be good over the *greatest* good: communion with God.

If all this were not bad enough, the Devil now has greater influence over the human person in tempting us to sin. To understand the Fall and appreciate the effects of Original Sin, we must acknowledge the reality of the Devil. Angels are the prominent created beings of the spiritual order as revealed by Scripture, and the Devil is a fallen angel, called Satan. The Greek *angelos* means "messenger," which describes angels' mission and function as servants and messengers of God. The angelic nature is purely spiritual, meaning that each angel has intellect and will and is therefore a person as well as immortal, but it does not have a material body. (This is why we were clear earlier to say that human beings were unique among *material* creation in having intellect and will; angelic beings do not have material form.) Among the whole range of created beings, the angelic nature surpasses all the rest of creation in its perfection. Because they are pure spirits, they are superior in intelligence and power to any other creature.

The Devil and his demons are angels created by God, and they were originally good, but through their own choice they fell from grace and became totally corrupted. Those fallen angels—demons—radically and irrevocably rejected God, turning them into spiritual monsters. There is no possibility for a fallen angel to repent since its decision to rebel against God and reject him is eternal. The Devil lives to hate God and destroy any relationship between individuals and God. What Satan considers to be a triumph is to instill sadness, despair, and division to cause damnation, undermining the work of Christ's redemption.

24. Gn 3:5.

The demonic tempter insinuated to our first parents that, by disobeying God's command, they would become like God with knowledge of good and evil.[25] Adam and Eve chose to be deceived by the Devil out of pride, mistrust of God, and envy of God's power over creation. The Devil's greatest harm was to effectively tempt Adam and Eve into bringing sin into the world. This sin has metastasized like an overly aggressive cancer and will remain until the end of time.

But there is good news—*the* Good News! God did not abandon us. As Genesis foretold, God would send a Redeemer to free everyone from sin and its destructive effects. The *Protoevangelium* (from the Greek for "First Gospel") is a passage in Genesis promising a Savior, born of a woman, who would wage battle with the demonic serpent. God assured Adam and Eve that through a special woman, whom we know to be the Blessed Virgin Mary, the head of the serpent would be crushed, achieving a final victory against forces of evil.[26] The Church calls the Savior the "new Adam" and his Mother the "new Eve" since their actions redeem us from the sin of Adam and Eve. The image of God, in which the human being was created, became disfigured by Original Sin, but through Christ, the Son of God and son of Mary, it can be restored. Jesus Christ, through his Death and Resurrection, restored what had been lost by Original Sin and offers all people a superabundance of grace and the opportunity to be healed of their sins and to become participants in the divine life of God.

The biblical story of the Fall often prompts the question of why God did not prevent the first man and woman from sinning. The answer is twofold: First, and this is no small point, God respects human freedom. He gave us freedom so that we can love. Even by restricting that freedom, essentially eliminating it, the inability to sin would be a lesser good than the ability to love. God "risks" human disobedience for the sake of the greater good of human love.

Second, not only does God preserve the higher good of human freedom; because he is *infinitely* good, God can draw an *even greater* good from this terrible evil. The graces and blessings showered on humanity through Christ far outweigh the evil and negative effects of Original Sin. The Church celebrates this in her liturgy during the

25. Cf. Gn 3:5.
26. Cf. Gn 3:15.

Easter Vigil: The poetic Easter Proclamation, often called the *Exsultet*, includes a reference to Original Sin as the "happy fault":

> O truly necessary sin of Adam,
> destroyed completely by the Death of Christ!
>
> O happy fault
> that earned so great, so glorious a Redeemer![27]

Faced with the mystery of evil in the world, what we need to remember is that evil is present on account of *our fault*, not in the original plan of God. Evil takes the form of not only natural catastrophes but also more acutely and formidably in the immoral conduct of people. God does not cause moral evils but rather permits them since, as just noted, he respects the freedom of spiritual beings and can, in every life, bring enormous good out of moral evil. The greatest sin in the history of the universe, the killing of the Son of God made man, led to the redemption of the entire human race. The existence of evil and suffering in the world is a mystery that is illuminated by the Passion, Death, Resurrection, and Ascension of Jesus Christ, who by his suffering vanquished it.

The tragic consequences of sin are a compelling appeal to the merciful, healing power and saving graces of Jesus Christ's redemption. If we hope to overcome sin in the world, our first step must be to overcome sin in ourselves, which we can only do by uniting ourselves to Christ, who restores our lost freedom and offers us eternal happiness with the Triune God.

27. RMiss, Easter Sunday of the Resurrection of the Lord: The Easter Vigil in the Holy Night, The Easter Proclamation (*Exsultet*), no. 19.

Chapter 4

Freedom and Happiness

Israel had long awaited the promised Messiah, who would bring liberation and peace—but it is clear from Sacred Scripture that not everyone understood the type of freedom the Messiah would bring. Some believed he would liberate the Hebrew people from the oppression of the Roman Empire and establish a new, earthly kingdom. This was not the salvation Jesus Christ came to offer. In preparation for Christ's message of salvation, God sent St. John the Baptist to preach *repentance and the forgiveness of sins*. Jesus himself proclaimed: "Repent, and believe in the gospel."[1] The Messiah came to liberate us from sin and all of the negative consequences that come as a result. He came to restore humanity's relationship with God. Accepting the reality of sin and seeking to overcome it in our lives is the first step toward restoring our communion with God.

What Is Sin?

Following the explanation of St. Augustine, sin is any deed, word, or desire that violates eternal Law. Eternal Law is the divine wisdom that directs all of creation. Part of this eternal Law includes the natural law, and so any violation of the natural law robs a person of dignity, reduces freedom and self-control, and creates a distance between the person and friendship with God. St. Thomas Aquinas's explanation focuses on the infractions of the Ten Commandments (or one of its immediate applications) and describes sin as a violation of the moral law. However one chooses to describe it, sin is any violation of the mind and will of God and constitutes an offense against God.

A person does not necessarily need to directly wish to offend God to sin. Offending God does not require a direct malicious affront. Many parents, for instance, feel offended when their children deceive them with the lie that they are at a friend's house when they're actually at an unsupervised party. Upon discovering the deception, parents understandably are hurt because of this outright lie, even though it was not told out of malice toward the par-

1. Mk 1:15.

ents. Thus, even without direct malice, the violation of any law that is derived from God's Commandments is still an offense against God.

Sin can also be understood as a disordered love for created things over God. Most instances of sin arise from an inordinate attachment to created goods on account of our unruly passions—thanks to our wounded human nature—which alienates, to some degree, the human person from God. Whether it pertains to robbery, theft, physical abuse, or lying, the common element is the pursuit of selfish motivations taking precedence over God's will. Like Adam and Eve, an *apparent* good is sought at the cost of a greater, or even the highest, good. In this sense, all sins manifest a form of idolatry in that the person places some other thing before God.

Sacred Scripture shows that sins are not all the same kind; neither are all immoral acts equally sinful. The most common classification of sin is according to whether it is a *mortal sin* or a *venial sin*. Mortal sin is a grave offense against God that destroys our relationship with him. By committing a mortal sin, a person willingly chooses a disordered act that separates him or her from God and his divine love. The *Catechism* lists three conditions for a sin to be considered a mortal sin: The act in question must involve a *grave matter* that is carried out with *full knowledge* and with complete *consent of the will*.[2] What can be noted here is that because it requires full knowledge and complete consent, there is no way to commit a mortal sin "by accident." It is possible, however, to commit a mortal sin without a desire to offend God directly or explicitly.

Venial sin is a less serious act that does not separate a person from God like a mortal sin does, but it does weaken that person's relationship with God. The *Catechism* distinguishes mortal and venial sins by the effects, stating:

> *Mortal sin* destroys charity in the heart... turn[ing] man away from God, who is his ultimate end and his beatitude.... *Venial sin* allows charity to subsist, even though it offends and wounds it.[3]

Though less grave, a constant unrepentant repetition of venial sins can lead to the committing of mortal sins and a life of vice. Unexamined habitual sin clouds the judgment and erodes a person's will to do good. If left unchecked, venial sin prepares the way to committing mortal sin by gradually eroding a person's love of God.

2. Cf. CCC 1858–1859.
3. CCC 1855.

"Mortal sin destroys charity." This is a tragic result. An interior emptiness and profound disillusionment visit the person in mortal sin. To know that something is against God's will and to do it anyway is a profound rejection of God's love. Why would a person take such a step? Why did Adam and Eve? Too often a person thinks that such an act is a form of liberation when precisely the opposite is the case. With mortal sin—sometimes also called serious, grave, or grievous, sin—comes a *loss* of freedom, where the person becomes enslaved to his or her passions and falls under the sway of the Evil One. Worst of all, the individual finds him- or herself alienated from God and everlasting life.

Authentic Human Freedom

Human freedom is at the heart of the question of sin and the presence of evil in the world. Free will is part of what distinguishes us from animals and is related to our capacity for reason, our ability to understand and discern good from evil, and the existence of our immortal soul. It was an abuse of freedom that caused sin to enter the world, and because of sin, the will is weakened—resulting in a loss of true freedom.

The loss of freedom caused by sin is generally misunderstood. Too often, freedom or free will is thought of as "the license to do whatever one wants." The most radical form of this misconception presupposes that our guiding light goes no further than our immediate physical desires. This would mean we have an open-ended freedom of choice, independent of any objective moral standard. In this view, our choices are not really a matter of choosing good over evil or a greater good over a lesser good. Every choice would be nothing more than an exercise of personal preferences of the moment, so much so that deciding whether to cheat on income taxes, shoplift, or commit adultery is erroneously perceived as what is "good for me" right now. Right or wrong would not transcend any personal disposition or inclination but solely rest on one's subjective perception. Following this view, anything that prevents me from doing precisely *what I feel like* doing in any given moment is a restriction of my freedom.

But that is not what free will is truly meant to be. As revealed in the creation narrative, God desires his people to follow him willingly and not through compulsion. God has endowed us with this freedom so that we can willingly, that is, *freely*, choose to embrace the moral law as the necessary first step in fulfilling Christ's Commandment to love as he loved.[4] Love, by its very nature, is a *free* gift of self. True love is free, not compelled; therefore, it is intimately linked to the exercise of freedom. From a moral perspective, for freedom to be used properly and develop, it must be guided by objective moral truth.

Considering the false view that the power to do what one pleases increases freedom, we find that the direct opposite is true. Adam and Eve, in their original holiness, had complete self-control over their minds, wills, and passions. Discovering the good, they were able at once to do it. As a result of the Fall, the human person suffers from a clouded mind, a weakened will, and disordered passions—passions that do not always obey our wills even when we know the good. Sin weakens our self-mastery and makes us less able to choose the good when it is inconvenient or requires sacrifice—and then our passions rule us rather than the other way around. I do not *want* to eat the cookie. I would *prefer not* to eat the cookie. I am compelled to eat the cookie and instantly regret it. My actions are not free; I am driven by my desires against my will.

This is not to say that the passions are inherently evil and to be eliminated. The *Catechism* teaches that passions can be either good or bad; they can be directed toward virtue or toward vice. The question is whether we control our passions or they control us. As the *Catechism* teaches: "The alternative is clear: either man governs his passions and finds peace, or he lets himself be dominated by them and becomes unhappy."[5] This is what Jesus meant when he said, "Every one who commits sin is a slave to sin."[6]

Authentic freedom is the power to do the good for which we were created. This requires that we first know what the good is. Our freedom must be guided by—and directed toward—the objective truth. Truth liberates us to know and choose what is ultimately best for us and leads to genuine, lasting happiness. We all desire happiness, but we must first know how to achieve it, and then we must have the strength of will to choose those means. The truest exercise of freedom is choosing to "do what one ought." This will always be

4. Cf. Jn 13:35.
5. CCC 2339.
6. Jn 8:34.

the will of God, which in turn is for the good of the person acting as well as for the good of others. Jesus explicitly stated that the truth of the moral law, perfected by his own example and teaching, perfects freedom: "If you continue in my word, you are truly my disciples, and you will know the truth, and the truth will make you free."[7] Sin, on the other hand, enslaves us to passions, which renders us incapable of love because passions are self-centered rather than other-centered. A self-centered life never leads to happiness.

Although God's natural law is inscribed in every person's soul, our sinful nature makes it difficult for us to make the right moral decisions on our own. Because of these inherited limitations, we need God's help to distinguish good choices from evil choices. Jesus himself taught that the precepts of the moral law are the first step toward salvation and a relationship with God. When the rich young man asked Jesus what he must to do to be saved, Jesus replied, "Why do you ask me about what is good? One there is who is good. If you would enter life, keep the commandments."[8] In his reply to the young man, Jesus expressed the nucleus and spirit of Christian morality. The answer to the question about moral goodness and its connection to eternal life can only be found in God. One cannot know what is good without knowing goodness itself. This is the liberation the Messiah came to offer: freedom from the slavery to sin—freedom to do what is good.

Authentic Human Happiness

The philosopher Aristotle (384–322 BC), based on natural reason alone, investigated what the proper goal, or end, of human life is and decided—like many other philosophers—that the goal of human life is to be happy. But what makes a person happy? As a good sculptor is someone who sculpts well, what does it mean to "be human" well? It cannot simply be existence, for the human person is more than a plant. It cannot simply be the pleasures of the senses, because all animals share this pursuit. The mere pursuit of physical pleasure, for Aristotle, would be a lower existence—what he called a "bovine" existence—beneath human dignity. The human person's good must be something that fulfills the needs of a rational soul. The good that makes for the happiness of a rational soul,

7. Jn 8:32.
8. Mt 19:17.

he determined, was virtue. Virtue—unlike fame, power, wealth, or any other fleeting good—is not left to chance or good fortune, is available to every human being, and is the product of human action and free will. Virtue produces a happiness that misfortune cannot take away. Happiness then, for Aristotle, is "an activity of the soul in accordance with perfect virtue."[9]

Virtue, however, is not given to human beings at birth. According to Aristotle (and later St. Thomas Aquinas), virtue is only a potential that must be actualized through practice. A person must habitually choose virtue and good actions to possess the happiness that comes from their possession. Our actions can create for us either a good or a bad disposition.[10]

The choice between good and evil will accompany all of us for the duration of our lives. The human preoccupation with the struggle of good versus evil has been the great drama of humanity throughout history. Great literature, profound philosophical thought, and the development of law all concern notions of good and evil. Because this universal struggle is at the very core of human experience, the study of ethics and moral theology is of vital importance to us all. The philosopher Socrates (470–399 BC) put it well when he said, "The science of good and evil" is the most important of all forms of knowledge because it places us on the road to true happiness. The philosopher Plato (424–348 BC) wrote similarly: "Still, I should like to examine further, for no light matter here is at stake, nothing less than the rule of human life."[11]

The fact that ancient philosophers, studying the human person using unaided reason and without the help of God's Revelation, could come to such similar conclusions is because of the natural law written in the hearts of all people. Though called "law," it is really our ability to discern God's plan through a study of his creation, including ourselves. "Natural law" refers to the objective order established by God that determines the requirements for people to thrive and reach fulfillment, enabling the human person "to discern by reason the good and the evil, the truth and the lie."[12]

---

9. Aristotle, *Nicomachean Ethics*, Book 1.13.
10. Cf. Ibid., Book 2.1.
11. Plato, *The Republic*, I, 352d.
12. CCC 1954.

St. Thomas Aquinas wrote that a great deal—though by no means all—of what the human person needs to know to be saved *could* be known through a study of creation based on reason alone, but it would then only be known by a few, and after much study, and still mixed up with many errors.[13] This can be demonstrated by the various codes of law of different civilizations throughout history: While they feature many similarities, they vary in how they regard failures of justice. God, therefore, reveals the moral law to give us certainty regarding the standards for human behavior.

When Moses went up to Mount Sinai to pray, God manifested himself and asked Moses to prepare the Israelites for a new stage in the covenant he had established through Abraham. Through this new covenant God would give his people a clear code of conduct by revealing the Ten Commandments to Moses. For the Israelites, the Commandments were the basic guidelines governing every aspect of human conduct—directives on the pursuit of moral good and the avoidance of evil. The Mosaic Law, or Old Law, which has at its heart the Ten Commandments, set the Hebrew people apart from the rest of the ancient world, but God's people did not view the reception of the Ten Commandments as an imposition. (This is not to say people did not find the Commandments burdensome from time to time, failing to obey them.) Having clear guidelines for maintaining a loving relationship with God and a society built on justice was a blessing and a cause for celebration. This attitude is reflected in the Psalmist's song:

> He declares his word to Jacob,
> his statutes and ordinances to Israel.
> He has not dealt thus with any other nation;
> they do not know his ordinances.
> Praise the LORD![14]

Though God, in his mercy, revealed the Ten Commandments, they are essentially an expression of the moral law written on every human heart. For this reason, the *Catechism* teaches: "The Decalogue contains a privileged expression of the natural law. It is made known to us by divine revelation and by human reason."[15] They are presented in the *Catechism*:

---

13. STh I, q. 1, a. 1.
14. Ps 147:19–20.
15. CCC 2080.

1. I am the LORD your God: you shall not have strange gods before me.
2. You shall not take the name of the LORD your God in vain.
3. Remember to keep holy the LORD's Day.
4. Honor your father and your mother.
5. You shall not kill.
6. You shall not commit adultery.
7. You shall not steal.
8. You shall not bear false witness against your neighbor.
9. You shall not covet your neighbor's wife.
10. You shall not covet your neighbor's goods.[16]

The Israelites knew their destiny—for better or worse—was tied to the fulfillment of the Commandments. This was their history. When the people of Israel worshiped God with fidelity, they prospered, but when they were not faithful, God permitted them to suffer. We do not necessarily see ourselves suffering when we do wrong and prospering when we do good, but this does in fact happen to us—a moral act always changes us for the better or for the worse. Even in applications that are less grave, keeping the Commandments makes us better and happier because they express what we are by nature. They are like the "operating manual" or "FAQ" for being a good human person. Likewise, when we keep God's Commandments, we affirm our faithfulness and open ourselves to the grace of the Holy Spirit. In effect, we tell God that we accept his will in our lives.

Christ and the Law of Love

The Old Law, which is summarized in the Ten Commandments, was only a stage of God's Revelation to his people, a preparation for the fullness of the New Law that would be revealed by Jesus Christ. While the Ten Commandments are binding, morality cannot be reduced to a list of "thou shalt nots" as though the moral law presents only prohibitions. When morality is only seen as a list of cold, rigid rules, it is easy to think of it in negative terms as a list of restrictions. This view misses the point. Christian morality is a *positive* morality that is essentially liberating as it puts the human

16. CCC, Part Three, Section Two; cf. Ex 2:2–17.

person in a position to achieve true fulfillment and to love well. The prohibitions in the Ten Commandments are designed to aid the person to dominate his or her passions and disordered appetites to be able to positively do something. This can be compared to physical health. The "rules" about diet and exercise are not just a set of limitations for their own sake but guidelines to an active and healthy life. Jesus' moral teachings stress the good we must do much more than the evil we must avoid. The "rules" are at the service of a just, happy, and fulfilled life that can only be fully found in Jesus Christ.

The New Covenant of Christ still *includes* the Mosaic Law. Despite the novel message preached by Jesus, he did not come to get rid of the Old Law but to perfect it:

> Think not that I have come to abolish the law and the prophets; I have come not to abolish them but to fulfil them. For truly, I say to you, till heaven and earth pass away, not an iota, not a dot, will pass from the law until all is accomplished.[17]

Following the teachings of Christ, Christians have always been admonished to keep the precepts found in the Ten Commandments. The New Law does not abolish the Old; it includes and surpasses it.

In some places in the New Testament, Christ explicitly offers an expansion of a particular law, such as in the Gospel of St. Matthew where Jesus revealed:

> You have heard that it was said, "You shall not commit adultery." But I say to you that every one who looks at a woman lustfully has already committed adultery with her in his heart.[18]

Here we find Jesus expanding the Law to include not only an external action toward one's neighbor but an interior disposition in accord with that right action. Not only our actions but also our attitudes ought to conform with the will of God.

In other places Christ's expansion of the Law can be seen in an overall understanding of its purpose. At the heart of Christ's fulfillment of the Law is his emphasis on the love of God and neighbor as the basis for all moral law. When Jesus was asked which Commandment was the greatest, he replied:

> You shall love the Lord your God with all your heart, and with all your soul, and with all your mind. This is the great and first commandment. And a second is like it, You shall love your neighbor

17. Mt 5:17–18.

18. Mt 5:27–28.

as yourself. On these two commandments depend all the law and the prophets.[19]

To love God with all our heart, mind, and soul is to desire his will. To love our neighbor means we consistently desire their good. Neither of these is possible without mastering our selfish desires in the pursuit of virtue because the love of which Jesus speaks, on which the entire moral law rests, is not a sentimental love of warm wishes that comes and goes depending on our moods. It is a challenging call to submit to the will of the Father and actively seek to do good for others.

At the start of this chapter, various ways of describing sin were offered. Throughout the Old Testament the overriding notion of sin is infidelity to a loving Father who lavishes his blessings on his people. In every phase in the history of God's chosen people, God wants his people to enjoy a healthy, peaceful, and long life: He wants them to be happy. Fidelity to his Commandments demonstrates love of God and, in turn, ensures God's promises of protection and generous assistance. Disobedience or rejection of the Commandments was not taken merely as an infraction of a law but as infidelity to God's covenant and ingratitude for his unmitigated love.

In the Old Testament Israel's sins are likened to marital infidelity. This image is striking because God, through the prophetic writings, discloses his dispositions toward his chosen people. His love for them is equated with the all-consuming devotion of a loving husband for his wife. Similarly, the sins of God's people are put on the same par as adultery. God, however, cannot persist in his anger and mercifully takes back his wayward wife—his chosen people—time and again. Though his "bride" does not honor the covenant and is unfaithful by committing idolatry, God never breaks his covenant with his people or the promise he made—to our first parents and through the prophets—that he would send a Savior to redeem the world.

The Son of God became man and, according to the plan of the Father, redeemed humanity from sin and saved them from death by undergoing unparalleled suffering, humiliation, and anguish. Jesus, who is God the Son, suffered on account of sin but more from *our loss* of dignity and happiness than any personal offense to himself. Since a person is ruined by sin, Jesus suffered out of love and com-

19. Mt 22:37–40.

passion for the one who has been injured. Christ, who "knew no sin," suffered only to save us from our own sin. This total outpouring of oneself for the good of the other is our "Model of all perfection."[20]

Christian morality, then, though grounded in the natural law and revealed in the Ten Commandments, goes much further than the precept "do no harm." It is a call to love as Christ loved by "laying down our lives" for one another out of love, no matter how small the act. The Church teaches that "everyone . . . is called to holiness" and defines holiness not as virtue pursued for its own sake, not as prayer and austerity, but rather as "perfection of charity."[21] Everything else is in service of loving God above all things and loving our neighbors as ourselves.

The connection between the prohibitions of the Ten Commandments and the call to perfection in charity might not be immediately obvious. It goes back to what was said earlier about God's gift of freedom and its purpose in making it possible for us to love. Because of Original Sin human passions are unruly and powerful. Through sin people can easily become slaves to their passions rather than exercising mastery over them. This turns a person in on oneself, causing him or her to seek self-gratification above all things—even above justice toward others. To truly love as Christ loves involves the gift of oneself to another since Jesus defines his love for friends as laying down his life.[22] To give ourselves, we must master our passions so we can exercise our freedom in choosing what is good. This is equally true for any virtuous act. To be just, merciful, chaste, or honest, we must have the freedom to choose these virtuous acts as well as the freedom to effectively convert these choices into actions.

To enjoy the freedom that comes from self-mastery, we must choose to live according to the moral law. It is precisely in choosing to follow the moral law that we become the true masters of ourselves and are in a condition to live self-giving charity. This self-mastery has the power to liberate us from inordinate passions and therefore make us truly free and ultimately happy. Charity is not possible if angry reactions, lustful desires, selfish greed, or consuming resentment drive our actions.

20. Cf. LG, no. 40.

21. Cf. Ibid., nos. 39–40.

22. Cf. Jn 15:13.

If in our freedom we enjoy a high degree of self-control, we can pray seriously, bear suffering joyfully for the sake of Christ, and find fulfillment in serving the needs of others. If we use this marvelous gift well, we can be transformed in such a way that the image of Christ clearly emerges in us. With the aid of grace, we can become empowered to love with the love of Christ himself.

Beatitude

Aristotle was right: The human person is made for happiness. God created us to be happy, both here on earth and in the next life. True happiness is only possible through union with Jesus Christ, who gives us a share in his very life. His life is manifested by a deep love for God and loving service to others. The Beatitudes, given by Jesus in his Sermon on the Mount, exemplify this spirit of love and self-giving, which will bring us bliss (the meaning of the word "beatitude"). In this way, the Beatitudes respond to the desire for happiness placed within the human heart by God himself.

The Beatitudes are the perfection of the Mosaic law. They command a disposition of the heart that radically breaks new ground in moral teaching. For most of the ancient world, happiness lay in power—the power of wealth, the power of authority, the power of strength. The people of Israel, to whom God revealed his Law, were called not to live by the rule of power but of justice. The Ten Commandments bade them to give God the worship he was due and to live in justice with their neighbors. The teaching of Christ in the Beatitudes goes further than the Old Law and flies in the face of the cultural norms of pagan society by calling us to actively give of ourselves for the good of others. Jesus calls "blessed" and "happy" those who are willing to suffer in pursuit of the good.

> Blessed are the poor in spirit, for theirs is the kingdom of heaven.
>
> Blessed are those who mourn, for they shall be comforted.
>
> Blessed are the meek, for they shall inherit the earth.
>
> Blessed are those who hunger and thirst for righteousness, for they shall be satisfied.
>
> Blessed are the merciful, for they shall obtain mercy.
>
> Blessed are the pure of heart, for they shall see God.
>
> Blessed are the peacemakers, for they shall be called sons of God.

> Blessed are those who are persecuted for righteousness' sake, for theirs is the kingdom of heaven.
>
> Blessed are you when men revile you and persecute you and utter all kinds of evil against you falsely on my account. Rejoice and be glad, for your reward is great in heaven.[23]

The Beatitudes run directly counter to the false promise that happiness comes from submitting without restraint to the desires of the passions and appetites. Christ taught that it was only in this sacrificial capacity for love that we can be happy and thrive as people and as a community. Simply avoiding evil and satisfying our duties to our neighbors in a minimalist way will never build a civilization of love. Here lies the importance of the Beatitudes: They point the way to a truly free, happy, and peaceful existence based on the love of Christ.

---

23. Mt 5:3–12.

CHAPTER 5
THE MORAL ACT

In the previous chapter we saw how the moral law is a first step toward being able to love as Christ loves. Put another way, this is because love first requires justice. As Pope Benedict XVI wrote, "If we love others with charity, then first of all we are just towards them."[1] Viewed in this way, the moral law, insofar as it is a guide to behavior, is a guide to just relations—between us and God, and with each other. Turning to the Ten Commandments, we see that they pertain to justice, that is, "giving to each what he or she is due." The first three Commandments pertain to the proper worship we owe to God. The last seven pertain to what we owe our neighbor in justice—do not take your neighbors' belongings, respect your parents, etc. Pope Benedict XVI's point is that, to charitably give a person something he or she is not owed, we must first be just by giving that person what he or she is due.

The precepts of the moral law are understood to be both objective and universal as they are ordered toward justice and rooted in the fundamental dignity of the human person. They are not meant for Catholics or Christians only. To say that a moral law is "objective" means that it is true regardless of anyone's opinion. This can be distinguished from a "subjective" morality that believes the "right thing to do" depends on the situation or the person's feelings. The problem here is that if morality is *all* subjective, then there is no basis for just relations between people. If every disagreement is only a matter of opinion, then a settlement cannot seek justice for all. Whoever has the most power simply gets his or her way. If it is not true that theft is a crime, then thievery is only a matter of getting away with it. If it is not true that every human person has inherent dignity, then racism and genocide can be justified by prejudice and power. As St. John Paul II wrote:

> If one does not acknowledge transcendent truth, then the force of power takes over, and each person tends to make full use of the means at his disposal in order to impose his own interests or his own opinion, with no regard for the rights of others.[2]

1. CiV, no. 6.
2. CA, no. 44.

There can be no justice without an objective law that all parties are obliged to obey.

The Moral Law as Justice

The teachings on moral behavior can be called "law" because they are linked to justice. To understand this more clearly, it might be helpful to study the idea of "law" itself. Any justice system that includes a court of law and the imposition of penalties implies the existence of a standard of morality. If the standards of the law have no source beyond that of the ruler—whether this be an individual or the will of the majority—then people are subject to a tyrant's whims. For law to be just, it must be objective. For such an objective standard to be possible, there must be a transcendent truth to which we are all subject.

The Greek philosophers were fascinated by this capacity of the human person to pursue, grasp, and communicate the truth. With Revelation, God's people can see the truth more clearly and—by his grace—obey it. God's chosen people in the Old Testament had a great love of Scripture because it was the Word of God. One of the many privileges they recognized was their ready access to the truth about the world, morality, and God himself. The law of the surrounding nations was subject to the changing decrees of their despotic rulers. Living in an age abounding in deceit, dishonesty, and treachery, Israel had assurance and security in God's Word and the fullness of truth it expressed. Even the King of Israel had to obey God's Law. This reaches its high point in the Incarnation with the surprising disclosure of God's Revelation that Christ himself is the truth. Not only did Christ "come into the world, to bear witness to the truth,"[3] but he also declares himself to be "the way, and the truth, and the life."[4]

For the law to be just, truth must be the origin of it. Since God is truth itself, all just law finds its origin in the mind of God. Catholic tradition distinguishes different types of law—natural law, revealed law, ecclesiastical law, and civil law—all of which find their origin in eternal Law, which is "nothing other than the plan of divine wisdom as directing all acts and movements."[5] Eternal Law is where

3. Jn 18:37.

4. Jn 14:6.

5. STh I-II, q.93, a.1.

all just law finds its origin. Every law—whether physical, moral, or man-made—is derived from God's eternal Law. God's plan for his creation is the foundation and basis of all true law.

When people speak of the "natural law," they are referring to the precepts that human reason can deduce from a study of creation as a guide for human behavior. Its fundamental precept is "do no harm," and a person need not believe in God to believe in the natural law. From a Catholic perspective, St. Thomas wrote that the natural law is "nothing other than the rational creature's participation in the eternal Law."[6] The natural law is simply the eternal Law as it is perceived and applied to human conduct. As we have seen in previous chapters, the natural law is written in the heart of every human person; this means that "deep down" in each person there is an innate sense of order, an awareness of right and wrong. The natural law shows us the inherent dignity of the human person and how to attain our proper end. It encompasses the essential precepts of the moral life and the principal precepts being expressed in the Ten Commandments. The natural law is universal, and its authority extends to all human beings. It is something that sets the human person apart from the rest of God's material creation.

We must also recall that the human person is set apart from the rest of material creation as being in possession of an intellect and a free will. Whereas physical laws are mechanical, the natural law is not; while the animals are compelled toward their good by instinct, human beings are not. If we want to boil water, we raise the temperature of the water high enough, and it boils. If the ponds start to freeze, birds fly south. By contrast, to obey the natural law requires an exercise of the mind and the will. Unlike physical laws or animal instincts, the natural law must be discovered and is never imposed. One chooses to obey or reject a moral principle.

The moral law is rooted in the natural law, which is in turn an expression of eternal Law. To go against the natural law knowingly and willingly is an offense against God and is termed "sin," but it is not just some arbitrary rule that is broken. When a person rejects these moral obligations, it is detrimental to his or her freedom, dignity, and happiness. A violation of the moral law is sinful because it harms the human person.

---

6. Ibid., q.91, a.2.

The natural law is expanded by revealed law. As discussed in the previous chapter, the precept, "Do no harm," does not approach the requirement of Christ's New Commandment of Love. Aristotle, who believed in a natural law, thought that suffering on purpose was folly. The true beauty of suffering in service to others is the product of God's Revelation in Jesus. Also called the "Law of Grace" or "Law of the Gospel," the New Law of Love makes it possible for us to model our lives after the life of Jesus.

Civil and ecclesiastical laws are made by people for the governance of the world. While these may sometimes seem arbitrary and subjective, to be just they must always be ultimately rooted in the natural law. For example, it is a completely arbitrary choice whether to drive on the right side or the left side of the road. There is nothing in the natural law that dictates one side of the road is good and the other side is evil. Care to protect the safety of the other people on the road, however, is a clear precept of the natural law, so for this reason it is necessary for civil authorities to choose one side or the other. For a law to be just, or even valid, it must reflect some aspect of the natural law, especially as articulated by the Ten Commandments. In fact, a civil law that is in contradiction to the natural law is not even considered a valid law and ought to be resisted.

The Moral Act Itself

Later chapters on the Sacraments of the Church will include more specific details on the precepts of the moral life. This chapter offers a general overview of the moral act itself, using the terms developed by Catholic moral theologians and found in the *Catechism*.

As used in philosophy and theology, the term "moral act" refers to any action that results from a deliberate choice between good and evil, or between different degrees of goodness. To be deliberate, it must be chosen freely. For example, the acts of breathing, walking, and yawning in themselves have no moral value because they are not the fruit of deliberation and choice. They are simply physical actions that are performed unconsciously. The action must also be a choice between good and evil. It is not a moral decision to decide whether to get rocky road or maple nut ice cream. Neither option would be considered wrong, nor is one choice inherently better than the other.

When it comes to moral choices, we have the ability and opportunity to reason and evaluate the various choices set before us along with their corresponding consequences. Then we must make a choice and determine to carry out the chosen act. This interplay between the mind and the will means a person is responsible for his or her actions and must bear the consequences of good or evil. A rooster is not at fault for crowing in the morning and punished for waking people. Unless there is use of reason and will, an action has no moral bearing. In fact, as we will see, even in a properly moral act where either knowledge is lacking or the person was coerced and not acting freely, the blame for the person acting might be diminished.

Some erroneously believe that identifying an immoral act as immoral is tantamount to an unfair judgment of a person; however, the judgment of a person and the judgment of an action are not identical. I can have sympathy for a desperate person holding up a liquor store, but I am not being "harsh" and "judgmental" if I still say robbery is a moral evil. Though an *action* might be sinful, a *person* may bear a greater or less amount of personal blame. While everyone can morally categorize a type of *act*—be it good or bad, moral or immoral—only God can judge the disposition of the human heart. Only God can truly judge the person.

Still, even as we affirm the wrongness of an action, we can consider what alters responsibility. We can judge a person's culpability, which is determining the extent to which a person is at fault, or "culpable," for the bad actions he or she commits. The two factors that impact a person's culpability, or blame, are the same that determine whether an action is a moral act in the first place—how much did this person know, and how freely did he or she act?

Because every human person has an innate grasp of at least some standard of good and evil, every person is accountable for his or her actions, but the knowledge that enters each specific act determines the corresponding level of moral responsibility. For example, an adult is more culpable for lying than a seven-year-old child since the adult has—or at least should have—a fuller grasp of the obligation to speak truthfully. The greater the knowledge of certain rules of good moral conduct, the greater the responsibility. Those who know the truth are held to a higher standard.

The requirement of knowledge means that a person who acts through an ignorance that cannot be overcome (that is, invincible ignorance) is not morally culpable. For an action to be considered sinful, the subject must be aware on some level that the act violates the moral law. For a person to be morally culpable for missing Mass on Sunday, he or she must first realize that it is a serious obligation to attend Sunday Mass. Complete, invincible ignorance of a moral teaching exonerates the person of moral responsibility for that act; partial, invincible ignorance will partially exonerate the person. Responsibility for an objectively sinful action will always depend on the person's actual awareness of the act.

This does not mean ignorance can be used as cover. If we have at least some suspicion that an action might be wrong, then we have a moral obligation to discover the truth before acting. If a person deliberately carries out a wrong action when he or she had prior doubt as to whether it was right or wrong, then that person has committed a sinful act because he or she did not bother to determine whether it was good.

A similar situation arises when free will is considered. Fear and duress — as well as other psychological and social factors — can lessen or even remove personal responsibility for a moral action. This is due to the nature of human freedom. A person acting under the effect of fear is not acting with full freedom, which, like lack of knowledge, limits his or her blame. It does not, as we shall soon discuss, change the nature of the action, only the amount of personal blame.

Moral acts involve the complete person — body and soul. This means they express who we are. As St. John Paul II wrote, "Human acts are moral acts because they express and determine the goodness or evil of the individual who performs them."[7] These actions are not only expressive but also formative. For better or for worse, moral acts contribute toward forming our character. Every moral act leaves us either better or worse off, more or less virtuous, closer to or further away from God. It never leaves us the same. If we perform virtuous actions, we become better people. If we commit sins, our moral quality as people diminishes. If, for instance, I strive to have gentle reactions in the face of anger, little by little, I become a meeker person. If, however, I consistently give in to anger and

7. VS, no. 71; cf. STh I-II, q. 1, a. 3: "*Idem sunt actus morales et actus humani.*"

react negatively, I will gradually become a more violent person. The actions I choose shape who I am.

Components of Moral Deliberation

Despite the effect of knowledge and freedom on blame, an action is still morally good or evil based on the act itself. The way circumstances can alter culpability is only one consideration of moral behavior. Every human act can be evaluated from three distinct perspectives: the object, the intentions, and the circumstances.

The *object* is the act itself, the "good toward which the will deliberately directs itself."[8] It is the action that is performed. Of the three sources of moral deliberation, the object carries the most weight for the simple reason that the object determines the objective morality of an action, how good or evil the action is. The *intention* is "a movement of the will toward the end: it is concerned with the goal of the activity."[9] If the object is "what" a person is doing, the intention is "why" he or she is doing it. Finally, there are the circumstances of the act. The *circumstances* are just what you would expect: all the details of time, place, location, and person that go into the performing of any given act. When? Where? By whom? These are questions about the circumstances.

Though the object is the weightiest consideration for determining the moral goodness of an act, for a human act to be considered morally good, *all three aspects* must be morally good. All three principles must function together toward the enhancement of the goodness of the act itself. If any one of them is lacking, then it can diminish or destroy the goodness of the action. For example, for a person to donate money to charity is a good object, but if his or her *intention* is to do it to win the prestige of peers, then this bad intention diminishes the merit of the good action. If a young man does the favor of shoveling the driveway of a young woman only as a means to seduce and then abandon her, then his good object is completely tarnished by his evil intention. *Circumstances* also play a role in determining the moral goodness of an act. It is an act of charity, for instance, to correct someone who is making bad choices that could have negative effects on that person or others; however, if it is done in front of other people and causes the person humili-

8. CCC 1751.
9. CCC 1752.

ation, the circumstances will have made the good action less good (more evil). Bad intentions and certain circumstances can take an otherwise objectively good action and make it morally evil.

While bad intentions and certain circumstances can diminish the good, the opposite is not the case. Good intentions or certain circumstances have *no impact whatsoever* on an objectively bad action. Good motives do not make an evil action good. Claiming "it depends on the circumstances" is not a good guide for moral decision-making. An objectively evil act can never be justified even with the most laudable intentions and exceptional circumstances. Simply put, a wrong action can never be made right.

What would it be like if every act was judged morally good or bad based on the intention alone? It would be a frightening world indeed. This false position would open a Pandora's box, allowing even the vilest actions to be considered good provided there was a good intention. Some people have tried to justify racism, abortion, adultery, euthanasia, and genocide under the guise of good motives. Recent history shows many oppressive political regimes and unjust wars have been justified by claiming good motives. Totalitarian regimes are notorious for trying to defend their oppression by saying their evil actions are necessary for the sake of the common good. From St. Paul,[10] to St. Thomas Aquinas, to today, the Church has taught that we cannot do evil so that good may come. For an act to be morally good, the object of the act, the intention behind it, and the circumstances surrounding it must all be good.

As with blame, a good intention might diminish the *gravity* of a sinful action. A woman might lie about her previous employment experience to secure a job that will better provide for her family, or a teenager might take his father's car against his will so that he can participate in a charitable activity with his youth group. These actions are still objectively the sins of lying and disobedience / theft, even if the intentions make the actions less grave, or serious. Circumstances, too, can lessen the gravity of a sin. To steal a bottle of water from a well-stocked grocery store, for example, is a lesser sin than to steal the last supply of water from a person who is destitute with little access to water. But *no intentions or circumstances can make an evil action good.* This is an erroneous way of thinking that often

10. Cf. Rom 3:8.

is described as "the ends justify the means." Evil and sin cannot be used even to achieve a good, positive goal.

Example: The Eighth Commandment

Dividing moral deliberation into the categories of object, intentions, and circumstances results in three moral principles: (1) Good intentions or circumstances cannot make an evil action good; (2) evil intentions or circumstances can make a good action bad; (3) intentions or circumstances can affect the gravity of and culpability for a sin. These principles mean that the context of the action can only make good actions wicked or make wicked actions *less bad*. To illustrate how this works, let us consider the Eighth Commandment: "You shall not bear false witness against your neighbor."[11]

While explicitly forbidding the spread of false statements, the Eighth Commandment requires us to be truthful in word and deed in all our dealings with others. Truthfulness is a virtue; it demands that we seek the truth and strive to put it into practice in our lives as well as share it with others. The *Catechism* teaches that truthfulness is "the virtue which consists in showing oneself true in deeds and truthful in words, and guarding against duplicity, dissimulation, and hypocrisy."[12]

As in all evaluations of moral actions, the object of the act must be determined. The object of a lie is to lead another person into error. A person lies when he or she deliberately says (1) something contrary to what he or she thinks or knows to be true or (2) something false to a person who has the right to be dealt with truthfully. Every lie is an evil act. If the object itself is different than this, then speaking falsehood is not an evil act. To transmit erroneous information unintentionally, through ignorance, or in good faith is an objectively different act and therefore not a lie.

While all lies are evil, the gravity of a particular lie is determined by "the nature of the truth it deforms, the circumstances, the intentions of the one who lies, and the harm suffered by its victims."[13] Objectively, a lie is a lie, even though the circumstances and intentions can affect how evil the lie is.

---

11. CCC, Part Three, Section Two; Ex 20:16; cf. Dt 5:20.

12. CCC 2505.

13. CCC 2484.

The nature of the truth deformed can be as minimal as whether someone looks good in a hat or as grave as *calumny*, in which someone's reputation is damaged or destroyed through false information. With the former, the truth might not necessarily have great consequence; with the latter, a person's very dignity is at stake. Once the nature of the lie is established, the intentions must be considered. One can lie, for instance, simply to avoid giving an embarrassing answer, or one can intend to inflict serious suffering through a false accusation of a crime. In the former case, the intention is not grave, so that person is culpable of a venial sin; in the latter, it is grave, so (depending on the circumstances) that person is likely culpable of a mortal sin. Although the intention can increase or diminish the gravity of a lie, it still can never erase its objective evil.

As in all moral acts, circumstances play a role in determining the degree of wrongdoing caused by a lie. If the person lies while under duress, it would reduce the gravity of the sin; if someone willfully constructs an elaborate narrative in order to cause another person's downfall, the seriousness of the deception is significantly intensified. As with intentions, the circumstances of the lie can increase or diminish the culpability of the person who lied but can never change the object of the act.

Another important part of the circumstances of an action is its effects on others. Every moral act affects others in some way. By its nature, lying deceives at least one other person. Recommending someone as an honest and virtuous person for a job while knowing that person is dishonest and troublesome, for example, would cause problems for everyone in the new place of employment. On the other hand, the effects might be minimal such as when a person gives false reasons for not going to a social event.

While the gravity of a lie can be greater or lesser, the overriding consequence of lying and deception is always the creation of mistrust, hostility, and strife among people who are victims of falsehood. *Objectively* the act of telling a lie is always wrong. As disciples of Christ, we should always be careful to avoid giving scandal through double-dealing, or duplicity, by acting or speaking differently depending on the circumstances. Such conduct gives rise to hypocrisy and reduces our effectiveness in spreading the truth of Christ.

This same process of deliberation applies to all violations of the moral law. Objectively a sin is a sin; only the gravity, the culpability, and effects are changed by circumstances.

The Loss of the Sense of Sin

God's abundant mercy and the possibility of committing a "less evil" act should not be taken as an invitation to be wishy-washy about sin. We cannot presumptuously commit a wicked action thinking, "That's okay; I'll just go to confession later" or, "I did a bad thing, but it wasn't *that* bad." This does not sufficiently acknowledge the reality of sin or the evilness of the act.

Some people, for various reasons, refuse to acknowledge sin as the reason for evil in the world. Others simply reject the whole idea of sin—or even God himself—in their lives. In many instances, sin is considered no more than a label placed on certain actions based on arbitrary social norms. This insensitivity to both the nature and evil of sin has led to severe moral and social problems. What would have been unthinkable in other times has now become widely accepted—and even welcomed—to the harm of human dignity and the social fabric.

The loss of the sense of sin has many contributing causes. Oftentimes it is simply through the repetition of habitual sin that a person's heart becomes hardened; this leaves him or her neither able to recognize the damage caused nor hear his or her own conscience. In the face of temptation, we might look for a way to rationalize our desires. Unfortunately, many voices today offer seemingly "intellectual" answers for why we need not worry about the idea of sin.

Faulty psychology is one such voice and occurs when the inferences and theories of this otherwise valid behavioral science go against the moral law. Psychology is a valid science that has made wonderful inroads in assisting the human person to overcome emotional and mental difficulties. Like any other discipline, however, it must base its premises and conclusions on objective truth. The Church teaches that the path to fulfillment lies in overcoming and mastering the impulses of the passions, but in some psychological circles self-control over the passions or appetites is labeled as an unhealthy repression resulting in self-imposed guilt. Certain thinkers characterize the experience of guilt and shame as the evil to avoid, when in fact the sense of guilt and shame is often a product of conscience and a symptom that something else has gone wrong. A psychology that encourages the expression of anger, self-absorption, or immoral sexual behavior would be a false psychology because it contradicts moral truth coming from God himself, who is the true guide for human happiness.

Other psychologists dismiss the concept of sin, attributing disordered choices to insecurity, trauma, poor upbringing, lack of parental concern, or other factors. Though these tragic effects can be the cause of sin and can offer valid mitigating circumstances, most often they do not exonerate a person from culpability of moral wrongdoing. For these psychologists, the remedy is to ventilate the negative feelings and thoughts through the application of mental techniques. Though this can offer relief, it does not get to the cause of the problem. Such a psychologist can be compared to a medical doctor who only seeks to eliminate the pain and totally ignores, or denies, its cause in a broken bone. While psychology has a very important role in remedying emotional and personality disorders, it can never serve as a substitute for actually *healing* the effects of *sin*. The remedy for sin is found through improving the quality of a person's actions and turning to the healing graces of Christ's forgiveness.

Confusion can also exist between what is moral and what is legal. Just because something is permitted by civil law does not mean it is a reflection of the natural law, that is, lawful in the eyes of God. First, civil authority cannot legislate and police every immoral act. A teenager lying to her mother will not land her in prison, but it is still a sin. More significantly, what is legal is not always morally correct. In fact, when civil law violates or opposes the fundamental tenets of the natural law, it must be rejected or disobeyed. The "Jim Crow laws" that enforced racial segregation in the United States of America in the first half of the twentieth century were an affront to human dignity and were rightly resisted. The legalization of abortion constitutes another glaring example of a civil law that contradicts the Law of God and warrants opposition. Civil law is not a complete guide to moral behavior.

Secular humanism is a philosophy that rejects the idea of sin. This intellectual system seeks the improvement of human society but only through human means such as scientific advancement and efficient social work. It tends to focus on a person's *material* welfare. While the goals of people who subscribe to secular humanism are often noble, their view of reality rejects any reference to God, religion, or objective moral values. Their secularist attitude has a narrow view of human dignity, ignoring the spiritual component of the human person. It therefore has no concern for moral rectitude and development. The rise in popularity of secular humanism in some segments of society has also contributed to the loss of the meaning of sin. This ultimately undermines the very goals secular humanists set out to accomplish. The problems of the world cannot be corrected without fully considering the reality of sin and acknowledging the true freedom that Christ bought for us.

These and other factors contribute to a growing sense of moral relativism in the world. Moral relativism is the belief that there are no objectively good or evil actions and there exist no moral standards applicable to all situations and circumstances. According to people who hold this, morality is relative to the person, the circumstances, the times, the culture, and the prevailing opinions. The "goodness" of an act depends upon a person's attitude or disposition rather than objective standards according to the natural law. In the context of moral relativism, the notion of sin becomes irrelevant since it is defined as an infraction of a law that does not objectively exist. The worst a person can do is contradict an accepted social custom, making every situation "your opinion against mine."

There are many "schools" of moral relativism. Each of them, in some fashion, rejects the position that the object of moral deliberation is good or evil *independent* of intentions or circumstances. For example, situation ethics maintains that the goodness or evilness of a given action is determined by the particular *circumstances*. The circumstances, or situation, according to this opinion, form the prevailing criteria concerning the morality of an action. A common example of the application of situation ethics takes the form of cohabitation of an unmarried man and woman. Some will admit that living together outside of marriage is wrong, but financial situations or the need "to know one another better" would warrant or at least allow unmarried couples to live together in a romantic relationship as if they were married. This is a clear claim of the situation overriding the standard guidelines of the natural law in the area of sexual morality. This branch of moral relativism does not summarily reject the natural law but rather holds that the circumstances are the main determining factor of the moral act.

One offshoot of situation ethics is consequentialism. People who hold this outlook judge an action to be good or evil by the consequences that follow it, not by whether the object of the action reflects the natural law. For consequentialists an act is good if the subject perceives a good outcome, while an act is evil if a bad result is anticipated. This is the clearest expression of the philosophy that "the ends justify the means." It is also seen in the notion that an otherwise evil act is permissible if "nobody gets hurt." Whether the act corresponds to objective truth for human behavior becomes, at most, a secondary consideration.

Consequentialism exhibits several flaws in its moral thinking. First, objective morality takes a back seat to the subjective standards of end results. According to this system, adultery is an evil action only if the end result is expected to have a harmful effect on a marriage and children; however, cheating on a spouse would easily be considered a morally good act if it were expected to somehow bring about a certain fulfillment that helped the adulterer become an ostensibly better or happier person. Consequentialism defies St. Paul's teaching that a person can never do evil to bring about a good.[14] A deeper investigation usually reveals that the so-called "positive" results are only euphemisms for selfish satisfactions that inflict much harm and pain on others. It also fails to consider that the person who commits an objectively immoral act is always damaged by it even if he or she is totally ignorant of that act's immorality. As in the example above, even if the spouse of an adulterer never finds out, the person committing adultery is damaged by the sin.

There is a general appeal to consequentialism regarding life issues. Some declare that assisted suicide in the case of someone suffering from a painful terminal illness is a kind and merciful act since the patient is relieved of his or her misery; however, in addition to the fact that euthanasia is objectively a murderous act, the true consequences of it have a devastating effect on the perception of human dignity. A person's right to life is shifted from an objective moral standard to the subjective decisions of doctors, family members, and civil authorities.

Another expression of moral relativism is proportionalism, which measures the moral goodness of an action according to a comparison between its good and evil *effects*. In this view, an action

14. Cf. Rom 3:8.

is good when the good effect proportionately exceeds the evil effect. On the other hand, an action is wrong when the evil effect is proportionately greater than the good effect. In practice proportionalists will maintain that an individual can disregard the natural law for a proportionately good reason.

The self-evident consequences of these erroneous perspectives demonstrate that the ethical criteria defended by these systems are not valid. Some of history's greatest injustices were supported by people using the arguments of proportionalism and consequentialism. These errors are rejected by the *Catechism*:

> It is therefore an error to judge the morality of human acts by considering only the intention that inspires them or the circumstances (environment, social pressure, duress or emergency, etc.) which supply their context. There are acts which, in and of themselves, independently of circumstances and intentions, are always gravely illicit by reason of their object; such as blasphemy and perjury, murder and adultery. One may not do evil so that good may result from it.[15]

Following Your Conscience

The requirement of knowledge for moral responsibility does not mean "ignorance is bliss," as though not knowing the moral law gives a person a free pass and an easier life. Although the responsibility for a moral act is mitigated by lack of knowledge about its sinfulness, the act still causes damage. For example, even if a person were somehow oblivious to and ignorant of the moral obligations to refrain from pornographic movies or magazines, the act nevertheless would cause negative moral effects on his or her mind, heart, passions, and will. Such a person would still become a slave to that sin. He or she would still be more susceptible to worse evils. The joy would still be emptied from his or her life. We might not blame an inexperienced drinker for overindulging and not fully understanding his or her actions, but that does not prevent the hangover. This makes it all the more necessary to eliminate our ignorance by learning the moral law, to discover what pleases God, and to make our choices according to his plan for our happiness.

One guide that every person has for making the right choices is the conscience, but this assistance can be misunderstood. Con-

15. CCC 1756.

science is often described as a "little voice" that prompts an action or to avoid an action. But everyone has many different "little voices," and those voices are not all urging good deeds. Conscience is also often confused with emotions, desires, or "gut instincts." A person might think there is nothing wrong with something he or she wants to do because "I *feel* okay about it." Feelings can be deceptive, and human beings are masters of rationalizing the things they desire. The word *conscience*, however, is from the Latin *cum scientia*, which means "with knowledge." Conscience is a process by which we can *know* whether something is good or evil. This knowledge may *prompt* certain feelings in response—like satisfaction when helping a neighbor or guilt upon harming a neighbor—but feelings alone are not a source we can rely on for decision-making.

Properly understood, conscience is a practical judgment of right reason made by the intellect regarding the good or evil of a particular act in light of objective moral standards—the moral law. Conscience is not a feeling, an emotion, or a hunch; neither is it the mere absence of guilt or regret. It is also not a *theoretical* judgment on whether something might be good or evil; rather, it is a practical judgment regarding a moral act. Since conscience is a function of reason and the intellect that evaluates the moral content of a given action, the person who acts according to conscience—or in opposition to it—is responsible for his or her actions.

Conscience is a vitally important faculty for the Christian striving to lead a moral life in Christ. How are we to consult our conscience, and how can we be sure that our conscience is telling us the truth? First, we should be aware of a few basic principles regarding conscience. The existence of the conscience is attested to throughout the Old and New Testaments, but it is recognized quite readily from human experience. When a mother asks her son a question about his conduct at school, for example, the son is prompted by an interior law that urges him to tell the truth. If he chooses to lie, his conscience indicates to him the wrongness of the lie even though he may proceed with untruthful statements. In the case of a lie, conscience informs the boy to experience a sense of guilt.

Within our human intellect there exists a practical moral deliberation. We constantly ask ourselves, "Is this the right thing to do?" or, "Does this act reflect what is morally correct?" We may ignore or barely notice the ethical question at the moment due to our blinding passions, weak will, or apathy, but the question is raised in the depths of our souls. The natural law is inscribed in the heart of every person. In the intimacy of our hearts, we can make free choices, and conscience will assist us in those choices. This assistance is always available to us even though the standards it sets cannot always be articulated immediately.

According to St. Paul, conscience in a certain sense confronts each of us with God's Law and thus becomes a "witness" for us—a witness of our own faithfulness or unfaithfulness to our moral beliefs. There exist innumerable examples where a person suffers a lifetime of sorrow after committing a gravely sinful action that went against conscience. Unless this guilt is relieved through repentance, especially in the Sacrament of Penance and Reconciliation, it can leave the person perpetually unsettled. Conscience is indeed a moral voice that does not keep silent but rather appraises and reprimands, exhorts and corrects. Only God has full access to that witness.

One of the biggest misconceptions regarding conscience is that it can create and apply its own moral standards. This belief is steeped in the error of subjective morality, discussed earlier. Conscience is not just another word for "personal preference." Conscience, if it is to be reliable, must make its judgments consistent with objective moral truth. If it does not, then that conscience is in error and is not to be trusted. In both the spiritual and physical worlds, truth is objective and must be obeyed and applied accordingly. A poorly formed conscience that acts against truth is no conscience at all. It is outside the power of a person's conscience to be the source of its own moral truth. Conscience is a practical *judgment* of right reason made by the intellect. There is always the possibility to err in that judgment.

Conscience seeks to do the good and avoid evil, but it is not always so easy to discern the right thing to do. We do not always know, and we often try to rationalize when we do not like what we do know. The presence of emotion, compassion, or strong loyalties can cloud conscience and adversely influence its discernment. There must be a commitment to the truth about what is good that will be maintained even in difficult circumstances. The gifts of the Holy Spirit—received at Baptism and strengthened at Confirmation—help to enhance the effectiveness of conscience in making sound moral judgments and remaining mindful of the natural law,

Christ's teachings, and the Church. A person's conscience is intimately involved in every effort of discernment, whether that discernment involves a moral decision, vocation, or self-examination of personal sins and virtues. "When he listens to his conscience," says the *Catechism*, "the prudent man can hear God speaking."[16]

As an operation of knowledge, conscience must be formed, or educated and nurtured. This formation begins with learning the basics of Christian conduct such as in the Ten Commandments and the Beatitudes, but it cannot end there. Proper formation also requires a spirit of humility. We must admit to ourselves that we do not know everything and we might sometimes mislead ourselves. If we turn to the Church for guidance, we are blessed with a body of teachings that has been preserved and developed over two millennia. Under the guidance of the Holy Spirit, these truths develop and grow in response to the different challenges of the times but never change. We can study the *Catechism*, read the lives of the saints, and seek out trusted holy men and women to achieve greater moral certainty in our choices and actions. Christ himself assured us that the Church would never err in her teachings on faith and morals.

Formation within the Church can be a challenge. Her principles will sometimes go against what we have learned from the culture or become accustomed to accepting or doing. If approached with humility and an openness to correction, instruction in the Church's teachings will reveal the beauty of the moral law. A person who gives habitual obedience to the teachings of the Church often finds that it leads to an even clearer and more profound understanding along with the testimony of greater happiness and peace.

Besides having a well-formed conscience, discerning God's will in the moment requires a personal relationship with God that only comes through the practice of prayer. Prayer is conversation with God. Through prayer God communicates his will and strengthens us. Prayer, therefore, must accompany the development as well as the deliberations of a well-formed conscience. These topics will be discussed more fully in later chapters, but prayer, meditation on the Scripture, and the grace received in the Sacraments—particularly reception of the Eucharist—are fundamental to the formation and strengthening of the conscience.

---

16. CCC 1777.

A well-formed conscience is a lifelong endeavor that requires nurturing and openness to conversion. The careful and prayerful interior evaluation of our thoughts, words, and deeds using the life of Christ as a standard and reference is called an *examination of conscience*. The entire Sermon on the Mount in the Gospel of St. Matthew[17] serves as a marvelous reference for self-examination. Jesus' teachings on mercy, judgment, humility, purity, and prayer—as well as the Ten Commandments and the teachings of the Church—are the guide by which we can evaluate our own behavior with an eye toward growth in holiness.

An examination of conscience, however, must go beyond a dry analysis of moral conduct. Acknowledging, "I did this bad thing this many times," is a start, but it does not produce growth. It must also lead to sincere contrition, which includes sorrow for our sins and the intention to avoid sin in the future. The examination of conscience—ideally performed daily, particularly at day's end before retiring for the night—must end with a firm resolution to avoid the sins and near occasions of sin that have confronted us. A person can, at any time, turn to God and ask for forgiveness. His mercy is boundless, but the goal of an examination of conscience is conversion of heart, leading to the Sacrament of Penance and Reconciliation, which is presented in Chapter 15. A sincere confession within the Sacrament of Penance and Reconciliation results in a cleansing of the soul and a strengthening of the will. Frequenting this great Sacrament with contrition and repentance is highly recommended since it serves as an invaluable means for not only the formation of conscience but also the strengthening of the will.

You Shall Know the Truth

God creates us in his image and likeness, gives us freedom, and invites us to cooperate freely in his plan of creation; however, we suffer from the consequences of Original Sin and it is only through the merits of Christ that we can have the freedom to love and seek God and to abide by his moral law. The freedom to choose correctly necessarily entails the option to reject God or to be indifferent to him and his will for us. Out of respect for the freedom he grants us, God neither forces us to make the right choices nor prevents us from making wrong choices; otherwise, we would not be free. Evil in the

17. Cf. Mt 5—7.

world, even that which reaches monumental proportions, is the bitter fruit of our evil choices. We cannot blame God for the evils that find their origins in our abuse of freedom. There are varying degrees of ignoring or violating God's Law for human happiness and the welfare of the common good. The more the human will conforms with God's plan, expressed in the natural law, the greater the benefit. By the same token, the more severe the rejection of standards of morality, the more dire the consequences.

Nevertheless, God's grace is offered abundantly to those who seek to live according to his plan. It is a gift that will assist every person who sincerely commits him- or herself to keeping the moral law. As human beings we lack the capacity to perfectly discern good from evil. Even after Baptism we still have the temptation to sin, but Jesus Christ's teachings and the grace he gives us assist in both living the Ten Commandments and following his New Commandment of Love. Those who lack that commitment and effort or who rationalize their own behavior as exempt from the moral law will not be aided by grace they have already rejected. In the case of every baptized person who truly tries to live the Commandments, however, God's grace will never be lacking. God's graces overcome all by supplementing the limitations in our human abilities and enabling us to follow him.

Even with God's grace, it must be admitted, the New Commandment of Love is still no easy task. Original Sin weakens both the intellect and the will, making it hard to know the good and to follow through on doing it. Our passions cloud our judgment. Our motives are often mixed. Even St. Paul, examining his own actions, wrote, "I am carnal, sold under sin. I do not understand my own actions. For I do not do what I want, but I do the very thing I hate."[18] When Jesus came to preach repentance as preparation for the kingdom, he also came to *offer forgiveness*, and Jesus offers forgiveness *abundantly*. When St. Peter asked Jesus how many times he should forgive his brother, probably thinking he was being magnanimous, he asked:

> "As many as seven times?"
>
> Jesus said to him, "I do not say to you seven times, but seventy times seven."[19]

18. Rom 7:14–15.
19. Mt 18:21–22.

We do not understand Our Lord, here, to literally mean 490 times and then we are done. Rather, Jesus figuratively multiplied to show one of his closest disciples just how stingy he was being. Forgive and then forgive again. No sin, no matter how objectively evil, is outside of God's forgiveness. When Jesus appeared to St. Faustina Kowalska with his message of mercy (more on her in Chapter 15), he said, "Let no soul fear to draw near to Me, even though its sins be as scarlet."[20] Jesus forgave even St. Peter, who publicly rejected him three times.[21] The only ways to fail to obtain forgiveness are to not repent and seek it or to reject it when it comes. God loves us infinitely more than anyone else who has ever forgiven us when we were sorry. This love was dramatically revealed when God sent his Only-Begotten Son into the world to become a man, suffer, die, save us from our sins, and bring us to everlasting life.

---

20. DSFK, no. 699, 10.
21. Cf. Jn 21:15–25.

CHAPTER 6

AND THE WORD WAS MADE FLESH

God created a perfect world and placed the man and the woman in the garden to be fruitful and multiply. Our first parents existed in a state of original justice and holiness and were in communion with God, each other, and the beautiful world around them. All of this changed when they disobeyed God and chose not to live according to his plan. Sin, alienation, and death entered the world. But we saw in Chapter 3 that, from the beginning, God had a plan for our restoration. Genesis offers "the *Protoevangelium* ('first gospel'): the first announcement of the Messiah and Redeemer, of a battle between the serpent and the woman, and of the final victory of a descendant of hers."[1] In fact, the entire Old Testament can be seen as a preparation for the coming of Jesus. As St. Augustine said, "The New Testament is hidden in the Old, and the Old is made manifest in the new." Jesus is prophesied and prefigured throughout God's Revelation as the Messiah that would come into the created world, to all the nations through Israel.

After the covenants with Noah, Abraham, and Moses, God established a covenant with David the King. God promised David that he would raise up an offspring from the line of David whose kingdom would be established forever.[2] Here begins God's promise to Israel that he will send his "Anointed One"—his *Messiah*—to rule his people and be their Redeemer. The prophets, too, would speak of the coming of the Messiah, in whose time the blind would see, the deaf would hear, and liberation would be given to those in captivity. He would be the Light of the World and the Prince of Peace. Though many in Israel expected the Messiah to be an earthly king who would liberate his people from worldly oppression and rule on a political throne, the prophets also foretold that the Messiah would willingly take on the world's suffering for the redemption of souls.

---

1. CCC 410.
2. Cf. 2 Sm 7:12–16.

As St. Paul taught, Jesus came "when the time had fully come,"[3] which means that he came at the absolute right moment in history. The chosen people had an established culture and religion based on the worship of the one true God that included fidelity to the Commandments revealed to Moses and trust in God's fidelity. They would provide the foundation and launching pad for the New Covenant of grace and charity founded by Jesus Christ. The world—gripped by sin and characterized by violence, hatred, lust, and pride—was deeply pining for relief and hope that only the Good News of the Gospel could bring. Not even the Israelites, who enjoyed the advantageous gift of God's Revelation, could have guessed that this Redeemer would be God himself, who would become a man to take on the suffering for our sins.

To state the obvious, then, Jesus Christ is the focal point of the Catholic faith. Our Catholic faith is not just a set of teachings but revolves around a divine Person who has become human. The solemnly proclaimed dogmas of faith, the Seven Sacraments, and the moral law are all pathways to an intimate life with Christ. All teachings, Sacraments, and Commandments are meant to lead us to friendship with Christ.

A serious Christian had a conversation with someone who was never exposed to the Christian faith and claimed to be an atheist. This person was curious to know what the distinguishing mark of Christianity was. The believer told the atheist that Christians believe that Jesus—while he was a baby, a carpenter, and a man dying on the Cross—is both God and man at the same time. The person was totally shocked and taken off guard that some people believed the man Jesus could actually be God—the same Creator who brought the universe into existence through his divine nature.

This idea was also shocking to the Jewish people of Jesus' time. How could this man claim to be God's Son? In Chapter 2 we looked at the beginning of St. John's Gospel, which reveals, "In the beginning was the Word, and the Word was with God, and the Word was God."[4] This Word—the Second Person of the Trinity—is eternally with God the Father. The central teaching of the Catholic faith is that this divine Person became one of us. God found a way not only to become part of our world but become one of us in everything but

3. Gal 4:4; cf. Eph 1:10.

4. Jn 1:1.

sin. Our God has a human face; he identifies with human suffering and sorrow. Our God has brought to light a way to become a baby, a worker, a slave, and a suffering Redeemer. It seems too good to be true; God must have gone "too far" in lavishing his love on us in such a radical way. The Incarnation of God the Son gives us a model of holiness and complete access to share in the everlasting life of the Blessed Trinity. "In him the whole fulness of deity dwells bodily."[5] The humanity of Jesus is the sign and instrument of his divinity and work of salvation. All his visible actions lead to the reality of his divinity.

Revelation of Christ's Divinity in Scripture

How exactly does a transcendent, all-powerful God truly become human at the moment of conception? The story is quite familiar but no less spectacular. The wildest fantasies of the imagination could not come up with a more fantastic script. A full treatment cannot be given here, of course, and readers are encouraged to read the Gospels to learn more about the life and death of Jesus. We will focus our treatment on the events that marked the Revelation that Jesus is the Messiah and the Son of God.

As we read in the first chapter of the Gospel of St. Luke, Mary of Nazareth, a teenage girl, was visited by an angel: the Archangel Gabriel, whose name means "Strength of God." He delivered a message that would dramatically change the course of history. This angelic messenger first greeted Mary, "Hail, full of grace."[6] He did not say, "You have been graced," but hailed her with the strange title "full of grace." It was an odd greeting. Scripture relates that Mary was troubled by it and wondered what it meant. The angel told her not to be afraid, that he had been sent from God to inform her that she has been chosen to be the instrument to usher in the Son of God, the long-awaited Messiah. She expressed her commitment to her Perpetual Virginity, that "I have no relations with a man."[7] Then the angel assured her that she would conceive the Son of God in her womb by the "power" of the Holy Spirit, who "will overshadow you"[8] without compromising in the least her virginity. Mary was to

5. Col 2:9.

6. Lk 1:28.

7. Lk 1:34 (New American Bible, Revised Edition).

8. Lk 1:35.

be the only woman in the history of humankind to conceive a child in her womb without the intervention of a man.

God prepared for his Incarnation by creating a woman totally free from Original Sin. She would be the counterpart of the first woman, Eve, who with Adam committed Original Sin. "In view of the merits of Jesus Christ, her Son and the Redeemer of the human race... [Mary was] preserved free from all stain of original sin";[9] this is called the "Immaculate Conception." For this reason, the Archangel Gabriel did not simply *describe* her as full of grace but rather *called* her "full of grace" as if that were her name. Given Mary's calling and singular condition of being preserved from all stain of sin, her beauty and holiness are unparalleled.

After some brief discernment, Mary proclaimed her *yes* to the archangel. The effects of this *yes*, given by Mary in full freedom, changed the course of history and continues to have ramifications until the end of time. The conception of the Second Person of the Blessed Trinity is called the Incarnation—literally, "into flesh." The physical component of Jesus' humanity would strictly come from Mary. By becoming Mother of Jesus, Mary becomes the Mother of every human being on the order of grace. As Eve—the mother by nature of the whole human race—who chose to say *no* to God's mandate, so Mary, completely sinless, chose to say *yes* to God's will, becoming the Mother by grace of all people redeemed in Christ.

Given her unique calling to be the Mother of Jesus Christ without the intervention of a man, the Tradition of the Church teaches that Mary's virginity was preserved before, during, and after the Birth of Jesus. Though the Gospels mention brothers and sisters of Jesus,[10] these terms in the ancient Jewish culture also included cousins and extended family as well. The people that are identified as brothers and sisters of Jesus could also be children of another Mary.[11] Her spouse, St. Joseph, also committed himself to celibacy to make himself totally at the service of protecting and caring for Mary and Jesus, to whom God the Father made St. Joseph the earthly father. Entrusted to St. Joseph was the education and formation of Jesus in his humanity. St. Joseph had a key role in preparing his adopted Son, Jesus, for his public life.

9. ID.
10. Cf. Mk 3:31.
11. Cf. Mt 13:55.

Not only was Joseph responsible for the care of the Holy Family but also it was his responsibility as father to name the child. From the earliest Old Testament times, a name would point to a special calling and mission. The name "Jesus" was not bestowed arbitrarily but was specifically indicated to St. Joseph in a dream by an angel: "You shall call his name Jesus, for he will save his people from their sins."[12] The name Jesus means "God saves." This name strikes at the very heart of Jesus' mission to redeem the world. The Son of God took on human nature to save the world from sin.[13] He came to reveal God's infinite mercy and to give every person absolute access to forgiveness from sin. God the Father through his Son Jesus Christ is the means for everyone to overcome despair and be enlivened with hope and joy.

A title frequently used for God the Son made man is "Christ." In fact, this title is so closely associated with him that it is practically used as a name. The word "Christ" is from the Greek *Christos*, a translation of the Hebrew *Messiah*, which literally means "Anointed One." So Jesus is the long-awaited Messiah. Being the "Anointed One" carries other meanings as well: In the Old Testament, kings, prophets, and priests were anointed with oil as a sign of their calling to God's service. This vocation involved governance, teaching, and worship. Jesus Christ—prefigured by the Old Testament kings, prophets, and priests—is invested in those distinct offices in a perfect, most complete way. Jesus is *the* perfect priest, prophet, and king, who mediates between God the Father and his people. In contrast to Old Testament times, the anointing of Jesus is not performed by means of oil but by the Holy Spirit himself. Kingship, prophecy, and priesthood culminate in Jesus Christ.

Two other titles that are attributed to Jesus in the Gospels are Son of God and Lord. The title "son of God" was used to describe angels, kings, and the chosen people in the Old Testament. In the New Testament "Son of God" refers exclusively to Jesus Christ in his divine nature. According to his divinity Jesus is the Only-Begotten Son of God the Father. Put in human terms, he is God the Father's natural son. Baptized Christians are God's sons and daughters "by adoption," but Jesus Christ, as the Second Person of the Trinity, is God's Only-Begotten Son by nature. To stress his natural filiation, or sonship, to the Father in contrast to our adoptive filiation, Jesus

12. Mt 1:21.
13. Cf. Jn 3:17–18.

addresses God the Father as "my Father," and the rest of us say "our Father."[14] Finally, in the Old Testament the title "Lord" refers to God. Since the Jewish people considered the name *Yahweh*[15] too sacred to use in ordinary speech, the Hebrew *Adonai*, or Lord, was often substituted for *Yahweh*. It was fitting, therefore, that the New Testament applies the title Lord to Jesus, who is God.

The Birth of Christ is of utmost importance in human history since God has entered our world of experiences, sorrows, and joys. God though he was, he did not make a grand entrance; on the contrary, Jesus saw the light of day for the first time in a primitive, grimy stable because there was no room in the local inn. His entourage consisted of a donkey and maybe a couple of lambs and cows. His crib took the form of a food-stained manger drooled over by countless animals. Protected from the harsh elements, he was wrapped in swaddling clothes while Mary, his loving mother, and St. Joseph, his earthly father, doted on him.

Jesus' first visitors were local shepherds—perhaps the lowest on the social scale at the time—before whom a host of angels appeared, announcing the Birth of Jesus. The angels describe the Savior of the World as "good news of great joy." The angels state, in no uncertain terms, that this divine infant is the secret to true happiness.

Some time after the shepherds made their appearance before the divine infant, three mysterious men from a faraway country also paid a visit to the Holy Family. These men did not constitute part of the chosen people but represented the rest of the world's Gentile population. Their presence before the Prince of Peace conveyed the deep significance that Christ was born for all people, both the Jewish people and others alike.

Through study and divine illumination, they had come to realize that a special king was to be born in Bethlehem. Perhaps their familiarity with the prophecies of Daniel together with the illumination of the Holy Spirit led them to embark upon the challenging journey to Bethlehem. This knowledge was reinforced by the appearance of the guiding star that would ultimately lead them to the Christ child. The narrative states that the star disappeared as they were approaching the city of Jerusalem. This disappearance prompted the Magi, or wise

14. Cf. Jn 20:17; Mt 6:9.

15. Ex 3:14: "I AM WHO I AM."

men, to consult Herod, the reigning king in Jerusalem at that time, concerning the whereabouts of the Birth of the King of the Jews. Herod had a reaction both angry and fearful over the prospect of a rival ruler. After mandating that experts in Sacred Scripture research where the Messiah was to be born, Herod was informed that Bethlehem would be the designated place. He encouraged the wise men to look for the child and said, "When you have found him bring me word, that I too may come and worship him."[16]

The star then reappeared, and the three Magi finally found Jesus, Mary, and St. Joseph and offered them gifts of gold, frankincense, and myrrh. The gold is a gift corresponding to a king; frankincense is used to give homage and worship to God; and myrrh consists of a substance for anointing cadavers. The three gifts symbolize Christ's kingship, divinity, and redemptive Sacrifice on the Cross. After their unforgettable visit, which would be joyously commemorated by future Christians for centuries to come on the Solemnity of the Epiphany of the Lord, the Magi returned through a circuitous route bypassing Jerusalem because they had been warned in a dream not to return to Herod.

Herod, realizing that he had been duped, decided to exterminate any potential king born in the region of Bethlehem by having every male child under two years of age mercilessly slaughtered. These children would be called the Holy Innocents. They were the first martyrs for Christ, and their Feast Day is still celebrated every year on December 28. To avoid this destruction, St. Joseph took the Blessed Virgin Mary and her infant Son to Egypt where they would sojourn until the death of Herod. We see that Jesus is a victim, even in his infancy, of suffering and persecution.

Despite the miraculous nature of Christ's conception and entrance into the world, the Blessed Virgin Mary and St. Joseph were always obedient to the customary Hebrew obligations. Eight days after Jesus' Birth, prior to the Holy Family's departure to Egypt, he was officially enrolled by means of circumcision as a member of the chosen people in conformity with Jewish Law. Forty days after his Birth, they brought the baby Jesus to the Temple for his Presentation to God the Father. This Jewish ritual served a dual purpose under the Mosaic Law: First, a woman who had given birth was considered ritually "unclean." Some weeks after childbirth, she was required

16. Mt 2:8.

to go to the Temple to offer a sacrifice for her purification. Second, every firstborn male of the Israelites belonged to God by virtue of the Passover, when he had spared the Israelites' lives while freeing them from slavery in Egypt. For this reason, the Law required parents to present every firstborn male to God in the Temple and redeem, or "buy back," the child.

Throughout the Gospels' infancy narratives, we are constantly reminded that Jesus is the ultimate meaning and fulfillment of every human being. During Jesus' Presentation in the Temple, a holy, righteous man named Simeon encountered the divine infant, and his canticle of prayer proclaimed Jesus as "a light for revelation to the Gentiles, / and for glory to thy people Israel."[17] Included in the Presentation is Simeon's painful prophecy to the Blessed Virgin Mary: "A sword will pierce through your own soul also."[18] This foreboding prediction specifically pointed to Jesus' future Passion and Death that would be witnessed and felt deeply by his Mother. For her this knowledge must have been a never-ending reminder amid the joys and the mirth of a happy Holy Family that a nightmarish end awaited her Son.

The Gospels, interestingly, say nothing of Jesus' early life—except when St. Luke narrates that a twelve-year-old Jesus was temporarily lost and found by his parents in the Temple. Jesus, the Blessed Virgin Mary, and St. Joseph had traveled to Jerusalem for the festival of Passover. This was the greatest feast of the Jewish year, and people gathered from all over the country and even from foreign lands to attend the celebrations. It was customary on these journeys to travel in large groups of family and friends, where the men would travel in one group and the women in another. The children would go back and forth between the two groups. For this reason, Jesus' Mother and earthly father did not at first notice that their son was missing for one full day after having left Jerusalem. Immediately, they went back to the city in search of him.

Upon finding Jesus, his Mother asked her Son why he had done this to them. His response marks his first recorded words of the New Testament: "How is it that you sought me? Did you not know that I must be in my Father's house?"[19] This reply indicates that Christ

17. Lk 2:32
18. Lk 2:35.
19. Lk 2:49.

was aware of his divine Sonship and understood his mission. In this instance, the divine adolescent reveals his inner sentiments, marked by an ardent desire to fulfill God's will above all else.

The otherwise almost total lack of reporting suggests that the hidden years of Jesus consisted of an ordinary life with a normal routine. These years saw no miracles or sermons but rather were characterized by growth and study, work, family life, and interactions with friends and neighbors. Those years were so typical for people of his time that when Jesus spoke for the first time in the synagogue, his audience was surprised and perplexed, asking themselves: "Where did this man get this wisdom and these mighty works? Is not this the carpenter's son?"[20] Those who knew him would not have expected this.

Jesus' time with his family and at his trade conveys the high importance of family and the workplace in the work of redemption. Jesus, the Blessed Virgin Mary, and St. Joseph were involved in the most pivotal moment in human history, but for most of their lives, they were engaged in standard activities no different from those of the majority of the population. Still, we can be sure that everything the Holy Family did—cleaning a room, repairing a roof, or cooking a meal—was done with unparalleled love for God and others. The Hidden Life of Jesus is a powerful lesson and instruction that the normal forum to follow Christ occurs in every person's daily life amid work and interaction with family and friends as well as in the experience of suffering.

Jesus began his public ministry, which culminated in his road to the Cross, when he was about thirty years old. He appeared at the River Jordan, where he approached his cousin, St. John the Baptist, who had been chosen by God to prepare the hearts of men and women for the Messiah.

St. John the Baptist also had a miraculous entrance into the world. He was conceived by his parents in their old age, and it was revealed to his father, St. Zechariah, that St. John would herald the coming of Our Lord. Scripture tells the story of young Mary going to visit her cousin St. Elizabeth, who was pregnant in her sixth month. St. Elizabeth's greeting, along with that of the Archangel Gabriel, forms the first half of the prayer *Hail Mary* and demonstrates St. Elizabeth's recognition of Jesus' special mission and divin-

20. Mt 13:54–55.

ity. As the Blessed Virgin Mary entered, St. Elizabeth exclaimed with a loud cry:

> Blessed are you among women, and blessed is the fruit of your womb! And why is this granted me, that the mother of my Lord should come to me? For behold, when the voice of your greeting came to my ears, the babe in my womb leaped for joy.[21]

In this scene from Scripture, both St. Elizabeth and her unborn child recognized Christ's divinity.

Many years later, St. John the Baptist was preaching and baptizing for the forgiveness of sins. As St. John saw Jesus from a distance he declared: "Behold, the Lamb of God, who takes away the sin of the world!"[22] Through the eyes of faith, St. John again recognized the person for whom he had been preparing the way. These words of St. John can still be heard, repeated by the bishop or priest during the celebration of Mass right before Holy Communion. Like St. John the Baptist, every person is called to recognize the presence of Christ through the eyes of faith.

Upon encountering St. John the Baptist, Jesus requested baptism from him who, acknowledging his own unworthiness, refused. The baptism offered by St. John was a purification ceremony that invited both repentance and conversion. Since Christ had committed no sins, he had no need of repentance or a change of heart. Even so, Christ insisted, telling him, "It is fitting for us to fulfil all righteousness."[23] Though sinless, Christ identified himself fully with sinners as part of his plan of redemption. The baptism of Jesus serves as a powerful sign of his solidarity with every human being born in sin. Since he mercifully and generously chose to take upon himself the entire burden of sin, it was fitting that he would allow himself to be baptized as if we were a sinner.

In this story that demonstrates Jesus' deep humility, we also witness another clear proclamation of his divine Sonship. Subsequent to Jesus' baptism, God manifested himself as a Trinity of Persons: God the Father is manifest in a voice from a cloud, God the Son is manifest in the presence of Jesus Christ, and a dove seen hovering over Jesus represents God the Holy Spirit. In this theophany, or visible manifestation of God, the Father invites every disciple of

21. Lk 1:42–44.

22. Jn 1:29.

23. Cf. Mt 3:15.

Christ to contemplate Jesus' words and life and follow him: "Lo, a voice from heaven, saying, 'This is my beloved Son, with whom I am well pleased.'"[24]

After his baptism Jesus withdrew into the wilderness, where he prayed and fasted for forty days. The number *forty* indicates a protracted period of trial and preparation, which he underwent before his public ministry. The forty days Christ spent praying and fasting are the prototype of the forty days of Lent, during which Christians prepare to experience anew the events of Our Lord's Passion, Death, Resurrection, and Ascension. This retreat into the desert with the purpose of praying and fasting shows every disciple of Christ that the foundation of Christian life is prayer and penance. As diverse as the saints are, they all share the common denominator of generous prayer and self-denial.

During this time in the wilderness, Jesus was sharing fully in the human experience of suffering and temptation. At his weakest moment he was tempted by the Devil. From the moment God foretold Satan's defeat in the *Protoevangelium* in the Book of Genesis, Satan had probably been waiting to discover the identity of the woman and her Son in order to engage them in a supernatural battle. Coming to tempt Jesus Christ, he was determined to find out if he truly is the Son of God, the promised Messiah. Satan began by tempting Christ in the flesh: "If you are the Son of God, command these stones to become loaves of bread."[25] This tactic had worked well throughout human history because one consequence of Original Sin is that the bodily passions and appetites are no longer completely subject to reason. Satan's first temptation was to entice Our Lord to pursue what yielded pleasure and comfort over the spiritual goods connected with bodily penance. Jesus warded off this temptation with his famous response, quoting Scripture: "Man shall not live by bread alone, but by every word that proceeds from the mouth of God."[26] The happiness of the human person consists not in the indulgence of physical desires but in embracing the Word of God.

Having failed in his first effort, Satan tempted Our Lord a second time. He took Christ to the top of the Temple in Jerusalem and told him to throw himself off, claiming if he were truly the Son of

24. Mt 3:17.

25. Mt 4:3.

26. Mt 4:4; cf. Dt 8:3.

God, angels would surely rescue him. This particular temptation of vanity and presumption was designed to impress the religious leaders of Israel with a great miraculous feat. Consequently, they would immediately proclaim him the promised Messiah without the ordeal of his redemptive Sacrifice on the Cross. Though this second temptation is open to many layers of interpretation, it is certain that Satan tempted Christ to pursue glory without the humiliation of his Passion and Death.

With this second temptation, the Devil also implied that Our Lord's toil and suffering was incompatible with the Revelation that he is the Messiah, the Son of God. At the time of Christ, many Jewish people expected a political or military Messiah who would "liberate" his people by defeating the Roman occupiers and restoring their temporal glory, hearkening back to the time of King David. Had Christ assured his people liberation from the yoke of Rome, he would have been proclaimed the king spontaneously. While Jesus is the rightful King of all peoples, his kingdom is not of this world and was obtained at the great price of his self-giving on the Cross. The liberation Christ offers is spiritual: liberation from the yoke of slavery to sin and the freedom to love and be in communion with God. Through his obedience to the Father, Christ would defeat Satan. Jesus understood perfectly that the nature of his mission was not one of human triumph and fame; to redeem the world, he had to suffer and die on the Cross and not "show off" his divinity. In response to the Devil's second temptation, Jesus replied, quoting Scripture: "You shall not tempt the Lord your God."[27]

Having failed twice, Satan tried a third time. The last temptation promised Jesus Christ tremendous worldly success and power if only Jesus would fall and worship him. This temptation is much more common than what it immediately appears to be. There are countless examples of people violating the moral law to get ahead in politics, academia, medicine, and every area of human endeavor. Advancement in many instances is predicated on compromising objective moral standards. Again quoting Scripture, Jesus replied, "Begone, Satan! for it is written, 'You shall worship the Lord your God and him only shall you serve.'"[28] After this, Satan finally left him. By his prompt rejection of the Devil's temptations, Jesus, the new Adam, counteracted the disobedience of the first Adam, who

27. Mt 4:7; cf. Dt 6:16.

28. Mt 4:10; cf. Dt 6:13; Mk 8:33.

surrendered to Satan's temptation to eat the forbidden fruit, thereby rebelling against God's Fatherhood.

After Jesus completed these forty days in the desert, he called his Twelve Apostles and began his ministry of teaching and healing. While Christ's preaching is often referred to under the heading of "Gospel" or "Good News," it is also known as the "proclamation of the kingdom." Though every word and action of Jesus is revelatory, the central message can be summarized in this proclamation: "The kingdom of God is at hand; repent, and believe in the gospel."[29]

The kingdom Christ proclaimed and taught was not the earthly kingdom of David for which some hoped. Throughout his public ministry Jesus declared that his kingdom was not of this world. Open admissions characterize this kingdom. The only condition for entrance is repentance and faith in Jesus' teachings. Since his kingdom is not of this world, it is strictly spiritual and is marked by peace, joy, truth, and freedom. The faith required for Jesus' kingdom include heartfelt contrition for sins, detachment from material things, willingness to serve the needs of others, and commitment to a serious prayer life.

Jesus explains the mystery of the Kingdom of God through a whole variety of parables. He uses the image of the seed to shed light on the workings of the Kingdom of God. Seeds grow from within, and they grow not just quantitatively but through constant transformations. If they grow to full maturity, they will bear fruit. To establish oneself in the Kingdom of God and extend his kingdom to others, that person needs to be totally committed to living out Christ's teachings. The saints have laid down their entire lives for Christ and subsequently have attracted many to Christ.

Jesus backed up his teachings on the Kingdom of God with spectacular miracles that had no natural explanation. With a mere word he would calm a storm, cure a leper, or restore sight to the blind. By the mere exercise of his will, he would cause preternatural phenomena like multiplying fish and loaves of bread to feed thousands. By a mere wish he changed water into wine and restored a withered arm to its normal size and ability. The miracles are an expression of Jesus Christ's absolute dominion over the laws of nature. Only God can suspend or bypass physical laws and, moreover, only God can forgive transgressions. An important facet of

29. Mk 1:15.

Jesus' prodigies was his superior power over the Devil. Throughout the Gospel Jesus casts out demons. His miracles that exhibited his total control over illnesses, the Devil, and physical laws are a clear sign of his divinity.

Perhaps the most dramatic event whereby Jesus' divinity is made manifest occurs later in the story, after he had called his Twelve Apostles and had been proclaiming the Kingdom of God through his teaching, healing, and miracles. His divinity emerged through a sudden and startling change in appearance. Jesus took three of his disciples, Sts. Peter, James, and John, up on a high mountain and "was transfigured before them, and his face shone like the sun, and his garments became white as light."[30] In order to inspire his Apostles' confidence in his Passion and Death and to show a foretaste of his Resurrection and future everlasting life in heaven, Our Lord worked an unprecedented miracle. This extraordinary phenomenon, in which Jesus presented himself in a glorified state and dazzled his Apostles with his radiating light, is called the Transfiguration.

To add to this extraordinary scene, Moses and Elijah appeared, speaking with Our Lord about his imminent suffering and death. The Old Testament Patriarch Moses represents the Law and the Old Testament Prophet Elijah represents the prophets. The Law and the Prophets had prepared the chosen people for the coming of the Messiah, and Jesus is the culmination and fulfillment of both the Law and the prophecy. Here, the Revelation of Christ's divinity along with his status as the promised Messiah unites the two ideas, affirming that the promised Savior had been God all along. Being present at the Transfiguration was an occasion for a deep mystical experience whereby St. Peter said, "Lord, it is well that we are here."[31]

This extraordinary phenomenon of Jesus' Transfiguration is the occasion of another theophany of the three Persons of the Blessed Trinity. God the Father is again present in the voice, God the Son is present in his humanity, and God the Holy Spirit is present in a bright cloud. The message is the same, but this time Christ is revealed as both Son and Word: "This is my beloved Son, with whom I am well pleased; *listen to him.*"[32] Jesus, the Son, is God commu-

30. Mt 17:2.
31. Mt 17:4.
32. Mt 17:5; emphasis added.

nicating himself to the world. His words form the contents of the New Covenant of grace and love.

Christology

The Revelation that God is one God in three Persons and that Jesus is true God and true man, though accepted in faith, took some time to be formulated into words. It is a mystery that surpasses reason, though by faith, we can grow in our understanding. Thus, in the first few centuries, the truth that Jesus Christ is both fully God and fully man prompted certain erroneous theological interpretations. The neo-Platonic philosophy that reigned in the early centuries AD understood divinity as so entirely transcendent that it was completely incompatible with material existence. In short, this neo-Platonic philosophy purported that God is too good to get messy down here on earth. Under the influence of this idea, certain thinkers denied either Jesus' humanity or divinity. A divine being, according to purely philosophical notions, could not be a baby, be hungry, suffer, and die. The proposition was impossible. Jesus could be either human or divine, not both. The position of the Church is that the relationship between Christ's human nature and divine nature could never compromise the integrity of either his humanity or divinity. If Jesus Christ were not perfect God and perfect man, the essence of the Christian faith would unravel.

Some Christians professed a doctrinal error called Docetism, which denied that Jesus had a real human nature. According to the Docetists, Jesus is a purely spiritual being, and he only "seems" (in Greek, *dokein*) to have a body, to suffer, and to die. In this heresy not only is the goodness of God's creation utterly rejected but also Christ's Sacrifice as the means of our salvation is completely lost.

Another doctrinal error went in the opposite direction and denied the divine identity of Christ. This heresy was called Arianism (named for Arius, its chief proponent) and put the infant Church through one of her severest trials. Arians did not deny that Christ is the incarnation of a supernatural being. What they did was strike at the heart of the Trinity by denying that the eternal Son was equal to God the Father. The Son, they taught, was the most exalted creature but a creature nonetheless; therefore, the being who became the man Jesus was not himself God. If Jesus is not God, every tenet of Christianity becomes meaningless. This crisis was resolved for a short time by an Ecumenical Council of the bishops of the whole world (Nicæa I, in the year 325) which declared, as we pray in the Nicene Creed, that Jesus Christ, the Father's Son, is "consubstantial [of the same substance or essence] with the Father."[33] Arianism had become so pervasive that another Ecumenical Council (Constantinople I, in the year 381) was necessary to lay this dangerous heresy finally to rest.

Not long after Arius, Nestorius taught a different doctrinal error, another threat to the faith. Nestorius was scandalized by the way Christians referred to the Blessed Virgin Mary as the "Mother of God" (in Greek, *Theotokos*, literally "Bearer of God"). How can an eternal being, he asked, have a human Mother? He argued that at most the Blessed Virgin Mary could only be the Mother of Christ (in Greek, *Christotokos*, "Bearer of Christ"). The implication is that there are *two* persons—one human and one divine—who are somehow mystically united with one another. This "mystical union" of two persons ultimately destroys the radical love expressed by the Incarnation—that God truly became man and that the Son "emptied himself, taking the form of a servant."[34] According to Nestorianism, God remains aloof and did not truly walk on earth with his people.

The Church clarified the issue by distinguishing between a "person" and a "nature." There cannot be two persons in Christ. There is only the one divine Person, who has a divine nature and took on a human nature also. This was defined and later elaborated on in the fifth century.[35] In theological terms, Jesus is *not a human person* but a divine Person. This divine Person, Jesus Christ, maintained his divine nature while, at a point in history, took on a human nature *as well*, uniting them in his one divine Person. The popular title of the Blessed Virgin Mary, *Theotokos*, is right and proper. As St. Cyril of Alexandria pointed out, mothers do not give birth to *natures*; they give birth to *persons*. The result of the Council Fathers' pronouncement at the Ecumenical Council of Ephesus produced euphoria among the townspeople, reaffirming that Mary is Mother of God.

Following these challenges to the divinity of Christ came further threats to his humanity. Some denied that he had a human soul, substituting the divine Word for the human soul. Some denied he

33. RMiss, The Order of Mass, no. 18.

34. Phil 2:7.

35. Bishops from around the world defined these at the Ecumenical Councils of Ephesus, in the year 431, and Chalcedon, 451.

had a human will, saying that he only has a divine will. Each time, the Church affirmed the full and complete humanity of Christ. He is like us in every way but without the slightest hint of sin. Jesus had a human soul that animated and configured his Body. Jesus had the whole array of human emotions, albeit under perfect control. Since he has both a divine and a human nature, Jesus possesses both a divine will and a human will, though his human will is in perfect harmony with his divine will. Since he is human, Jesus grew in knowledge and character through experience, education, and formation while improving in work skills, character, and virtue. Humans by our very nature need training and education since we are not governed by instinct. It therefore follows that Jesus has both a human intellect and a divine intellect; however, because Christ's human nature is united to the Person of the divine Word, on earth he enjoyed a direct knowledge of God the Father. In fact, on a deeper level, he also enjoyed the Beatific Vision. This preternatural knowledge enabled Jesus to penetrate the deep recesses of the human heart. This union of his human nature to the Second Person of the Blessed Trinity is called the "hypostatic union." It is a mystery of faith since it can never be fully comprehended, but it is the radical, beautiful, joyful proclamation at the heart of the Catholic faith. "God so loved the world that he gave his only Son, that whoever believes in him should not perish but have eternal life."[36]

Jesus As God's Word

We have seen twice already that St. John's Gospel reveals the "Word." When the text does so—for example, "The Word was with God, and the Word was God"[37]—it uses the Greek *Logos*. Christ, the Second Person of the Trinity, is also called the divine *Logos*. This Greek term carries various meanings. In Greek it can mean law, speech, reason, idea, wisdom, or story. *Logos*, despite its varied meanings, comes from the Greek *lego* ("I say") and is most typically understood theologically as "word." As St. John's Gospel relates, "all things were made through [the Word], and without him was not anything made that was made."[38] As discussed in Chapter 2, God the Father generates an idea of himself, personified in the Second Person of the Trinity, and consequently all possible beings through

36. Jn 3:16.

37. Jn 1:1.

38. Jn 1:3.

the personified idea of himself. God's Revelation, his communication to us about himself, is present in seed in creation and more fully expressed in the Revelation of the Old Testament; but God's self-communication was most fully expressed to humanity when his divine Word became man and dwelt among us. As the Father said from the bright cloud at Christ's Transfiguration: "Listen to him."[39]

Through his Incarnation, Jesus speaks to every person and makes God visible with a human face. Jesus is the Word of God made flesh, which signifies that he is the personified language of God the Father. Both Jesus' witness and his words speak directly to every human being about the love of God the Father. "In many and various ways God spoke of old to our fathers by the prophets; but in these last days he has spoken to us by a Son."[40] It can be said that through the humanity of Christ, God translates himself into our language so we can relate to God on our own terms.

Heretics like Arius and Nestorius, though ultimately misguided, were on to something. God, in his infinite transcendence, cannot be known directly but only indirectly by his effects in creation. We cannot "climb up" to God on our own power. What their flawed beliefs failed to accept was God's power to come down to us, to join himself to his creation. In his infinite love for each of us, God made himself visible by taking on a human nature without losing his divine nature. Christ translated infinite divine love into human form and revealed God's love for us. By entering into human history and taking on the human condition from infancy to death, God becomes visible. The proverbial question of what God is really like can be answered with a simple response: "Look at Christ."

Everything Jesus did and said points to the love of the Father since Jesus in his divinity is the mirror image of his Father. His display of mercy and compassion for the sorrowful and suffering, his love for sinners, all reveal the love of God in a very poignant way. His poverty enriches us, his obedience to his parents during his Hidden Life atones for our disobedience, and his suffering and Death reveal the self-worth of every individual. His words instruct, purify, and transform his listeners. In healing diseases and casting out demons, he demonstrates that he bears all our infirmities. Through his Passion we are redeemed since he has made reparation

39. Mt 17:5.

40. Heb 1:1–2.

for our sins by overcoming sin and death. By his Resurrection he offers us eternal life. Jesus' entire mission is to raise us up to be children of God—as was the original plan for human beings—and to have direct access to everlasting life. God so badly wants us to have everlasting happiness that, even though he is infinitely perfect and complete in his own divinity, he took on our suffering by becoming human and dying on the Cross.

Jesus Christ, though, is both God *and* man, so "look at Christ" is also the answer to what it means to be human. Jesus is our perfect model and example of the meaning of personal perfection. He calls each of us to become his disciple and follow him. This discipleship involves duplicating his dispositions and actions and implementing his teachings. The wonderful charm of the Gospel is that all its contents can be applied and adapted to everyday life. Through his example of love and mercy, he invites us to draw strength and consolation in prayer to him. Through his poverty and suffering, we are encouraged to accept the difficulties, deprivations, and pain that come our way in union with his Cross. Through his ministry of compassion and mercy, we are called to be compassionate and merciful. His obedience to the Father even unto death teaches us that nothing in this life should be exchanged for doing the will of God. We are not supposed to simply admire Christ or merely address him from time to time; rather, we are called to live in him by integrating our life into his. We are called, in a certain sense, to identify our biography with that of Jesus. Words and actions are all potentially incarnational since they are all meant to be practiced and ingrained into every human life regardless of the circumstances. They are meant to become incarnate in us.

The teachings of Jesus do not constitute some new "philosophy" as though it were only a new way of thinking about things. The imitation of Christ's life, especially sharing in his suffering, will bring about a personal *transformation*. The saints are people who have undergone total transformations in Christ. In many instances, grave illnesses, experiences of failure, or loss of loved ones serve as crosses that lead to greater intimacy with Christ and profound conversion. People begin to reflect Christ's compassion, mercy, affection, and joy through their faith in embracing his Cross. For most of us, this transformation is the work of a lifetime, but in every episode of Christ's life there lies, for each of us, hidden practical applications that lead to conversion and transformation.

A woman once spoke about her experience of meeting the gaze of St. John Paul II while he was Pope; he blessed her mother in a wheelchair after celebrating Mass. She stated that she was overcome with emotion because she felt that she had seen the eyes of Christ in the Holy Father. As can be seen in the lives of the saints, contemplation of Christ's life with the eagerness to practice is the means to "put on the Lord Jesus Christ."[41]

After Jesus had completed his task of teaching—backed by his mighty deeds—he was ready to enter the next phase of his sojourn on earth. He wrapped up his public life by warning his Apostles that his life would end soon with terrible suffering and a horrific death; however, it is precisely his painful sacrificial offering that would save the world and bring about everlasting life to every person who desires it.

41. Rom 13:14.

CHAPTER 7

THE PASCHAL MYSTERY

The Paschal Mystery of Jesus Christ was prefigured centuries earlier by the Israelites' Passover, when God liberated his chosen people from the Egyptians. In the Book of Exodus, the final plague God sent upon Egypt was the death of all the firstborn of Egypt. The Israelites, however, would be spared. Each Israelite family was instructed to find an unblemished lamb and mark the doorposts with its blood before roasting the lamb and sharing the meal. This blood on the lintels of the Israelites' homes would set them apart from the Egyptians. As God describes to Moses: "The blood shall be a sign for you, upon the houses where you are; and when I see the blood, I will pass over you, and no plague shall fall upon you to destroy you, when I smite the land of Egypt."[1] It was this last plague that finally prompted the frightened Pharaoh to release the Hebrew people from their bondage. After agreeing to release the Israelites, Pharaoh changed his mind and pursued them in their departure. Here God performed another great miracle when, through Moses, he parted the Red Sea so that his people could cross safely—and then returned the flow of the water to engulf the Egyptian army. Having passed through the waters from death to life, Israel moved on to the Promised Land.

This spectacular prodigy prefigures the redemption of Christ, the "Lamb of God."[2] By Christ's Blood, we are redeemed from death and liberated from bondage to sin and the Devil. We go from death to life through the cleansing waters of Baptism, and the gates of heaven—the Promised Land—are open to all the redeemed. The definitive perfection of the Israelites' Passover (in Hebrew, *Pesach*) celebration is the Paschal Mystery, which is the redemptive work of Christ in his Passion and Resurrection.

THE LAST SUPPER

The Last Supper is the final episode in Christ's life before his Passion and Death. This event, charged with the emotion of some-

1. Ex 12:13.
2. Jn 1:29.

one bidding a final farewell to his loved ones, is the setting for Our Lord's greatest legacy: the institution of the Holy Eucharist. Throughout the evening Jesus gave a *tour de force* of profound spiritual and theological teaching to his Apostles. The words and teachings on that unforgettable night of Holy Thursday are so important that a significant portion of Catholic doctrine—including the priesthood, the Eucharist, and his New Commandment of Love—derives from that one evening.

The central event of the Last Supper is the institution of the Holy Eucharist, which constituted the first Holy Mass. Jesus and his Apostles came together to celebrate the Jewish feast of Passover. This time, however, where the meal would normally proceed to the sharing of the Passover lamb, Jesus blessed the unleavened bread and offered it to his disciples, saying, "Take, eat; this is my body." Taking the cup, he gave thanks to God and said, "Drink of it, all of you; for this is my blood of the covenant, which is poured out for many for the forgiveness of sins."[3] At the Last Supper Jesus Christ changed bread and wine into his own Body and Blood even though they still maintained the appearance of bread and wine. Jesus himself had become the Lamb of sacrifice.

At the moment of the institution of the Eucharist, Jesus offered himself to his Apostles in an unbloody manner; the next day he would offer himself in a slow, agonizing death on the Cross. This first Mass, celebrated by Our Lord in the Cenacle, or Upper Room, with his Apostles, highlights how Jesus' Sacrifice transcends time and place. At the Last Supper Jesus offered a *re-presentation* of his redemptive Sacrifice *in anticipation* of its occurrence in time. That is, this first Mass celebrated by Christ before his physical self-offering on the Cross already shows the unity of the unbloody *re*-presentation of Christ's Sacrifice of the altar with the bloody Sacrifice on the Cross itself. Both present the one offering of Christ to the Father. In the Last Supper and in his Passion, Christ offered one and the same redemptive Sacrifice. The Holy Eucharist is God's greatest gift to the Church and humankind: Not only is it the Real Presence of Jesus Christ in both his divinity and humanity under the appearance of bread and wine but also it is a participation in the one perfect offering of Christ on the Cross.

3. Mt 26:26–28.

St. Matthew's Gospel speaks of the "blood of the covenant,"[4] emphasizing Christ as the Lamb of God. In St. Luke's account, Jesus speaks of the "new covenant."[5] Having continually renewed his covenant with his chosen people, in Christ God now offers the final, definitive covenant with all of humanity. The covenant with Abraham, whose visible sign is circumcision, prepared a chosen people for God. The covenant with Moses, whose privileged expression is the Ten Commandments, taught God's people obedience to his Law. The institution of the Eucharist ushered in the New Covenant of grace and love, perfecting the Mosaic Law. The New Law of Grace, established through the Blood of Christ on the Cross, goes beyond the basic moral rudiments of the Ten Commandments. Through the graces of the Eucharistic Sacrifice, every disciple of Christ can aspire to live the life of Christ, which is to love as Christ loved.

At the Last Supper Jesus Christ commanded that the Eucharistic Sacrifice be perpetuated until the end of time. To this end he instituted the priesthood and bestowed on his Apostles and their successors the sacred power and authority to act in his place (to act *in persona Christi*: "in the Person of Christ"). Priests of the New Covenant receive the power to offer the Eucharistic Sacrifice in Christ's name. Every time a priest repeats the words of consecration during the Mass, the same Sacrifice of Calvary is re-presented on the altar in a sacramental and unbloody manner. The first Mass, celebrated by Christ with his Apostles at the Last Supper, is re-presented in every age and in every place, thus enabling the faithful to share in the Paschal Mystery directly through the liturgical actions and worship of the Holy Mass. Though every Sunday is a participation in the Last Supper, Holy Thursday of Holy Week—a few days before Easter Sunday—is specifically focused on commemorating this moment in the life of Christ.

While no description can do justice to the depth and scope of the meaning of the Last Supper, it is accurate to say Christ's message describes the principal consequences of his redemption. The Last Supper narrative in St. John's Gospel contains five chapters of teaching and meditation, much of which is Jesus' elaboration on the life of charity to which he calls his disciples. It is telling that Jesus offers these reflections within the context of the first Mass. No one can fulfill Christ's Law of Love without first being united to him,

4. Mt 26:28.
5. Lk 22:20.

and there is no more profound unity with Jesus than receiving him in the Holy Eucharist. This mystery of intimate union with Christ is explained by his allegory of the vine and the branches:

> I am the vine; you are the branches. He who abides in me, and I in him, he it is that bears much fruit, for apart from me you can do nothing.[6]

Jesus Christ emphatically stressed that for his disciples to be fruitful, they must be united to him as a branch is united to its vine.

Holy Thursday, in a sense details the requirements for a full life in Christ. The perfection and hallmark of every Christian is marked by his or her replication of Christ's charity, drawn from the graces of the Holy Eucharist. Fruitful Christian discipleship consists of an intimate union with Our Lord, by which a person exhibits a joy and peace the world cannot give.[7] This faithful reflection of Christ's wisdom and love is crucial to the work of evangelization.

Jesus does not simply teach through words. Prior to all that he said to his disciples at the Last Supper, he did something that shocked them: He washed their feet. In the time of Jesus and the Apostles, it was customary to wear sandals in a dry and dusty climate. Offering a basin of water for guests to wash their feet was an expected part of hospitality. To wash *another person's* feet was a sign of servitude and humility; only a servant would wash another's feet. Christ, by washing his disciple's feet, embodied the depth of charity he was about to ask of his disciples. "A new commandment I give to you, that you love one another; even as I have loved you, that you also love one another."[8] His disciples must love as he loves.

Jesus' display of radical love by washing his disciple's feet served as a proximate preparation for his supreme act of love the following day on Calvary. The Crucifixion, in which Christ laid down his life for the redemption of every human being, is the greatest display of charity. "Greater love has no man than this, that a man lay down his life for his friends."[9] This ability for such colossal love is available to anyone who wishes to follow him, given through the graces

---

6. Jn 15:5.
7. Cf. Jn 14:27.
8. Jn 13:34.
9. Jn 15:13.

merited by the redemption. "You are my friends if you do what I command you."[10]

Though free cooperation is vital, Christ's Law of Love is impossible without the supernatural graces he won for us on the Cross. His New Commandment is only possible through the union of one's heart with the heart of Christ. The grace to love as Christ loved is given initially in Baptism and bolstered through frequent reception of the Holy Eucharist, which is the sacramental manifestation of the Paschal Mystery instituted at the Last Supper.

The Agony in the Garden

The first stage of Christ's Passion began with his Agony in the Garden.[11] After the Last Supper Christ left the Upper Room with three of his disciples for the Garden of Gethsemane on the Mount of Olives. Jesus frequently went there to pray. He came there to pray for strength to endure the merciless suffering he was destined to endure; on this particular occasion Christ was put to a much more severe test than the Devil's temptations in the desert. As both God and man, Christ had a profound knowledge of every human heart. His Agony in the Garden was unique because of that burden of sin weighing on his mind and heart. What made matters worse was the realization that, despite his imminent Sacrifice, his loving gift of redemption would be rejected by many. His deeds of loving self-sacrifice would prove futile for so many who would insist on refusing his friendship and mercy. This knowledge added dramatically to his terrible pain.

Jesus' sorrow for the many wayward sons and daughters who would refuse his gift of forgiveness and eternal life caused him a punishing agony. St. Luke records, "His sweat became like great drops of blood."[12] Some have speculated Our Lord experienced a rare medical condition called *hematohidrosis,* in which a person who is undergoing intense anxiety literally sweats blood. Under severe strain the capillaries surrounding the sweat glands burst, causing blood to mingle with sweat. No matter what is the exact physical nature of the phenomenon, his physical suffering powerfully attests to the severity of Christ's agony.

---

10. Jn 15:14.

11. Cf. Lk 22:41–45.

12. Lk 22:44.

In addition to the ostensible failure of his mission, human fear and dread over his future suffering was also a major source of Christ's anguish and grief. He was very much aware that his Father's plan for salvation involved his suffering and Death. This foreboding reality was frightening and troubling. In fact, Jesus asked his Father to remove "this cup": "My Father, if it be possible, let this cup pass from me; nevertheless, not as I will, but as thou wilt."[13] This special prayer serves as the perfect template for our prayer in times of trouble and hardship. Christ is teaching us how suffering becomes meritorious.

Suffering is not good in and of itself, and it is not wrong to seek to alleviate it. Jesus' obedience to the Father's will makes his suffering a "fit offering." Comparing the fall of Adam to the redemption of Christ, St. Paul wrote: "As by one man's disobedience many were made sinners, so by one man's obedience many will be made righteous."[14] Though Jesus asked that his cup of suffering might pass, he accepted and expressed a preference for the will of the Father. Jesus not only reveals to us how to pray in adversity but also offers a model for how our suffering should be borne with faith in God's plan.

Through his experience of such intense anguish, Our Lord also demonstrated solidarity with all who suffer. Our Redeemer desired to unite himself with everyone who experiences loneliness, emotional anxiety, distress, and physical infirmity. In both the Garden of Gethsemane and through his self-offering on the Cross, Christ literally felt and understood everyone's pain. As God, Jesus understands human suffering infinitely more than all people combined. As man, he is not only familiar with the human condition but also with its trials and tribulations, as he has undergone almost every kind of suffering that can afflict a human being. Our God has literally and physically "felt our pain."

During his Agony in the Garden, Our Lord was accompanied by the same three Apostles who had witnessed his Transfiguration. He urged them to persevere in praying with him for an hour. Sadly, they fell asleep while he prayed. Our Lord woke them and admonished them to pray during this severest of trials. While Christ wanted his Apostles to pray, he also wanted to instruct all his disciples how to

13. Mt 26:39.

14. Rom 5:19.

obtain the strength and courage to bear their own crosses. "Watch and pray that you may not enter into temptation."[15] Jesus is teaching that only with prayer can a disciple believe and find strength in the power of the Cross. Only when a person "watches and prays" can he or she follow Christ closely by living a life of sacrifice.

After Jesus' hour in Gethsemane, Judas, the disciple who had plotted with the chief priests and the Pharisees to aid in the arrest of Jesus, arrived with a band of soldiers. To identify Jesus, he approached and kissed him. "Judas," asks Jesus, "would you betray the Son of man with a kiss?"[16] Christ was then arrested and put on trial before the Sanhedrin, the ruling council of the Jewish people, where he was falsely accused of blasphemy.

The Causes of Jesus' Crucifixion and Death

In St. John's Gospel, while Jesus was preaching, he declared: "I and the Father are one."[17] At this proclamation, the Jewish people listening took up stones to stone him. Jesus patiently responded by saying, "I have shown you many good works from the Father; for which of these do you stone me?"[18] Jesus had only taught love and brought healing, so why would they want to put him to death? "It is not for a good work that we stone you but for blasphemy; because you, being a man, make yourself God."[19]

Our Lord's style and message had already clashed with the mindset and customs of the Pharisees, priests, and scribes. Specifically, his display of power to expel demons and heal the sick on the Sabbath day of rest and forgiving sins on his own authority certainly rankled the Jewish authorities. The company he kept with moral outcasts and public sinners added to their bitter resentment toward him. Their antipathy was so severe that they accused him of being in league with evil spirits and possessing demonic powers.

Jesus also took it upon himself to interpret and perfect the Mosaic Law, frequently criticizing the way the Pharisees interpreted the Law. (The Pharisees were a Jewish sect distinguished by strict

15. Mt 26:41.
16. Lk 22:48.
17. Jn 10:30.
18. Jn 10:32.
19. Jn 10:33.

observance of the written law.) First, Jesus illuminated the true spirit of the Old Covenant and rejected their clever but unsound interpretations and useless legalism, which violated the spirit of the Law and the intention of the divine Legislator.

> Woe to you Pharisees! for you tithe mint and rue and every herb, and neglect justice and the love of God; these you ought to have done, without neglecting the others.[20]

Jesus' outright criticisms of the Pharisees' senseless accumulation of endless minutiae profoundly upset them. Moreover, Jesus interpreted the Law in his own name. Unlike the prophets, he did not profess to have received a message from God to relate to his chosen people. Jesus spoke with authority: "I say to you...."[21] His interpretations did not abolish the Old Covenant laws but brought them to perfection. He transferred the Mosaic Law from Commandments written on tablets of stone to the human heart, elevated and assisted by grace. All combined, this made Jesus a threat to the authority behind the leadership of the Pharisees, priests, and scribes.

What really put the Jewish authorities on edge, though, was that Christ identified with God by both his words and gestures. He mingled lovingly with sinners and outcasts, assuring and consoling them with the forgiveness of their sins. He lavishly showed mercy on individuals who were alienated from God through habitual and serious sin. The Pharisees realized that only God was capable of and authorized to forgive sin. Connecting the dots, the authorities realized that Jesus was attributing powers to himself that were exclusively divine. Their outrage over Jesus' perceived blasphemy reached its climax when he basically gave himself the sacred name *Yahweh*, by saying, "Before Abraham was, *I am*."[22] He also proclaimed, "I and the Father are one."[23]

After being betrayed by Judas and arrested, Jesus was first led to the home of the high priest, Caiaphas, where they were seeking false testimony against Jesus. The first accusation leveled against Jesus was someone's recollection that Jesus had said that the Temple of God would be destroyed, and he would raise it up again in three days. Speaking of the Temple's destruction would certainly get the attention of the Jewish leadership; it was the sacred center of the

20. Lk 11:42.
21. Mt 5:18 and many other verses.
22. Jn 8:58; emphasis added.
23. Jn 10:30.

Jewish religion. This was the place of worship and spiritual destination for all the members of the chosen people. When Jesus was referring to the Temple in this particular context, he was speaking about his own Body. The Crucifixion would destroy the bodily temple of Christ, and it would be reconstructed at his Resurrection. This rebuilding of "the temple" would usher in the New Covenant of Grace whereby true worship would take place in the newly rebuilt Temple, the Person of Jesus Christ.

The accusation that Jesus threatened to destroy the Temple was insufficient for the purposes of the Jewish leadership. The high priest finally asked Jesus outright whether he claimed to be the Messiah. "You have said so," responded Jesus, "But I tell you, hereafter you will see the Son of man seated at the right hand of Power, and coming on the clouds of heaven."[24] This was too much: "Why do we still need witnesses? You have now heard his blasphemy."[25] They sentenced Jesus to death.

Condemnation of Jesus

The Sanhedrin declared the most infamous verdict in human history. Jesus was stating under no uncertain terms that he is divine. Indeed, claiming to be the Son of God *would* have been blasphemy, a crime punishable by death under the Mosaic Law, were it not true. If they had truly been children of God, Jesus told them, they would have recognized him for who he is.[26] Instead, his proclamations only enraged them, and they sentenced the Messiah to death. The Jewish authorities, however, had no civil power to execute a criminal; that authority was reserved to the Roman governor of Judea, Pontius Pilate.

To bring Christ before Pilate, however, the Jewish authorities needed a charge other than blasphemy, which carried no weight under Roman law. So, the Jewish leaders told Pilate that Jesus had claimed to be a king, which was a usurpation of the emperor's authority. To Pilate, they threatened: "You are not Caesar's friend; every one who makes himself a king sets himself against Caesar."[27] This shrewd tactic placed Pilate in a difficult position. He was torn

24. Mt 26:64.
25. Mt 26:65.
26. Cf. Jn 8.
27. Jn 19:12.

between political ambition and his conscience, which indicated unequivocally that Christ was not guilty of their accusations. Though he preferred not to enter what he considered a religious squabble, Pilate was obligated to come face-to-face with Christ to determine if he was guilty of any crime. After interrogating Our Lord, Pilate felt compelled to release him and looked for a way out of the awkward situation.

Pilate thought he had found a solution to this dilemma upon learning that Christ came from Nazareth and, therefore, was under the jurisdiction of King Herod, the Roman tetrarch of Galilee. He sent Jesus to Herod, who was in Jerusalem for the Passover. A sadistic individual, Herod had looked forward to this encounter but soon grew bored when Jesus would not answer him. To ridicule him, Herod dressed Our Lord in regal apparel and sent him back to Pilate.

While Pilate wrestled with the fateful verdict, his wife sent him word about a disturbing dream that indicated he should not be a party to Christ's condemnation. Attempting to escape his predicament, Pilate invoked the Passover custom of releasing a condemned prisoner. Pilate gave the agitated crowd a choice between Barabbas, "a notorious prisoner"[28] and "robber,"[29] or Jesus of Nazareth, the King of the Jews. The crowd, stirred up by the Jewish authorities, bellowed, "Not this man, but Barabbas!"[30]

Pilate again desperately looked for a way to avoid condemning an innocent man to a cruel death. Hoping to placate the crowd, he ordered Our Lord to be scourged. This form of torture consists in brutal flogging with a whip of cords containing sharp pieces of bone or metal at their ends. Scourging tears flesh and muscle and damages nerves and internal organs. Many victims of this traumatic ordeal die from blood loss or internal injury. After the horrendous scourging, the Roman soldiers proceeded to ridicule, mock, and taunt Jesus. They slapped him and spit in his face. Mockingly, the Roman legionaries dressed him as a king, complete with a crown of thorns. Christians should never grow accustomed to Our Lord's extravagance of love in allowing himself to undergo this unbearable torture. It is important to bear in mind that the Person going through

28. Mt 27:16.
29. Jn 18:40.
30. Ibid.

this cruel ordeal is God the Son, who merits infinite homage and adoration. Pilate himself was, on some level at least, so moved with pity by the pathetic sight of this broken man that he made one last effort to appeal to the crowd. He presented them with a Christ covered with gaping wounds and bruises through the relentless flogging and crowning with thorns and shouted a phrase that has remained ingrained in the consciousness of Christian posterity: "Behold the man!"[31]

Despite this, the mob was not satisfied and clamored for Jesus' Crucifixion all the more: "Crucify him, crucify him!"[32] The risk to his political career proved too much for Pilate, and he finally sentenced Jesus to death. In a feeble attempt to deny responsibility for the deed, he washed his hands, saying, "I am innocent of this man's blood."[33] The image of Christ bathed in blood; crowned with thorns; and covered with welts, bruises, and gashes reveals a God of infinite love. "Behold the man!" The battered and broken Christ is a symbol of people's violent rejection of God's loving offer of salvation through the forgiveness of sin. It is an allegory of their attitude and treatment of God and his Laws; nevertheless, God awaits every person's change of heart.

The Crucifixion and Death of the Redeemer

After Pilate's sentence of death by crucifixion, Our Lord embarked on what is called the Way of the Cross. Christ was forced to carry his heavy Cross from Pilate's *praetorium* to Golgotha (from the Hebrew for "skull"), also called Calvary (from the Latin for "skull"). Given Jesus' weakened condition, loss of blood, physical shock, and trauma, this last journey involved indescribable agony. According to the traditional devotion of the Stations of the Cross, Christ fell three times as he summoned every ounce of strength to carry the Cross to the place of his Crucifixion. Seeing that he could not continue under his own power, the Roman soldiers "compelled a passer-by, Simon of Cyrene,"[34] to help Jesus carry his Cross. This encounter between Christ and St. Simon reveals that every Christian must be willing to help Christ carry his Cross.

31. Jn 19:5.
32. Jn 19:6.
33. Mt 27:4.
34. Mk 15:21.

This part of his Passion, marked by Our Lord's extraordinary effort to reach the place of his execution, is a powerful reminder that Christ is intimately familiar with fatigue and exhaustion. Everyone who is crushed by the burdens and cares of life will find compassion from the one who carried his Cross amid such excruciating pain. Christ's Passion reached its climax at the moment of his Crucifixion. He was nailed to the Cross through his hands / wrists and feet. Crucifixion kills its victim by horrifically slow asphyxiation. Christ's every breath became increasingly labored, causing him dreadful suffocation, accompanied by major blood loss.

Even still, in this agonizing scene we witness the love of God and the victory of life over death. Hardly had he been lifted up on the Cross when Jesus made a heartfelt appeal to his Father: "Father, forgive them; for they know not what they do."[35] Affixed to the Cross with his arms outstretched in a symbolic embrace of the whole human race, Christ became the image *par excellence* of charity and mercy. After he paid the price of our redemption in full, he declared from the throne of his Cross these last words: "It is finished."[36]

KENOSIS

In his Epistle to the Philippians, St. Paul gives his celebrated description of Jesus Christ...

> who, though he was in the form of God, did not count equality with God a thing to be grasped, but *emptied himself*, taking the form of a servant, being born in the likeness of men.[37]

This passage is known as Christ's *kenosis*, which is Greek for "an emptying." These words refer first to the Son of God's self-emptying in taking on our human nature, being born of a woman in a humble stable. They also encapsulate Christ's whole life of sacrificial love and bring out the essence of his entire existence. Every action of Christ on earth was redemptive. In the same way, his *kenosis* permeated his whole life of obedience and service. It reached a crescendo between his Agony in the Garden and his last dying breath on the Cross.

The immediate reason for this supreme Sacrifice of his life was his great love and desire to atone for the sins of every human being. He wanted people to recover their lost happiness, for which they

35. Lk 23:34.

36. Jn 19:30.

37. Phil 2:6–7; emphasis added.

had been created. In perfect obedience to his Father and out of love for every person, Christ willingly laid down his life in a most sacrificial manner. His life was ended neither by the chief priests nor by the Romans, but through his own willing obedience to God's plan for our salvation:

> For this reason the Father loves me, because I lay down my life, that I may take it again. No one takes it from me, but I lay it down of my own accord.[38]

Christ's total gift of himself on the Cross is most dramatically displayed when "one of the soldiers"—to be certain that Jesus was truly dead—"pierced his side with a spear, and at once there came out blood and water."[39] In his beautiful Eucharistic hymn *Adoro Te Devote*, St. Thomas Aquinas petitioned "Lord Jesus" in a poetic fashion that, given who Christ is, he could...

> Wash me clean with your Blood,
> one drop of which can free
> the entire world of all its sins.[40]

Our Lord, to show the superabundance of his love for us, pours out every drop of his Blood for our redemption.

Why Did Jesus Have to Die?

There are some pitfalls to avoid when contemplating the Death of Jesus. It is important, first, to note that the whole of the Jewish people of that time are not to be considered culpable for Jesus' sentence of death. It is a grave injustice to look askance at the Jewish people on account of Jesus' Passion and Death on the Cross. The Israelites, the chosen people of God, were the people through whom God would save the whole world. The Redeemer of the world comes from the Jewish people. The nascent Church's members were all Jewish people who followed another Jewish rabbi, Jesus Christ. The Church's foundation and pillars are the Apostles, who were all initially Jewish people. The two greatest Christian models of discipleship are the Blessed Virgin Mary and her spouse, St. Joseph, who were both Jewish. It would, therefore, be grossly unjust and historically inaccurate to intimate that the Jewish people were responsible for Jesus' Death. In terms of particular individuals, Judas, some of

38. Jn 10:17–18.

39. Jn 19:34.

40. "I Devoutly Adore You (*Adoro Te Devote*)," in HBP, 287.

the Jewish authorities, Pontius Pilate, and the Roman soldiers had major parts to play in Jesus' suffering and execution. It does not make sense to pin the blame on all Jewish people for Jesus' Crucifixion, just as it would be illogical to blame all Roman people. Every Christian must remember that the Savior of the world came from the chosen people and that the first Christians were all ethnically Jewish.

Palm Sunday and Good Friday, which we commemorate during Holy Week, are centered on Christ's Passion. During the Gospel reading at Mass on these days, the congregation proclaims the words of the crowd, shouting, "Crucify him!"[41] This serves as a vivid reminder that *we are all* responsible for Jesus' Death. Fallen humanity is responsible for the Death of Our Lord. Jesus Christ died to remove the sin of Adam and Eve, wounding their nature. They then passed on human nature, which is wounded, to all their descendants, so *every person* has a part to play in Jesus' painful demise. The staggering number of personal sins comprise the ingredients for Jesus' anguish, which was payment for the reparation and restoration of life to a fallen world. Since Jesus is God the Son, there is an eternal dimension to his suffering, meaning that everyone's forgiveness and salvation were present at his redemptive Sacrifice. It is not a mere pious exaggeration, then, to say that every sin adds to the pain our incarnate God endured on the Cross. In light of these considerations, the Good Friday event commemorated yearly becomes painfully personal for every Christian.

The fatal brutality experienced by our Savior was not simply a regrettable tragedy but rather God's eternal plan for our salvation. This was the eternal plan of God for the redemption of the sons and daughters of Adam and Eve. God promised salvation in the *Protoevangelium* in Genesis. The entire history of Israel is a preparation for the coming of the Savior. The prophets foretold of his coming, and while they prophesied a king in the line of David who would bring peace and justice, they also predicted that he would suffer greatly. The numerous scriptural passages—written many centuries before the actual episode of this horrible execution—attest to a well-thought-out plan. It is interesting to observe in the Old Testament writings, especially those of the psalms and the prophets, the amazing amount of detail about the Messiah as a Suffering Servant. The prophet Isaiah most explicitly relates how the coming

41. *The Book of the Gospels*, 2nd Edition (Downers Grove, IL: Midwest Theological Forum, 2022), Good Friday of the Lord's Passion [40], 173.

Messiah will have to suffer to save his people. In what is called the "Song of the Suffering Servant," Isaiah foretold of Jesus:

> He was wounded for our transgressions,
> he was bruised for our iniquities;
> upon him was the chastisement that made us whole,
> and with his stripes we are healed.
> All we like sheep have gone astray;
> we have turned, every one, to his own way;
> and the LORD has laid on him
> the iniquity of us all.
>
> He was oppressed, and he was afflicted,
> yet he opened not his mouth;
> like a lamb that is led to the slaughter,
> and like a sheep that before its shearers is dumb,
> so he opened not his mouth.[42]

Jesus Christ's willingness to serve by making satisfaction for our sins was especially expressed by his Passion and Death on the Cross. In his sacred humanity Jesus underwent a most severe physical, psychological, and moral suffering. His entire Body was covered with bruises and lacerations. He was exhausted, thirsty, and wracked with pains that exceeded the limits of human endurance. Psychologically and emotionally, Our Lord suffered from fear of impending pain and death, loneliness, and abandonment, witnessing the sorrow of his loved ones (especially his Mother), and outrage at the injustices being inflicted on him. Perhaps most of all, Christ experienced moral suffering—while he was innocent of any moral wrongdoing, he took upon himself everyone's guilt and experienced the full extent of the ugliness and evil of sin. This is why Christ deserves the title "Man of Sorrow." He certainly is the Suffering Servant foreseen by the prophet Isaiah.

Christ suffered, though, without bitterness, with willing obedience to the Father's plan, and out of love for all of us. Throughout his painful ordeal he entered into deep solidarity with every person undergoing suffering of any kind. We all can encounter Jesus Christ, the Suffering Servant, through personal difficulties and painful situations. Through Christ's Passion, suffering itself has new meaning. If we bear our trials with patience and trust, we can join Jesus in his redemptive suffering and thus experience the great joy of the Resurrection.

---

42. Is 53:5–7.

But why should this be so? Why would God's plan require such a price? "Redeem" is from the Latin *redimere*, which means "to buy back." God's justice requires atonement, but what mortal can make restitution to the infinite God? Only God himself could satisfy justice. As the psalmist begs of God, "Enter not into judgment with thy servant; / for no man living is righteous before thee."[43] Our Lord Jesus, the Word made flesh, though perfectly holy in both his humanity and divinity, allowed God the Father, who "made him to be sin,"[44] to serve as a substitute for every sinner. God the Son made reparation and atonement by "buying back" humanity through his redemptive Sacrifice on the Cross. The merciless killing of Christ was the exorbitant price tag of our liberation from sin and death. Hence St. Peter's words: "you were ransomed from the futile ways inherited from your fathers... with the precious blood of Christ."[45] In simple terms, Jesus' redemption involved death through his humanity, while his divinity gave the merits of this Sacrifice infinite value.

Another way of looking at Christ's redemptive Sacrifice is according to his obedience. Adam rejected God's will, disobeyed him, and sin entered the world. Christ, in all his life and most dramatically from Gethsemane to Calvary, demonstrates total obedience to God's will, restoring the right relationship between the rest of humanity and God. He "became obedient unto death, even death on a cross."[46] He willingly laid down his life, trusting in God's eternal plan. This is why so many martyrs have been able to follow in Christ's footsteps—they accepted their fate by trusting in the one who went before them and who had a plan for their salvation.

It is wrong to view Christ's suffering as the act of a vengeful God. The entire point is that it is *God himself* who takes the penalty *upon himself* to spare all of his children. When we remember that Jesus is God, dying on the Cross for our sake, it becomes for Christians a dramatic demonstration of God's love—not wrath—for us. Our Lord's painful journey to Calvary, the place of his execution, is the ultimate manifestation of divine love for every person expressed graphically in Jesus' lacerated Body. The sight of our God-man's self-immolation for each of us personally should banish any sense of low self-esteem. The Crucifix tells us who we are in the eyes of God and

43. Ps 143:2.

44. 2 Cor 5:21.

45. 1 Pt 1:18–19.

46. Phil 2:8.

our true self-worth. "God so loved the world that he gave his only Son."[47] Jesus Christ utilized his all-powerful divinity to lay down his life for every person as if he or she were the only one to exist. Every person can rightly say, "Jesus died to save *me*."

Through his Passion and Death on the Cross, Jesus Christ offered a perfect Sacrifice, totally acceptable and pleasing to God the Father. This supreme offering therefore merited the reconciliation of the human race to God and repaired, once and for all, the sin of Adam. Jesus is the new Passover Lamb who takes away the sins of the world, winning the grace of our salvation and sanctification. The consequence of Christ's redemptive Sacrifice is that every person, through the grace of Baptism, attains such access to God that he or she becomes a child of God. Moreover, every person does not simply relate to God as creature to Creator but rather as *daughter or son* to a loving Father.

He Descended to the Abode of the Dead

The death of a human being involves the separation of the soul from the body. Once the body is no longer animated by the soul, it undergoes corruption. The soul, however, is immortal and continues in existence without the body. Like every human person, Jesus' Death consisted of a separation of his soul from his Body. "Father, into thy hands I commit my spirit!"[48] Following his Death, Christ descended to *Sheol* (Hebrew for the "abode of the dead") that is, the state of all who had died before the redemption, which was not heaven. Up to that point access to everlasting life in heaven was barred, even for the righteous, until Our Lord's redemptive Death on the Cross and Resurrection paid the entrance fee for the entire human race. These souls eagerly awaited the redemption to open the gates of heaven. Included among these just souls were the innumerable holy men and women of both the chosen people and non-Israelites. The details of this period between Jesus' Death and his Resurrection have not been revealed, but one can imagine the holy men and women of Israel entering Paradise with St. John the Baptist and St. Joseph among the first.

Many of the just in *Sheol* had not conformed their lives to totally fulfilling God's will and consequently needed purification before

47. Jn 3:16.

48. Lk 23:46.

entering heaven. Part of Christ's descent to the dead was to confirm with these souls that their entrance into heaven would occur after the necessary purification in purgatory. Another group of souls were the souls of the damned. Because they chose to reject any relationship with God and had fully refused to follow his will during their lives, they lamentably brought eternal punishment upon themselves. These individuals, despite God's many overtures to them, chose to be separated from God's love and friendship during their lives; therefore, this separation would continue eternally in hell. Christ's "descent into hell" has a number of meanings that involve the state of different categories of souls who had died before Jesus' redemptive Sacrifice. Heaven, hell, and purgatory will be discussed further in the presentation of the Anointing of the Sick in Chapter 16.

The Resurrection

Throughout the biblical narrative of Christ's life and Death, we find reference to the people's perception that the Messiah, the King descended from David, would bring about an earthly paradise. Israel would reign again. Time and again, Jesus tries to explain that this is not the kingdom he came to inaugurate. Pilate, faced with the accusations of the chief priests that Christ had made himself a rival of Caesar, confronted Jesus directly on this point: "Are you the King of the Jews?" Jesus replied, twice over, "My kingship is not of this world."[49]

One can imagine, though, the thoughts that might have occurred to those who expected the Messiah to be an earthly king, as they watched him tortured and mocked while he died the most shameful death of crucifixion. They would have immediately concluded he was a charlatan. Even the disciples, whom Jesus had expressly warned about his suffering and Death, were scared and confused. How could they know that his Death was, in fact, a victory? The greatest sign of Christ's victory is that after three days he rose from the dead. The entire Christian faith hangs on this wonderful truth: Christ is risen from the dead, and he is alive in the fullest sense of the word.

Over the years, there have arisen several false interpretations of the Resurrection that argue either explicitly or implicitly that it should not be taken as a literal or a historical event. Some opine that the Resurrection is a myth that evolved from the great admiration

49. Jn 18:33, 36.

the early Christians had for Jesus Christ. They speculate that his disciples, with the passage of time, only gradually claimed Christ rose from the dead and deified him. Others claim the Resurrection was the result of mass hysteria by which early Christians convinced themselves he had risen.

A more diligent study of the Gospel accounts shows that the Resurrection is a historical event. Christ truly, bodily rose from the dead. In the Gospels, St. Mary Magdalene, Mary the mother of James, and a woman named Salome went to anoint Christ's dead body and were the first to see the empty tomb and then the risen Lord. Both afraid and joyful, they ran to tell the Apostles. Instead of accepting and believing, the Apostles' response was one of disbelief along with a bit of ridicule. Even after seeing the empty tomb for himself, St. Peter did not draw any conclusions. In fact, there is absolutely no hint that any of the Apostles expected Jesus to rise again. When Christ appeared to the Apostles to demonstrate he had indeed risen from the dead, only then did they come to believe. Only through an encounter with the Risen Christ were the Apostles able to believe he had truly risen from the dead.

According to St. Paul, about 500 people saw Jesus Christ after his Resurrection. In his Epistles in the New Testament, St. Paul states clearly, "If Christ has not been raised, then... your faith is in vain."[50] People would still be prisoners to sin. Men and women would not have been redeemed, forgiven, or adopted as children of God. Those who have died following Christ would have died in vain. Christians, thus, would be the most pitied of people.

In the modern era, faith in the Resurrection is based on the account of those Apostolic witnesses who saw the risen Christ. He appeared so that this glorious event could serve as the foundation of the Christian faith. At least as much as any reliable historical record, the Gospels and the rest of the New Testament—together with the writings of the early Fathers of the Church—should be given full credence. Is there reason to doubt the honesty and integrity of the Apostles and Evangelists who wrote the Gospels? Unlike St. Thomas the Apostle, who doubted the other Apostles until he could see and touch the risen Lord for himself,[51] our faith must begin by trusting

50. 1 Cor 15:14; cf. vv. 14–19.

51. Cf. Jn 20:24–28.

the testimony of others and listening to our friends. "Blessed are those," said Jesus, "who have not seen and yet believe."[52]

The risen Lord also shows in many ways how everything is different. The human condition is changed. He has made "all things new."[53] It is clear from the accounts following the Resurrection that Christ's relationship with his Apostles and disciples had dramatically changed. No longer did Christ live among them as before, address large crowds, or heal infirmities. According to the Gospels, he appeared and disappeared: "He vanished out of their sight."[54] With his glorious, resurrected Body, Jesus is able to pass through the walls and locked doors. His glorified Body is no longer subject to suffering or the strictures of space and time.

In his glorified Body Christ must not have appeared exactly in the same manner as he existed before his Death for the simple reason that his disciples did not always recognize him at first. Jesus would have to open their eyes—then they immediately knew that it was he. For St. Mary Magdalene, the recognition of Jesus occurred after he spoke her name.[55] When Christ spoke with two of his disciples on their way to Emmaus, they recognized him only after he had sat down to table with them and celebrated the "breaking of the bread,"[56] a phrase the early Christians used to describe the Eucharist. Only then did they realize their mysterious companion was none other than the risen Christ. Upon their realization, he vanished from their sight.

Such events after Our Lord's Resurrection signified much more than simply a restoration to life or resuscitation; rather, they involved the glorification of a once mortal Body. Christ's Resurrection was inherently different from the likes of the son of the widow of Nain[57] and Lazarus,[58] whom Christ had brought back to life during his public ministry; they were restored to their natural life and later died. The Resurrection of Jesus Christ is the sign that Our Lord's Passion and Death has overcome the power of Satan, sin, and death.

---

52. Jn 20:29.
53. Rev 21:5.
54. Lk 24:31.
55. Cf. Jn 20:16.
56. Cf. Lk 24:35; cf. vv. 30–31.
57. Cf. Lk 7:11–17.
58. Cf. Jn 11:38–53.

The Resurrection is a compelling invitation for every Christian to believe that Jesus Christ lives. Now that, in his humanity and divinity, he transcends space and time, everyone can have an intimate, personal relationship with him. The transcendence of Christ's glorified Body makes him present everywhere: in the Church, in the Sacraments, and in the lives of his disciples. In heaven the faithful will contemplate the risen Christ directly and eternally, but during our sojourn on earth, we encounter him on the level of faith and love. Therefore, the ultimate Good News is not just Christ's exalted moral teachings or even his New Commandment of Love—it is that he lives!

The Resurrection imprints a kind of seal of victory on every human effort performed in the name of Christ. Because our Savior conquered sin and death by rising from the dead, everything done or suffered to promote his kingdom will prove successful in the end. Considering Christ's victory, St. Paul aptly stated: "We know that in everything God works for good with those who love him, who are called according to his purpose."[59] Perhaps the greatest confirmation of the victory of the Resurrection is the lives of the saints. Their days were marked by suffering and hardship; at the same time, they reflected Christ in their lives and attracted many others to him. The joy, peace, and love manifested in the lives of conscientious Christians attest to the power of the Resurrection working through the supernatural grace obtained by the redemption. The Resurrection and its effects give great confidence to proclaim the Good News to everyone.

Forgiveness of Sin as the First Fruit of the Resurrection

The Resurrection of Christ is a divine message that sin has been conquered and the human race's bondage to Satan has been shattered. Every sin, no matter how serious or heinous, can now be forgiven if the sinner has faith in Christ and offers the proper dispositions of sorrow and purpose of amendment. The purpose of God's plan of redemption is to restore all people to their full dignity as children of God. No amount of sacrifice or personal sorrow would have been sufficient or effective in removing sin. Only God-made-man was capable of making full reparation for sin and winning the

59. Rom 8:28.

grace to be reconciled with God. The forgiveness of sins appears as the first revealed fruit of the Resurrection.

During his time on earth, the people marveled that Jesus forgave sin on his own authority. It scandalized the Pharisees that a mere man would claim an authority that only belonged to God. Even after his Death and Resurrection, most failed to recognize this sign that Christ was indeed God among them. Having conquered sin and brought forgiveness, Jesus went on to bestow this authority on his ministers in the world. On the evening of the Resurrection, Our Lord appeared to his Apostles, and said: "Peace be with you. As the Father has sent me, even so I send you."[60] He established their mission of extending his work of redemption to the whole world. The Evangelist narrates what happened next:

> He breathed on them, and said to them, "Receive the Holy Spirit. If you forgive the sins of any, they are forgiven; if you retain the sins of any, they are retained."[61]

Christ gave his Apostles authority to forgive sins in his name so that all who want their sins forgiven, no matter how grave, will find reconciliation and healing in him. The Apostles extended this mission to others through the laying on of hands so that throughout all time the bishops—the successors to the Apostles—and the priests—their coworkers—might extend Christ's mission of mercy. This ministry of Christ continues in the Church today, primarily through the Sacraments of Baptism and Penance.

St. Peter was one of the first beneficiaries of the forgiveness of sins after the Resurrection. At the Last Supper St. Peter had fallen into pride since he stated under no uncertain terms that he would be more faithful than the other Apostles. As Jesus immediately predicted, before the cock had crowed the next morning, St. Peter had denied him three times. After the Resurrection Jesus sought out St. Peter to lavish his loving forgiveness on him. St. John's Gospel relates that, while the Apostles were fishing from their boats, they spotted Jesus on the beach; he urged them to cast their nets to the right side. They subsequently caught a great quantity of fish. After they had hauled in their catch, Jesus invited them to have breakfast he had prepared beside a charcoal fire, reminiscent of the charcoal fire before which St. Peter had denied him three times. Having eaten,

60. Jn 20:21.
61. Jn 20:22–23.

our Lord turned to the sorrowfully guilt-ridden St. Peter, who was his chosen Head of the Apostles. In a moving dialogue, Jesus Christ gently led St. Peter to repentance by asking him three times to affirm his love and fidelity, thereby nullifying his triple denial of Christ.[62] Jesus forgave St. Peter and simultaneously reaffirmed him as chief shepherd over the whole Church.

The Ascension

The Resurrection signified Christ's victory over sin and death and initiated his glorification; nevertheless, this glorification would not be fully accomplished until his return to the Father. Christ spent the days between his Resurrection and Ascension instructing his Apostles and confirming their faith in his Resurrection, preparing them to receive the Holy Spirit at Pentecost. This outpouring of the Holy Spirit would transform the Apostles, enabling them to be bold witnesses of the Gospel, even to the point of martyrdom. Christ's mission on earth was fulfilled, and his glorification was completed when he ascended into heaven. With his Apostles gathered around him, Jesus ascended—Body and soul—into heaven in a clear manifestation of his divinity.

Christ's victory over sin and death takes on an air of moving triumph with his glorious return to heaven, body and soul. The crowd of disciples present at Jesus' Ascension can be likened to a festive parade led by a victorious general. His rightful place in heaven is at the right hand of the Father. The Ascension of Christ into heaven also reveals that his kingdom will have no end. By ascending, our Lord personally opened the gates of heaven for the rest of his Church. His grand entrance into heaven gives his disciples hope that one day all the faithful will join him in his glory.[63] In heaven Christ constantly intercedes on our behalf before his Father. Christ's final instructions before his Ascension define the mission of the Apostles and the Church until the end of time: to evangelize all nations.

Divine intervention was necessary for the Apostles to accomplish this staggering task, so Our Lord assured the Apostles they would receive special powers to complete his work. "You shall receive power when the Holy Spirit has come upon you."[64] After his Ascen-

62. Cf. Jn 21:15–17.

63. Cf. Jn 14:2.

64. Acts 1:8.

sion into heaven, Christ and his Father would send the Holy Spirit, who would give the Apostles the graces needed to evangelize the world. By virtue of these graces merited by the Paschal Mystery, the Holy Spirit would transform each of Christ's disciples so he or she could become the light of the world and salt of the earth in Christ. The Ascension of Christ into heaven was the preliminary condition for the Holy Spirit to descend upon the Apostles, Our Lady, and the other disciples with them on the day of Pentecost.

The Ascension of our Lord initiated another kind of relationship between himself and his Church, founded on a life of faith, hope, and love. His return to the Father makes it possible for Christ to live in his disciples through the work of the Holy Spirit. He left these comforting words: "Lo, I am with you always, to the close of the age."[65] In a certain sense, the Ascension of Christ and the subsequent Descent of the Holy Spirit made Christ more accessible than he was during his public life. At the right hand of God the Father, Jesus Christ intercedes as our Eternal High Priest and Mediator. Last, with Jesus' Ascension into heaven, the plan of redemption is completed. Bringing about the effects of the redemption would officially start with the Descent of the Holy Spirit on the day of Pentecost.

65. Mt 28:20.

CHAPTER 8

THE HOLY SPIRIT

During his sojourn on earth, Jesus announced the Kingdom of God and the Good News of our redemption. After his Death and Resurrection, Jesus' instruction to the Apostles continued as he provided all the teaching necessary for salvation and sanctification until the end of time. But Christ did not merely leave us with wise words to follow. Upon the Apostles Christ *founded a Church*—a community of love. The Church serves as Christ's instrument in proclaiming the truth that saves and offers the grace that heals and sanctifies. Through his Church, Jesus reconciles the citizens of the world back to the Father. Now that Christ's redemption has made full and definitive reparation for all past, present, and future sins, it is time for the Holy Spirit to make the merits of the redemption accessible to all, for it is the Holy Spirit who applies the grace of the redemption through Christ's Church. By the Holy Spirit the Church develops, grows, and carries on Jesus' mission.

God is one, but it is still appropriate to distinguish different "roles" for the different Persons of the Trinity. St. Catherine of Siena, the great fourteenth-century mystic and Doctor of the Church, wrote about the work of the Trinity in the Eucharistic celebration of the Church and described their unique roles according to a banquet feast. The Father, according to her, is the "table" that offers us the food. Jesus, the Lamb of God, is the "food" we are being offered. The Holy Spirit is the "waiter" who serves the food.[1] Like any good waiter, the Holy Spirit can sometimes go unnoticed as he serves this heavenly feast of grace.

Though the work of the Holy Spirit is hidden within the human heart, he is fully a Person of the Blessed Trinity. St. Josemaria Escriva once lamented in a homily that, for too many people, the Holy Spirit is the "Great Unknown" rather than a "Someone... with whom we can talk and with whose life we can live."[2] As St. Josemaria pointed out, the story of the Early Church in the Acts of the Apostles is filled with the action of the Holy Spirit, but he stressed that this is not

1. Cf. Suzanne Noffke, *The Prayers of Catherine of Siena*, 2nd Edition (2001), Prayer 12.
2. CPB, no. 134.

a mere "remembrance of the past." The Spirit fills the Church now and forever as promised by Christ:

> The Holy Spirit is present in the Church of Christ for all time, so that it may be, always and in everything, a sign raised up before all nations, announcing to all men the goodness and the love of God.[3]

In the presentation of the Ten Commandments and the moral law in Chapters 4 and 5, the point was made that the moral law is not just a list of things to avoid but rather a preparation for the fullness of God's plan and the New Commandment of Love. Christian morality is a *positive* morality that is essentially liberating; it puts the human person in a position to achieve true fulfillment. Such fulfillment is found only in a loving communion with God and is possible only through his action. We cannot achieve fulfillment by our own efforts. This is the work of the Holy Spirit, and it is why Christians should regularly pray, "Come, Holy Spirit!"

Jesus Promises the Holy Spirit

Jesus, in preparation for his departure from the world, promised his disciples that he would send another divine Person, the Holy Spirit. The Holy Spirit heals and renews every person by uniting him or her ever more deeply with Jesus, who is the source of our communion with the Father.

This is not to say that the Spirit of God was not already in the world *at all*. In addition to many instances of God's "Spirit" at work in the Old Testament, it was the Holy Spirit who first prepared the Blessed Virgin Mary to become the Mother of Jesus through his most spectacular work, the Incarnation. The phrase that best describes Mary, "full of grace," denotes the fullness of the Holy Spirit. In anticipation of the redemption, the Third Person of the Trinity prepared the perfect dwelling for the Son of God's entrance into this world. Mary, through the intervention of the Spirit, was conceived without any stain of sin and is, for that reason, full of grace. Through the overshadowing of the Holy Spirit in synchrony with Mary's profound *yes*, God entered our world and became one of us in everything but sin. The Spirit was present at the major theophanies of Jesus' baptism and Transfiguration. The entrance of God the Son into the world as a man is marked by the presence and action of the Holy Spirit and ushers in a new age for the Spirit. As St. John the Baptist

3. Ibid., no. 128.

proclaimed of the Messiah, "I have baptized you with water; but he will baptize you with the Holy Spirit."[4]

Though the Spirit was already at work in the world and intimately connected to the incarnate Son, once Jesus died on the Cross and rose from the dead he promised, in union with the Father, to send the Holy Spirit upon his Apostles and, through them, upon all who are united in his Church. This Descent of the Holy Spirit took place at Pentecost. From that moment, the Church found herself in the age of the Holy Spirit because the communication of the merits of Christ's redemptive Sacrifice corresponds to the Spirit's work. The Spirit is sent to sanctify what Jesus Christ has redeemed.

At the beginning of his public life, Jesus invited his disciples to embrace his teachings and accompany him in his sufferings. He invited all his disciples to imitate him. At the Last Supper, as he drew near to the end of his sojourn in this world, he spoke of a more radical unity. Looking ahead to his own Death, Resurrection, and Ascension, Jesus spoke about the expediency of his departure because he would then be able to send the Holy Spirit. In St. John's Gospel Jesus first encouraged his disciples to keep his Commandments and then reassured them, "I will pray the Father, and he will give you another Counselor, to be with you for ever, even the Spirit of truth."[5] Though Jesus must soon leave his beloved disciples, he assured them, "I will not leave you desolate; I will come to you."[6] Jesus would no longer physically be with them, but would still come to them in the outpouring of the Spirit.

According to these words of Jesus to his Apostles, his departure from them and return to the Father opened a new and even deeper form of communion with him, in the sending of the Spirit. This he compares to the life-giving relationship between a branch and the vine: "I am the vine, you are the branches. He who abides in me, and I in him, he it is that bears much fruit, for apart from me you can do nothing."[7] What Jesus established was not merely a way of life or even just a novel religion, but a new, more profound relationship between God and the human person. The redemptive Sacrifice of Jesus achieved the capacity for everyone to share in the very

4. Mk 1:8.
5. Jn 14:16–17.
6. Jn 14:18.
7. Jn 15:5.

life of God through grace. His work boggles the mind. The Christian is invited not merely to know about Jesus but furthermore to share in Christ's very life. This communion is made possible by the Holy Spirit, who joins the Christian to Christ and assists him or her in penetrating and personalizing his words and putting them into action. Though we cannot see Jesus Christ with our eyes—because our union with Christ is by the Spirit—we can become so radically united to him that this union surpasses the one he had with his disciples during his public life. We can "abide" in him, and it is the Holy Spirit who is the "life force" that unites the *branch* to the *vine*.

As part of his promise, Jesus also explained the work of the Holy Spirit, the "Spirit of Truth" who will enlighten every mind. Jesus continued:

> The Counselor, the Holy Spirit, whom the Father will send in my name, he will teach you all things, and bring to your remembrance all that I have said to you."[8]

The Holy Spirit has always been associated with understanding. Four of the seven traditional "gifts of the Holy Spirit" involve enlightenment: wisdom, understanding, counsel, and knowledge. Prior to his suffering and Death, Jesus assured his Apostles, the future leaders of his Church, that he and the Father would send the Spirit to guide them. Until the end of time, by the grace of the Sacraments, all Christians receive this gift of the Holy Spirit, who serves as a translator of Jesus' teaching and example so that each one of us can personalize it and apply it to our own lives of discipleship. The Holy Spirit enables the Christian to discern not only God's Laws but also God's will, which is always the plan that will lead to our ultimate happiness.

The Holy Spirit was also established as the principle of growth for Christ's emerging Church. Continuing his lesson, Jesus told his Apostles, "I have yet many things to say to you, but you cannot bear them now. When the Spirit of truth comes, he will guide you into all the truth."[9] Jesus inaugurated his Church and entrusted his Apostles with the mission to carry the Gospel message "to the end of the earth."[10] Jesus assured them that the Holy Spirit would "guide" them in their understanding of all that Jesus has taught them and

---

8. Jn 14:26.
9. Jn 16:12–13.
10. Ibid.

the fullness of the Good News. The Church, by that same Spirit, is guided to this day.

In his preparatory teaching at the Last Supper, Jesus also established the full divinity of the Third Person of the Trinity. His instruction on the Holy Spirit came to an end as he added:

> He will not speak on his own authority, but whatever he hears he will speak, and he will declare to you the things that are to come. He will glorify me, for he will take what is mine and declare it to you.[11]

Far from putting the Spirit on a "lower" level, this is precisely how Jesus expressed his own unity with the Father:

> I can do nothing on my own authority; as I hear, I judge; and my judgment is just, because I seek not my own will but the will of him who sent me.[12]

As Christ's divine authority is the authority of the Father, so the Spirit is united to both the Father and the Son. The Spirit is presented as another divine Person in union and on a par with both the Father and the Son.

Before returning to the Father at his Ascension, Christ repeated this promise to his disciples: "You shall receive power when the Holy Spirit has come upon you."[13] Given the power of the Spirit, Jesus said they would then give witness to him "to the end of the earth."[14] Here, Christ's instruction adds that the Holy Spirit provides not only the ability *to understand* God's will but also the power *to act* on it. He is the source of the graces that will empower the Apostles—and by extension all Christians—*to do* what God is asking of them. This "power" of the Spirit is represented in the other three traditional gifts of the Holy Spirit: fortitude, piety, and fear of the Lord. A person might work to achieve virtue through natural means, obtaining even a high degree of self-discipline and control over his or her passions, but the capacity to replicate the life of Christ, to love as Christ loved, is humanly impossible. It is only possible through the work of the Holy Spirit.

---

11. Jn 16:13–14.
12. Jn 5:30.
13. Acts 1:8.
14. Ibid.

Pentecost

During the interim between Christ's Ascension and the Descent of the Holy Spirit, the Apostles, together with the Blessed Virgin Mary and other disciples of Our Lord, devoted themselves to intense prayer in preparation for Pentecost, the due date for the arrival of the promised divine Advocate. The word "Pentecost" means "fiftieth [day]." It is the Greek name of the Jewish "Festival of Weeks," which takes place fifty days after Passover. While the event is typically portrayed as limited to the Apostles and the Mother of God, Scripture suggests there may have been up to 120 people gathered together during this time. On the day of Pentecost, a great tumult was heard in the Cenacle, or Upper Room, where they were gathered, when "a sound came from heaven like the rush of a mighty wind."[15] Following the loud noise, the Holy Spirit manifested himself in the form of tongues of fire over the head of all present and they were "filled with the Holy Spirit."[16]

Filled with the Holy Spirit, the Apostles' first inclination was to go out and proclaim the Good News of salvation from Christ—and on this occasion a great miracle occurred. Because of the festival of Pentecost, Jewish pilgrims from all over the Roman Empire were in Jerusalem. Many gathered at the sound of the noise, and each of them—from diverse parts of the world—could hear the disciples preaching in his or her native tongue. The Spirit manifested itself in wisdom and understanding—not only in the preaching of the Apostles but also in the ability of all gathered to comprehend their meaning.

Just as Jesus had said, the Spirit also brought the Apostles power: St. Peter stood up and boldly preached in the name of Jesus. This St. Peter—the same man who had denied Jesus three times before his Crucifixion and had hidden himself away with the other disciples after Jesus' Death out of fear of what the Jewish authorities might do to him[17]—now boldly stood before the crowd and preached Christ crucified as Lord: "Let all the house of Israel therefore know assuredly that God has made him both Lord and Christ, this Jesus whom you crucified."[18] This episode marks the "birthday"

15. Acts 2:2.
16. Acts 2:4.
17. Jn 20:19.
18. Acts 2:36.

of the Catholic Church. It also demonstrates the role of the Holy Spirit in conversion, for Scripture relates that some 3000 people were baptized that day.

What exactly happened to the Apostles when they received the fullness of the Holy Spirit? We can recognize here, and throughout the Acts of the Apostles, all the gifts of the Spirit: wisdom, counsel, understanding, knowledge, fortitude, piety, and fear of the Lord.[19] The history related in Scripture through the rest of the Acts of the Apostles gives ample testimony to how the members of the nascent Church also produced the "fruits of the Holy Spirit": charity, joy, peace, patience, kindness, goodness, generosity, gentleness, faithfulness, modesty, self-control, and chastity.[20] These gifts and fruits are offered to all who strive to live their lives in the Spirit. Through the invisible work of the Paraclete in the deep recesses of the human heart and soul, every person begins to exhibit the fruits of the Holy Spirit as he or she becomes more and more united to Christ.

This new association with Christ is the fruit of a supernatural rebirth through the work of the Holy Spirit by means of Baptism, which incorporates a person into the Mystical Body of Christ. This Sacrament is how he or she first begins to "abide" in Christ. Baptism is not simply a rite of passage that gives a person access to a community. In uniting each person to Christ, the Holy Spirit effects a personal transformation. Every baptized person is a work of the Holy Spirit in progress. As we strive to imitate Christ, the Holy Spirit increasingly enhances our heart's capacity to love with the merciful heart of Jesus. A Christian's every spiritual action is attributed to the action of the Holy Spirit. St. Paul taught that even the pious mention of the name Jesus Christ can only occur through a movement of the Spirit.[21] The desire to repent, convert, and embrace holiness all reflect the hidden action of the Holy Spirit on the soul.

You Will Know Them by Their Fruit

Christ taught the Apostles at the Last Supper that everyone "who abides in me, and I in him, he it is that bears much fruit."[22] This is how we can see the invisible work of the "great unknown" in

19. Cf. CCC 1831.
20. Cf. CCC 1832.
21. Cf. 1 Cor 12:3.
22. Jn 15:4.

the heroic and sacrificial lives of those who love Jesus and follow his Commandments. As Jesus himself pointed out, you can only judge the goodness of a tree by its fruit.[23] The work of the Holy Spirit, invisibly operative in the human heart, is only detected in the fruit we witness in the disciples of Christ.

One striking example of the work of the Holy Spirit is St. Maximilian Kolbe, a Polish Franciscan who died at Auschwitz.[24] Prior to his arrest, St. Maximilian had already lived a life of heroic virtue, giving witness to the great works of charity that a human person united to Christ by the Spirit can accomplish. But the heroic virtue of his life is most dramatically evident in the manner of his death. After a prisoner had escaped from Auschwitz, the guards randomly chose ten men to be killed by starvation as a deterrent against future escape attempts. One man chosen cried out, "My poor wife! My poor children!" St. Maximilian, also a prisoner, stepped forward and offered to take the man's place.

Self-preservation is the most basic animal instinct. To overcome this drive for self-preservation and, like Christ, to "lay down his life for his friends"[25] is possible only through the power of God's grace. Even further, witnesses relate that during the period of their starvation, St. Maximilian continued to work as a priest, leading his fellow inmates in prayer and remaining peaceful to the end. After every person had died of starvation, only St. Maximilian was left alive. Wanting to be finished with it, the guards gave him a lethal injection, which witnesses say he patiently endured. Such heroic virtue is the fruit that comes from a life lived in the Spirit and a heart transformed into the heart of Jesus.

Another striking example of the work of God's grace by the Holy Spirit is the story of St. Maria Goretti. St. Maria's family were poor farmers, and her father died when she was very young. They shared a home with another family, the Serenellis. When Maria was only eleven years old, the Serenellis' son, Alessandro, attempted to rape her. He threatened to stab her with an awl if she did not sub-

23. Mt 7:16–17.

24. Auschwitz, in southern Poland, was the largest of the Nazi concentration and death camps. During World War II (1939–1945) Jewish people, people with mental and physical handicaps, Romani, homosexuals, artists, educators, political prisoners, Communists, and other suspected enemies of the State were used as slave laborers and exterminated, often in gas chambers. More than 1 million people, by some accounts, lost their lives at Auschwitz.

25. Jn 15:13.

mit. St. Maria staunchly refused, proclaiming that it would be a sin and accepted death rather than displeasing God. Alessandro, in a rage, stabbed her fourteen times. But what is perhaps even more remarkable than the bravery of St. Maria in the face of evil is that this young girl, when told in the hospital that she would not survive her injuries, offered her full forgiveness to her attacker and said that her hope was to see him one day in heaven.

The amazing power of the Holy Spirit did not end at this point in an already remarkable story. Alessandro, while in prison, had a miraculous conversion that he attributed to the prayers of the little St. Maria. On the day of his release, he went to St. Maria's mother to plead for her forgiveness. Assunta Goretti freely forgave him, and the two received Holy Communion together the next day. Alessandro Serenelli, the man who had murdered this young saint, was even present at her canonization in 1950. Such unbounded mercy and forgiveness are only possible when a person's heart has been truly transformed into the merciful heart of Jesus by the Holy Spirit.

These are but two of many stories in the life of the Church showing the fruit that grows on the branches united to Christ in the Spirit. Every age witnesses the courage of the martyrs, the bravery of the missionaries, and the tireless works of charity and service offered by Christ's disciples. And this is only to mention the most dramatic. The work of the Holy Spirit is seen in countless ways in every type of life. The Spirit is seen in the father who patiently works every day to support his children, in friends who reconcile their disputes and heal their relationship, and in a kind neighbor who cares for another's family when they are ill. Those who truly become Christ-like produce all the fruit by which we can recognize the work of the Holy Spirit. A person might have all the natural gifts a person could ask for: intelligence, energy, creativity, etc. Such a person might be highly successful in his or her career or personal life, but if the gifts of the Holy Spirit are lacking, no matter how materially successful or well liked that person might be, he or she will be a withering branch that "proves unfruitful"[26] and is not fit for the kingdom. Instead, cultivating the fruits of charity, joy, peace, patience, kindness, goodness, generosity, gentleness, faithfulness, modesty, self-control, and chastity is a sign of conforming a heart to the loving heart of Jesus.

26. Mt 13:23.

Baptism, as we shall see, does not automatically make a person perfect. Grace is not magic, and God does not impose himself against our will. As stated above, everyone is a work of the Holy Spirit *in progress*. The power of the presence of the Holy Spirit is best recognized in those who have completely given their lives over to Christ—like St. Maximilian Kolbe, St. Maria Goretti, and the many special holy men and women that we have in our lives.

CHAPTER 9

THE CHURCH OF CHRIST

The Holy Spirit ushers in the last phase of salvation history, called the "end times." This period does not signify that the end of the world is coming soon but rather that Divine Revelation has been completed, and it is now a question of extending the merits of Christ's redemption to everyone. Pentecost was not a solitary event but the beginning of the permanent indwelling of the Holy Spirit in the Catholic Church, the Kingdom of God on earth. The Church, a communion of persons reflecting the Trinity, has become the medium through which the Holy Spirit acts in his role of teaching and sanctifying. Since Pentecost until the end of time, the Holy Spirit will serve as the soul and inspirational force of the Church. This divine Advocate is present in Sacred Scripture, the pronouncements of the Church, the Sacred Liturgy, and the daily lives of Christ's disciples. There is no facet of a person's life or the life of the Church where the Holy Spirit is not present.

The "normal means" for the Spirit to impart sanctifying grace is through the Church's celebration and administration of the Sacraments. This is not the *exclusive* manner by which God works in people's lives; it is, however, the *primary* route for the bestowal of God's grace upon his children. The Descent of the Holy Spirit at Pentecost began the life of the Church so that the Spirit of God can continue to descend upon and sanctify his disciples by means of the Sacraments through the Church.

CHRIST FOUNDED A CHURCH

In modern times people give many reasons for rejecting the notion of what is called an "institutional" Church. A person might say that what matters is only to learn from Jesus and connect with him, and it is not necessary to officially join a Church. Others with good intent will say they have no use for organized religion since it suffices to simply be a Christian and follow the teachings of the Gospel. Some complain that the superabundance of Catholic teachings and mandates stifle a simple Christian life by distracting people from the essentials of following Jesus. "I believe in God, but I'm not very *religious,"* others will sometimes say, perhaps adding that they feel closer to God when experiencing nature than they do when participating in religious services.

These biases come from a caricature of the Catholic Church and her teachings. The Catholic Church does not "separate" people from access to Jesus. In reality, Jesus Christ himself speaks, sanctifies, and governs through the Church. A favorite image of the Church handed down by the Early Church Fathers is that the Church can be likened to the moon illuminated by the sun, which symbolizes Christ, the Light of the World. According to this analogy, the light of Christ reaches every person *through the Church,* represented by the moon, amid the darkness of the world.

The Magisterium aimed to better express the Church's mission and structure in the last century at Vatican II. The Council Fathers drew on the wisdom of the Early Church Fathers, stating that as the soul is the animating life force of the human body, so the Holy Spirit is for the Church. When the Church teaches, preaches, and sanctifies through the Sacraments and governs through the hierarchy of bishops in union with the Pope, the Holy Spirit is the ultimate inspiration of all those facets of the Church's work.

As we saw in the previous chapter, the Holy Spirit was sent to fulfill the Church's "work." The Church community is the primary means intended by God to unite people more closely to himself. As the same Council Fathers taught:

> When the work which the Father gave the Son to do on earth[1] was accomplished, the Holy Spirit was sent on the day of Pentecost in order that He might continually sanctify the Church, and thus, all those who believe would have access through Christ in one Spirit to the Father.[2]

God can certainly be experienced in creation, and a person can be united to Jesus through the reading of Scripture. We all experience God's presence in the company of our loved ones. God is not limited to the walls of a church building. But incorporation into the Church with access to the Sacraments is the great gift Christ left to deepen our communion with God the Father. The Church is not an earthly gathering invented by people like a club or mutual support group. The Church is an assembly of believers in Christ called together by the Father and guided by the Holy Spirit.

1. Cf. Jn 17:4.
2. LG, no. 4; cf. Eph 1:18.

The history of salvation begins with God forming a people to be his own. The covenant with Abraham established the chosen people as a nation set apart. From Israel came the Messiah, who brought God's salvation to the whole world. The Church of the New Covenant began in seedling form when Jesus Christ gathered around himself the Twelve Apostles and his other disciples. He saw those disciples as his flock and family, and he led and served them like a Good Shepherd. The foundation of the Church that would last until the end of time would be his Twelve Apostles, prefigured by the patriarchs of the Twelve Tribes of Israel. These Apostles would serve as the first link to Jesus in governing, teaching, and sanctifying in his name through his newly formed Church. They received the authority to transmit and interpret Jesus' teachings and impart forgiveness as his representatives. The Apostles would then pass on Jesus' teachings and the authority invested in them to successors in an unbroken line for all of history. In the Acts of the Apostles, St. Peter and the others ordain successors through the power of the Holy Spirit by the laying on of hands. This "tactile" succession is unbroken to this day in the bishops who continue as the Apostles' successors.

It is a good thing to study the history of the Church, but it is important to remember the Church established by Christ is not just another human institution. It remains a mystery that surpasses full comprehension by the light of unaided reason. Like all mysteries, it is best described using the language of poetry and metaphor. Our Lord frequently taught using stories, parables, and images. One of the more common images of the Church is the "People of God" derived from the writings of the Old Testament. The people of Israel were "God's chosen people." In Christ, a personal relationship with God is open to all the nations—and the Catholic Church is the new "People of God," whose head is Jesus Christ.

In keeping with this image of a united people, Christ often depicted himself as a shepherd tending his flock. Jesus is the "good shepherd [who] lays down his life for the sheep."[3] Using images with which his listeners would be familiar, Jesus revealed, "My sheep hear my voice, and I know them, and they follow me."[4] This image especially strikes at the heart of the relationship of Christ and his

3. Jn 10:11.

4. Jn 10:27.

Church—he is the Good Shepherd who cares for every person as a shepherd tends his flock of sheep.

The image of a building also has special significance. Jesus associated his Body with the Temple in Jerusalem,[5] and St. Paul referred to Christ as the cornerstone of the household of God. The foundational stones of the building are the Twelve Apostles, and the living stones that form the rest of the building are the members of the Church.[6] Christ, together with his Apostles, gives the Church an everlasting bedrock. This edifice made of living stones serves as the lodging of the Family of God, the Church.

The most prominent image of the Church, however, is that of a Body. This image has many facets and has been used by the Church to describe its "corporate" existence from the New Testament until today. First, the Church is the "Body of Christ." Through Baptism every Christian is incorporated into the "Mystical Body of Christ," and through frequent reception of Christ in the Eucharist, the members of Christ's Body are more fully united to Christ's own Flesh. Christ, in this image, is "the head over all things for the church, which is his body."[7] The riches of Christ's life are communicated to his whole Mystical Body.

The image of the Body also highlights the organic communion that exists among the "members" of the Church. The Law of Love requires us to love God above all things but also our neighbor as ourselves. Being united with Christ, the members of his Mystical Body are thereby more united with one another. The teaching of the Church on communion frequently repeats St. Paul's words: "Just as the body is one and has many members, and all the members of the body, though many, are one body, so it is with Christ."[8] If one member of the Body suffers, all suffer; if anyone rejoices, all rejoice. When one member leads a saintly life, the whole Mystical Body benefits, and when a baptized Christian sins, the negative effects of those actions redound on the rest of the faithful—like a physical sickness affecting the whole body. It is an "organic communion" where all the members are united with one another in Christ.

5. Cf. Jn 2:19–21.

6. Cf. Eph 2:19–22.

7. Eph 1:22–23.

8. 1 Cor 12:12.

It should be clear from this vision of the Church that the call to follow Christ is not only for the sanctification of the disciple. Integral to the uniting of a person to Jesus is committing him- or herself to the service of others. As St. Paul revealed regarding the varied gifts of the Holy Spirit: "To each is given the manifestation of the Spirit *for the common good*."[9] This presence of the Holy Spirit extends from Jesus Christ to everyone who forms part of the People of God, and each member is called to radiate Christ's love to the world.

The Body of Christ is not limited to those presently in the Church on earth. The Church is a "Communion of Saints" that includes not only the members on earth in this present moment but also the Church in heaven and in purgatory. As we pray for our deceased brothers and sisters in the faith, we obtain spiritual goods for the souls being purified in purgatory. From the earliest times the Church has had the tradition of praying for the dead. Their intercession for the Church on earth is especially effective. We also invoke the intercession of the saints in heaven—both those officially recognized and those recognized only by God—for their powerful prayers. These saints are most intimately united to Christ as they directly contemplate his face. Because of this unique intimacy with God, their prayers in heaven for the People of God on earth are extremely efficacious. There are scores of stories of saints in modern times whose intercessory prayers have resulted in cures of terminal illnesses, the conception of children after many years going childless, and most importantly, spiritual conversions.

The image of the Body also demonstrates that the Church offers more than a one-to-one communion between the individual Christian and God. The Church is called a "Sacrament of Unity" because the goal is a deeper communion with God and with one another—love of God and neighbor. The members of the Church work together for the salvation of all, not for themselves with no thought for their brothers and sisters. The unity of the Church is also meant to spill out into the rest of the world. While the Church is a sign of God's love and the pursuit of each person's everlasting life, an ambitious objective of this instrument of divine care is the unity and solidarity of the whole human family.

Since the Church is at the service of the holiness of its members, she is designed to bring peace and harmony to the whole human

9. 1 Cor 12:7; emphasis added.

race. The daily news virtually never fails in reporting suffering and tragedy as a result of war, natural disasters, terrorism, domestic violence, and every other evil. It is clear that the world is fraught with the scourges of hatred and brutal violence. This sad state of affairs finds its remedy in the peace and love Jesus Christ wants to lavish on everyone through the work of his Church. The Church is designed to be an effective instrument in making this world a happier, more peaceful place; she proclaims her teachings and generously administers the life-giving Sacraments of Christ so that everyone can live up to the dignity of his or her calling.

Being a member of the Church is, then, not just "organized religion" in the sense of people coming together and forming a structure to control behavior within an established community. In contrast to a natural society, where many civil laws are derived from the natural law, there is only one Law in Christ's Church: the Law of Love. This begins with the power to overcome one's appetites and achieve true freedom. Every person's actions can make him or her more or less capable of making the sacrifices necessary to love. Grace builds on nature; it does not control anyone like a tyrant. The Holy Spirit, interacting with human free will, makes a person Christ-like according to our nature. But to love as Christ loved is a work of God's grace, achieved most immediately within the community of the Church and by the Sacraments.

VOCATIONS

Another way the organic communion of the Church is expressed is in the unity among the various vocations found in the Church—to married life, to Holy Orders, and to the consecrated life—all have their special "charisms," or gifts, to be used to serve others. The call to holiness; the threefold mission of priest, prophet, and king; and the charge to evangelize and spread the Gospel belong, as we shall see, equally to every member of Christ's Mystical Body, but there are different ways to fulfill this call.

The governance of the Church is entrusted to the bishops as successors of the Apostles in union with the Pope, who occupies the See of Peter. Every bishop is the head and teaching authority over a diocese, which is a geographical territory of people. The bishop has legislative, executive, and judicial powers within the ecclesiastical law, or law of the Church. The Council Fathers of Vatican II taught,

"By Episcopal consecration [ordination as a bishop] the fullness of the sacrament of Orders is conferred."[10] The bishop "impresses" some of his authority, as it were, on other men—priests—who are given the "power" to preach, offer the Eucharist, and absolve sins. The priests of a diocese care for the people in a parish, a section of that diocese, as coworkers with their bishop.

Though each bishop is responsible for his own diocese, all the bishops as a group are called the "episcopal college," or College of Bishops, because the universal Church is a communion of the faithful. The College of Bishops, however, has no authority on its own unless they are united to and under the Bishop of Rome, the Pope. The Pope is the successor of St. Peter, the Rock upon whom Christ built his Church: "I tell you, you are Peter, and on this rock I will build my church, and the powers of death shall not prevail against it."[11] The Pope is the visible and permanent foundation of unity of the Church on earth. This fact is especially experienced in gatherings with the Holy Father. Especially at a papal audience or a solemn Mass at St. Peter's Basilica in Rome, people from every corner of the globe are enthusiastic and excited to be in the presence of the Holy Father. Whether someone is from Canada or Burundi, all equally recognize the Pope as their spiritual father and the successor of St. Peter.

To ensure that the faithful receive the truth that saves and sanctifies, the Magisterium possesses the gift of infallibility regarding faith and morals under certain narrow conditions. This infallibility is most typically exercised in an Ecumenical Council, which is, as you remember from Chapter 1, a meeting of all the bishops of the Catholic Church in union with the Pope as the head. We have seen teachings on various subjects from the Second Ecumenical Council of the Vatican (Vatican II) throughout this book, on the Trinity from the Ecumenical Councils of Nicæa I and Constantinople I in Chapter 2, and on the Person and natures of Jesus Christ from the Ecumenical Councils of Ephesus and Chalcedon in Chapter 6. The teaching of an Ecumenical Council is authoritative when all the bishops, united to the Pope as their head, agree upon it. This confidence comes from the promise of Jesus that the Holy Spirit would always preserve the Church. Infallibility is not based on any special natural genius of the men gathered; rather, this charism is given through faith in the

10. LG, no. 21.
11. Mt 16:18.

guidance of the Holy Spirit when all the bishops are in accord under the leadership of the Pope. When they teach on a matter of faith or morals in an Ecumenical Council, it must be held as a matter of belief. With the charism of infallibility, the Church is guaranteed to profess and teach the faith without the possibility of error.

The Pope has the gift of infallibility by virtue of his office of Vicar of Christ and the successor of St. Peter. He can infallibly declare on his own authority a particular tenet of faith or morals. This does not mean that every word he utters is prophetically true. There are certain circumstances that must be met for the Pope to speak infallibly:

> When the Roman Pontiff speaks *ex cathedra* ... he defines a doctrine concerning faith or morals to be held by the whole Church, he possesses, by the divine assistance promised to him in blessed Peter, that infallibility which the divine Redeemer willed his Church to enjoy in defining doctrine concerning faith or morals.[12]

First, papal infallibility is a matter of content. The Pope, like the Bible and the Magisterium as a whole, is infallible when he teaches "concerning faith or morals." God's Revelation does not disclose the natural order; he has left that discovery to human ingenuity. Revelation is focused on what is necessary for our salvation. Second, papal infallibility is a matter of context. If the Holy Father were discussing theology at a backyard cookout with his friends, his words would not suddenly be binding on all the faithful. The Pope must explicitly intend to speak *ex cathedra*, or "from the chair [of St. Peter]" as the visible head of all Christians. Very rarely in the history of the Church has a Pope spoken *ex cathedra*. The Pope, however, apart from infallibility, is trusted by the faithful to interpret the Gospel through the special guidance of the Holy Spirit.

But Holy Orders, as great as it is in dignity, is far from the only vocation in the Church.

The faithful in the consecrated life are those men and women who are given a vocation to a state of life characterized by the practice of the evangelical counsels—poverty, chastity, and obedience—which provide a radical means of growing in holiness in imitation of the life of Christ. Most people in the consecrated life are called "religious," which in this context means they make public professions and commitments to the evangelical counsels. These formal

12. First Ecumenical Council of the Vatican, Dogmatic Constitution on the Church of Christ *Pastor Æternus* (July 18, 1870), ch. IV, no. 9.

promises and commitments are called "vows," and they are binding in conscience. A rich diversity exists among the men and women who make these vows. Some religious orders focus on teaching; some care for the sick; some are devoted to Eucharistic Adoration; and some others spend their time in quiet, contemplative prayer. The common vocation of all religious is to give witness to the Kingdom of God that is to come. Making vows to practice the evangelical counsels is neither a renunciation of the goodness of this life nor a rejection of material goods, marriage, or freedom. The vows provide the means for these dedicated men and women to put aside their own desires in service to the coming of God's kingdom. They do this not only for themselves and their own salvation but also so they can better serve those around them, whether through prayer or by corporal and spiritual works of mercy. Those consecrated to Christ in the religious life are a sign of Christ's self-emptying out of love for every person. They also serve as a model for all Christians to carry out God's will in service to his kingdom.

St. Therese of Lisieux, lovingly called the "Little Flower," offers an example of the beauty and simplicity of the religious life. Many people have been inspired by her autobiography, *The Story of a Soul*. Her "little way" teaches that the path to holiness does not depend on grandiose actions of vast importance, but rather on countless little acts of love done throughout the day. She lived a short but joyful life of prayer and devotion to Jesus. Her life in the convent was not lived only as a witness for other women living lives in the convent. Her lessons on the spiritual life have been embraced by people from all walks of life—from the lay faithful to bishops—and her story has caused many conversions.

The great majority of the Church's faithful are lay people whose mission is to share in Christ's work of teaching and sanctifying amid their family life and work. As the Council Fathers of Vatican II taught, lay Christians are not simply "all the faithful except those in Holy Orders and those in the state of religious life."[13] Lay Christians have a positive mission:

> What specifically characterizes the laity is their secular nature.... The laity, by their very vocation, seek the kingdom of God by engaging in temporal affairs and by ordering them according to the plan of God.[14]

13. LG, no. 31.
14. Ibid.

The vocation of every lay Christian carries the heavy responsibility of bringing Christ's light into the world through everyday life: in family life, in the workplace or school, with friends, and in every situation. By virtue of Baptism the lay faithful have the divine calling to inspire everything they do with the spirit of the Gospel. Through their work they contribute to the common good and to improving the quality of life in society. Lay Christians strive to make decisions and carry out actions—political, economic, scientific, etc.—with a Christian spirit and the Catholic Church's moral guidance. The extension of the Kingdom of God into the modern world will grow to the degree that the lay faithful bring the life of the Church into their temporal affairs; they express their personal sanctity, or holiness, in the way they work, speak, and act.

There are innumerable examples of lay Christians who have lived a life of quiet holiness. As the *Catechism* teaches, holiness is "perfection of charity."[15] It can be pursued by everyone, even a person in the most humble or difficult circumstances. The saints are not all great founders of religious orders, bold missionary priests, or brave martyrs who died heroically for their faith. The Church has canonized many lay people who died peacefully at home after an exemplary life of charity, and there are countless others whose names are known only to God—and maybe known to a few relatives and friends.

One inspiring example is St. Giuseppe Moscati, who was a physician, medical school professor, and pioneer in biochemistry in the early twentieth century. His life was one of not only intellectual accomplishment and physical healing—he was renowned for his ability as a doctor—but also of consistent, beautiful acts of charity toward all people. A pious man, he went to Mass daily and began each workday with prayer, but his communion with God expressed itself in the world in all that he did. He encouraged his interns to treat patients as whole human beings—mind, body, and spirit—not just ailments to be healed. He treated the poor free of charge, often slipping money into their prescription envelopes to help pay for their medication. His life is filled with acts of service, both small and great. When Mt. Vesuvius erupted in 1906, he personally helped evacuate a nursing home. During the cholera epidemic of 1911, he went above and beyond the call of duty. He treated thousands of

15. CCC 2013.

soldiers in World War I. Though he was a gifted physician and hospital administrator, it was the holiness of his life of charity that truly set him apart.

The Four Marks of the Church

The Church herself also has certain marks, or characteristics, given to her by God, yet for which we are always laboring. In the Creed at Mass the Catholic faithful profess that the Church is "one, holy, catholic and apostolic."[16] Jesus Christ, through the workings of the Holy Spirit, imparts these special and enduring marks to his Church.

The Church is One

The ultimate source of the Church's presence in the world is the work of the Blessed Trinity, one God in three divine Persons. In all things the Church is "One." Both the unity, or "oneness," of the Church and the ever-growing number and rich diversity of her members reflect the oneness of the Triune God. The Church can be One—in spite of the sins of her members—because Jesus Christ unites all his faithful to God the Father through his redemptive Sacrifice on the Cross. Every member finds salvation in union with him via his Church. The great diversity in the Church is a sign not of disunity but rather of an abundant variety of God's gifts. The treasures of every person, culture, and age serve the good of the whole Church, particularly when they are used in service to others. The Church's unity is expressed through the bond of charity her children exercise.

The Church's unity is also expressed through common adherence to the authentic teachings of Christ. There is one faith; one Baptism; one Eucharistic celebration; and one head on earth, the Pope, who is the Vicar of Christ. Tragically, the unity of believers has been damaged by heresy, apostasy, and schism. Succeeding generations have inherited the effects of these divisions within the Church. Especially since Vatican II in the 1960s, there has been a wonderful eagerness and effort to mend fences and restore unity with Orthodox, Anglican, and Protestant Christians. The Popes of the modern era have worked to explicitly heal the divisions among Christians.

16. RMiss, The Order of Mass, no. 18.

The lack of visible unity among members of the Church—while it is a cause of sorrow—should not come as a surprise. The principal effect of the fall of Adam and Eve was alienation and division. Frequently, the New Testament Epistles St. Paul addressed to his newly formed Church communities focus on calling them back to communion with one another, eliminating divisions. The Church, in herself, is One; but her members come to the Church—as a popular description describes her—as "a hospital for sinners, not a hotel for saints." Her members stand in constant need of repentance and renewal.

The Church is Holy

In a similar fashion, the Church will always be "Holy" because Christ, who is fully God and fully man, has constituted his Church as his Mystical Body. The image of the Body, discussed earlier, has a further application in perhaps the most beautiful image of the Church as the "Bride of Christ." Marriage, as we will see in Chapter 17, is one of God's favorite images for his relationship with his people. It is often pointed out that the Bible begins with a marital union in the Book of Genesis—Adam and Eve become "one flesh"[17]—and ends with "the marriage supper of the Lamb"[18] in the Book of Revelation: "I saw the holy city, new Jerusalem, coming down out of heaven from God, prepared as a bride adorned for her husband."[19] As Israel in the Old Testament was so often spoken of as the "faithless wife"[20] of God, Christ is the "Bridegroom" who comes to sanctify and make his "Bride" holy.[21] This is one reason why the Church is traditionally referred to as "she" rather than "it." Through this union with Christ, the Church is invariably and totally Holy. Every activity of the Church is at the service of sanctifying its members.

If the Church is Holy, why is there such rampant sin among so many Catholics? One response is that the holiness of the Church should not be judged by those who refuse to live according to her teachings or try but fail to live it fully; rather, her holiness is evident in people who eagerly strive to live the Gospel message in its entirety. Sanctity, or holiness, is especially exemplified in the lives

17. Gn 2:24.
18. Rev 19:9.
19. Rev 21:2.
20. Cf. Jer 3:20.
21. Cf. Rev 21:2.

of the saints since the holiness of Christ is made manifest in their own personal lives. The practice of charity, spelled out by the Gospel and lived perfectly by the Church's founder, especially reveals the holiness of the Catholic Church. When everything is said and done, it is precisely saintly men and women who renew the Church in all periods of history. But everyone who struggles to implement the Church's teachings in his or her daily life and take full advantage of the Sacraments—even when he or she falls but repents and gets up again to trust in God's mercy—will most definitely grow in holiness and consequently serve as a witness to the world that the Church is Holy.

The sins committed by the members of the Church also remind us that it is Christ himself who makes his Bride Holy. Christ laid down his life for the Church...

> that he might present the church to himself in splendor, without spot or wrinkle or any such thing, that she might be holy and without blemish.[22]

Even with the heroic example of so many saints, the saints would be the first to remind us that it is Christ who makes us holy, and it is by his Blood that we are made clean.[23]

The Church is Catholic

"Catholic" does not, in the sense of the marks of the Church, refer to the "Catholic Church," understood as distinct from an "Orthodox Church," the "Anglican Church," or the "Baptist Church." The word "catholic" has been used since at least the fourth century to describe a *quality* of the Church, and is still used by non-Catholic Christians who, although they might have a slightly different understanding of the word, continue to profess this same Creed.

"Catholic" is from the Greek for "universal." The universality, or catholicity, of the Church is exhibited from several perspectives. Since the fullness of Christ's Mystical Body subsists in the Church, the totality of the means to salvation and sanctification can only be found there. Christ is the one Lord. He is not another prophet, or guru—another option among options. The fullness of the contents of the faith and the sacramental life of grace that flows from the Church is meant universally for all people. Because the teachings

22. Eph 5:27.
23. Cf. Rev 7:14.

and the Sacraments of the Catholic Church are meant for every human being, her mission is to evangelize everyone.

There's plenty of room for everyone: the sick and the healthy, the poor and the rich, the sinner and the saint. Inside the physical edifice of a Catholic church, at Mass it would not be unusual to notice a whole array of people of different ethnic backgrounds, professions, and ages all worshiping God with the same beliefs and desires for a more perfect union with Christ. Though each diocese or parish is a very small part of the Church, they do reflect the universality of the Church. An Australian—for example, despite cultural differences in music, art, or even the language itself—would still be comfortable and feel at home in a Catholic church in Korea. The universality of the Church also means that salvation in Christ is meant for all time periods, both before and after the historical span of Christ's time on earth. The Gospel does not become "outdated," as it is the *universal* means of salvation for every person.

The Church is Apostolic

The fourth characteristic of the one true Church is that she is "Apostolic": She was founded on the Apostles, whom Christ directly taught, formed, and commissioned. The teachings of Jesus, called the "Deposit of Faith," were entrusted to his Apostles. They are the first recipients of the whole Deposit of the Faith that they were instructed to hand down to every generation of the faithful until the end of time. The Apostles, in turn, chose successors to continue the work of evangelization they had initiated. It was the will of Jesus that St. Peter have direct successors to lead the universal Church. The same applies to the order of bishops who succeed the Apostles without interruption. This Apostolic Succession is, of course, guided by the Holy Spirit throughout history.

In the Early Church, it was common for bishops to "trace their lineage" back to the Apostles in order to establish that their teaching was true. If they could not show their continuity with the Apostles—and thereby with Christ—then their teaching and authority was "of man" and "not from God." The Church, guided by the Holy Spirit, continues to transmit and interpret these teachings in every time period and culture without deviating from the original Deposit of Faith. To be united authentically to Christ, the Church must be Apostolic.

Degrees of Communion with Christ's Church

If the salvation of Christ is communicated to the world through his One, Holy, Catholic, and Apostolic Church, then how do Catholics regard those outside of visible communion with the Catholic Church? Does the Catholic Church have a "monopoly" on God's grace? Is everyone else doomed? The Council Fathers of Vatican II taught, "Many elements of sanctification and of truth are found outside of its [the Catholic Church's] visible structure."[24] These elements are found in varying degrees of concentration, from those who embrace the totality of Christ's teaching to those who do not even believe in God.

These varying degrees can be understood as different levels of participation, a sort of "imperfect communion." Many Christians share in the Sacrament of Baptism; some Christians share in the Sacrament of the Eucharist, but are not in communion with the Pope; still other Christians follow Christ but do not accept the Seven Sacraments as efficacious signs of grace. Other people believe in God but do not accept Jesus Christ as the divine Messiah. Finally, there are many people who live the natural law but do not believe in God, some even having no contact with Christianity. Having all Seven Sacraments, the Orthodox Churches have much in common with the Catholic Church; their imperfect communion with the Church is closer than other non-Catholic Christian ecclesial communities, which, in turn, are in a closer relationship than non-Christian monotheistic religions.

Among the monotheistic religions, the Jewish religion enjoys a very special connection to the Catholic Church since it served as the indispensable preparation for the coming of the Messiah. It was from the special nation of God's chosen people that the Messiah and Savior of the world came. The Church's relationship with other non-Christian religions is found in their common origins in our first parents, directly created by God. Thus, the Church also has a relationship with the Muslim people; they both worship one God as the Creator and consider Abraham their father in faith. In each case, "many elements of sanctification and of truth"[25] are found outside of the Church.

24. LG, no. 8.

25. Ibid.

There is, however, an ancient axiom of the Church: "Outside of the Church there is no salvation." If misinterpreted or misunderstood, this declaration can be quite disheartening, to say the least. The meaning of this ancient teaching in no way says that there is no hope of salvation for anyone outside of the visible confines of the Catholic Church. The Church teaches that people...

> can attain to salvation who through no fault of their own do not know the Gospel of Christ or His Church, yet sincerely seek God and moved by grace strive by their deeds to do His will as it is known to them through the dictates of conscience.[26]

Even those who "without blame on their part" have no knowledge of God won't be denied the "helps necessary for salvation."[27] God is Creator of the whole world and of all people, and whatever is good and true comes from and leads to God; therefore, whatever good or truth is found in groups outside of Catholic communion "is looked upon by the Church as a preparation for the Gospel."[28]

What the statement, "Outside of the Church there is no salvation," *is* saying is that the grace of Christ comes to everyone, whether they realize it or not, through Jesus' Mystical Body, the Church. As St. John Paul II explained, for those ignorant of the Gospel due to the circumstances of their life, "salvation in Christ is accessible by virtue of a grace... having a mysterious relationship to the Church."[29] The relationship is "mysterious" because it is not explicit, yet the grace still comes from Christ because of his Sacrifice and is communicated by the Holy Spirit. Those who, through no fault of their own, are not in full communion with the Church but seek God by leading a moral life can achieve salvation. God never denies his saving grace, which is imparted through the Church, from anyone.

If people outside of the Church can be saved, the next question one might logically ask is, "Why evangelize?" Not only is salvation outside of the Church possible, but the Church even teaches that a *greater* responsibility is placed upon those who *do understand* that the Church is necessary and founded by Christ. Would it not be better to leave people in the spiritual state where they find themselves? The first thing to say in response to this question is to point out

26. Ibid., no. 16; cf. Mk 4:14.

27. Ibid., no. 16.

28. Ibid., no. 16; cf. Lk 12:32.

29. St. John Paul II, Encyclical Letter on the Permanent Validity of the Church's Missionary Mandate *Redemptoris Missio* (December 7, 1990), no. 10.

that the advantages of being in full communion with the Catholic Church are quite significant. Sharing in the life of Christ through Baptism, reception of the Eucharist that contains Christ's Real Presence, and the certainty of forgiveness of sin through the Sacrament of Penance and Reconciliation are of inestimable value. In addition to the Sacraments, the sure teachings of the Church, which enjoys continuous guidance of the Holy Spirit, is another luxury Catholics have that is obviously meant to be shared.

The teaching on the possibility of salvation outside of the Church is based on the presumption that such people are seeking the truth, which means they are in reality *seeking Christ*. It would then be of even greater importance to evangelize so that the Church might bring them what they already so ardently long for—the truth that comes from God and a deeper relationship with God in Christ. For those reasons and numerous others, the Church is committed to doing everything possible to bring the Gospel message to everyone. Jesus commissions his disciples to "make disciples of all nations."[30] God is love, and he glories in the happiness of every person; he wants to share his life with every human being by way of his Church.

It is also the goal of the Church to draw all separated Christians back to full unity with each other. This accomplishment will come as a miraculous gift from Christ since this objective goes way beyond the ambit of good will and human effort. Though human effort is necessary, alone it does not stand a chance of remedying the rifts and scars of past misunderstandings and injuries. What brings much hope is that divine intervention, in response to prayer and charity, will bring about this greatly desired unity. Thus, the means to reach full communion requires personal conversion and a holy life. Common prayer, fraternal charity, dialogue, and mutual collaboration are all vital ways to reach this goal. More than convincing one another who is right or wrong, the charity of Christ will ultimately draw Christians to greater love and understanding.

Mary, Mother of the Church

The Church has a hierarchical structure, and this hierarchy is represented by ordained men, causing some to argue that the Church as an organization represents a sort of repressive patriarchal system. The all-male priesthood will be discussed in Chap-

30. Mt 28:19.

ter 19. What we note here is that the Church is not the same as her structure. The full mystery of the Church is not fully expressed by her hierarchical structure and should not be limited to this single dimension. The whole purpose of the hierarchical structure is to be in service to the holiness of her members, which in turn immediately prompts the image of the Church—both men and women—as "the Bride," who, as St. John Paul II wrote, "responds with the gift of love to the gift of the Bridegroom."[31]

Church teaching frequently points out that it is precisely in the Blessed Virgin Mary, the Mother of Jesus, that the Church is first prefigured. It was Mary, "full of grace," who brought Christ into the world through the work of the Holy Spirit. In an analogous way, the Church brings Christ to every person willing to have faith in him. Mary gave birth to the Son of God, who in turn founded his Church, which is a mystical extension of his very Body. Since Mary is the Mother of Jesus, she is the Mother of the Church, her Son's Mystical Body. Being Mother of Jesus and of his Church makes Mary the Mother of all the baptized. She is our Mother in the order of grace. She is an image of the goal of the Church in her totally purified, sanctified form. Mary, in addition to being the Mother of Jesus—fully God and fully man—is Christ's greatest disciple. Therefore, her example makes her the role model and hope of all Christians. As St. John Paul II wrote:

> From this point of view the "woman" is the representative and the archetype of the whole human race: she *represents the humanity* which belongs to all human beings, both men and women.[32]

Far from being repressively patriarchal, the Church manifests both the masculine and the feminine. As St. John Paul II put it, "the Church is both 'Marian' and 'Apostolic-Petrine.'"[33] Both men and women share, though in diverse ways, in the Eternal High Priesthood of Christ; both men and women must represent, though in varying ways, the holiness of the Blessed Virgin Mary as the archetype of all that it means to be a disciple of Christ.

---

31. MD, no. 27.
32. Ibid., no. 4.
33. Ibid., no. 27; cf. H. U. von Balthasar, "*Neue Klarstellungen*: Address to the Cardinal and Prelates of the Roman Curia (December 22, 1987)," in; *L'Osservatore Romano* (December 23, 1987).

CHAPTER 10

CHRISTIANITY AND THE COMMON GOOD

The presentation of Christian morality, in Chapters 4 and 5, focused on moral behavior as more of a personal quest. The human person—subject to sin but liberated by Christ—can overcome, with the help of God's grace, the inherited tendency to selfishness and the inordinate pursuit of pleasure in order to live an upright, holy life. This growth in holiness is meant to both purify each person for his or her own sake as well as to enable him or her to be more capable of loving others as Christ calls. We can compare this to physical health. A person who chooses to eat a healthy diet and exercise will grow stronger and healthier. This is a fine goal, but if it is pursued as an end in itself, it is a somewhat selfish goal; it does no good for anyone but the individual person. If he or she pursues health and physical fitness to do a better job at work, to be able to engage in more activities with their children, or simply to live longer for the good of his or her family, then that personal growth also serves others. The pursuit of holiness is similar. Our growth in holiness should make us better at loving others—not only those in our immediate circle of acquaintances but also all our neighbors, serving the common good of all.

The communion sought by the pursuit of holiness can also be viewed from the other side of the coin, from the perspective of sin. There is a common distinction in moral theology between "individual sin" and "social sin." The idea is that some sins primarily hurt the individual committing the sin and other sins are more directly the cause of harm to others or a community. While it is a useful distinction, it is only a logical distinction. As members of the Body of Christ, we know that every sin—even our most private or those committed in secret—causes the entire Body to suffer.

For many so called "private" sins, we do not have to get too esoteric to recognize that every action has wider social implications. The use of pornography is a good example. A person might think that pornography use "is not hurting anyone else," even if he or she has an inkling that he or she should not be engaged in this behavior either. If we look at the situation more closely, though, it is clear that it has a tremendous impact on others. First, there are the men and women who are being degraded by being the subject of pornographic content; second, there is the manipulation and corruption present in the industry of pornography; and finally, widespread use of pornography causes a significant decrease in respect for the dignity of others which, as it spreads, can shift a culture from one that respects others to one that easily sees others as objects of self-gratification rather than human persons with dignity. There is, strictly speaking, no such thing as a purely "individual" sin. Every sin impacts other people.

All that being said, the logical category of "social" morality is useful. There is something different about a pickpocket taking one person's wallet versus a cohort of industry leaders banding together to defraud thousands or millions of workers of their just wages. Certain individual actions can have a greater or lesser impact on the common good. Christians are called to overcome sin not only in themselves but also in their families, workplaces, and societies. As St. Josemaria Escriva wrote:

> A man or a society that does not react to suffering and injustice and makes no effort to alleviate them is still distant from the love of Christ's heart.[1]

This chapter will look more closely at what is called the Church's "social teaching"—a body of teachings addressing those sins that cause more direct harm to society at large—and at what Christ's New Commandment of Love requires of Christians in service to the common good.

In the initial presentation of the Ten Commandments, we saw the first three Commandments refer to the love that we owe to God, and the remaining seven direct us toward the love of neighbor. The Commandments that require honor for God, for his name, and for the Sabbath were discussed in Chapter 2, and the Eighth Commandment—against false witness—was used as an example in Chapter 5 on the moral act. In this chapter the discussion of the Commandments will continue with the Seventh, Tenth, and Fifth

1. CPB, no. 167.

Commandments: "You shall not steal,"[2] "You shall not covet your neighbor's goods,"[3] and, "You shall not kill."[4]

The Human Person Is Social by Nature

No human being is an isolated entity. It is human nature to interact with others at home, at school, at work, and in recreation. The social nature of the human person has been accepted by philosophers for millennia and is attested to in the first chapters of Genesis when God, having created Adam, "said, 'It is not good that the man should be alone; I will make him a helper fit for him.'"[5] Every human being, regardless of the circumstances that precede or follow, comes into the world as a member of a family. The gathering of people into a family is the basis on which societies form. Individual people do not come together to form tribes and cities—groups of families do. The family, as the Church teaches, is the "basic cell" of society.

It is from the social nature of the human person that we derive the legitimacy of familial relationships all the way up to political and public authority. The social character of every human being and the interdependence of the whole human "family" require that there be an established authority to facilitate harmonious relationships among members of society as well as protect them as people with human dignity. This is the duty of civil authority: to facilitate relationships and protect individual rights, or in other words, to protect the common good. Herein lies a difficulty in human organization: If we were all just rugged individuals, doggedly seeking our own personal interests, decisions would be much easier. On the other hand, if all that mattered were the group, or the collective society—and individuals were merely cogs in a machine or drones in a hive—decisions would also be much easier. A system based on either of these premises could be much more efficient and easily run.

The problem is that neither premise reflects reality. The nineteenth century in the Western world offers an example of what happens when individuals seek their own good without any sense of social responsibility. The great wealth produced by the free market

2. CCC, Part Three, Section Two; Ex 20:15.

3. CCC, Part Three, Section Two; cf. Ex 20:17; Dt 5:21.

4. CCC, Part Three, Section Two; Ex 20:13.

5. Gn 2:18.

and industrialization was channeled to serve a small number of people, while the mass of workers lived from hand to mouth in great poverty. In the twentieth century, Nazi Germany and Soviet Russia both created societies where the state was all, and the individual was reduced to a mere tool that existed only to serve the state. Individual rights vanished. Catholic teaching rejects both views of society. Every human person has an immense personal dignity but is also called to live in relationship with others, not only respecting the fact that others have the same dignity but also that our relationships with them form us as human persons.

The interplay between individual dignity and the social nature of the human person was expressed well by the Council Fathers of Vatican II. They pointed out that when Jesus revealed the Triune nature of God—three Persons eternally in relationship with one another—he also revealed something about the human person created in God's image. They first pointed out that the human person "is the only creature on earth which God willed for itself."[6] The Church affirms the infinite value of each individual person uniquely willed by God. God does not "will" a person "to be" simply because he wants more people around; God personally wills each individual human person for his or her own sake. We are not the random result of interactions between reproductive adults. Each one of us is individually, personally, uniquely desired by God. This gives each human person radical importance and dignity—such that St.Thomas Aquinas wrote that one human person is worth more in the eyes of God than the rest of the material universe combined.

The Church's teaching on—and defense of—the dignity of each individual person, though, is not cause for a self-centered or individualistic attitude. First, we must recognize that *every human person* has this dignity. At minimum, everyone must at least respect this dignity in others. Further, not only is every person created for his or her own sake, but a person "cannot fully find himself except through a sincere gift of himself."[7] God's plan for every human person is to become who he or she is meant to be and reach his or her potential through the ways in which a person can make him- or herself a gift to other people.

6. GS, no.24.

7. Ibid.; cf. Lk 17:33.

The reality of our individual dignity, coupled with the call to be self-gift, permeates every aspect of Christian life—from the most basic pursuit of a moral life, to marriage and family, to Christian discipleship, to the building of a more just world. In this chapter the focus will be on how the love to which Christ calls us must radiate out into the world. As Pope Francis said:

> True faith in the incarnate Son of God is inseparable from self-giving, from membership in the community, from service, from reconciliation with others.[8]

Catholic Social Teaching

Moral theology has always been concerned with "social issues." In the Old Testament the Israelites rejoiced in the gift of the Law because it meant they were ruled by God's justice rather than a powerful human leader's personal whims. God's justice rules all people in fairness, and even Kings of Israel had to submit to it. The Psalms are full of praise for God, who rules the world with equity and fairness.[9]

God's rule over his chosen people meant that the powerful were not left at liberty to exploit the weak. The prophets of the Old Testament, who called Israel back to God's ways, presented three recurring themes for condemnation: idolatry, sexual impurity, and abusive treatment of the most vulnerable in society—the poor, the foreigner, the orphan, and the widow.

> Render true judgments, show kindness and mercy each to his brother, do not oppress the widow, the fatherless, the sojourner, or the poor; and let none of you devise evil against his brother in your heart.[10]

The Old Covenant's teachings are clear that God has special concern for those who are most vulnerable, and the people of Israel would be judged according to their treatment of the poor. Jesus, ever expanding on the Old Law, called his disciples to offer kindness even to an enemy, and taught that any good done to those in need would be treated as a good done to himself.[11] "Social" teaching is part and parcel of building the Kingdom of God.

---

8. EG, no.88.
9. Cf. Ps 9:8; 67:4.
10. Zec 7:9–10.
11. Cf. Lk 6:27, 35.

There is, however, a special body of teaching referred to as the "social doctrine" of the Church, or "Catholic social teaching." At the end of the nineteenth century, there were significant social transformations. The Western world saw rapid industrialization, the fall of mercantilism with the rise of free market economies, and the proliferation of democratic ideals and secular government; social relationships were transformed politically and economically. These changes also created new opportunities for the "unscrupulous strong" to exploit the weak, as St. John XXIII pointed out: "Men of this stamp are always in evidence, and, like cockle among the wheat, thrive in every land."[12]

To address these problems as well as respond to the emerging Marxist ideology, in 1891 Pope Leo XIII wrote a famous encyclical letter, *Rerum Novarum*, to all the faithful. This letter marked the beginning of modern Catholic social teaching and was read by Catholics and non-Catholics alike. Subsequent Popes have published encyclical letters on various anniversaries of *Rerum Novarum*, and these papal teachings constitute the main source of the Church's modern social doctrine. Catholic social teaching is far-reaching and encompasses virtually every form of human relationship. In her moral teachings the Church is concerned not only with individual moral conduct but also with the justice of economic and political systems and the world of labor. Catholic social teaching covers labor rights, just wages, private property and its social function, the right to belong to associations and labor unions, the defense of justice, the rights of families, the condemnation of racism and sexism, the protection of the natural environment, and more—everything related to the common good, social justice, and authentic human development.

A summary of Catholic social teaching shows its general principles: human dignity, service to the common good, solidarity, subsidiarity, the right to private property, the priority of persons over other created things, the preferential option for the poor, and others. Applying these principles to particular circumstances, specific elements of Catholic social teaching are applied to the modern world: that wages must be just and not determined simply through competition, that workers have a right to form associations, that property must be used in accordance with the common good, that the family has rights that precede the state, and others.

12. St. John XXIII, Encyclical Letter on Christianity and Social Progress *Mater et Magistra* (May 15, 1961), no. 58.

One thing to be aware of when studying Catholic social teaching is the distinction between what the *principles* are and the *application* of those principles using "prudential judgment." The principles of social teaching are perennial; grounded in the Gospel, they do not change from generation to generation. Every situation, though, requires prudence in the application of these principles. As the world's problems are always changing, so the faithful in every generation might apply the principles of Catholic social teaching anew to address the needs of the day. Pope Leo XIII, for example, knew in the late nineteenth century that both socialism and a lopsided distribution of wealth were against human nature and the Gospel, so his focus was to give a strong defense that *every* person has the right to "the owning of private property."[13] But Pope Francis focused in the early twenty-first century on "the idols of profit and consumption" and "the culture of waste."[14] Why did Pope Leo XIII not speak more about materialism? Why did Pope Francis emphasize the harmful effects of consumerism? Such differences do not represent a change in the principles of the teaching but rather the application; they are different emphases and tailored responses to the differing needs of the times.

A full treatment of the social doctrine of the Church is too broad a subject for this book. To round out our study of both the Ten Commandments and the moral teaching of the Church, this chapter will focus on a few particular areas of the Church's social doctrine—the role of government in preserving rights, the basis of rights in the dignity of the human person, the right relationship with material goods, and the call to solidarity.

The Role of Government

From the Sacred Authors' writings in the Old Testament to St. Paul's teachings in the New Testament, it is abundantly clear that all legitimate authority comes from God. Though rulers established in authority are human—they are and have been flawed both in morals and in leadership—their authority still comes from God; therefore, they must be obeyed in everything that is not immoral. This authority, like society itself, is derived from the model of the family. The Fourth Commandment calls each of us to "honor your

13. RN, no. 8; cf. nos. 15, 47.

14. Cf. Pope Francis, *General Audience* (June 5, 2013).

father and your mother."[15] This has particular bearing on the family, as will be discussed more in Chapter 18, but it is from this lawful authority of the parents in the family that the lawful authority of civil leaders is derived.

The Church teaches that all legitimate civil authority—unlike the call to honor our parents—depends on the consent of the governed. For this reason, one people might be ruled by a monarch, another by a parliament, and another by a president of a republic. God wills that an established ruler and his collaborators govern society *well*, but God does not specify *how* this authority should govern. The reason that government can legitimately wield *any* authority is because God has established the role of authority in society based on the model of authority in the family. Any organization of people in a community requires a leader or leaders whose vision encompasses the common good in order to facilitate harmonious relationships among members, protect individual rights, and preserve the rule of law.

Based on the Fourth Commandment, the Church teaches that *any* lawful authority deserves respect, whether it be a parent, a president, a mayor, a teacher, or an employer. Because authority ultimately comes from God, rulers and their representatives merit respect and obedience. Disobedience to civil law warrants punishment by civil authorities, and the State, according to the Church, has the right to impose taxes. Anarchy or even radical libertarianism does not find much support from the Church's understanding of government.

On the other hand, the State is not "all" and does not wield *its own authority* over its citizens. Its authority is dependent on its adherence to the natural law, truth, and justice. Every Christian has the obligation in conscience to obey the established ruler and his or her representatives as well as the laws of the State in all things that are just—but this means Christians must use moral discretion. They can and *must* disregard any mandate to act immorally. Unjust laws that violate the moral standards of the natural law must not be obeyed. For instance, laws that legislate the option of destroying unborn life or usurp parental rights in the education of their children should be challenged and resisted with measures taken to overturn them. As the *Catechism* teaches:

15. CCC, Part Three, Section Two; Ex 20:12.

> The citizen is obliged in conscience not to follow the directives of civil authorities when they are contrary to the demands of the moral order, to the fundamental rights of persons or the teachings of the Gospel.[16]

It is not hard to conjure up more vivid acts of grave injustice and oppression that have been perpetrated under the cover of law by government authorities throughout history.

Besides the requirement that the laws enacted by the State must accord with the natural law, there are other limits to the State's authority. The purpose of civil authority is not power for the leader but service to the people. A person in civil authority has *power* precisely because it must *serve* the society, just as parents have "power" over their children for the purpose of the good of their children. Public authority is obliged to respect the fundamental rights of the human person as well as to guarantee the conditions that make the exercise of these rights possible. A general rule of thumb is a phrase of Pope Leo XIII, repeated time and again by subsequent Popes: "The State has for its office to protect natural rights, not to destroy them."[17] The laws enacted by the state must support—not threaten—individual or family rights.

This principle of government rests on a correct understanding of the dignity of the human person. The State does not *confer* rights; rather, the State is called to protect the rights of all people, which according to the Church, belong to every human person *by nature*. Grave injustice has been caused throughout history when civil authorities have concluded that the State is the *source* of rights. If it were the *source* of human rights, then the State could, at its pleasure, take those rights away from all people or from specific groups of people deemed "less human." Socialism, for example, removes the right to own certain forms of property from all citizens. Some societies have segregation laws that deny one group of the population their basic human rights. These laws are illegitimate and rightly resisted by citizens and movements for civil rights. Human rights come from God and are inscribed in human nature; they are not social constructs dependent upon the State. The State's job is to recognize and protect human rights.

16. CCC 2242.

17. RN, no.51; cf.CA, no.7.

By bearing in mind that (1) laws must be based on justice and truth and (2) the State's job is to protect natural rights rather than stifle them, the authority of a government is kept from becoming tyrannical.

Another important guide for the use of power in society is the *principle of subsidiarity*. The State is not expected to solve every problem. Put simply, the principle of subsidiarity states that a community of a higher authority must not interfere with that of a lower authority without necessity and only for as long as required. The higher levels of government or society should not usurp the authority of lower and more local government, except when absolutely necessary, and should withdraw once the matter has been resolved. The State must not intervene in the role of parents to raise their children unless there is a grave necessity or a violation of rights within the family. Once remedied, the civil authority should withdraw. In this way, freedom and self-agency are preserved within a structure of authority and mutual aid.

Human Dignity

The Church's social doctrine rests on the conviction that every uniquely created person possesses the dignity of a child of God, redeemed by God, and destined for God. A primary purpose of society is to preserve the dignity of the human person rather than leave the protection of our rights and the fulfillment of our potential to the "law of the jungle" or the "survival of the fittest." Without a sound legislative and juridical framework, without some authority that oversees the common good, the vulnerable—be they disadvantaged financially, physically, intellectually, or otherwise—are left at the mercy of what St. John XXIII called the "unscrupulous strong." It is the conviction that *every* human life has dignity and *every* human person has rights that guides Christians in their decisions regarding the common good.

Violations of human dignity are, however, a sad reality in our world, and people's failure to live an authentically Christian life. Pope Francis reminded all people about one of the consequences of failing to live Catholic principles:

> The Catholic faith of many peoples is nowadays being challenged by the proliferation of new religious movements, some of which tend to fundamentalism while others seem to propose a spiritual-

> ity without God. This is, on the one hand, a human reaction to a materialistic, consumerist and individualistic society, but it is also a means of exploiting the weaknesses of people living in poverty and on the fringes of society, people who make ends meet amid great human suffering and are looking for immediate solutions to their needs.[18]

This is but one example of all the varied reasons human rights are violated in our world. Pope went on to describe entire populations that are deprived of housing, basic sustenance, and other requirements of a dignified life. There is much work to be done to create a more just society that respects the dignity of every human person.

The Church has always maintained, however, that the fundamental basis for all rights is the right to life. St. John Paul II maintained that the struggle for rights in society—to housing, to work, to health, to family, to culture, and others—is "illusory" if a society does not *first* defend the individual person's right to life.[19] Understanding that all rights must be defended, we will focus here on the right to life and the Fifth Commandment: "You shall not kill."[20] If we assume that God did not toss the Ten Commandments out randomly, there is something to be learned from the fact that *immediately* after the three Commandments focused on the love of God, the Fourth Commandment is, "Honor your father and your mother,"[21] and then the Fifth is to respect the lives of others.[22] The Fifth Commandment also offers another example of how the pursuit of holiness and the life of discipleship begins within ourselves and then radiates out toward others.

In the creation accounts in Genesis, the human being, having been made in the image and likeness of God, is given stewardship over the material world, but it is God who has dominion over the human person. God alone has absolute power over human life. He alone has the authority to grant life and to take it away; therefore, every human life is sacred and must be protected and nurtured. As the *Catechism* teaches:

18. EG, no. 63.
19. Ibid., no. 38.
20. CCC, Part Three, Section Two; Ex 20:13.
21. CCC, Part Three, Section Two; Ex 20:12.
22. Cf. CCC, Part Three, Section Two; Ex 20:13.

> Every human life, from the moment of conception until death, is sacred because the human person has been willed for its own sake in the image and likeness of the living and holy God.[23]

The main thrust of the Fifth Commandment is the absolute duty to respect, defend, and protect human life. The Commandment, "You shall not kill,"[24] essentially means that killing an innocent person is a flagrant violation of the natural law and, therefore, a most grave sin.

The worth of every person is particularly demonstrated by Jesus Christ, who became man, suffered, and offered his life in Sacrifice for our sins on behalf of our redemption. In light of the Revelation of Jesus Christ, every person must be viewed not only as created in God's image and likeness but also redeemed by the Blood of Christ and destined to be with God forever in heaven. Here, too, the Beatitudes of Jesus expands on the Old Testament restriction against murder. In his Sermon on the Mount,[25] Jesus stipulated a merciful heart as the proper attitude toward all people, particularly those alienated from God. As Christians we are expected to love everyone, even those who may injure or hate us. Our Lord revealed that even anger has no place in the hearts of his disciples. Our hearts must be free of resentment and rancor if we are to worship God properly. A forgiving heart, free of enmity, is necessary for any meaningful relationship with God. The precept against killing is understood in the light of the New Commandment of Jesus: "Love one another; even as I have loved you, that you also love one another."[26] This Commandment of charity thus enriches the Fifth Commandment, as it does all Commandments, beyond its Old Testament interpretation.

Respect for the Gift of Our Own Life

Not only are modern cultures far from fulfilling Christ's Law of Love, but also human history presents a poor track record of keeping even the minimum requirement of the Old Testament prohibition against murder. Time and again we have had to be reminded that "Every human life, from the moment of conception until death, is sacred."[27] Sometimes, although it is often not the first place we look, the problem begins with a person's lack of respect for *his or her own*

23. CCC 2319.
24. CCC, Part Three, Section Two; Ex 20:13.
25. Mt 5–7; cf. Lk 6:20–49.
26. Jn 13:34.
27. CCC 2319.

dignity. Respect for all life must first begin with gratitude for the life that every person has been given and an understanding that his or her own life is a gift from God. "Do you not know," asked St. Paul...

> that your body is a temple of the Holy Spirit within you, which you have from God? You are not your own; you were bought with a price. So glorify God in your body.[28]

Every person is obligated to respect his or her own life as well as the lives of others. We can fail to respect our own lives and dignity in a variety of different ways, but some of the more serious and common sins that show a lack of respect for one's own life include suicide, cult of the body, gluttony, and substance abuse.

Suicide usurps God's exclusive right to call his adopted child out of this present life. Suicide is a very serious evil, but the *Catechism* teaches, "We should not despair of the eternal salvation of persons who have taken their own lives."[29] Remember the components of moral deliberation in Chapter 5: object, intention, and circumstances. Looking at the *object* of the act, it is a grave evil for a person to kill him- or herself. There are, of course, many *intentions* and *circumstances* that diminish the subjective culpability of this kind of tragic action. Many people who think seriously about killing themselves lack the nurturing love and attention required for healthy emotional and psychological growth and development. Severe psychological problems may significantly diminish responsibility. God, in his mercy, has his own ways of offering the opportunity for repentance.

A more grave temptation to kill oneself can develop when love for God is replaced with an idol of achievement, money, physical appearance, success, fame, or any other created good. These poor substitutes fail to satisfy us or bring true meaning, and a sense of emptiness ensues that can lead to despair. Worse still, these substitutes are temporary, and when a person bases his or her happiness on such fleeting pleasures, the sense of loss can be devastating. The only true, lasting good that brings ultimate meaning to human life is the love of God, commitment to love and service for others, and humble acceptance of God's forgiveness and redemption.

Suicide represents the most radical failure to respect one's own life, but there are many less dramatic ways a person can fail to honor

28. 1 Cor 6:19–20.
29. CCC 2283.

the life God has given. Those who willfully engage in actions that harm the body are guilty of breaking the Fifth Commandment. Gluttony, for example, is incompatible with human dignity. This intemperance has unhealthy and even life-shortening effects on the body. Moderation in eating, along with appropriate attention to physical exercise, results in significantly better health while showing respect for the body, an understanding of our own personal worth and dignity, and gratitude for the gift of our life.

Gluttony focuses on our consumption of food, but substance abuse is also seriously sinful. The Fifth Commandment strongly urges prudence and moderation in drinking alcoholic beverages. Excessive consumption of alcohol causes intoxication and inebriation, which is objectively evil as a serious violation of human dignity. The state of intoxication relinquishes self-control and impairs proper judgment and use of reason, which can give way to offensive and even tragic situations, including automobile accidents, acts of violence, abusive behavior, and inappropriate sexual activity—not to mention the potential for sullying one's reputation, giving scandal to others, and being embarrassed in front of family and friends. The same goes for recreational drug use, many of which even more than alcohol present a danger to bodily health and safety. Even occasional recreational drug use at parties is like playing Russian roulette with our lives.

The respect we should have for the human body is so great that it is immoral to disfigure or mutilate one's body intentionally. Enhancement of the beauty of the body that contributes to human elegance is a natural way of emphasizing human dignity, but when ordinary attention to sound health and well-being give way to obsession, it then becomes the cult of the body. Excessive food deprivation; inordinate body piercing and extensive tattooing; extreme efforts at bodybuilding; and radical, unnecessary plastic surgery violate the Fifth Commandment as offenses against the human body. We must instead respect the life given to us by God along with the body he chose for us—with all its quirks and beauty. A healthy and just self-love respects the beauty of the human body. The fact that God the Son assumed a human nature to carry out his redemptive work indicates the human body must be considered sacred, as it is both an integral part of the human person and an instrument of salvation, sanctification, and evangelization.

Another attack on one's own bodily integrity is direct sterilization such as a vasectomy or tubal ligation, which is the alteration of the reproductive organ with the intention of depriving a person of his or her procreative capability. We have no authority to destroy our procreative faculties; therefore, the Church teaches that voluntary sterilization employed toward contraceptive ends is gravely evil. It is a sin against the Fifth Commandment because it is not only a mutilation of the body but also an attack on the integrity of the human person.

Indirect sterilization is a secondary and *unintended* result of a medical procedure directed toward the cure of a patient or an accident. The Magisterium teaches that indirect sterilization is morally licit *only under necessary medical conditions* such as, for example, a woman whose ovaries must be removed because of ovarian cancer. In this situation, the operation is performed for a legitimate medical reason, namely, recovery from cancer. Unlike direct sterilization, which is an affront to the beauty and dignity of the body, indirect sterilization resulting from the preservation of life respects a person's life and dignity.

One particularly grave form of personal mutilation is the growing occurrence of cosmetic surgery and hormone therapy to alter a person's sexual characteristics. Many people struggle with gender identity, and their challenges should not be taken lightly. Every person who struggles with gender dysphoria must be loved for the beautiful child of God that he or she is; nevertheless, surgery to change his or her sexual characteristics is gravely evil. It is immoral precisely *because* it is an act that does *not* show the proper love for a person as a child of God. Besides being a desecration of the human body, which is a sacred component of the human person, it is also a falsification of the true identity of that person. The body and soul are united in the one person uniquely willed by God. Any change through the means of merely cosmetic surgery is not only a rebellion against God's will in creating that particular individual but also a radical departure from what he has planned for that person's fulfillment and happiness. The temptation to "play God" is very strong, particularly when human science discovers techniques to manipulate human life, but experience shows us that in the long run the lack of respect for the human being results in serious moral disorders.

> *Human nature* must be understood on the basis of the *unity of body and soul,* far removed from any sort of physicalism or naturalism,

> since [it is] "in the unity of his spiritual and biological inclinations and of all the other specific characteristics necessary for the pursuit of his end."[30]

Beyond the question of whether the action is evil, "gender reassignment" surgery or hormone therapy reveals a tragic inability to love oneself as the person God created and loves. Our purpose in life should be to discover who God made us to be. To be perpetually at war with his purpose is to never find peace with our own identity. Gender reassignment surgery, far from solving the question of gender identity, only perpetuates the struggle for meaning and a sense of true self. This problem is becoming more prevalent in society; many who have changed the appearance of their biological sex continue to struggle with depression, substance abuse, and high suicide rates. To truly love people suffering from gender dysphoria is to help them learn to love themselves just as they are and affirm they are loved by God, who made them.

One last way people can tragically fail to respect their own lives is when, to please other people, they abandon their rights. A young person might give up his or her right to privacy or chastity to impress someone or to maintain a relationship with someone they care about. Allowing oneself to be taken advantage of, abused, or used by others is a failure to respect one's own dignity. In situations of racism, or sexism, or exploitation, the Church—besides condemning the unjust actions—urges victims of abuse to stand up for and respect their rights. As Pope Leo XIII wrote, "Self-preservation is a law of nature, which it is wrong to disobey."[31]

A person might wonder—if Jesus willingly accepted the suffering of the Cross and taught his disciples to be meek: "If any one strikes you on the right cheek, turn to him the other also"[32]—how can self-preservation be an obligation of nature? What about the martyrs who freely gave up their lives in imitation of Jesus? Amid abusive situations people are sometimes confused into believing that the Law of Love requires them to persist and ignore the affront to their dignity out of a false sense of what it means to be meek or charitable. This, of course, is a manipulation of the truth. Jesus, who was the incarnation of self-gift and love, accepted suffering that was

---

30. Congregation for Catholic Education, *Towards a Path of Dialogue on the Question of Gender Theory in Education* (June 10, 2019), no. 32; quoting VS, no. 50.

31. RN, no. 44.

32. Mt 5:39.

a consequence of his proclamation of the truth. His witness reflected his unparalleled dignity as he held to the truth in the face of unjust persecution. The martyrs, too, are willing to face death rather than deny the truth about Christ. In both cases, a sacrifice is made in service to the truth and the authentic good of others. In the case of people who allow others to take advantage of or abuse them, it is not a matter of standing up for the truth but relinquishing their rights, dignity, or physical and emotional well-being to serve the selfish interests of an abuser. The abuse is sinful and involves compromising their dignity. Turning the other cheek requires a spirit of service, patience, and forgiveness. It means refraining from violence. It does not mean being a doormat or allowing the sinful actions of others to rob us of our own dignity for their sinful "gain."

Recalling what was said at the start of this chapter, the sins that violate respect for one's own life are not purely "individual" sins. Suicide, in particular, is terribly damaging to those who love the person who has died, and that pain ripples out into the community. Likewise, respect for our own lives as a precious gift from a loving Father ought to extend outward to our respect for all life. The issue becomes a matter of "social" concern as we try to *build a culture* that respects all human life.

The Right to Self-defense and Just War

Before looking at the various ways the respect for life is threatened in society, it is important to note that the Fifth Commandment does not mean Christians are all called to be pacifists. The right to self-defense is an extension of the inalienable right to life. Every person is justified in defending and protecting him- or herself and others against an unjust aggressor. The act of self-defense, even though it may involve harm and injury inflicted on the assailant, is compatible with the Fifth Commandment. The spirit behind the Commandment is to respect and protect innocent life.

There are, of course, certain criteria that need to be met for the moral use of self-defense. It must be a true act of self-defense, and the use of force must be in proportion to the aggression sustained. You cannot swing a baseball bat at someone who shoved you. The act must also be only as much as is necessary to thwart the attack, not to render revenge or heap abuse upon the attacker. The purpose of self-defense is not to harm the aggressor; rather, a person must use the minimum amount of force necessary to protect him- or herself and others.

The right to self-defense extends to those in a position of authority and tasked with the responsibility of protecting others; examples include police officers and security guards. The use of proportionate means also applies. Brutal violence that causes serious injury or even loss of life in response to violations of the law that would not endanger someone's life or cause physical harm to another is gravely evil. A person responsible for maintaining security is authorized to use all measures at his or her disposal to protect the lives of others, as long as he or she maintains the principles of proportionality and last resort. Unfortunately, serious physical injury and even death sometimes result from these protective efforts. If a police officer uses disproportionate force or had other means available to prevent crime or injury, he or she would be guilty of perpetrating violence on the community rather than protecting and serving it.

The right to self-defense also applies to the community as a whole or the nation. War is always a tragedy. When nation rises against nation or opposition forces revolt within their own nation, the pain and suffering for the dead and wounded, their families, and the nations themselves are immense and incalculable. War is never a desirable option. Under certain conditions, however, a nation's participation in a war can be morally justified.

For a nation's participation in war to be morally just, it must fulfill principles like those for legitimate self-defense. First, the war itself must be an act of self-defense against an unjust aggressor. The act of war must be taken only as a last resort after all diplomatic means have been exhausted. Perhaps the most difficult component of the just war criteria is that for a military action to be justified, it must have a reasonable chance at victory. If defeat is almost certain, then the loss of life is meaningless. Also, like individual self-defense, the use of force must be proportional or no greater than what is required.

The mere fact that a country is engaged in a just war does not grant it license to disregard the moral law, especially the Fifth Commandment. Even if a country is justified by all the above criteria and chooses to attack, the moral considerations do not end there. Every battle or military action within that war must also fulfill the just war conditions. In addition, it is always morally wrong for a military force to target noncombatants and unarmed people. Sadly, contemporary history recounts horrific violations of human dignity with indiscriminate bombings of residential areas and massacres of innocent people. Two very dark episodes in World War II caused mass destruction of human life: one was the Allied forces' firebombing of Dresden, Germany, and another was the United States' use of atomic bombs on Hiroshima and Nagasaki, Japan. These acts were not aimed at military targets; rather, they were meant to kill and wound wide swaths of innocent people to exert pressure on opposing civil authorities. The fact that the Japanese surrendered within days of dropping two atomic bombs does not legitimize their targeting civilian targets. The twentieth century is infamous as the era of far too many grave violations of far too many people's rights in almost every region of the world.

The Gospel of Love articulated by Catholic social teaching is radically opposed not only to targeting innocent people but also to kidnapping, torture, hostage-taking, and terrorism. A war policy that allows for such violent abuse of the innocent alongside the guilty is a flagrant violation of the Fifth Commandment. The imposition of justice or the effort to win a war can never take the forms of barbaric inflictions of pain and of fearful dread.

Similarly, the Church has always criticized the amassing of weapons in what is known as an "arms race." Following World War II, many nations began to build weapons of mass destruction as a preventive measure against attacks from other countries. This resulted in an arms race, in which nations invested much of their economic resources in the stockpiling of weapons. The Council Fathers of Vatican II addressed this issue; in short, an arms race is not a safe way to preserve a sure, authentic peace in the world. Furthermore, the money spent on these weapons contributes to the economic miseries that afflict the modern world. They called on society to look for new approaches to promote peace and free themselves from the slavery to war.[33]

The question of legitimate self-defense and cases where the Fifth Commandment is not automatically broken by a loss of life brings to mind the debate over the use of capital punishment. Civil authorities have the right to impart just punishments after due process in proportion to particular crimes. According to strict justice,

33. GS, no.81.

the state has the option to hand down even the death penalty for crimes involving the murder of innocent persons or high treason. Nevertheless, there is a law higher than that of strict justice: the law of compassion and charity based on the inherent dignity of human life. The Church does not teach capital punishment is intrinsically morally wrong, but it does state that the death penalty should be used only as an extreme measure when it is absolutely necessary to protect society from the convicted person. Given the prisons and security systems available in most parts of the contemporary world, "'the death penalty is inadmissible'[34] and the Church is firmly committed to calling for its abolition worldwide."[35] The teachings of the contemporary Church most strongly discourage the use of the death penalty.

From the perspective of the Gospel, the purpose of the imposition of justice is not so much retribution as it is to seek the spiritual and moral rehabilitation of the person guilty of the crime. Capital punishment, although it sometimes may satisfy the demands of strict justice, often does not serve as a deterrent from future crime and denies the criminal the opportunity to experience conversion, repentance, and healing. It may even serve to perpetuate a diminished view of the value of human life in society that leads to capital crimes in the first place. Capital punishment is often opposed on the grounds that the criminal justice system is fallible, and innocent people will inevitably be executed by mistake. In such situations, capital punishment excludes the possibility of reversal and reparation of damages wrongly inflicted.

These instances—self-defense, just war, and capital punishment—recognize that while the taking of human life is always a tragic outcome, it is not always a sin against the Fifth Commandment. Other than these qualified instances, which at root seek to serve the protection of life, "murdering the innocent" is a ubiquitous principle. Most if not all cultures have accepted it, even if only for their own citizens. In our modern society, however, certain types of killing have entered what some believe to be a "gray area" where the killing of the innocent is permissible beyond self-defense such

34. Pope Francis, Address on the Twenty-fifth Anniversary of the Promulgation of the *Catechism of the Catholic Church* (October 11, 2017).

35. FT, no. 263; cf. Congregation for the Doctrine of the Faith, "Letter to the Bishops Regarding the Revision of No. 2267 of the *Catechism of the Catholic Church* on the Death Penalty (August 1, 2018)," in *L'Osservatore Romano* (August 3, 2018), 8.

as euthanasia, assisted suicide, and abortion. The Church, honoring God as the Author of life and the dignity of the human person, has always rejected these practices, even in the face of criticism.

Building a Culture of Life

Rights, as pointed out earlier, are given by God and belong to every human person by nature. The right to life is not something a person "earns." The value of a life as a human being is not determined by secondary characteristics such as how a person looks, his or her place of origin, the state of his or her health, or how useful other people find him or her. It is not based on a person's fame, skills, wealth, or accomplishments but by the simple fact that he or she is a beloved child of God who was created in his image. At the root of every genocide is the idea that one person can decide whether another person's life has value. Sadly, this notion has gained traction in our time in a more widespread cultural erosion of the dignity of each person. An incapacitating sickness or severe suffering does not diminish the value of a person; a terminal illness or debilitating physical condition is never an occasion to usurp God's exclusive right to call his adopted child out of this world through death; the size or stage of development of an unborn child can never serve as a measuring stick for his or her worth.

Euthanasia, sometimes called "mercy killing," involves the decision by doctors, family members, or public officials to end the life of a person who has been given little or no chance of recovery and is thought to have a poor quality of life. One cautionary episode came between 1939 and 1941 when the Nazi government of Germany euthanized more than 75,000 of its own citizens—and as many as 250,000 by the end of World War II—who had mental or physical disabilities; this served as a model and precursor to the eventual execution of 6 million Jewish people, people with mental and physical handicaps, Romani, homosexuals, artists, educators, political prisoners, Communists, suspected enemies of the State, and others also deemed unfit for life. This demonstrates quite vividly what is at stake with the question of euthanasia.

Who decides whose life is worth living? Typically when people have determined that another person's life is "not worth living," what they are really struggling with is that *they*, for one reason or another, find that person's life irritating—he or she might struggle with poverty, be elderly and a burden, or have an inconvenient mental illness. Once one person claims the power to decide questions related to death over another, it becomes too easy to wield for trivial reasons such as professing a different religion or having a different skin color. No one has the power to decide that someone else's life is "not worth living" and rationalize it by calling it an act of "mercy."

But what if a person is suffering and wants to die? Assisted suicide is distinct from euthanasia in that the person who is suffering requests help in ending his or her own life. In such cases, would it not be a "mercy" to end that person's suffering? Why should people suffer? Though it can be hard to watch someone we love suffer, we must still have faith in God's plan for this person's life and death. This form of killing is another egregious offense against God's love and a violent disruption of his plan for every person and his or her eternal life. Suffering is a great mystery, but the witness of Christ's suffering on the Cross brings meaning to human suffering. Christ willingly endured suffering and brought redemption to the world. Our suffering, when patiently accepted and united to Christ's, is also redemptive, both for ourselves and for others. Those who shoulder these special crosses—Alzheimer's, terminal cancer, physical paralysis, or other ailments—carry within themselves the power of God. Only from the perspective of the crucified Christ can we realize that human dignity reaches its finest hour when suffering is joined to the Cross of Christ. Those who are ill need those around them to help them cherish and love the life they have, with all its hardships, rather than encourage them to despair of God's plan.

Someone who suffers from an illness or a condition that will end in death can still refuse what are called *extraordinary or disproportionate means* of sustaining life when there is virtually no hope for recovery. Measures that were quite extraordinary in the past have now become standard procedure for medical practice. Considering these great strides in medical science, the Church has indicated that extraordinary means, which only prolong the imminent dying process or that impose an undue burden on the patient and family, do not need to be taken. The spirit behind this guideline rests on the fact that God's will to call someone out of this world must be respected. Respect for a person in a terminal situation will involve allowing him or her to suffer and die in the most dignified way possible.

The right to refuse extraordinary measures does not apply to nourishment, hydration, and medication to sustain life; these are ordinary means of medical treatment. At times, trustworthy people need to be consulted regarding the right moral course of action to be taken in these matters. The well-publicized case from the late 1990s and early 2000s of Terri Schiavo, a Florida woman in a *persistent vegetative state,* gave the nutrition-hydration issue unprecedented national attention. While some doctors considered Terri brain dead and incurable, family members and some other doctors disagreed, stating that they recognized some cognitive response in her. Terri's husband, who had denied Terri any rehabilitative therapy for most of her convalescence, ultimately prevailed in a long legal dispute with Terri's parents over his wish to remove Terri's feeding tube. Terri thus was deprived of food and water, which led to her death.

The sins of euthanasia and assisted suicide are not simply "individual morality." The whole culture is profoundly affected by the attitude people take toward life. Pope Francis wrote about the struggle to overcome the culture of death with the culture of life. Using the example of abortion—but it is applicable to other issues equally well—he showed how everything can build a culture of life:

> Since everything is interrelated, concern for the protection of nature is also incompatible with the justification of abortion. How can we genuinely teach the importance of concern for other vulnerable human beings, however troublesome or inconvenient they may be, if we fail to protect a human embryo, even when its presence is uncomfortable and creates difficulties?[36]

To be "prolife" in most of the world is considered a purely religious position. Although nowadays that term almost exclusively means "against abortion," the orientation toward life extends to all aspects of life. Many argue that there is no place in politics for prolife talk or legislation. Though Christ illuminates the meaning and dignity of the human person, the Church has always maintained that the right to life is a natural right and the need to defend it is acquired by reason, not Revelation. It falls to civil authorities to defend and not undermine this natural right. Though the Church, as part of her witness to the dignity of the human person, defends the sacredness of all human life, to be prolife is not necessarily a religious principle. At the same time as the right to life is under attack, other people make claims for false rights that do not exist like the

36. LS, no. 120.

"right to die" for suicide. This strikes home for most Catholics with the debate over the so-called "right" to an abortion.

Abortion has touched, and continues to touch, an increasing number of people. Some estimate that one in four people have been personally involved in an abortion in one way or another. Only the persons involved can understand the pain and heartache that goes into making such a decision; oftentimes, such enormous pressure is placed upon the woman in her duress that her culpability can be greatly diminished. Women who have felt compelled to take this drastic measure frequently deserve compassion more than censure. No one who has participated in an abortion should ever despair because anyone who turns to Jesus with true sorrow for sins and a firm resolution not to repeat those sins finds mercy, forgiveness, healing, and love.

But our compassion cannot prevent us from affirming that at the very moment of conception, a new human person, made in the image and likeness of God, comes into existence. The unborn child developing in his or her mother's womb is the most innocent and defenseless of all human persons. It is at this vulnerable time that the human person deserves all that society can offer for his or her protection, health, and development. The Church teaches, in fact, that those who are most vulnerable deserve *more* attention and care—this applies to both the unborn child and the mother who is in crisis.

One argument in support of abortion is that the fetus is not yet a person. There is no basis in truth, scientifically or morally, to claim the embryo or fetus is not a person on the grounds that he or she has not yet reached full development. Every human being is a person simply by virtue of being human. From a strictly biological perspective, the fertilized egg in the womb is a completely new organism with its unique genetic code, the blueprint of a fully developed being. Abortion providers try to soften this grave evil by calling it "termination of pregnancy" or instead lumping it into a sanitized category of "family planning" or "reproductive services," seeking to avoid all reference to the human person. Since the unborn person is seen as having no real value, abortion enters the picture to sidestep moral responsibility and to resolve the inconvenient and sometimes painful situation of an unwanted pregnancy.

Remember the components of moral deliberation in Chapter 5: object, intention, and circumstances. Looking at the *object* of the act, it is a grave evil to kill an innocent person. There are, of course, many *intentions* and *circumstances* that diminish the subjective culpability of this kind of tragic action.

The reasons men and women give for procuring an abortion are many. Some find pregnancy an obstacle to their career or educational goals. They may not want others to find out about the pregnancy. Parents, boyfriends, or husbands sometimes pressure the woman into having an abortion to avoid their own responsibility for the child. The new parents may believe they are too young or too old; they might not want any more children than they already have because they cannot handle the burden emotionally or financially. A child may present an undesired change of lifestyle. The parents themselves might already be living in challenging circumstances and not want to bring a baby into a difficult life. In some cases, the fetus may have been diagnosed with a birth defect, or the pregnancy may have been the result of rape or incest.

While we must be sympathetic and willing to help those who find themselves in difficult circumstances, none of the reasons above can ever justify an abortion. The unborn child is neither a commodity nor a possession, let alone an obstacle or disruption that can be discarded if unwanted or inconvenient. Even in the case of moral tragedies such as rape or incest, the fetus is an innocent person willed into existence by a loving God and made in his image. It is important to separate the irresponsible or sinful actions, which resulted in conception, from the reality of the newly created human being, who deserves all the rights and safeguards intrinsic to human dignity. Likewise, physical or mental deformity does not detract from the dignity of being a person created in the image of God. Every child, from the moment of conception, is a human person created by God and endowed with all the human rights and dignity of any other person—made to love and be loved in return.

Despite claims of a "woman's right to choose," abortion is also a threat to *her* dignity. First, the proabortion mentality makes the woman's reproductive faculty an "illness" to be treated and the miracle of pregnancy a "problem" to be eliminated. Abortion also shows disrespect for a woman by arguing she is not capable of facing the challenges her pregnancy may bring. Rather than being told that their fertility is a failure and that they're too weak to be mothers, women need a message of love and support when faced with pregnancy.

The act of abortion has wreaked untold emotional and psychological pain in women, many of whom are left to carry this burden on their own. In addition to deep psychological wounds, abortion can have severe adverse physical effects on the woman, including sterility or cancer, not to mention the harm done by the actual abortive procedure. Entire counseling ministries reach out to women who have aborted one or more children, have come to regret those choices, and need healing and compassion. The same is true of the fathers of these aborted children, who often are opposed to the abortion or regretful for facilitating the abortion or not standing up for their child. The Church and all Christians need to extend the utmost compassion to post-abortive women and men and to affirm and transmit to them the love and forgiveness of Jesus.

Lack of respect for the human rights of the unborn is also found in the practice of *in vitro* fertilization (IVF), a medical technique commonly used by couples who are unable to conceive children. *In vitro* is Latin for "in glass," referring to the fertilization of the egg in a test tube or petri dish. The procedure involves the removal of a number of eggs from the woman, which are then fertilized in the laboratory with sperm taken from the man. The embryo or embryos are then inserted into the woman's uterus.

This procedure raises several moral issues. The conception of human life in a laboratory setting is a gravely evil act, contrary to the moral law because it is opposed to the dignity of the person, who should be the fruit of the loving conjugal union between husband and wife—an issue we will examine in more detail when we discuss the Sixth and Ninth Commandments. But related to the present matter of the Fifth Commandment, IVF involves the selection and final disposal of fertilized embryos, each of which is a human person. As the process must often be repeated, more embryos are created than desired, then later discarded or frozen for possible use in the future. Fertility specialists may produce as many as one or two dozen fertilized embryos for a particular couple. By genetic testing, they may euthanize those embryos that seem weaker or have discernible defects. When they finally implant one of the embryos into the mother's womb, the remaining embryos are either euthanized or frozen according to the wishes of the parents. Many thousands of such frozen embryos are presently being held in fertility clinics throughout the Western world. Most of these embryos, frozen in a limbo made by human hands, will likely be disposed of or used for experimentation. Such practices show no respect for the gift of human life.

The sinfulness of the act, however, does not diminish the dignity of the person who is conceived. Children conceived via IVF are still uniquely willed by God, loved by God, and created in his image and likeness. In God's infinite wisdom and providence, he utilizes sinful or distorted actions to draw good out of them and accomplish his will. God can draw good from even the worst of human actions, and every new life comes from God and is desired by God, regardless of the circumstances surrounding a person's conception.

Another procedure that takes the life of the unborn and is an affront to the dignity of the human person takes place in embryonic stem-cell research. Scientists study stem cells — cells that are "pluripotent," meaning they have the capacity to adapt and repair any human organ — in the hopes that they may someday provide a cure for presently incurable conditions such as Parkinson's disease, juvenile diabetes, certain neuromuscular disorders, and spinal cord injuries. While stem cells are present in adults, some researchers insist they need stem cells from human embryos to conduct the research necessary to find these cures. They either create a fertilized egg in the laboratory or accept donated embryos from fertility clinics for this purpose. These newly formed human embryos are then "harvested" so their stem cells can be used in research. When the stem cells are extracted from the embryo — usually at eight to twenty-one days of age — the embryo dies.

The Catholic Church does not oppose *adult* stem-cell research. Stem cells can readily be obtained through sources other than human embryos — umbilical cord blood, adult skin cells, bone marrow, and others — all of which involve no harm to the donor and are, therefore, morally licit. Recent studies show that stem cells from nonembryo sources have as much potential for finding cures as embryonic stem cells. Research announced in late 2007 revealed that stem cells taken from the skin of human adults show the same "pluripotence" as cells from embryos. These adult cells have another distinct advantage: They can be taken from the very person who will benefit from the cells, reducing the chance of incompatibility from getting genetically different cells from another person.

Each of these different practices—euthanasia, assisted suicide, abortion, IVF, and stem-cell research—are often regarded as falling into some sort of "gray area" where, even though someone's life has been taken, there is no crime of murder. Widespread use of such practices feeds the "culture of death," which fails to see a fellow person as a child of God to be loved and respected. It is not simply a matter of killing. In each of these cases, one person has made the decision that another person's life is not as valuable, desirable, or acceptable as others, and therefore they feel they have the right to end a person's life. As this attitude prevails, widespread injustice becomes easier. The Council Fathers of Vatican II forcefully condemned all attacks on human life:

> Whatever is opposed to life itself, such as any type of murder, genocide, abortion, euthanasia or wilful self-destruction, whatever violates the integrity of the human person, such as mutilation, torments inflicted on body or mind, attempts to coerce the will itself; whatever insults human dignity, such as subhuman living conditions, arbitrary imprisonment, deportation, slavery, prostitution, the selling of women and children; as well as disgraceful working conditions, where men are treated as mere tools for profit, rather than as free and responsible persons; all these things and others of their like are infamies indeed. They poison human society, but they do more harm to those who practice them than those who suffer from the injury. Moreover, they are supreme dishonor to the Creator.[37]

One important phrase in this passage from the Church is that actions in opposition to life "poison human society." This means that the State, whose reason for existing is to preserve the common good and protect the rights of all, has a key role to play in preserving the right to life for all people and enacting laws that protect the lives of every human person, regardless of how others value the worth of their life. The Nazis began with euthanasia of the ill and ended with the attempted genocide of an entire people. The State's job is to protect rights, not eliminate them.

The Fifth Commandment, "You shall not kill,"[38] refers most explicitly to the direct murder of the innocent but extends much further. It is not as though we can say to ourselves, "Well, at least

37. GS, no.27.

38. CCC, Part Three, Section Two; Ex 20:13.

I've never done *that*; I've never *killed* anyone," and feel as though this Commandment has been obeyed. That's a very minimalist look at the moral life, which does not acknowledge the radical transformation of the world by the Incarnation.

In precise terms, the Fifth Commandment prohibits the taking of human life, but because of the innate sacredness of every human person, violations against human dignity go far beyond *murder* and *violence* resulting in physical injury inflicted upon another. In his Sermon on the Mount, Jesus extended this Commandment to also encompass the root causes of murder.[39] Any preliminary actions or attitudes that could lead to the destruction of the life of another are also severely prohibited, including hatred, physical violence, and uncontrolled anger. The more common sins against the Fifth Commandment specified by Jesus include anger, hatred, abusive language, resentment, omissions of service, racism, and failures to treat an enemy or oppressor with love.

Particularly heinous is the sin of racism, the immoral belief that all members of a race share certain characteristics or abilities that distinguish them as inferior, even subhuman. This attitude historically has led to terrible injustices and untold suffering by those so oppressed. Racial prejudice contradicts in a dramatic way the unconditional love that Jesus has for every person. Every person is uniquely willed by God and cannot be repeated. Every person is likewise born into his or her own unique circumstances of family, culture, and context. God is the author of this diversity and wills that all his children form one human family. Racism is part and parcel of the attitude that denies the dignity of the human person created in God's image and likeness. In the words of the Council Fathers of Vatican II:

> With respect to the fundamental rights of the person, every type of discrimination, whether social or cultural, whether based on sex, race, color, social condition, language or religion, is to be overcome and eradicated as contrary to God's intent.[40]

On the other hand, revenge, vindictiveness, and the desire to hurt those who have hurt us is not the solution to racism, prejudice, or other forms of abuse. Vengeful retaliation stems from the same root as the injustice that inspires it and is often marked by the same

39. Cf. Mt 5:21–22.

40. GS, no. 29.

hatred, abusive language, and resentment it seeks to combat. The Old Law in the Old Testament provided for a system of justice based on "an eye for an eye, a tooth for a tooth." This sounds to modern ears like a rather harsh judicial system. It was, in fact, much more just than the systems based on retribution where if someone took your eye, you had your revenge by taking their life—the mafia mentality: If they kill my brother, I kill their whole family. "An eye for an eye" provided a limit to the vindictive desire to destroy a wrongdoer through intense retaliation. But this is still a narrow view. Jesus, as with all laws of simple justice, brought this concept to a new level with his New Commandment of Love.

> You have heard that it was said, "An eye for an eye and a tooth for a tooth." But I say to you, Do not resist one who is evil. But if any one strikes you on the right cheek, turn to him the other also....
>
> You have heard that it was said, "You shall love your neighbor and hate your enemy." But I say to you, Love your enemies and pray for those who persecute you.... For if you love those who love you, what reward have you? Do not even the tax collectors do the same?[41]

The sense of Christ's teachings here is not that his disciples must be pacifists or allow themselves to become victims of violence and wrongdoing; rather, our response to our enemies should be grounded in love and a deep respect for the fact that they, too, are human beings created in the image and likeness of God. We must never lose sight of the presence of God in every human person; the moment we do, we fail to recognize that person's dignity and status as a child of God. The goal in conflict should always be to achieve justice and, where possible, reconciliation, but not the destruction of an opponent. Recall from a few pages ago that acts opposed to life "do more harm to those who practice them than to those who suffer from the injury."[42] We trash our own dignity when we try to retaliate with the same anger and violence as our abusers.

Revenge or vindictiveness also has no place in a Christian's heart. An incredible example of what it means to follow Christ can be found in the actions of St. John Paul II. In 1981, while entering St. Peter's Square, the Pope was shot four times by Mehmet Ali Agca. Two years later, the Pope visited Agca in his prison cell, asked everyone to pray for him, expressed his full forgiveness, and lobbied for

41. Mt 5:38–39, 43–44, 46.

42. GS, no. 27.

his pardon with the Italian president. As a model of Jesus, the Pope returned love for injury.

According to the Law of Love, even an omission in service—if we can serve someone in need but fail to act—can be a breach of the Fifth Commandment. As St. Ambrose once said, "Feed him who is dying of hunger; if you have not fed him you have killed him."[43]

Speaking the Truth

The Eighth Commandment, "You shall not bear false witness against your neighbor,"[44] is a mandate to speak the truth. This Commandment is also a requirement of the moral law ordered toward the common good—"against your neighbor." To articulate a falsehood is a violation of a person's human dignity. A lie is always an injustice because it invites the listener or reader to accept false information as if it were true. The *Catechism* teaches, "A lie does real violence to another" and affirms that "lying is destructive of society." Lying destroys trust in our neighbors and "tears apart the fabric of social relationships."[45]

One particular outcome worthy of a closer look is the evil of sullying the good name or reputation of another person through false information or accusations. These evil acts include calumny, slander, detraction, and rash judgment. Violations of truthfulness and honesty often come in the form of exaggeration expressed in insincere flattery and bragging.

Calumny or slander involves a lie that falsely accuses another of a wrongdoing or vice. This evil act is directly forbidden by the Eighth Commandment. Every person has a right to a good name by virtue of his or her dignity as a child of God. It is an obligation both of justice and charity to protect and, if possible, build up the good reputation of another. Calumny, which often arises out of envy or hatred, is especially ugly because it robs someone of his or her good name through lies and false accusations.

Detraction involves hurting someone's good name through the disclosure of an incriminating truth. Reference to a person's mistakes or misbehavior is not a sin of detraction when his personal

43. St. Ambrose of Milan, *Exposition of Psalm 118*, Sermon 12, 44; quoted in *Loci Theologici*, vol. II, 406.

44. CCC, Part Three, Section Two; Ex 20:16; cf. Dt 5:20.

45. CCC 2486.

welfare or the common good requires it. If a person is taking drugs, stealing, or habitually cheating an employer, for instance, justice would require that this misconduct be reported. However, unless it is necessary to eradicate a personal evil or danger to others, a person's defects or mistakes should not be communicated to another party. As St. James warned in the New Testament, "Do not speak evil against one another."[46] This kind of talk is often the essence of gossip. Christians have a responsibility to avoid gossip by unnecessarily repeating statements, true or not, that would damage the character of others without cause.

Rash judgment involves a judgment that questions someone's character or concludes a moral defect without sufficient evidence. In rash judgment the facts do not logically lead to an accusation of guilt. This kind of judgment is evil because the verdict could very well be false. Insincere flattery, though usually not a serious infraction of the Eighth Commandment, is a form of lie that falsely attributes qualities that may not exist or are exaggerated. The purpose of insincere flattery is to praise in an exaggerated way to obtain a favor or to win over someone's affection. Bragging is a form of self-flattery whereby personal qualities are embellished to impress others. Since insincere flattery and bragging convey a certain degree of falsehood, they are evil and should be avoided.

We focus on these particular vices for a variety of reasons. First, the defense of the dignity of the human person demands truth. Additionally, these individual vices can spread within the culture and, as already stated, destroy trust and just relations among people and nations. In our time the sins against the Eighth Commandment are most hotly contested in the media realm—the commercial media and especially social media, which has a tremendous impact on social relationships in our world.

The first practical way of abiding by this Commandment is to always speak truthfully. Truth in speech involves expressing what the individual perceives as corresponding to reality. Justice requires that everyone receive truthful information and not be deceived or misled; therefore, it is an injustice to intentionally transmit false information.

But the command to be truthful does not only apply to "fake news" and the intentional spreading of misinformation. An important aspect of the Eighth Commandment concerns the discretion

46. Jas 4:11.

necessary to uphold and protect someone's good name or in maintaining silence regarding sensitive material. Silence is not only permitted but it is also a duty when another person *does not* have a right to certain information or if the reputation of another must be upheld. Not everyone should have access to all information; this is the basis for confidentiality. The public at large has no right to kinds of private information such as health histories, certain internal workings of a corporation, military intelligence, or someone's voting record. Social media should not be used to slander a person's good name, destroy his or her reputation, or spread gossip.

Sometimes the protection or welfare of an individual or society may warrant disclosure of classified information. Withholding certain information under the intention of loyalty, friendship, or discretion could result in terrible tragedies. Moral issues, though, may also arise from the public diffusion of information. Reporters and writers can violate their natural duty of protecting a person's good name. Scandalous details of celebrities' private lives, in many instances, offer information that is morally unhealthy for the consumer and exposes this personal wrongdoing to an entire population. Producers of media must consider whether these disclosures will truly benefit the common good or will simply feed on people's weakness for scurrilous sensation, contributing to the general lowering of morality in society. Consumers of media should be mindful of whether they derive unjust pleasure from dwelling on the faults of others. Sharing links to inappropriate stories is akin to gossip, detraction, and possibly calumny.

Nowadays it is not only the professional media outlets that can cause this kind of damage. Anyone with Internet access can spread misinformation and information that others do not have a right to know. Social media can do great good in bringing communities together, uniting people from faraway places, and sharing common joys and sorrows. On the other hand, if improperly used, they can be veritable hot beds of detraction, flattery, bragging, calumny, rash judgment, and a whole host of other sins against the Eighth Commandment that are destructive to the human dignity of particular people and the entire social fabric.

The virtue of honesty also requires us to keep secrets that we have promised to keep, our profession requires of us, or the good of our neighbor demands. Unless it is necessary to correct a serious wrong or avoid terrible harm, we are obliged to keep secrets. Breaking a promise to another person is bad enough, but publicly posting information that no one has a right to know is a grave sin, and the consequences can be devastating to the injured party. The Eighth Commandment should guide the actions not only of professional journalists but all who share information publicly.

Every child knows that it is wrong to lie, yet given the broad scope of truly honest behavior, a lie seems to be one of the easiest sins to rationalize. Speaking the truth can also be among the most daunting of tasks when it can so often bring negative consequences from others who do not want to hear the truth or do not want the truth to be known. Christ himself is the truth, and the ultimate love for the truth is to witness it with one's very life, as he did. The first Christians preferred torture and execution to withdrawing their belief in the truth of the Christian faith. Though most disciples of Christ will not be in a position to sacrifice their lives for the truth, every one is nonetheless called to live the virtue of fortitude and "lay down his life"[47] for Christ through the ordinary activities that mark a person's life. We must keep always in mind the words of Jesus: "He who is faithful in a very little is faithful also in much; and he who is dishonest in a very little is dishonest also in much."[48]

Human Dignity and Material Goods

Another topic at the heart of human dignity is the possession and distribution of material goods. In order to live, people need things. It is a fact of human existence. To acquire material goods, people need to work. A great deal of Catholic social teaching is focused on the issues that arise around labor, private property, and distribution. The Church does not approach these questions as experts on the economy; neither do the writings propose practical solutions or a political agenda. Catholic social teaching is, above all, a *moral* teaching on how people ought to shape the culture in which they live to best preserve human dignity and the common good. The teachings of the Church outline what we learn from shedding the "light of the Gospel" on modern problems.

The questions around the acquiring and distribution of material goods, perhaps more than any other area of human life, highlights

47. Jn 15:13.
48. Lk 16:10.

the need and the challenge of preserving both individual rights and dignity and the good of the entire community. Both "rugged individualism" and "totalitarian collectivism" are rejected as dangers to the good of the human person. An individualistic society fails to live up to the social needs of the human person and the building of community. Much like the Church is the Body of Christ, where each member is important and all are united, the whole world is one human family. On the other hand, the "common good" is not the same as the good of the "collective"; rather, it is the good of *all* and of *each* person. A society that places the State above all reduces the human person to a cog in the machine—without rights, freedom, or personal initiative. The State is meant to serve the good of the human person; the human person is not created to serve the State. Achieving this balance can be challenging, particularly when it comes to the distribution of the world's resources, but the Church has always defended both the individual right to private property as well as the social nature of property in both justice and charity.

To illustrate using one of the more basic principles, the Church affirms the individual right to own things privately. During the pontificate of Pope Leo XIII, Marxism was rising in popularity, though it was not yet implemented anywhere as a political system. He wrote *Rerum Novarum* to address the problems that had arisen within capitalist economies; chief among them:

> The hiring of labor and the conduct of trade are concentrated in the hands of comparatively few; so that a small number of very rich men have been able to lay upon the teeming masses of the laboring poor a yoke little better than that of slavery itself.[49]

But the first topic that Pope Leo XIII addressed in detail was the fact that socialism *was not* the solution. Besides other problems inherent to Marxism—its atheistic basis and threat to the family—human beings have a right to own private property that no state can take away. In fact, Pope Leo XIII argued that socialism would cause problems far worse than the ones it promised to solve.[50]

The right to private property has had an interesting philosophical history, and many different natural law theories are used in its defense. From Aristotle to St. Thomas Aquinas to John Locke, multiple complementary arguments have been offered in defense of

49. RN, no. 3.

50. Cf. ibid., nos. 4, 18.

people owning material goods as their own. For the Christian the most basic starting point is that God condemns taking someone else's created goods: "You shall not steal,"[51] says the Seventh Commandment. Stealing, or theft, is the act of unjustly taking another person's property without permission or legal right and without intending to return it.

The spirit of the Seventh Commandment, like the Fifth, applies beyond the limited, literal interpretation. Acts of stealing include vandalism, cheating on exams, reporting more payroll hours than a person worked, price gouging, shoplifting, wasting time at work, and keeping found valuables without an honest attempt to find the rightful owner. In addition, although direct stealing is not involved, failure to pay taxes and bills, overspending the money of another person, failing to put in an honest day's work, and making fraudulent products all constitute evil acts against the Seventh Commandment. Excessive gambling involves squandering money destined for the support of oneself and one's family; this vice, then, is also a violation of the Seventh Commandment. In general, any misuse or unjust acquisition of another's goods is at least indirectly linked to stealing and therefore a sin against the Seventh Commandment. Robbery, or taking the property of another by force, adds malice to stealing. Damage to goods may involve either private or State property, and all who effectively cooperate in doing damage are morally obliged to make restitution.

Because everyone has a right to life that involves nourishment, clothing, medicine, and shelter, every person has the right to avail him- or herself of material goods. In the case of extreme necessity, an individual may take some private possessions from another if it is required to preserve life. For example, a person with diabetes who will die without a shot of insulin may be morally right in breaking into a closed pharmacy; it would not be stealing if he made every attempt to make restitution.

This brief overview of the moral teaching surrounding the ownership of goods demonstrates the need for society to respect the rights of property. Pope Leo XIII, building on the thought of St. Thomas Aquinas and other more modern philosophers, offered a natural law argument in favor of a person's right to own things in *Rerum Novarum*. The socioeconomic issues in society at the end

51. CCC, Part Three, Section Two; Ex 20:15.

of the nineteenth century—especially the vast wealth disparities and the threat of socialism—called for a wider appraisal of what it means to have a right to own things. For one thing, society is more orderly and peaceful with a system of private property, and people are more incentivized to work when they know they are working for themselves. Pope Leo XIII added that a worker has a right to the fruits of his or her labor. Human beings, being rational, seek to plan for future needs, which also depends on private ownership. This defense of private property has been echoed by subsequent papal teachings.

The complexity of social life, however, offers varied ways of unjustly appropriating the goods of another. Paying an unfair wage, for example, is one of what the Church traditionally calls the "sins that cry to heaven"[52] for justice:

> The wages of the laborers who mowed your fields, which you kept back by fraud, cry out; and the cries of the harvesters have reached the ears of the Lord of hosts.[53]

So, while a person does have a right to private property, it is not an unlimited right. Manipulating the system to selfishly generate personal wealth at the expense of others cannot be justified by this right.

No human being owns anything *absolutely*. Everything is absolutely God's property, and he bestowed the gift of "stewardship" of the earth on the human race.[54] The Church teaches that the important question is not *how much* or *how little* property we own; what matters is how we *use* it.

Pope Leo XIII taught that it was one thing to say a person has a right to private property, but it is another thing to say he or she a right *to use* it however he or she desires. People do not. In fact, Pope Leo XIII argued, echoing St.Thomas Aquinas, that people ought to *use* their material goods *as though they were common*, always considering the greater need or right.

One guide for the right use of goods is a principle called the "universal destination of goods." Divine Revelation explicitly tells us that God created the world to serve the needs of all people. Among other things, every person has an innate right to life and

52. CCC 1867.

53. Jas 5:4; Dt 24:14–15.

54. Cf. Gn 2:15.

nourishment, and the created goods of the earth are destined to benefit everyone, not just a small segment of the population. As the *Catechism* teaches, "The goods of creation are destined for the whole human race."[55]

In the universal destination of goods, the Church does not find cause for socialist or communist systems of distribution, but she does teach that an economic system must be structured so the right to private property is subordinate to the universal destination of goods. When only a few people possess most of the goods, it becomes impossible for the majority of people to live in accordance with basic human dignity. In such instances God's plan is not fulfilled. "The *universal destination of goods* remains primordial, even if the promotion of the common good requires respect for the right to private property and its exercise."[56] The ownership of private property does not conflict with the common good when there is a fair distribution of the goods of creation.

Private property, though lawful and necessary for the good of society, is a *means* of distributing material goods. To say that private property is a "right" means not only that one person cannot take another person's things but also that everyone should enjoy that right. If the rules surrounding the acquiring and holding of property *thwart* distribution and are unjustly ordered to favor one group over another, ownership becomes illegitimate. A common example is the holding of a monopoly, which most States restrict by law. Another example is requiring a just wage so the owners cannot channel all the profits to themselves and leave their workers destitute. When problems arise in the economic practices of a society, Church teaching, in general, favors corrections that come from the free decisions of cooperating parties, but the State should intervene if necessary as part of its responsibility to protect people's rights.

The goal of achieving a fair distribution is an obligation and therefore a matter of justice, but the Church has perennially repeated that this does not eliminate the need for charity in a good society. The State cannot, and should not try to, eliminate every problem, and the Christian is never content with merely doing what is required of him or her in justice. The "culture of life" is not satisfied simply by doing no harm. Christ calls his disciples to expend

55. CCC 2402.

56. CCC 2403.

themselves in *doing good* to others; this lies at the heart of the call to self-gift. The rich teachings contained in the twenty-fifth chapter of St. Matthew's Gospel, in particular the Parable of the Sheep and the Goats, amply illustrate what Christ expects. To those who will be invited to the Kingdom of God:

> The King will say…"Come, O blessed of my Father, inherit the kingdom prepared for you from the foundation of the world; for I was hungry and you gave me food, I was thirsty and you gave me drink, I was a stranger and you welcomed me, I was naked and you clothed me, I was sick and you visited me, I was in prison and you came to me."[57]

By contrast, those who failed in such acts of charity will not be invited to the kingdom.

At the same time, situations of injustice cannot be glossed over by calling people to "be more charitable." Many such examples include factories or workshops where workers are employed at very low wages for long hours and under poor conditions. Populations of poor people, with little recourse to other opportunities, generate wealth by their labor to help only those few at the top. The workers' lives are improved very little. While such a situation calls for great charity and service, the solution must be larger; it must include overcoming the injustice of the situation.

Strangely enough, people engaged in programs to help those in need will sometimes argue over what is the best way to help society: justice or charity. Some people working for justice argue that charity can be an insult if the need is caused by prejudice, racism, or exploitation. Some people engaged in charitable work hold up the greater transcendent beauty that comes from personal sacrifice and love.

The Church, on the other hand, has always seen justice and charity as part of the same work, which Pope Benedict XVI described well. Justice is giving another what he or she is *due*; charity is freely giving something rightly owned to another out of love. Pope Benedict XVI pointed out that these are not two different ways of dealing with the problems in society; they are part of the same path:

> I cannot "give" what is mine to the other, without first giving him what pertains to him in justice. If we love others with charity, then first of all we are just towards them.[58]

57. Mt 25:34–36.

58. CiV, no. 6.

We will never build a society so just that charity is unnecessary, but our charity is empty if we ignore situations of injustice. As Pope Benedict explains:

> Not only is justice not extraneous to charity, not only is it not an alternative or parallel path to charity: justice is inseparable from charity,[59] and intrinsic to it. Justice is the primary way of charity.[60]

Christians are called not only *to be* just, but to work for a more just world. This includes working to achieve a distribution of goods that is based in justice. The universal destination of goods, though, will never be achieved through just laws and regulations alone. The common good requires that we go beyond simply giving people what they are *due* and give to them out of fraternal love. The right to private property, then, is also limited by the principle of "common use."

As mentioned earlier, it is one thing to say people have a right to *own* things but another to say that they can *use* them however they want. How is my property to be used? As Pope Francis taught:

> The right to private property is always accompanied by the primary and prior principle of the subordination of all private property to the universal destination of the earth's goods.[61]

If I still have a surplus after (1) I am in possession of property that does not belong by right to another person, (2) I have treated others with justice, and (3) my own needs and the needs of my family have been met, then the Church teaches that I am bound by the Law of Love to use my wealth for the good of others. While civil laws might not be able to compel such charity, Jesus was quite clear on the matter.[62] In considerations of how we ought to use what we own, we must always consider our neighbors in need.

The universal destination of goods should direct not only national economies but also relations between nations. Contrary to the views of those who would advocate national policies of isolation, concern for the common good does not stop at a country's borders. By virtue of the principle of the universal destination of goods, one nation cannot take advantage of another nation for its own financial gain. The globalized economy following the Industrial Revolution

59. Cf. St. Paul VI, Encyclical Letter on the Development of Peoples *Populorum Progressio* (March 26, 1967), no. 22; GS, no. 69.

60. CiV, no. 6.

61. FT, no. 123; cf. LS, no. 93; EG, nos. 189–190.

62. Cf. RN, no. 22.

has helped many poorer nations and the potential to help many more, but it has also led to the exploitation of many nations by multinational corporations that make use of their resources and workers without attention to stewardship and human rights. International financial institutions are called on to take steps to ease the burden of developing nations to assist them in securing economic independence and paths to true economic and social development.

The solution to helping the poorer countries of the world is admittedly complex. The overarching premise is that no people should suffer in squalor while others are able to live quite comfortably. Although prosperity and its pursuit are not inherently wrong, richer nations and individual people are called, in justice and charity, to substantially assist less fortunate nations and people and to take some responsibility for their progress. It is an offense against justice and a grave neglect of basic human rights to ignore groups of people suffering misery and destitution while other nations have a surplus of riches at their disposal.

SOLIDARITY

Thinking back to Chapter 9 on the Church, part of the Church's mission is to build a community of love where every person is respected and an organic communion is built among all, united together for one another's good. While this type of communion is much easier to achieve in the Church, where all are united by Christ in the Sacraments, it is also a goal to be achieved in the whole world where all are united at least by a common humanity. As we read earlier, the human person, each one uniquely loved by God, "cannot fully find himself except through a sincere gift of himself."[63]

The call to communion, brotherly love, and friendship applies to all areas of society where there is instead division, rancor, and strife. When considering the material goods of the earth, this call applies to the use of resources and wealth. The Seventh Commandment forbids stealing another person's goods, and Tenth Commandment forbids even enviously desiring them: "You shall not covet your neighbor's goods."[64] Our natural appetites lead us to desire things that are good in themselves, but an excessive desire leads to sins of *greed*, *avarice*, and *envy*.

63. GS, no.24.

64. CCC, Part Three, Section Two; cf. Ex 20:17; Dt 5:21.

These sins, in some fashion, make the possession of material things an absolute good. *Greed* is the desire for earthly goods that are not truly needed for a Christian life. It is the act of acquiring things solely to look rich and powerful in the eyes of one's neighbors or simply for self-gratification. *Avarice* is the inordinate desire of accumulating and hoarding wealth. The avaricious person becomes hardhearted, unjust, and deceitful in his effort to hold on to his or her wealth. Ebenezer Scrooge at the beginning of Charles Dickens's *A Christmas Carol* is an enduring model of an avaricious person. *Envy* is the wrongful desire for things possessed by another or unhappiness at another's good fortune. Besides being evil, it leads directly to hatred and the desire to acquire the desired goods by illicit means. By way of distinction, avarice is the sinful desire for wealth, while envy is the sinful desire for the goods of one's neighbor. They are grave sins that easily lead to moral deterioration.

The sins of greed and avarice have profound social ramifications, particularly if they become the cultural mindset. In his writings on social justice, Pope Francis traced the evils in society to an all-consuming desire for material gain to the detriment of the poor and the worker. He laments that wealth coupled with a high quality of life is limited to a small percentage of the world population in contrast to the inordinate number of underprivileged and destitute people:

> A tiny minority of the world's population owns half of its wealth.
>
> For all our deeply-held convictions that all men and women are created equal, many of our brothers and sisters in the human family, especially those at the margins of society, are effectively excluded from the financial world.... New and creative forms of social, political and economic participation must be devised, sensitive to the voice of the poor and committed to including them in the building of our common future.[65]

This consumerist attitude obfuscates the high value placed on the dignity of others—or love. Profit and power may not be pursued without being limited by any other value: the dignity of others, the rights of others, the law of justice, love, or any other virtue. These sinful attitudes held by people are the root cause of the evil structures that come to exist in the world. Placing wealth and power above every other value makes it impossible to love God and neighbor as Christ calls us to. Material things have value and are good in

65. Pope Francis, *Letter to the Participants in the 2021 Spring Meetings of the World Bank Group and International Monetary Fund* (April 4, 2021); cf. FT, no. 169.

themselves, but they are only a means to an end and can never be treated as absolute goods and ultimate ends.

In our fallen state, however, the human heart can become overly consumed with material possessions, suffocating the life of the spirit and the ability to serve others. The remedy for greed, avarice, and envy is in taking to heart Our Lord's first Beatitude: "Blessed are the poor in spirit, for theirs is the kingdom of heaven."[66] Poverty in spirit involves much more than a lack of material goods; it requires a general detachment from the things of this world. This spiritual poverty encourages the firm conviction that our happiness does not lie in material possessions and only God can fill the human heart.

The practice of poverty of spirit requires habitual meditation on the life of Christ, frequent examination of conscience regarding any possible disordered attachment to earthly goods, and a general desire for total identification with Christ and an imitation of his life of loving service. It also requires a firm conviction about the dignity of the human person. Persons are greater than things. As the *Catechism* teaches, "Society is essential to the fulfillment of the human vocation.... [R]espect must be accorded to the just hierarchy of values."[67] As Pope Francis reminded business leaders:

> The noble vocation of business leaders will be evident in the measure that all human activity becomes a witness of hope in the future and an incentive to greater social responsibility and concern through each person's wise use of his or her talents and abilities.[68]

Individual people, corporations, and nations cannot put the pursuit of wealth above the good of the human person. Owners cannot put profit above workers. International investors cannot ignore the good of the people in the community where they will invest. Any person can fail in this regard if he or she puts gaining "things" above *his or her own dignity* as a person, making that more important than virtue, relationships with others, or his or her ultimate good. "The dignity of each human person and the pursuit of the common good," wrote Pope Francis, "are concerns which ought to shape all economic policies."[69]

---

66. Mt 5:3.
67. CCC 1895.
68. Pope Francis, *Address to the International Christian Union of Business Executives* (November 28, 2018).
69. EG, no.203.

To offset the two "sins" of the "desire for profit" and the "thirst for power" pursued "at any price," St. John Paul II promoted what he called the virtue of solidarity. The term "solidarity" can mean different things to different people. For some, solidarity implies standing with the oppressed in the fight against the oppressor. While this might be a great act of solidarity, in St. John Paul II's understanding, solidarity is a virtue that focuses not on the *fight* but rather on the *communion* that should exist among all people. In his words, solidarity...

> is a firm and persevering determination to commit oneself to the common good; that is to say to the good of all and of each individual, because we are all really responsible for all.[70]

The virtue of solidarity encompasses both the struggle for justice and the call to love. It pertains to justice in that we are "responsible" for one another. It pertains to charity because it calls us to go beyond ourselves in service to our brothers and sisters. It is the sense we have that not only can we do no harm to others but we must also work for the good of others. In this way, solidarity can overcome the sins of greed and avarice. A person with a strong sense of solidarity certainly refrains from putting "profit" and "power" above other people; moreover, he or she is willing to sacrifice in order to achieve the good of other people. This is the path offered by Christ that can transform society.

While the focus so far has been on material goods, both their ownership and their use, the good of the human person cannot be limited to this one dimension. Though the human person needs things, people are greater than things. Material goods and wealth are just a means of achieving the good of the human person, and even then it does not achieve their highest good. The pursuit of wealth and "things" as the sole purpose of life stifles the good of the person while the higher goods—for example, friendship, virtue, and communion with God—can remain totally unfulfilled.

As Christians we must realize that the true development of the human person has a spiritual as well as a material aspect. Authentic development that attends to the whole person, body and soul, looks at a wide range of needs: cultural, educational, moral, and most importantly spiritual. People deserve to have sufficient mate-

70. St. John Paul II, Encyclical Letter for the Twentieth Anniversary of *Populorum Progressio, Sollicitudo Rei Socialis* (December 30, 1987), no. 38.

rial resources to lead a dignified life, but they also need the riches of the Gospel message brought to them as well. The disciple of Christ is called to relieve the rampant poverty in the world, both material and spiritual. By addressing the development of the whole individual, every person is given the means to respond to their Christian vocation.[71]

The need to see the good of all and of every whole person means the teaching on solidarity goes far beyond the question of material goods. Solidarity does not simply mean "with the poor" but that "all are responsible for all." Christians should have this sense of solidarity with all people. The call to build a better society that protects every unique person's dignity includes, as does Catholic social teaching, the call to eliminate all threats to human dignity. We can stress here the havoc wreaked in society by racism, sexism, ageism, and other forms of prejudice.

The Church also teaches that the environment and its protection must be embraced by all in solidarity. Part of our consideration of the distribution of the world's resources and our own poverty of spirit is the manner in which we treat the beautiful world God created. We are called to be faithful stewards of the earth, not plunderers extracting wealth and leaving other nations or future generations with a polluted world and depleted resources.[72] Increasingly, recent Popes, most notably Pope Francis, have turned their attention to this issue. Environmentalism, though, should not be turned into a modern form of "nature worship." Our goal is to be good stewards of the beautiful gift of creation, respecting God's plan, and the thriving of the whole human race.

Lay Vocation

In Chapter 9 on the Church, the different vocations within the Body of Christ were briefly described — to married life, to Holy Orders, and to the consecrated life. Each one has a unique and important role in fulfilling God's plan. Often in the history of the Church, the role of the lay faithful has been misunderstood and downplayed as though lay Catholics were "second-class citizens" in the Church. Nothing could be further from the truth.

71. Cf. CCC 2461.
72. Cf. LS, no. 50.

The Council Fathers of Vatican II gave a great deal of attention to the lay vocation, with the goal of offering a "positive" definition rather than a "negative" definition. "Positive" means the definition of the lay vocation should not be what the lay person lacks, say, the lay person is *not* a priest or religious; rather, the lay person's vocation should be understood according to what it *is*. Priests, by their vocation, are ordained to the sacred ministry, preaching, and offering the Sacraments. Religious, by their vocation, serve as a witness that ultimate happiness does not come from this world but in the Kingdom of Heaven. Lay Christians, who are intimately engaged in the world, are called to transform the world according to the Gospel message of truth and love. As the Council Fathers put it:

> The laity, by their very vocation, seek the kingdom of God by engaging in temporal affairs and by ordering them according to the plan of God.[73]

It is in the very activities of regular life that the lay person lives out his or her vocation and works to further the Kingdom of God.

Christian discipleship cannot be satisfied merely with practicing an individual morality, but rather must do whatever possible to create a society based on a fair distribution of goods and solicitous concern for every individual, especially the underprivileged. Not only is it a moral duty to cast votes from a Christian perspective of justice, but it is also all the more necessary for the conscientious Christian to either directly participate in public life or to establish some role in contributing to a more just society.

If we were to live our lives in accordance with Christ's Sermon on the Mount, especially the Beatitudes, we would fulfill the Commandments and become faithful disciples of Christ. This cannot be done, however, without the grace of God. The challenge to love everyone as Jesus loves requires serious prayer and a sacramental life. These supernatural measures give the disciples of Christ the necessary strength and assistance to reach the levels of love and charity required of every Christian. The next chapter will introduce the graces that flow from God through the sacramental life of the Church.

---

73. LG, no.31.

CHAPTER 11

SACRAMENTAL CONTACT WITH CHRIST

Anyone with the experience of having read the Gospels realizes that, among the many images of Jesus Christ, his miracles of healing are especially moving. In these miraculous cures, which defy immediate scientific explanation, both the humanity and divinity of Christ work in perfect synchrony. Jesus healed a withered arm with a touch of his human hand. He restored the sight of a blind man by applying a mixture of spittle and clay. He cured a person riddled with leprosy by uttering a word with his human voice. What especially calls the attention of the Gospel reader is Jesus' bout of weeping over his dead friend Lazarus, whom he later brought back to life with a mere command. In each event, the divine action of Christ worked in and through his humanity.

These miracles are part of the historical record of Jesus' public life. Given his display of power to heal and circumvent physical laws, he undoubtedly garnered attention. Throngs of people felt the compelling need to seek him out and receive his medicinal touch. In one instance a woman forced her way through the crowds, and it sufficed for her to touch the hem of his garment to be restored to health. Jesus drew huge crowds because it was soon patently obvious that Jesus' medical success rate was off the charts.

These are not, however, mere stories from the past to fascinate us today, the way we might read about the conquests of Alexander the Great or the construction of the Great Wall of China. Being both human and divine, Jesus operates in time and also transcends the temporal order. This fact, cloaked in an air of mystery, means that what Jesus did historically, he continues to do eternally. Everything that happened 2000 years ago is meant for every person of every era. Jesus had every person present in his mind and heart at his Birth, at his miracles, and at his Death and Resurrection. His sojourn on earth is not simply consigned to the period of history in which he lived but extends to every person until the end of time.

Viewing Jesus through the prism of eternity, his public life—though forming a concrete period of history—extends invisibly to every person. This is why reading the Gospel is not just a refresher on the rudiments of Christianity or an interesting history of the life and words of the man called Jesus. The Gospel is an inexhaustible well of teaching that can speak to us personally at every juncture of our lives. Taking this consideration one step further, what Jesus did physically in terms of cures also applies to all of us today.

We point to numerous stories of miraculous physical cures received in response to prayers, but these occurrences are not the norm and occur according to God's mysterious plan. But what Jesus did historically by way of healing is still available to everyone, only now invisibly and spiritually. It may be helpful, in the spirit of the ancient Christian writers, to see Christ's miracles as not just historical events but allegorical teaching. In this analogy the throngs of sick people wracked with gruesome infections and severe disabilities represent the human soul that suffers from the infirmity of sin. These spiritual infirmities rob the soul of joy, peace, and freedom; the physical maladies that disfigure and limit the body represent a spiritual and moral loss of dignity. Leprosy, a devastating illness, is an apt physical symbol of what the soul experiences when deformed by sin. What the divine Physician did for the physically ill, he does for the spiritually and morally sick. Now that Jesus Christ has ascended and is "seated at the right hand of the Father,"[1] he provides an abundance of grace for spiritual renewal and healing. Every spiritual malady finds a remedy through Jesus' constant intervention. This is the reason Christ came: to save us from our sins.

Despite having departed from this world to be with his Father, at least in terms of his historical humanity, Jesus Christ continues to do this work of healing through a combination of both the physical and the spiritual. Christ's work of spiritual renewal, purification, and strengthening is performed through material signs and spoken words in the Church's celebration of the Sacraments. These sacramental rituals have been directly prescribed by Christ as a means of interacting with his people. Through these Sacraments Christ brings the spiritually dead back to life, cures the infirm, and strengthens the weak. Through the Sacraments Christ's power is bestowed on the soul by the action of the Holy Spirit. The following can serve as

1. RMiss, The Order of Mass, nos. 8, 18.

a simple definition of a Sacrament: an outward sign instituted by Christ to give grace; alternatively, a visible sign of a sacred reality.

The Divine Institution of the Sacraments

Since the Sacraments are conduits of the grace of salvation, only Jesus Christ, the Redeemer, could institute them. It is from Christ himself that the Sacraments derive the power to heal and sanctify. He was the one who established these sacred signs through which he would bestow his graces of redemption and sanctification. He began the process of instituting the Sacraments before his Death, but only when the work of redemption was fully complete with his Resurrection did the Sacraments become fully effective.

The number of Sacraments instituted by Christ is a point of contention among the various Christian denominations, but the Catholic Church affirms that all seven of the Sacraments—Baptism, Confirmation, the Eucharist, Penance and Reconciliation, Matrimony, Holy Orders, and the Anointing of the Sick—were each instituted by Christ himself. Some have claimed that the number of Sacraments evolved over the course of time, with the Church adding some not originally instituted by Christ. Undoubtedly the rituals and celebrations that accompany the Sacraments have changed with the needs of different cultures and historical eras, but the essential signs explicitly instituted by Christ were present from the beginning.

In two of the Sacraments, Christ explicitly spelled out the sign and formula connected to them. Baptism, the Sacrament necessary for salvation and incorporation into the Mystical Body of Christ, was clearly specified in both its sign and words. The Holy Eucharist, the greatest of all the Sacraments, was celebrated for the first time by Jesus Christ himself. It is the only Sacrament whereby we can read Our Lord's mandate to his Apostles to do what he precisely did and said during the Last Supper. The Eucharistic celebration is narrated in all three synoptic Gospels (Sts. Matthew, Mark, and Luke), and St. John's Gospel records Our Lord's extensive discourse on the Eucharist as the Bread of Life. These explicit instructions and elaborate theological explanations attest to the fact that the Eucharist is the Sacrament of Sacraments and "the source and summit of Christian life."[2]

2. LG, no. 11; quoted in CCC 1324.

The other five Sacraments are clearly and explicitly instituted by Christ, though the Evangelists do not record detailed instruction on the exact words and gestures that accompany their sacramental signs. Except for Baptism and the Eucharist, Christ left instructions to his Apostles—as part of Sacred Tradition—and to his Church the precise words and rituals for each Sacrament. It is to be expected, then, that as the Church grows in the Spirit, she refines her celebration of the Sacraments and allows for adaptations of the rituals according to culture and history.

Since the Seven Sacraments were instituted by Christ, they are here to stay. The Church cannot replace them—let alone eliminate them—since their required celebration is explicitly mandated by Christ himself. Though instituted by Christ, the Church has the right and duty to make modifications on *how* the Sacraments should be celebrated. The Catholic hierarchy can modify the wording for the sake of precision and greater understanding. Without changing the essentials, the celebration of the Sacraments can be more adapted to various cultures. In fact, presently, the sacramental rituals enjoy a more elaborate liturgical celebration with selected readings, hymns, and the allowance for preaching. There used to be less emphasis on explicit instruction through the celebration of the Sacrament; nowadays the whole ritual is a teaching moment, shedding light on the meaning of the Sacrament being administered.

Each Sacrament serves as a vehicle of the Church to bring Christ's redemptive graces to people. Through this supernatural gift of grace, a Sacrament truly provides healing, strengthening, nourishment, and special powers for the soul. The basic goal of all the Sacraments is to bestow grace for a real participation in the life of God. The contact point for intimate union with the three Persons of the Trinity is always the Sacraments.

Basic Components

Early Greek-speaking Christians used the word *mysterion,* and Latin-speaking Christians used *sacramentum* to describe a "Sacrament." Each language distinctly emphasizes the same reality. *Mysterion* means "mystery" in the sense of a secret or hidden teaching; this is apt because the effects of a Sacrament is hidden beneath its material signs. In the Eastern Churches the Sacraments are called "Mysteries." The English "Sacrament" is derived from the Latin *sac-*

ramentum. In the ancient Roman world, a *sacramentum* was a solemn oath or obligation. In ecclesial Latin this came to signify something sacred, especially a sanctifying object or action. In every administration and celebration of a Sacrament, the recipient is sanctified by the Holy Spirit through the Church's sacred action. Both *mysterion* and *sacramentum* complement the nature of a Sacrament as a visible sign of the mystery of divine action on the soul.

As a general principle all the Sacraments are God's plan to communicate his grace to his people through material signs and symbols. They correspond to the mission of Christ himself, who, though God, entered into our world as a human being in the flesh. This means that the sacramental principle of the Church is an extension of the Incarnation of God's Son. The Sacraments not only reflect the Incarnation, but also—in what is called the "sacramentality" of the Church—speak of the goodness of God's creation. Contrary to the Docetists' belief (see Chapter 6), God is not too spiritually transcendent to work through his material creation. The sacramentality of the Church also reflects and speaks to the nature of the human person as both body and spirit.

Sacramental theology distinguishes three basic features of each Sacrament: *matter, form,* and *minister;* in addition, each Sacrament has a proper *recipient* and the right *intention* of the minister. While all the Sacraments offer sanctifying grace and greater union with God, each Sacrament confers its own specific grace, or "effects." This chapter will provide a general overview of these terms and ideas as a foundation for successive chapters devoted to individual Sacraments.

Matter and Form

Following Aristotelian classifications, physical reality consists of two metaphysical principles: matter and form. "Matter" comprises the physical underpinnings of an entity, while "form" gives the thing its nature. For example, a bird and a squirrel are composed of similar matter, but they have different forms that make them distinct beings. For both animals, the matter includes organic compounds, hydrogen, oxygen, lipids, proteins, and many others, but each one's form is "bird" or "squirrel," respectively. For another example, both a chair and a table can be made of the same matter—wood from a tree—but their forms—"chair" and "table," respectively—differ. The wood is the raw material, and a carpenter gives each a distinct form.

Similarly, each Sacrament possesses a material substance or gesture accompanied by specific words. Since the words spoken give nature to the physical signs and gestures, the words used in the sacramental celebrations correspond to the form. For example, the matter of Baptism is water, and the form is the words of Baptism: "[Name], I baptize you in the name of the Father, and of the Son, and of the Holy Spirit."[3] The form defines the spiritual effect of the matter while the new child of God is being immersed in the water or having the water poured over his or her head. For another example, the matter of the Holy Eucharist is bread and wine, and the form is the words of consecration: "This is my Body.... / This is the chalice of my Blood."[4] The form defines the spiritual effect of the matter while the bishop or priest takes up the bread and wine for the Holy Spirit to make it the Body of Christ.

Each Sacrament consists of its own matter (a sign) and form (words).

Minister, Recipient, and Intention

Christ works in the Sacraments through his earthly ministers. The true minister of each Sacrament is Jesus Christ, who entrusted the Sacraments to his Church, and the Church in turn ordains people to administer his Sacraments.

Each Sacrament has an ordinary minister. This use of "ordinary" does not mean the minister is nothing special or is just the person who happens to celebrate a Sacrament most of the time; this refers to the minister being in the proper "order"—group or rank—of the Church. The ordinary minister administers the Sacrament proper to his or her order; an extraordinary minister may be permitted under certain circumstances. For example, the ordinary minister of the Sacrament of Baptism is a bishop, priest, or deacon, but anyone may celebrate Baptism in danger of death. For another example, the ordinary minister of the Sacrament of Confirmation is a bishop, but he may allow a priest to celebrate Confirmation at times. It often comes as a surprise to people that the ordinary ministers of marriage is the couple themselves: the bride and the groom.

---

3. OBap, no. 97. Alternatively, in the Eastern Churches, "The servant of God [Name] is baptized in the name of the Father, and of the Son, and of the Holy Spirit."
4. RMiss, The Order of Mass, no. 89.

Though the Church appoints a minister for each Sacrament, it must always be remembered that the power of the Sacrament does not come from its earthly minister. The power of the Sacrament comes from Jesus Christ. It is common to hear people resist the idea of confessing sins to a bishop or priest, saying, "I do not need some person to forgive me." That statement is correct in a sense: No one can forgive a guilty person except the injured person, and in the case of sin, God himself is primarily injured. But there is something important missing from that statement: it is ultimately *not* the minister who forgives the penitent but Christ working through his bishop or priest in the Sacrament of Penance and Reconciliation. The minister signifies the reality that it is always Christ who heals, sanctifies, and saves.

Each Sacrament also has a proper "recipient." For example, to receive the Sacrament of the Eucharist, a person must be baptized and free of mortal sin. For another example, to receive the Sacrament of Matrimony, a person much be baptized, meet a minimum age and other requirements, and not be under another oath or vow.

It is not enough, though, to have the right people in play; the proper "intention" is also necessary. The form of a Sacrament is not some sort of magic formula totally divorced from the intentions and will of the minister, and it is not enough to give grace to an unwilling recipient. It is not like a spell cast at Hogwarts. The celebration of a Sacrament needs at least an implicit intention.

First, the minister of the Sacrament must have the proper intention. Even for the extraordinary minister of Baptism, as the *Catechism* teaches, "The intention required is to will to do what the Church does when she baptizes."[5] If a person is acting in a movie, playing in a swimming pool with his or her nieces and nephews, or otherwise says the form of Baptism without the proper intention, another person is not magically or automatically baptized. The minister must intend to do what the Church does.

Second, the recipient must at least implicitly desire to receive the Sacrament. The matter and form, though necessary, are not enough in themselves. A person cannot be baptized or ordained without the implicit willingness to receive the Sacrament. A person coerced into a wedding does not receive the grace of the Sacrament of Matrimony, and a bishop cannot ordain a man who does not

5. CCC 1256.

have the intention of serving as a deacon. Although the sacramental encounter may be valid, the benefits of the Sacrament would not be received due to the recipient's lack of intention. It is possible, however, for the graces of the Sacrament to take effect when the right dispositions are restored through repentance, for example, when a person receiving the Sacrament of Confirmation had committed a mortal sin but later repented and atoned in the Sacrament of Penance and Reconciliation.

The intention of the recipient was at the heart of early debates over infant Baptism. Some Christians thought it is not appropriate to baptize an infant since he or she cannot explicitly desire the Sacrament. The Church's clear and consistent response to that doubt has been that baptizing an infant rests on the Church's faith that incorporation into the Body of Christ is the one true means of salvation meant for all people. Every infant, therefore, implicitly desires Baptism[6] through his or her ongoing formation in the faith, which the Church entrusts to the parents and godparents. To baptize anyone who has use of his or her reason and will, though, requires explicit assent. No one can—and no one should!—be baptized against his or her will.

Effects of the Sacraments

Each Sacrament, by virtue of its celebration, is an effective conduit of grace that flows from the heart of Christ by the action of the Holy Spirit. As long as the minister uses the specified sign in conjunction with the matter and the appropriate words and has the intention of doing what the Church wills, the grace of the particular Sacrament is invariably transmitted. The gift of grace does not depend on the minister's qualities but rather on the work of the Holy Spirit through the action of the Church. For example, if a priest—the proper minister—were to use tea in place of wine or use his own words in place of the words of consecration, the Body and Blood of Christ would not be sacramentally present. On the other hand, if that same priest had committed sins but still used the proper form and the proper matter, his human failings would not invalidate the Sacrament, and the faithful would certainly receive the Body, Blood, Soul, and Divinity of Christ.

6. Sacred Congregation for the Doctrine of the Faith, Instruction on Infant Baptism *Pastoralis Actio* (October 20, 1980), nos. 16–22.

Recall the simple definition of a Sacrament from earlier in this chapter: an outward sign instituted by Christ to give grace. The Sacraments are "effective" signs because they actually do—they "effect," or really bring about—what they mean. In our everyday lives water cleanses us, so it is a sign of cleansing; the water in Baptism truly cleanses the recipient's soul. In our everyday lives oil fortifies our food and strengthens our skin, so it is a sign of strength; the oil in Confirmation truly strengthens the recipient to bear adversity and profess the faith. If, hypothetically, traffic signs were *effective* signs, then a stop sign would not simply offer guidance about how to safely operate a vehicle, but rather it would *actually stop* the vehicle. The Church, from her very beginning, has taught that Sacraments are signs that truly produce the signified effect on the soul. Grace will invariably be bestowed in the celebration of the Sacrament.

It is this divine guarantee that makes the Sacraments such a tremendous gift. Surely, God works in a multitude of ways, bestowing graces on his children. Faced with a difficult exam, a student who prays might be given strength and focus or peace of mind to accept the outcome. Unsure of how to help her children, a mother who prays might receive wisdom and courage to do what is best for them. The work of conversion that leads a person to the Sacraments in the first place is already the fruit of God's grace. Such incidents are built on the person's faith—but with the Sacraments, the recipient can be confident that what Our Lord has promised is being received.

The person receiving a Sacrament, however, does not invariably receive the full effect of its graces. In addition to the requirement that the recipient desires the Sacrament, his or her "dispositions" determine how much benefit is derived from the graces of the Sacrament. God freely gives his grace, but he does not force it on us. It must also be freely received. The Sacraments by no means work independently of a person's freedom and dispositions but benefit the recipient according to the quality of his or her desires and interior conditions.

In addition to greater confidence in the bestowal of grace, the Sacraments offer a special kind of grace called "sanctifying grace." In the examples above of the student praying before a test or the mother praying for guidance, such recipients receive "actual grace." Actual grace is an intervention by God in the moment for a particular need. Sanctifying grace is a "habitual gift, a stable and supernatural disposition that perfects the soul itself to enable it to live with God, to act by his love."[7] Sanctifying grace comes to us for the very first time in the reception of Baptism. Once in the state of grace, that same grace can increase in intensity so that a person can truly reflects the heart of Christ. Holiness can never be reached without an abundance of sanctifying grace. For this reason, the Blessed Virgin Mary, whom the archangel called "*full* of grace,"[8] is the greatest of all saints. Everyone who is considered very saintly has a high intensity of grace, even though this added quality to the soul cannot be quantified.

Besides increasing sanctifying grace, each Sacrament gives a particular, "sacramental" grace directly connected to the Sacrament being celebrated and received. By reflecting on each of the Sacrament's signs, the specific kind of grace can be deduced. Water in Baptism is an effective sign of cleansing, oil in the Anointing of the Sick is an effective sign of strengthening, and the vow of a lifelong covenant is an effective sign of Matrimony.

These specific sacramental graces also respond to key stages of human life. Baptism corresponds to birth and newly born life; for this reason, it is the first Sacrament of Christian Initiation. Confirmation corresponds to the growth of the human person; it is the second Sacrament of Christian Initiation. The third Sacrament of Christian Initiation, the Holy Eucharist, the greatest of all Sacraments, corresponds to the lifelong need for nourishment and growth in charity. The Eucharist initiates the soul into direct communication and a more profound friendship with Jesus Christ. (This is true despite the Eucharist usually being received before Confirmation in the Western Church.) Matrimony corresponds to the domestic and reproductive components of human life. Holy Orders corresponds to need for governance in society and services that promote the common good. Penance and Reconciliation corresponds to the continuing need to cleanse ourselves when we are soiled and marred by the activities of life. Last, the Anointing of the Sick corresponds to strength and preparation in the face of illness and danger of death. Thus the Sacraments address in a spiritual manner the main stages and needs of human life from birth to death. Christ, by the power of the Holy Spirit, walks with Christians through their lives by means of his Sacraments.

7. CCC 2000.

8. Lk 1:28; emphasis added.

Each Sacrament is a sign of holiness since it signifies the common objective of a holy life. Whether the Sacrament is Matrimony, Holy Orders, or the Anointing of the Sick, the goal is always holiness. The aim of each Sacrament is to transform a person in such a way that he or she can say with St. Paul, "It is no longer I who live, but Christ who lives in me."[9] God does not desire the Christian to merely "get by" or "hang in there" but rather vibrate with Christ's merciful, loving heart.

The ultimate meaning of each Sacrament, regardless of its particular objective, is intimate union with Jesus Christ. These signs of grace bespeak a calling to a serious practice of Christ's teachings. Each Sacrament, therefore, signifies the universal call to holiness but from a distinct perspective. For example, the immediate aim of the Eucharist is to enhance the human heart so that it becomes the heart of Christ. Analogous to the transformation of bread and wine into the Body and Blood of Christ, the Eucharist transforms the recipient into "another Christ." For another example, the immediate aim of Matrimony is to help the couple's love for each other reflect the love Jesus Christ has for his Church. All these sacramental signs serve as a call to a deeper life in Christ, which means they cannot be received as mere Catholic observance that have no bearing on everyday life. Some people enjoy the pomp and ceremony of the Sacraments—to have an extravagant party for their child's baptism or to have a big "church wedding." The Sacraments of the Church, though, are not empty ritualized milestones. They are *effective* signs. They unite us with Christ to the extent that we have the disposition to receive the graces and seek to live out our Christian vocation.

And we should desire these effects. A life of grace is a life filled with joy. Holiness, which unites us more closely to God, brings a happiness that the world cannot give; it is a joy that endures even during tribulation. The human person has God as his or her source and final goal, so all the Sacraments point to the ultimate goal of everlasting life in heaven. The Sacraments give us a share—already here on earth—in eternal life, which begins in Baptism, is strengthened in Confirmation, is nourished in the Eucharist, is regained in Penance, brings solace and strength in the Anointing of the Sick, and at the service of others in Holy Orders and Matrimony.

9. Gal 2:20.

The whole purpose of Christ's redemption was to open the gates of heaven, which were closed as a result of Original Sin and personal sin. Though each Sacrament enjoys its own perspective on our share in eternal life, it is a sign of that same joy in the next life. To reach heaven a person is required to die in the state of sanctifying grace. The Sacraments are all ordered either to put a person in the state of grace or to increase sanctifying grace in his or her soul in preparation for the Beatific Vision, which is heaven.

In this way each Sacrament points to the Paschal Mystery—Christ's work of redemption through his Passion, Death, Resurrection, and Ascension. The fundamental tenet of our faith is that Jesus Christ redeemed the world through his suffering and Death on the Cross. Each Sacrament draws from the merits of Christ's redemption. Jesus has literally bought this grace with the payment of his life, his painful Sacrifice. The Sacraments apply the effects of his redemption. We can imagine the merits of Jesus as an infinite reservoir of grace present at the foot of the Cross. To transport that grace to an individual person, metaphorically speaking, a plumbing system must be designed. The Sacraments serve as the pipeline between the merits of the redemption and the Christian soul.

Sacramental Character

The Seven Sacraments, as conduits for sanctifying grace, can transform a person so that he or she becomes increasingly like Christ himself, increasingly capable of loving God and others. Three of the Seven Sacraments, moreover, *permanently* change the person by imparting what is called an "indelible mark," or character, on the soul. This is why these three Sacraments—Baptism, Confirmation, and Holy Orders—can be received only once. (Holy Orders can be received only once for each of the degrees: deacons, priests, and bishops.) Their reception is effective once and for all.

The Latin *signaculum* was a distinguishing sign or image that set people or things aside for public functions. Legal documents were stamped with official seals or characters. During the first centuries the Fathers of the Church compared the invisible, permanent character the soul received in Baptism and Confirmation to a seal imprinted with lead or wax onto a document indicating the authority from which it came. It could be likened to the seal of a certain department of government imprinted on an envelope and letterhead.

Reflecting on the contents of the New Testament, especially the Epistle to the Hebrews, the Fathers of the Church took note of the phrase that Christ "reflects the glory of God and bears the very stamp of his nature."[10] Every baptized and confirmed Christian bears and reflects the glory of the Father in his or her union with the character of Christ through the work of the Holy Spirit. Even the most grave sin cannot cause the sacramental character to be removed. Once this character is received, the person is configured to Christ through participation in his Eternal High Priesthood. The Sacrament of Baptism, for example, through the imprint of this indelible mark, empowers a Christian through his or her sharing in Christ's Eternal High Priesthood, to join in Jesus' redemptive Sacrifice and receive the other Sacraments. The newly baptized person shares in the common priesthood of Christ, which involves personal union with him through every facet of human life. The Sacrament of Confirmation, for another example, enhances the Christian's participation in the Eternal High Priesthood of Christ through an additional character. This Sacrament assists the recipient not only in being united to Christ's redemptive sacrifice but also in proclaiming the Gospel through example and word. If needed, this Sacrament can give the Christian so much strength that he or she can give witness to Christ to the point of martyrdom.

The imprinted character in the Sacrament of Holy Orders is essentially different than the previous two. The power derived from Holy Orders enables a man to directly act in Christ's place as if Christ himself were present. This ministerial share in the Eternal High Priesthood of Christ is essentially distinct from the common priesthood shared by all baptized Christians since the ordained solely take the place of Christ in the celebration of the Sacraments. In addition to the administration of the Sacraments, the bishops—with his coworkers, the priests, and his helpers, the deacons—preach the Word of God and govern the Church in the name of Christ. Through the power of this indelible mark, a bishop or priest can forgive sins in Jesus' name. Most incredibly, a bishop or priest can change bread and wine into the Body and Blood of Christ as he re-presents Jesus' redemptive Sacrifice in the Holy Eucharist.

10. Heb 1:3.

A Sacramental Church

Jesus Christ, in his infinite wisdom and mercy, designed the Sacraments to fit human nature like a glove. As beings with a material existence, we learn, communicate, and grow through our interactions with the sensible world. As beings with a spiritual existence, though, the impact of what we learn and communicate has a deeper, spiritual effect, commensurate with our material-spiritual way of being. Since every human person's actions are an interplay between the activities of the senses and the exercise of the mind and spirit, the Sacraments function in a similar manner. The Sacraments begin with a physical substance or action accompanied by words that culminate in a spiritual effect. Just as sensation precedes the spiritual activity of thought and love, so the tangible sacramental signs precede the spiritual action in the soul.

This interplay of material and spiritual—body and soul—was instituted by Christ to confirm the goodness of the human body and of all material creation. The Catholic faith is not "disembodied." Despite the dangers of the passions of fallen humanity, which require us to have dominion over our bodies, the human body and all of creation are good. Some Eastern mystical traditions have the goal of "escaping" the body, but the goal of Christianity could not be further from this. The moral life teaches that, because of our fallen nature, the desires of our bodies can sometimes overcome our reason and cause us to sin, but the sacramental life assures us of God's plan for creation, which is its full restoration, healing, and redemption. After all, as we affirm in the Apostles' Creed, "I believe in... the resurrection of the body."[11]

The Church's mission of spreading the Gospel is intimately tied to the administering of the Sacraments. In a wider sense, though, we can talk about the Catholic Church as "sacramental." The Church herself is a type of Sacrament—a visible sign of a sacred reality. The Catholic Church also functions in a sacramental fashion. It is common to refer to the "smells and bells" of Catholic liturgy: art-covered churches, incense, music, and an emphasis on physical posture. The whole person—body and soul—participates in the liturgical worship of God in the Church.

There are many customs and practices of the Church—many traditional and some newer—that are not Sacraments but are

11. RMiss, The Order of Mass, no. 19.

referred to as "sacramentals." Like the Seven Sacraments, every sacramental includes a concrete sign and a prayer. Though these signs prepare a person to receive grace, they are not sources of sanctifying grace like the Seven Sacraments. Sacramentals were instituted not directly by Christ but by the Church over the course of her history. The effects of these signs come from the prayer of the Church.

One of the most common uses of sacramentals is crossing oneself with holy water, which is a recollection of the Blessed Trinity as well as of the gift of Baptism, fostering a desire for God's forgiveness and purification from sin. The laying on of hands, the veneration of the Cross, and the imposition of a scapular are examples of some of the many sacramentals. There are also sacramental blessings such as grace before a meal or before a trip or important task. Since all graces find their source in Our Lord's redemption, many blessings are accompanied by the Sign of the Cross over the person or object. Blessings deal with virtually every aspect of human life. For this reason, there are blessings for pregnant women, liturgical vestments, houses, and sacred objects, to name but a few.

There are also sacramentals focused on protection from the influence of the Devil. During the rituals within the Order of Baptism, for instance, there is a rite of exorcism: The oil that the deacon, priest, or bishop uses to anoint the baby's chest is a sacramental.[12] The general use of Holy Water is an ordinary means of protection against the Devil. Many Catholics have the custom of making the Sign of the Cross with Holy Water before going to bed. The graces of both Sacraments and sacramentals are derived from Christ's redemption and will always overcome the demonic forces of evil.

In addition to these and many other sacramentals of the Church, there is the practice of popular piety that spurs the faithful to praise God and petition his assistance. These practices form part of the communal prayer life of the faithful; examples include the Stations of the Cross, the recitation of the Holy Rosary, and Eucharistic and Marian processions. Many traditional devotions are typical of a given region or culture and, in most instances, arise from the people. Some forms of popular piety such as the recitation of the Holy Rosary and the Divine Mercy Chaplet are practiced by the universal Church. Other forms of popular piety are limited to a region of the world since they are derived from a certain historical or miraculous event.

12. Cf. OBap, no. 87.

For example, devotion to Our Lady of Guadalupe began with a miraculous apparition 500 years ago in Mexico. Other saints usually have an annual day of festivity in the region where that saint lived, during which veneration of and blessing with a relic of that saint might form part of the celebration.

Sacraments, sacramentals, and popular piety respond to the human need to adore, praise, and petition God by means of tangible signs. Every practice of true piety and devotion is aimed at intimate friendship and union with God the Father, God the Son, and God the Holy Spirit through the humanity of Jesus Christ. It is important that these different expressions of faith, hope, and charity be performed with love, not in a routine manner or with a superstitious spirit. It is an important aspect of our human experience that external manifestations of devotion lead to interior contemplation. If these practices are performed in such a way that the exterior, physical dimension is considered the only thing necessary, then they will bear no fruit for the soul. Making the Sign of the Cross, for example, is not a magical "ward against evil"; it must be accompanied by an interior movement of faith and love. Since the human person is composed of body and soul, we must worship and praise God with both body and soul.

The need to be fully engaged, of course, does not mean distracted or unemotional prayer and participation is pointless. As Jesus so aptly said of his disciples who could not stay awake with him in the garden of Gethsemane, "The spirit indeed is willing, but the flesh is weak."[13] We should not feel discouraged if our prayers are dry or we sometimes get distracted in prayer, even during Mass. What matters is to persevere and to keep returning to Christ to receive the graces he offers through his Church.

During our earthly participation in eternal life, we cannot sufficiently marvel at the abundance of means Jesus Christ has left us so that we can literally stay in touch with him. By internalizing the external meaning of both Sacraments and sacramentals, little by little we become transformed in Christ. This transformation gives credibility to Jesus' celebrated words: "You are the salt of the earth.... You are the light of the world."[14]

13. Mk 14:38.

14. Mt 5:13–14.

CHAPTER 12

BAPTISM: NEW LIFE IN CHRIST

The next few chapters will focus on each of the Sacraments, beginning with Baptism. The Sacrament of Baptism works a colossal miracle in our soul: It achieves the humanly impossible outcome of giving each of us a share in the life of Christ. By this union with Christ, we acquire an incredible relationship with God as a son or daughter ranked among God's definitive chosen people. If we remain faithful, an unimaginable inheritance of everlasting life awaits us in heaven.

The bylaws of this New Covenant consist in embracing the teaching of Jesus. Once we are grafted onto Christ through Baptism, we are called to grow in our union with him by means of the other Sacraments. The purpose of the rest of the Sacraments is to more deeply enhance our union with the Blessed Trinity through Jesus Christ. Baptism is the gateway to this life of grace. This Sacrament offers the forgiveness of Original Sin and personal sin, purification of the heart and soul, and elevation to the dignity of a son or daughter of God in Christ. All these perspectives on the effects of Baptism rest on the fact that Christ is the Head of his Mystical Body, the Church, of which the baptized are members.

"Baptism" is derived from the Greek *baptizein*, which means to "immerse" or "plunge." As St. Paul revealed, this immersion into water and emerging out of it symbolizes dying and rising with Christ.[1] Since Jesus' Death and Resurrection merited everlasting life once and for all, the ritual of entrance into and rising out of the water is an effective sign of sharing in Christ's Death and Resurrection. This plunging into and emerging out of the water also signifies becoming a new creation, which is why Baptism is also called the "Sacrament of rebirth." The washing, regeneration, and renewal by the Holy Spirit refers to a true spiritual rebirth.

The baptized person enters into the life of Christ, who is the Light of the World, which is why Baptism is also called "enlighten-

1. Rom 6:4.

ment." Not only does the newly baptized share in the life of Christ, but he or she also becomes a light. The *Catechism* quotes St. Gregory of Nazianzus, who uses the term "gift" in reference to Baptism. The word "gift" is especially appropriate since the soul gratuitously receives a spectacular grace to share in the divine nature. No one can merit this sanctifying grace by personal effort; it is "conferred on those who bring nothing of their own."[2] It is also called "clothing" because it covers the shame of sin, "bath" because it washes, and "seal" because it marks us as Our Lord's.[3]

Baptism in Scripture

Throughout the Old Testament the image of water is most conspicuous. In the Book of Genesis, water is depicted as a source of life for the entire physical world.[4] In addition to water, the wind blowing on the water, which was part of the creation process, would ultimately lead to the creation of life of all stripes: "The Spirit of God was moving over the face of the waters."[5] The Hebrew *ruah*—which is translated here as "Spirit"—means "wind,""breath," or "spirit," so the Sacred Author reveals a connection between the wind that moved over the surface of the waters and the work of the Holy Spirit. Since Baptism is the means of *re*-creation in Christ, the work of the "wind / Spirit" at creation is the first prefigurement of Baptism.

By observing the role of water in the history of the Hebrew people, we will grow in our appreciation and understanding of the Sacrament of Baptism. The Book of Genesis narrates the account of Noah and the ark. Because of the predominance of a sinful people, God chose to destroy them by means of severe flood waters, but God wanted to spare the few people who were not steeped in sin. Thus, God commanded Noah to construct an ark to save his chosen ones from the Flood. The entire population—except Noah and his family—perished. By means of the ark, Noah and his people survived the destructive waters of the raging Flood. The destruction of evil people by means of water serves is a prefigurement of the remission from sin and the defeat of the Devil through the waters of Baptism.

2. CCC 1216.
3. Cf. ibid.
4. Cf. Gn 1:20.
5. Gn 1:2.

The future Sacrament of Baptism, administered through the Church, is wonderfully symbolized by the ark.

Later in history, God made a covenant with the father of a people, Abraham. God promised Abraham that his descendants would be as numerous as the stars in the sky, and in return required Abraham to be faithful to his commands. The sign of this covenant was circumcision for Abraham, his sons, and all their male descendants. Entrance into the Abrahamic Covenant by circumcision is a prefigurement of entrance into the New Covenant in Christ through the Sacrament of Baptism; this comparison is quite developed in the New Testament Epistles of St. Paul. Just as circumcision of the flesh signified entrance into the status of God's chosen people, so Baptism is a "spiritual circumcision" whereby the old nature—characterized by sinful ways—is eliminated and replaced by a new life of holiness, offering entrance into Christ's Mystical Body, the Church.[6]

One of the most important prefigurements of the Sacrament of Baptism recorded in the Old Testament is the liberation of the Hebrew people from slavery in Egypt by passing through the Red Sea. This is the culmination of the Passover: The angel of death "passed over" the Israelites, and Pharaoh finally allowed them to depart. Pharaoh went back on his word, so as Moses and his people approached the Red Sea, they saw Egyptian forces in hot pursuit. Moses—at God's command—pointed his rod in the direction of the Red Sea, and its waters parted in two, leaving a path of dry ground for the Israelites to safely cross through the water. As the Egyptians pursued along the same route through the sea, the waters flowed aggressively back, drowning the entire Egyptian force, including its chariots and horses. This miraculous escape of the chosen people from slavery in Egypt through the waters of the Red Sea marks their departure to the Promised Land of freedom and prosperity.[7]

This singular event—one of the most important episodes in the history of the Hebrew people—is symbolic of Baptism. The deliverance of Israel from slavery in Egypt signifies liberation from the misery of and slavery to sin and the oppression of the Devil. The waters of Baptism, symbolized by the Red Sea, free the recipient from sin and from the sway and deceptions of the Evil One. The Egyptians, led by Pharaoh, represent the Devil and his minions, and

6. Cf. Col 2:11–13.

7. Cf. Ex 14.

thus sin, slavery, and evil are swept away by the rushing waters. The Promised Land signifies everlasting life, which can only be reached through the waters of Baptism.

Another powerful Old Testament prefigurement of Baptism is the water gushing out of the rock at Meribah. After Moses and the Israelites had passed through the Red Sea and were journeying to the Promised Land through the desert, they suffered from terrible thirst. An absence of water seemed to be leading to their demise. God instructed Moses to strike the rock at Horeb, and when he did, water gushed from the rock to quench their thirst.[8] Though this extraordinary phenomenon met a vital need for the chosen people in the literal sense, it also has tremendous spiritual value regarding both the origin and nature of Baptism. This scene conveys three symbolic references to Christ's Baptism: the striking of the rod against the rock, the rock itself, and the water.

The rod of Moses signifies the power of Jesus' Cross. The rock is a traditional symbol of Christ, as St. Paul reveals in the allegorical sense: "They drank from the supernatural Rock... and the Rock was Christ."[9] Striking the rock is also an allegorical description of Christ's Passion and Death on the Cross, which is how we can achieve everlasting life. When the soldier pierced the heart of Jesus on the Cross, Blood and water flowed from his wounded side. The Blood flowing from Christ's side signifies the Eucharist, the summit of the Sacraments, and the water signifies Baptism, the Sacrament that grants admittance to the other Sacraments. The water flowing from the side of Christ, like the water flowing from the rock in the desert, will quench our thirst for the grace of salvation and prevent the eternal death of damnation.

Even the desire for Baptism is prefigured in the Old Testament. Throughout the Old Testament—particularly in the Book of Psalms—the grace, favor, and protection of God is likened to water. The Psalmist describes the desire for God as a thirsting for water: "Like the deer that yearns for running streams, / so my soul is yearning for you, my God."[10] Again the Psalmist prays, "I stretch out my

8. Cf. Ex 17:2–7; Nm 20:2–13.

9. 1 Cor 10:4.

10. Ps 42:1; quoted in RMiss, Masses and Prayers for Various Needs and Occasions: 13. For Religious B, Communion Antiphon.

hands to thee; / my soul thirsts for thee like a parched land."[11] Or again the Psalmist prays:

> O God, thou art my God, I seek thee,
> my soul thirsts for thee;
> my flesh faints for thee,
> as in a dry and weary land where no water is.[12]

These prefiguirements of Baptism in the Old Testament come to immediate fruition at the beginning of Christ's public life. Just before the beginning of his ministry of preaching and performing miracles, Jesus went to the Jordan River, seeking to be baptized by St. John the Baptist, whose prophetic deeds included a baptism of repentance. Jesus insisted on being baptized—not because he needed it but to exemplify the Baptism that he would institute in his New Covenant. Jesus' mission on earth involved standing in the place of sinners to remove sin through his immolation on his Cross. Allowing St. John to baptize him, although sinless himself, served as a strong gesture of bearing the guilt for our sins, thereby being in solidarity with all sinners. Christ was not cleansed by St. John's baptism; the waters themselves were made holy by Christ. The baptism of Christ inaugurated a New Covenant that would take effect in each person once he or she received the Sacrament of Baptism in the New Covenant. Immediately after Jesus emerged from the waters of the Jordan, the Holy Spirit—represented by a dove—hovered over him. The Holy Spirit's presence at this scene in the Jordan hearkens back to the dawn of creation when the wind / Spirit breathed over the waters, inaugurating the creation of the world.

It is worthwhile to take a moment here to quote the Christian writer Tertullian, who died in the early third century, to illustrate the importance of the sacramental sign of water:

> Never is Christ without *water*: if, that is, He is Himself baptized in *water*;[13] inaugurates in *water* the first rudimentary displays of His power, when invited to the nuptials;[14] invites the thirsty, when He makes a discourse, to His own sempiternal *water*;[15] approves, when teaching concerning love, among works of charity, the cup

11. Ps 143:6.
12. Ps 63:1.
13. Mt 3:13–17.
14. Jn 2:1–11.
15. Jn 7:37–38.

> of *water* offered to a poor (child);[16] recruits His strength at a *well;*[17] walks over the *water;*[18] willingly crosses the *sea;*[19] ministers *water* to His disciples.[20] Onward even to the passion does the witness of baptism last: while He is being surrendered to the cross, *water* intervenes; witness Pilate's hands: when He is wounded, forth from His side bursts *water;* witness the soldier's lance![21]

Baptism is such a special Sacrament that clear references to it appear three times in Jesus' public life. First, St. John the Baptist predicts a new Baptism that will transcend his own. St. John's baptism was an invitation to repentance and a preparation for the Messiah's coming; St. John prophesied a new Baptism that would be imparted not just with water but with the Holy Spirit and fire, which signifies the charity of Christ.[22] A second reference is when Jesus, in his dialogue with Nicodemus, stipulates that entrance into his kingdom requires being "reborn" of water and the Spirit.[23] Last, upon departing from this world at the moment of his Ascension, Jesus' final instruction to his disciples was to go to people of all nations, "baptizing them in the name of the Father and of the Son and of the Holy Spirit."[24]

The Celebration of Baptism

Baptism, along with Confirmation and the Eucharist, is one of the "Sacraments of Christian Initiation." The Sacrament of Baptism is the first step in uniting our life to Christ in his Mystical Body, the Church, and opens the doorway to the life of sacramental grace. Since the purpose of Christ's Passion and Death is to rid the world of sin, Baptism—in which we die and rise with Christ—is naturally the first Sacrament to channel Jesus' grace for the forgiveness of all sins. The various rituals of the ceremony offer marvelous instructions on the Sacrament's supernatural effects on the soul. The Order of Baptism begins with tracing the Sign of the Cross on the forehead of the recipient. The graces given in all the Sacraments come from

16. Mt 10:42.
17. Jn 4:6.
18. Mt 14:25.
19. Mk 4:36.
20. Jn 13:1–12.
21. Tertullian, "*De Baptismo*," ch. 9; quoted in ANF, vol. 3.
22. Cf. Lk 3:16.
23. Cf. Jn 3:5.
24. Mt 28:19; cf. Mk 16:16.

the Cross, and Baptism opens the first door to access the merits of the redemption of Jesus Christ, obtained at this very costly price.

The proclamation of the Gospel is also prominent in the Order of Baptism. Jesus' words enjoy special significance since the desire for Baptism is an act of faith in the Gospel, and its celebration includes references to what Jesus Christ did and taught. This act of faith also includes the acceptance of everything the Church teaches since she has the grace and authority to interpret the meaning of Jesus' words. Since the virtue of faith is a theologically infused virtue, the gift of faith often comes to the recipient in anticipation of the celebration of this Sacrament. Once the Sacrament is received, however, that faith is enhanced and is there to stay unless it is voluntarily rejected. This new supernatural faith gives the new Christian the light and capacity to embrace all of God's revealed truths.

When our first parents ushered sin into the world, a certain bondage to the Devil ensued. Up to the time of Jesus' redemptive Sacrifice, the Evil One had a degree of control over the human population. The Cross and Resurrection of Jesus Christ changed that sad state of affairs by defeating the Prince of Darkness and breaking his oppressive fetters on humanity. For this reason, prayers of exorcism and a renunciation of Satan form a key part of the Order of Baptism.

The Prayer of Exorcism is immediately followed by an anointing with oil blessed for this purpose. The "Oil of Catechumens" is one of three Holy Oils blessed by the bishop every year at the Chrism Mass on the morning of Holy Thursday. "Catechumen" is derived from the Greek *katekhoumenos,* meaning "being instructed." This word describes a person studying for and awaiting Baptism (more on this in a few pages), so it is also the name of this Holy Oil. Since oil is a sign of spiritual purification and strengthening, the Church's Tradition uses anointing to signify protection against Satan's snares.

While the symbolism of anointing is rich, water, of course, is the chief baptismal sign and essential element of the Sacrament of Baptism. To continue the theological language of the previous chapter, water is the matter of the Sacrament. Though not absolutely necessary (unblessed water will still produce the full effects of Baptism), barring an emergency, the water should first be blessed for this sacramental liturgy. A prayer of blessing calls on the presence of the Holy Spirit to descend on the water to truly make it a vehicle of cleansing from sin and insertion into the life of Christ. The recitation of this prayer of blessing—with the right hand of the minister touching the water—is fitting since the accompanying prayer beautifully describes the powerful effects of Baptism by means of this water.[25] Moreover, it corresponds to the Spirit of God moving over the waters at creation, prefiguring the new creation of Baptism.

The Church has maintained from her beginning the Tradition of baptizing by bodily immersion three times in a pool of water. Though baptizing by pouring water three times over the candidate's head is more common today in the Western Church, both practices can be found. Neither method is more "right" or "wrong"; either the immersion into water or the pouring of water over the recipient's head symbolically represents dying and rising with Christ. The minister immerses / pours water over the recipient's head three times while reciting the words of Baptism: "[Name], I baptize you in the name of the Father, and of the Son, and of the Holy Spirit."[26] This triple immersion / pouring corresponds to the three Persons of the Blessed Trinity that are being invoked, because, as in all other things, every divine action is always the work of the three Persons of the Blessed Trinity.

In the administration of Baptism—whether by immersion or pouring—the water must touch the head of the person being baptized. This Sacrament signifies the cleansing of the soul, and the head is the part of the human body that most traditionally represents the seat of the soul.

The formula, "[Name], I baptize you in the name of the Father, and of the Son, and of the Holy Spirit,"[27] is the form of the Sacrament. These precise words are necessary for the Sacrament to be valid. Jesus expressly stated that his disciples should baptize "in the name of the Father and of the Son and of the Holy Spirit."[28] With such clear instructions, the Church does what Jesus said to do. Alterations to this formula have been attempted: some ministers have begun, "We baptize..." instead of, "I baptize...." Others have substituted titles for the names of three Persons of the Trinity, for

25. OBap, no. 91: "May the power of the Holy Spirit, / O Lord, we pray, / come down through your Son / into the fullness of this font, / so that all who have been buried with Christ / by Baptism into death / may rise again to life with him."

26. Ibid., no. 97. Alternatively, in the Eastern Churches, "The servant of God [Name] is baptized in the name of the Father, and of the Son, and of the Holy Spirit."

27. Ibid.

28. Mt 28:19.

example,"...in the name of the Creator, and of the Redeemer, and of the Sanctifier." The Church has consistently taught and acted against the validity of such attempts to baptize.

These minimal requirements raise an interesting fact about the Sacrament of Baptism in the eyes of the Catholic Church. All that is needed for a Baptism to be valid is water (the matter) and those words (the form), along with, as always, the proper dispositions. This means that most non-Catholic Christians are baptized because their Baptisms are perfectly valid. There is no other Sacrament that the Catholic Church accepts in this way. If a non-Catholic Christian has been baptized, then he or she is not offered Baptism when coming into full communion with the Catholic Church. What a gift it is that many non-Catholic and Catholic Christians already share some kind of communion—albeit imperfect—in Jesus Christ.

Why does the Church accept the Baptism of other Christian denominations but not the other Sacraments? As discussed in Chapter 11, the Sacrament of Baptism does not require an ordained minister or even a Catholic to perform it. Yes, the *ordinary* minister of Baptism is a bishop, priest, or deacon. And since the person is being baptized in the name of the Persons of the Blessed Trinity, it is fitting that an ordained minister celebrate Baptism. An ordained minister is set aside by God as a representative of Christ who mediates between God and his people; however, any person who uses the matter and form of Baptism—immerses / pours water while reciting the Trinitarian formula—and intends to do what the Church intends with Baptism will have validly administered Baptism. Even a non-Christian or nonbeliever can baptize in danger of death. Our Lord has given everyone this power as a way of making this important Sacrament accessible to everyone at all times.

Another important symbol included in the Order of Baptism is the putting on of a white garment. This explicitly refers to St. Paul's admonition, "Put on the Lord Jesus Christ."[29] This part of the ceremony serves to emphasize that the baptized person has become inserted into Christ's life, which is compared to a garment becoming one with the body. The white garment also serves as a marvelous image of the exalted holiness of Jesus Christ and the new Christian's call to the practice of the virtues and the pursuit of holiness.

---

29. Rom 13:14.

Another rich symbol within the Order of Baptism is the handing on of a lighted candle. A member of the recipient's family lights a candle directly from the flame of the traditionally large paschal, or Easter, candle, and he or she gives it to the newly baptized (or, for example, in the case of an infant, to one of the parents or godparents). By virtue of Baptism the new Christian is called to witness the light of Jesus Christ by radiating peace and joy. Lighting a candle off the Easter candle reminds us that Baptism involves living in the light of the Risen Christ.

Holding the lighted candle signifies a Christian's share in the life of Jesus Christ, giving us the capacity to both share and radiate his light and life to others. The first part of the Easter Vigil—the anticipatory evening celebration of the Resurrection of Jesus Christ—begins with the preparation of the paschal candle, sometimes called the Easter candle. It represents the Risen Christ as the Light of the World.[30] A dramatic part of the Easter Vigil is when, in a darkened church, the priest lights his smaller candle from the paschal candle, who in turn lights the candles of some of the faithful, who light others' candles, who light still others', until everyone's smaller candle is ablaze. The dark interior of the church is gradually and beautifully illuminated by the lighted candles. The fire on each candle burns as its wax is consumed. The wax sacrificing itself for the sake of the illuminating flame signifies Our Lord's Sacrifice for our redemption, and the fire on top of the candle signifies the charity of Christ, who is the Light of the World.

In addition to the Oil of Catechumens mentioned earlier, another Holy Oil, called "Sacred Chrism," is used for an anointing in the Order of Baptism. Sacred Chrism is olive oil perfumed with a fragrance called balsam; this Holy Oil is also blessed by the bishop at the Chrism Mass. "Chrism" is derived from the Greek *khrisma*, meaning "anointing." This name speaks directly to anointing, and Sacred Chrism is used in the Sacraments of Baptism, Confirmation, and Holy Orders.

The Threefold Mission of Priest, Prophet, and King

Anointing with oil in the Old Testament was associated with a particular calling as priest, prophet, or king. When God chose

30. Cf. Jn 8:12.

the Tribe of Levi to be priests for Israel, Aaron and his sons were anointed and consecrated.[31] In the Books of Samuel and Kings, King David and the kings who succeed him were anointed.[32] The Prophet Isaiah revealed, "The LORD has anointed me / to bring good tidings to the afflicted."[33] No one could become a priest, prophet, or king without an anointing for that mission. Before Christ the office of priest, prophet, and king were never shared by one person; the Messiah, however—the Anointed One *par excellence*—fulfilled to perfection all three of these missions. Jesus is the Eternal High Priest, the very Word of God, and the King of Heaven and Earth. Our anointing with Sacred Chrism at Baptism calls to mind that the newly baptized shares in Christ's triple office and mission as priest, prophet, and king. All lay Christians share in Christ's redemptive work, and it is worth looking more closely here at this threefold mission bestowed at Baptism.

The mission of a priest is to offer sacrifice and praise. Christ was himself both priest and victim in the perfect offering he gave to his Father on the Cross. As the Church teaches, all the ordinary activities of the lay faithful—in their families, in their labor, in their relaxation, in their rejoicing, and in their suffering—is a "spiritual offering acceptable to God."[34] Their activities must be done in the Spirit and their hardships patiently borne, but all their daily living can be offered to God and then united to the offering of Christ in the Eucharist.[35] As St. Josemaria Escriva writes:

> As Jesus, who is our Lord and Model, grows in and lives as one of us, he reveals to us that human life—your life—and its humdrum, ordinary business, have a meaning which is divine, which belongs to eternity.[36]

A prophet is called to preach the Word of God both when it is fashionable and when it is not, giving witness to the truth. Though the lay Christian is not called to preach from the pulpit or to teach on behalf of the Magisterium, he or she, too, fulfills the mission of Christ the Prophet. Every disciple of Jesus first accomplishes this task by witnessing the love of God through his or her ordinary

31. Cf. Ex 30:30; Lv 8:12.

32. Cf. 1 Sm 16.

33. Is 61:1.

34. St. John Paul II, *General Audience* (April 15, 1998), no. 2.

35. Cf. LG, no. 34.

36. St. Josemaria Escriva, *The Forge* (Princeton, NJ: Scepter Publishers, 1987), no. 688.

actions, drawing people to Christ through the joy of a life lived in Christ. There is perhaps nothing more prophetic than a virtuous life lived with joy. Pope Francis frequently called attention to this joy, the result of a personal encounter with Christ; early in his pontificate he pointed out that some of the greatest examples of Christian joy he has ever witnessed have come from people in materially poor circumstances.[37] The Pope reminded us, "Whoever wants to preach must be the first to let the word of God move him deeply and become incarnate in his daily life."[38] Such a life is *prophetic* because it gives witness to the fact that only in Christ can a person be truly free and happy.

The prophetic mission does not end with the witness of a life well lived. Every Christian is called to defend the truth and to teach the moral law and the Gospel not only by good example but also by verbal instruction, capitalizing on all occasions. "Always be prepared to make a defense to any one who calls you to account for the hope that is in you."[39] This admonition, taken from the Church's first Pope, summarizes the prophetic work of every Christian, who must explain the reason for his or her joy and selfless love.[40]

The task of a king is to rule. In their kingly mission, the baptized are called to a life of holiness by which they "rule" over themselves and overcome sin. The more we are able to govern ourselves, the better we are able to love and serve our neighbor. The good king or queen, after all, is the one who works for the good of his or her people and not for personal power or glory. This self-mastery makes it possible to "rule" as Christ, "that King for whom to serve is to reign."[41] Christ's kingship is an authority of service and humility. The more we show love and serve those in need, the more we reign with Christ.

The kingly mission of the baptized also requires them to work to direct society toward Christ. Christians are called to restore creation to its original value and help to create "a kingdom of truth and life, a kingdom of holiness and grace, a kingdom of justice, love and peace."[42] How this task is accomplished varies depending on a per-

37. EG, no. 7.
38. Ibid., no. 150.
39. 1 Pt 3:15.
40. Cf. LG, no. 35.
41. Ibid., no. 36.
42. Ibid.

son's circumstances: vocation, talents, family life, level of education, and everything else. The great bulk of kingly work is entrusted to the lay faithful since they are most engaged in the everyday world. Accepting the obligations of their kingly mission means that the work of Catholic social teaching—promoting justice and peace; working for a just distribution of goods; defending the dignity of the human person; overcoming racial, economic, and national disparity; etc.—falls primarily on lay Christians. In the everyday circumstances of family life, the workplace, the culture, politics, and every other realm, they are "led by the spirit of the Gospel [to] work for the sanctification of the world from within as a leaven."[43] The Sacred Chrism is a bountiful sign in the Order of Baptism.

Recipient of Baptism

Every human person who has been born, regardless of age—adult and infant alike—is a candidate for Baptism. In the case of an adult, it is most advantageous to spend a period of time in preparation for this important Sacrament. Baptism is much more than a formal religious and cultural rite of passage; rather, it is a serious commitment to wholeheartedly embrace the Gospel message. In the case of an infant, the parents must be committed to his or her ongoing instruction in the faith.

The extraordinary graces of Baptism build on knowledge of the faith and a grounded moral life. For the grace of Baptism to fully transform the candidate, he or she must be well disposed through both knowledge and practice. Baptism is certainly not a form of magic that automatically changes and transforms the person regardless of personal cooperation. Like each Sacrament, for Baptism to have its intended effect, the recipient must have good will and make a serious commitment to practice the Christian faith. The graces of Baptism would be greatly hampered if the candidate saw no need to attend Mass or approached Baptism with hardly any knowledge of the Catholic faith. Hence, the usual process of preparation for Baptism entails starting out first as a catechumen.

Recall that a catechumen is a person studying for and awaiting Baptism; this is why the Anointing before Baptism, as described a few pages ago, uses the Oil of Catechumens. Becoming a catechumen entails enrolling as a candidate for Baptism, engaging

43. Ibid., no.31.

in "catechesis," from the Greek for "instruction." The status of a catechumen reflects a serious desire to be baptized and the firm willingness to invest the time and effort in doctrinal and spiritual preparation.

Although instruction and personal commitment are necessary for catechumens who have reached the age of reason, it is still highly appropriate and much desired to baptize infants. Since the redemption of Christ is for all people, infants are understood to have an implicit desire for Baptism, but they still need to be instructed in the faith. Parents of infants assure the Church that the child will be brought up and instructed in the basic tenets of Catholicism. Babies should not be baptized indiscriminately or just for the sake of a gathering of family and friends. Out of respect for the dignity of the Sacrament, there should be sufficient probability that the child will have a Catholic upbringing. There needs to be a moral certainty that the baptismal graces will take effect since grace builds on nature. This assurance that the child will be brought up in the faith is given by the parents of the child and then *doubly* guaranteed by the godparents. It would be an abuse of the Sacrament to baptize a child who will most likely not be raised in the Catholic faith.

From the earliest times in Christian history, it has been strongly recommended to baptize infants as soon as possible. Considering the many graces and gifts offered by this Sacrament, it would be unfair to the child to wait until he or she is of mature age to decide whether or not to be baptized. It is not in the least a violation of human freedom to guide a growing child to be endowed with all the spiritual gifts for salvation and everlasting life. In a parallel to physical needs, it would be a misguided notion of freedom to refuse to feed, bathe, comfort, and clothe a child until he or she could request it explicitly! Parents are careful to provide their children with the best physical care, mental education, and character training. Such parental care strongly contributes to an enhancement of freedom—certainly not its repression. Should they not do as much for the health of their children's souls?

St. Augustine, the great theologian of the fourth and fifth centuries, wrote about the effects of his own "delayed" Baptism in his autobiography. Though infant Baptism has been the norm throughout Church history, many in his day were misguided by delaying Baptism until adulthood or even until the moment of death. The rationale was to cleanse a person of sin late in life—after getting all his or her sins "out of the way"—to better guarantee entrance into heaven. This was, of course, risky business. As St. Augustine wisely noted, "In regard to bodily health we do not say: 'Let him inflict more wounds on himself, for he is not yet cured.'" St. Augustine, whose life went dramatically off the Christian path in adolescence, strongly opposed the delay of his own Baptism; he felt cheated out of the graces to help him avoid sin:

> How much better then, had I been at once healed; and then, by my friends' and my own, my soul's recovered health had been kept safe in Thy keeping who gavest it. Better truly.[44]

Baptism and Salvation

Our Lord has made it abundantly clear that Baptism is necessary for salvation. Only through the application of the merits of the redemption through Baptism can a person be forgiven of Original Sin and be given a share in eternal life. Only divine power, in response to Jesus Christ's redemptive Sacrifice, can simultaneously cleanse and elevate the soul. The grace of Baptism is totally gratuitous: It can never be merited or earned. Knowing Baptism's invaluable benefits, it would be seriously wrong to avoid it.

This tenet of faith poses a very serious question, though. In light of this teaching, is the possibility of eternal life put in jeopardy for the great majority of the world's unbaptized population? As in all areas of Catholic teaching, both faith and reason need to work together. God, being all-powerful, does not have his hands tied by the need to receive the Sacraments; in other words, while *we* might be bound to seek out the Sacraments, *God's* intervention is not in the least restricted to the administration of the Sacraments. God can forgive sins, if he wills, outside of the parameters of the Sacrament of Baptism (or outside of the Sacrament of Penance and Reconciliation).

How are these acknowledgments of God's freedom compatible with Christ's Revelation that Baptism is the necessary means to salvation? The Church teaches that the Sacrament of Baptism can produce its effects even if not actually administered or received; these two ways are called "Baptism of Blood" and "Baptism of Desire."

---

44. CSA, Book I.

In the case of a person who dies for his or her faith in Christ before Baptism, he or she is said to have received Baptism of Blood. Such a person not only benefits from the effects of Baptism but has also reached holiness. To die for Christ presupposes a powerful desire for Baptism that leads to receiving its effects.

Baptism of Desire similarly consists in either an explicit (external or obvious) or implicit (hidden) desire for Baptism. For instance, if a catechumen were to die before the celebration of Baptism, he or she would certainly benefit from the effects of Baptism without being baptized; this would be an explicit desire. Another person might receive the salutary effects of Baptism by striving to lead a good moral life. The rationale behind this conclusion rests on a sincere disposition to identify with God's will, clearly demonstrated by a consistent moral life. This habitual effort to live according to the standards of the natural law certainly reflects an implicit desire to follow Christ. Such a person would most likely want to be baptized if the occasion would present itself and he or she had access to the knowledge of the Christian faith, so the Church teaches that he or she can receive the merits of Baptism through implicit desire.

Despite the teaching that the actual reception of the Sacrament of Baptism is, in some cases, not required, the grace to live the moral law in a habitual way still comes to every person through Christ and his Mystical Body, the Church. The truth that salvation comes exclusively from Christ and his Church has not changed whatsoever. Since the grace of God is the only way to integrate the principles of the objective moral law into a human life, the Church teaches that living an integral moral life reveals the grace of salvation. Since this grace comes exclusively through the merits of Christ—the graces of which are administered by the Church—it is still by Christ that all people are saved.

Recall from Chapter 9 that the possibility of salvation outside of visible communion with the Church does not circumvent the tremendous advantages of receiving Baptism. The benefits of sacramental Baptism are enormous: The person knows with certainty that he or she has been grafted onto the life of Christ. The possibility for the reception of the rest of the Sacraments and their graces alone makes the reception of Baptism extremely advantageous. Yes, every baptized Christian must still struggle against sin and grow in holiness, but this struggle, as St. Augustine noted a few pages ago, is greatly aided by the graces of Baptism. Only the actual reception of Baptism imprints the indelible mark that signifies union with Christ, the Eternal High Priest. Baptism of Desire *presumes desire*, meaning the "recipient" would *rejoice* to receive the Sacrament of Baptism given the opportunity and understanding.

The Church has not made an explicit declaration concerning children who die without Baptism. What happens to infants who die before birth through miscarriage or abortion? We know that God is infinitely merciful, with a special affection for children.[45] Jesus died for every human person precisely because he ardently desires the salvation of all. Though we cannot point to a dogmatic pronouncement regarding the death of infants without Baptism, we can be morally certain that Our Lord's standard procedure is to lavish mercy on those infants:

> The magisterium of the Church has shown an increasing openness to the possibility of the salvation of unbaptised infants, and the *sensus fidelium*[46] seems to have been developing in the same direction. Christians constantly experience, most powerfully in the liturgy, Christ's victory over sin and death,[47] God's infinite mercy, and the loving communion of the saints in heaven, all of which increases our hope.[48]

Effects of Baptism

The Catholic Church has taught from time immemorial that on account of Adam and Eve's first sin, every person born into the world is in need of redemption from the inherited Original Sin. Because the nature of every human being is ultimately derived from the wounded human nature of Adam, every human person—except the Blessed Virgin Mary by means of her Immaculate Conception, presented in Chapter 6—is born with the stain of Original Sin. Only the redemptive power of Jesus Christ can remove Original Sin. No effort, good deed, or life of stoic virtue can overcome being born with a wounded nature. Even infants require this cleansing. We tend

45. Mt 18:14; 19:14.

46. The supernatural sense of the faithful.

47. "Christ is risen from the dead. By death he conquered death, and to those in the grave he granted life" (*Easter Troparion* of the Byzantine liturgy). This paschal verse is sung in the Byzantine tradition many times on each of the forty days from Easter to the Ascension. It is, thus, the principal Easter hymn.

48. International Theological Commission, *The Hope of Salvation for Infants Who Die Without Being Baptised* (April 19, 2007), no. 78.

to talk about the "innocence of babes" because they have not yet done anything wrong. But St. Augustine speculated that infants are the best proof of Original Sin, crying and fussing to get their way! We only smile at their fits and tantrums because we trust that they will outgrow their bad behavior.[49] They are not culpable because they do not know what they are doing, but their behavior demonstrates the inherent selfishness of Original Sin. Everyone stands in need of purification through Baptism. Though some of the effects of Baptism have already been discussed above, it is worth considering them again comprehensively.

As water is commonly designated for washing and cleansing, it is fitting that the sacramental waters of Baptism are the effective sign that actually washes away Original Sin and other personal sins. The waters of Baptism are like an all-powerful soap that can remove any spiritual impurity left by sin. Baptism leaves the soul sparkling clean.

On the natural level water is indispensable for the birth and growth of new life. The waters of Baptism are the indispensable entryway into the new supernatural life in Christ. The supernatural life consists in sharing in Christ's life through the gift of sanctifying grace. The developmental changes caused by water in natural life are also reflected in the waters of Baptism, which opens the recipient to a life of grace. Baptism is a vehicle for the capacity for growth through many conversions toward the goal of loving as Jesus loved.

Water cleanses, refreshes, and renews—but also destroys. The Old Testament reports the destructive power of water in the great Flood and the destruction of the Egyptian army in their attempt to cross the Red Sea. The violence of raging waters is aimed at destroying anyone opposing God's will, as in the case of the sinful people of Noah's time and the Egyptians' evil pursuit of the Hebrew people. The slavery of the Hebrews under Pharaoh symbolizes the Evil One who held humanity under slavery to sin. The Prayer of Exorcism and the Renunciation of Sin within the Order of Baptism convey Baptism's power to effect liberation from Satan. The grace of Baptism assures the newly baptized that the Devil will never get the upper hand. The destructive capacity of water also symbolizes our own death to sin: in Baptism the recipient dies and rises again with Christ.

49. Cf. CSA, Book I.

Baptism gratuitously puts the recipient in the state of sanctifying grace. The state of grace elevates human nature and gives it a participation in the divine nature. This new sharing in the life of Christ gives the recipient the raised status of a child of God. Through Baptism people obtain a new way to relate to God the Father; this relationship is not best described as "creature to Creator" but rather as "son or daughter to a Father." Being a child of God also involves the indwelling of the Holy Spirit—the same Spirit who elevates the soul, uniting it to Christ. The Christian, born anew in union with Christ as a child of God the Father by the power of the Holy Spirit, is now a host to the life of the Blessed Trinity.

This sanctification of human nature involves the infusion of the theological virtues of faith, hope, and charity. Now the Christian can know God with his very knowledge and hope in his mercy and everlasting life. He or she acquires charity, which gives the capacity to love God and others with the heart of Jesus Christ. Through the exercise of the theological virtues, every Christian can become more and more like Christ. In addition to the infusion of the theological virtues, a whole array of moral virtues is infused. This does not at all imply that the newly baptized has all the habits of moral virtue without lifting a finger; these infused moral virtues are inclinations that only evolve into full-fledged virtues through perseverance and the repetition of action. In this struggle the baptized are again supported by the graces of the Sacrament. Baptism is tantamount to the anointing of the Holy Spirit, and so, in addition to the infused virtues, the gifts of the Holy Spirit are given to facilitate the practice of virtue and the quest for holiness.

Every baptized Christian is a member of the Mystical Body of Christ. Being part of Christ's Mystical Body is analogous to the organs and appendages of a physical body being connected to the head. Just as there is an organic unity in the anatomy and physiology of a human body, so the members of the Body of Christ are united to each other through sharing in the life of Christ, the Head of his Mystical Body. Hence, as mentioned in Chapter 9, when one member progresses in holiness, it redounds throughout the whole Body. The opposite is true as well: When one of the members fails, the whole body suffers.

Finally, it bears repeating that being grafted onto Christ's Mystical Body results in specifically sharing in three facets of Christ's mission as priest, prophet, and king. This share in Christ's triple office is exhibited in the sacramental seal that comes with the reception of Baptism. This indelible mark, or character, is an invisible insignia that the baptized belongs to Christ. This mark remains on the soul not only in this life but throughout eternity.

These wonderful truths about Baptism reveal a universal call to holiness. This extraordinary insertion into the life of Christ is meant to initiate a steady growth in holiness. It would certainly be an impoverishment of the Sacrament to simply celebrate it as if it were a mere traditional event or rite of passage; it is meant to be the driving force to a life of holiness and apostolate. Every Christian finds his or her hope in answering the call to holiness that flows from the Sacrament of Baptism. The baptized should recall their baptismal gifts with profound gratitude, seeking always to live up to the graces they have received.

CHAPTER 13

CONFIRMATION: ANOINTED IN THE HOLY SPIRIT

The urgent need to spread the light of Christ to a world in spiritual darkness makes a Sacrament like Confirmation especially meaningful. In the earliest years of Christianity, it was patently clear that divine intervention was crucial for the first evangelizers to effectively draw people to Christ. This divine intervention by means of the Sacrament of Confirmation is as equally vital today as it was in the first centuries of the nascent Church. The heart of the Christian vocation is to bring the Gospel message to everyone. This feat certainly requires the special power that comes from Confirmation when the Holy Spirit pours out his graces and gifts upon those anointed.

In a world pining for the consolation and healing of Christ's Word and grace, an ardent need arises for people who can deliver Christ's message to others. Ignorance of God's love and the subsequent despair over the emptiness of the fleeting goods of this world has become the norm rather than the exception. The self-inflicted damage to people due to both an indifference to and rejection of God's Law calls for immediate, urgent assistance. It is tragic that most people do not realize the profound healing, hope, and joy intimately linked with Christ. This generalized alienation from God, through a refusal of God's invitation for a relationship, or just the simple ignorance and lack of exposure to the rudiments of the Christian faith call for a mobilization of modern disciples of Christ who will take on the sweet burden of introducing many to Jesus. The widespread failure to know that Jesus is the Son of God who was made man and died for our sins must serve as a powerful incentive for every Christian to teach others about Jesus Christ.

THE TASK OF EVANGELIZATION

So many well-intentioned people believe that they more than sufficiently fulfill their Christian calling by practicing devotions—and leave it at that. They spend their time at prayer and believe their discipleship is fulfilled. Others feel that the heart of their Christian witness consists in combatting the current moral ills that afflict society. Commitment to promoting the right to life or the sacredness of marriage is of paramount importance, but more must be done. Both spiritual devotions and serious moral causes play a significant role in the Christian life, but they can never replace the sweet obligation to introduce others to Christ. Jesus commissioned his disciples to bring the whole world to him by first starting with their city of origin: "You shall be my witnesses in Jerusalem and in all Judea and Samaria and to the end of the earth."[1] The task will not be completed until the Good News of the Gospel reaches every nook and cranny of this world.

That immediate objective of introducing people within the surrounding areas of Jerusalem to the Gospel, though very challenging, may have seemed somewhat attainable. Taking this message to the very ends of the earth, however, could have come across as an adventure in reckless insanity. It appeared to be doomed to failure since almost every aspect of the Gospel message flew in the face of the mores of the ancient world. The moral character of the Roman Empire was at a very low point, marked by unbridled hedonism and violence. Power and pleasure were the primary goals of existence for most. The superlative ideals of Jesus' teaching—especially on the virtues of humility, chastity, and charity—would be totally foreign concepts since they radically contradicted the collective lifestyles of people in the ancient world. Adding to the hardships awaiting the first Christians were cultural and linguistic differences characterizing the vast areas that needed to be traveled. But what is humanly impossible is divinely possible, and Twelve Apostles fearlessly set out with faith in God's assistance. The disciples would undergo a profound transformation whereby they were likened to Jesus Christ, and what seemed impossible became possible.

The promise of special divine assistance to Jesus' disciples in their efforts to extend the Gospel would prove successful. Two millennia of history attests to the extraordinary penetration of Christianity deep into every continent of the planet. How were the first evangelists capable of even attempting to fulfill such a task? How did a handful of men and women transform their entire culture? Jesus reassured his disciples: "You shall receive power when the Holy

1. Acts 1:8.

Spirit has come upon you."[2] In Chapter 8 of this book we read how, on the day of Pentecost, those gathered were filled with the Holy Spirit and immediately turned from hiding in the Upper Room to boldly preaching Christ to all those gathered—and 3000 people chose to be baptized.[3] The effect of the Holy Spirit is like a spiritual magnetic force attracting others to Jesus Christ.

In a similar way, at Confirmation the Holy Spirit unites himself to every disciple so that he or she will become likened to Jesus Christ, sharing in his wisdom and love. Without losing their personalities, the new evangelizers will share the common denominator of Christ's heart. The lives of the saints who have especially allowed the Holy Spirit to do his work in the intimacy of their souls have made Christ very real to all the people who encountered them. The arrival of this divine Person will give the new Christian the ability to witness and preach the Gospel in any kind of environment.

Undoubtedly, the trouble awaiting the evangelizer can be quite overwhelming and discouraging—but throughout the ages, the Holy Spirit has given Jesus' disciples an indomitable love and courage that has overcome all odds. What leaves the spectator of history in awe is that the early Christians made major inroads in changing the prevailing pagan culture. The peoples of the ancient world were converted to Christ in an environment that was extremely hostile to the Gospel message. The power of the Holy Spirit has not changed. The contemporary apostle of Christ can repeat what was done in the Roman Empire millennia ago because the same special assistance from the Holy Spirit that came to the Apostles at Pentecost is given through the Sacrament of Confirmation.

The real challenge, however—surpassing the inherent difficulties of a skeptical and hedonistic culture—is the lack of personnel who faithfully mirror the life of Jesus Christ. If a person is docile to the promptings of the Holy Spirit, he or she will find that this divine Person packs a strong spiritual and evangelical punch. The person who is especially receptive becomes, in the words of Jesus, "the light of the world."[4] That person can penetrate the words of Jesus, explain them cogently, and incarnate them in his or her life. Being the light of the world is tantamount to being an up-and-coming saint.

2. Acts 1:8.

3. Cf.Acts 2.

4. Mt 5:14.

As in every age, but especially now as the Church takes on the formidable task of the New Evangelization, the modern Christian is summoned to a high level of holiness. Holiness, in the eyes of the Church, is not equated to only devotional acts like prayer and fasting, though these are necessary to grow in holiness. Holiness is not a radical departure from the world, though some very holy people are called by God to that lifestyle. Holiness, in the eyes of the Church, is perfection in charity. It can be pursued under every circumstance and in every manner of life. "Grow where you're planted," as the saying goes, but the disciple of Christ must now give a witness of habitual, genuine joy and love that has the power to prove that Jesus is the Way, the Truth, and the Life. In today's culture, with its staggering crisis of truth and hope, the Christian needs more than ever the powerful graces of the Holy Spirit (derived from Confirmation) that served the Early Church so effectively.

The incredible events of Pentecost (described more fully in Chapter 8 of this book) are supernatural phenomena meant to last until the end of time. The Descent of the Holy Spirit continues in many hidden ways but most directly through the Sacrament of Confirmation. Along with Baptism and the Holy Eucharist, Confirmation is one of the three Sacraments of Christian Initiation. Through the sacramental seal of Confirmation, the recipient becomes more united to the Church and is given a greater capacity to witness and profess the Catholic faith, even under very difficult circumstances. This completion of the grace of Baptism provides the recipient with gifts to proclaim the Christian faith, mostly by replicating Christ's love within very personal circumstances.

This demonstration of the heart of Christ includes the courage to speak about Christ and his teachings in both favorable and unfavorable situations. At times, this profession of faith will involve a charitable defense of objective tenets of the moral law even amid possible hostile reactions. A person might refuse to follow his or her friends in an immoral activity, change the subject when a conversation becomes impure, or stand up for the inalienable rights of all people on the margins, including those not yet born. It might be as simple as correcting someone who has a false view of Christians. Not everyone is called to preach like St. Peter preaches or to suffer like St. Paul suffered, but every baptized Christian is given the threefold mission of Christ to be priest, prophet, and king—and will therefore face opportunities to give an account for what he or she believes. Confirmation completes the work of Baptism by strengthening and completing those first graces, making the recipient more capable to live his or her mission in the world.

The Order of Confirmation

The remote celebration of the Sacrament of Confirmation, like Baptism, begins with the blessing of Sacred Chrism by the bishop at the Chrism Mass. The requirement to use Sacred Chrism is a sign that Confirmation associates us with the entire Church, represented by the bishop of the diocese. The work of professing and defending the faith by building up the Kingdom of God on earth is not a solitary job. Every person who takes up this challenge does his or her work as a member of the Mystical Body of Christ.

Though one of the rites in the Order of Baptism is an anointing with Sacred Chrism, Confirmation completes and perfects this first anointing. Sacred Chrism functions as a sign in Baptism, but it is not the essential *matter* like it is in Confirmation. The anointing with Sacred Chrism in Confirmation creates a more intimate sharing in Christ's life as priest, prophet, and king as the person receives a further outpouring of the Holy Spirit in union with Jesus Christ, the Anointed One. In this case, the oil carries the specific meaning of a full consecration to serving Christ as a soldier who will fight to transform the world according to God's plan and bring others the Gospel. The word "soldier" is intentionally used by the Church, but it is not meant to encourage a combative or confrontational attitude; rather, it is meant to highlight the fortitude necessary to combat evil and spread joy and peace. The Law of Christ is the New Law of Love; through charity and exquisite respect for the dignity of every person, the Christian draws others to the Gospel message.

In Confirmation the Sacred Chrism (oil) takes on added dimensions. In the Old Testament oil signified a certain wealthy abundance expressed in joy. Oil also pointed to purification since it was used to cleanse the body before and after bathing. Athletes of old covered their bodies with oil to loosen up their muscles so they would be more nimble and compete effectively. From time immemorial, oil served as a healing ointment for cuts, scrapes, and bruises. Even in modern times, first aid includes oil-based topical medicines. Oil also enhances beauty by producing a shimmering radiance. Finally, the fragrance given off by the balsam in Sacred Chrism points to the

Christian's spiritual union with Jesus Christ; in the words of St. Paul: "We are the aroma of Christ to God."[5] Such an array of meanings of strength, healing, and beauty is why oil is a most fitting sign for Confirmation.

All these meanings of oil signify the actual effect on the soul upon receiving the Sacrament of Confirmation, for they describe the multifaceted work of the Holy Spirit. This functional diversity of oil reveals the kind of transformation that will occur, provided there is a willing correspondence to grace. As we saw in Baptism and with all the Sacraments, grace is a free gift; it is not a magic trick. The gifts of the Holy Spirit work in conjunction with the virtues, which must be practiced and lived to take root and grow in a person's life and actions. To continue with the imagery of a soldier, the gifts of the Holy Spirit are the "arms" of the Christian soldier[6]—but soldiers will not improve at using their weapons if they never enter the battlefield.

Since Confirmation completes the graces and gifts received in Baptism, the proper recipient of this Sacrament must already have been baptized. Until the person is confirmed, his or her initiation into the life of Christ's story will be rendered incomplete. The spiritual life and work of evangelization will be stunted. In the Early Church it was common for candidates to receive all three of the Sacraments of Christian Initiation at the same time—Baptism, Confirmation, and Eucharist. In the Eastern Churches, Confirmation is administered by a bishop or priest immediately after Baptism regardless of the recipient's age. In the Western Church, Confirmation is usually reserved for the bishop, which typically means it is received later in time. We know from observation the age of a person's body does not necessarily correspond to the maturity of the soul. Though the body may be young in years, the soul could very well reflect the gravity of a mature adult. In fact, children frequently give the best witness to a life of faith, and many have willingly died for their faith out of deep love for and fidelity to Christ.

Like Baptism, to receive full benefit from the Sacrament of Confirmation, the recipient should receive age-appropriate preparation and be offered ongoing instruction to grow in the faith. Instruction before Confirmation should include a Christian's duties and respon-

5. 2 Cor 2:15.

6. Eph 6:10–18.

sibilities. Every recipient should cultivate an eagerness to profess and witness the faith. This desire to evangelize goes far beyond the realm of a mere vague agreement to stand up for the teachings of the Gospel. At the heart of being a good Christian disciple is a robust life of prayer since the knack for leading people to Christ is the direct fruit of a flourishing spiritual life. The preparation for Confirmation should, therefore, include a greater union with Christ through reading and reflecting on the Gospel and a growth in love for God through recourse to the Sacraments of Penance and the Eucharist.

To derive benefit from Confirmation, the recipient should be in the state of grace. It is highly recommended that the person should make a good confession (cf. Chapter 15) as immediate preparation for receiving the gifts of the Holy Spirit. The effort to connect with Jesus Christ in prayer and in the Sacraments will lead to the proper dispositions for the reception of the Holy Spirit. We must remember that there was a ten-day period of deep prayer that marked the immediate preparation of the Apostles for the reception of the Holy Spirit at Pentecost. The Holy Spirit greatly assists the disciple of Christ to the degree that he or she cultivates the best dispositions possible to welcome this divine guest.

In the Western Church, the bishop is the ordinary minister of the Sacrament of Confirmation, though he can delegate this power to his priests for a special reason.[7] At Confirmation, after the recipients have renewed their baptismal vows, the bishop extends his hands over all those about to be confirmed. From apostolic times, this gesture has signified the outpouring of the Holy Spirit and the transmission of the Holy Spirit's gifts and graces. It is especially fitting that the bishop perform this liturgical action since he enjoys the fullness of the priesthood. A priest receives his power and permission to act from his bishop, but it is the bishop who is the direct successor to the Apostles. To represent Jesus Christ, the Eternal High Priest, who enjoys the plenitude of the Holy Spirit, the bishop is the best sign of that fullness when transmitting the Holy Spirit in the Person of Christ.

This action of the laying on of the hands was performed from the very outset of Christianity. The New Testament, in the Acts of the Apostles as well as the Epistles of St. Paul, both mention the laying on of the hands in addition to the reception of Baptism:

---

7. OCon, nos. 7–8.

> [The Apostles St. Peter and St. John] laid their hands on them and they received the Holy Spirit.[8]
>
> It is God who establishes us with you in Christ.... [H]e has put his seal upon us and given us his Spirit in our hearts as a guarantee.[9]

This liturgical act is a continuation of Pentecost, albeit without the dramatic appearance of tongues of fire. What *is* imparted is a completion of the bestowal of the gifts of the Holy Spirit coupled with a spiritual seal establishing the recipient as an apostle empowered to witness, proclaim, and heroically live out the Gospel. This gives every disciple of Christ the spiritual wherewithal to proclaim and defend the truth of the Gospel with zeal.

The essential sacramental celebration of Confirmation in the Western Church consists in anointing the forehead with oil while the minister lays his hand on the recipient's head. The form is, "[Name], be sealed with the Gift of the Holy Spirit."[10] In the Eastern Churches, the anointing includes the forehead, eyes, nose, ears, lips, chest, back, hands and feet. Concluding the Order of Confirmation is a sign of peace between the minister and the newly confirmed Christian. This gesture of fraternity is symbolic of the person's union with the bishop and all the faithful.

The Gifts of the Holy Spirit

The gifts of the Holy Spirit, first received at Baptism and perfected at Confirmation, can be compared to a sail on a rowboat. A person can sail to his or her destination by rowing alone, but it takes much unnecessary effort; hoisting a sail would add to the speed and efficiency of the rowing and lessen the energy needed to row. The gifts of the Holy Spirit facilitate the quest to be united to God and profess the Catholic faith. Without these gifts, Christian growth would be much more labor intensive. In Baptism the Holy Spirit grafts the recipient into the life of Christ, and in Confirmation, in addition to imparting a greater union with Christ, facilitates spreading the faith to others in both word and deed.

The gifts of the Holy Spirit were revealed by the Prophet Isaiah: wisdom, understanding, counsel, fortitude, knowledge, piety, and

8. Acts 8:17.
9. 2 Cor 1:21–22.
10. OCon, no. 27. Alternatively, in the Eastern Churches, "The seal of the Gift of the Holy Spirit."

fear of the Lord.[11] These gifts are at the service of professing the Gospel message and persevering in a life of virtue and holiness; rhetorical devices, oratorical skills, and academic prowess are not among these special gifts. This powerful infusion of the Holy Spirit is at the service of revealing the face of Christ by both example and word. Ideally, the presence of the Holy Spirit in a person should catch the attention of others. Every disciple of Christ should be noticed for having an uncanny love for others, upright life of integrity, and ability to explain Christ and his teachings in a convincing way.

Wisdom is the gift of the Holy Spirit that assists the Christian in seeing God's love and intelligence as the ultimate cause behind creation and every person's life. This gift prompts an acknowledgment that God is the ultimate fulfillment of the human person. A rejection of God and his Commandments would usher in sadness and an interior emptiness, so wisdom brings about a clearer vision of God that leads to a deeper love for him. The realization that all of creation mirrors the eternal wisdom of God provokes deep respect and love for what is behind that colossal beauty and goodness. Through the prism of wisdom, suffering ceases to be simply a bout of misfortune but rather an opportunity to share in the cross of Jesus and "the wisdom of God."[12] St. Francis of Assisi saw the whole cosmos as one huge sacramental of divine wisdom. He regarded the sun as a symbol of Jesus, the Light of the World; a lamb as a representation of the Lamb of God; a stream of water as a reminder of everlasting life. Whether it is through the Cross or the beauty of God's creation, the gift of wisdom draws us to a deeper contemplation of God. This divine wisdom helps people direct their affairs and the world around them according to God's plan.

Understanding is the gift of the Holy Spirit that assists the Christian, already endowed with the light of faith, to penetrate the mysteries of faith more profoundly. The Holy Spirit can be compared to a private tutor who gives personal instruction on the subject of the faith; consequently, the student of the faith will have a firmer grip and command of the subject matter. To profess the Gospel more convincingly, every disciple of Christ must truly understand its mysteries insofar as possible to explain it in such a way that it gives a certain intellectual satisfaction to the listener.

11. Cf. Is 11:2–3.

12. 1 Cor 1:21.

Counsel is the gift of the Holy Spirit that illuminates the Christian mind, which provides light for discerning God's will in particular situations. The disciple of Christ needs to choose courses of action that lead to salvation and give glory to God, usually within the ordinary circumstances of everyday life. These possible actions are meant to serve as concrete pathways that lead to holiness and more faithful discipleship. This could be the formulation of a resolution to spend some quiet time in prayer or to spend more time with family rather than so much at work. This gift is also vital for advising others in making decisions and choices that would lead to a greater union with God. When a person seeks to fulfill God's plan in his or her life, the gift of counsel is essential.

Fortitude is the gift that contributes to a Christian's ability to profess the faith with loving clarity. Every disciple of Christ will find many opportunities—at work, at home, with friends, and in every situation—to kindly state religious and moral convictions amid strong opposition. Fortitude strikes at the heart of the Holy Spirit's work. In every age including the present time, courage as well as humility are vital for living and proclaiming the truth. The truth, at times, can produce a negative reaction exhibited in ridicule or accusations of intolerance, narrow-mindedness, or other unjust labels. In many eras and in many parts of the world, the reaction to Christians' presence has resulted in grisly violence and loss of life. Even though most Christians will not have occasion to die for their faith, they may be called to sacrifice their popularity or reputation because of their moral integrity and clear positions on the truth. Often, simply doing the right thing will come at a high price of losing friends, a job, or facing mockery.

Knowledge is the gift of the Holy Spirit that gives the Christian a greater understanding of the created world and where it falls within the divine plan. In the work of evangelization, it is fitting that the evangelizer transmit the truth that the created goods of this world are the means to lead people to God and to serve others. This gift helps every person see that the affairs of his or her family, profession, and social relationships form the tapestry of God's plan and the arena to put the teachings of Jesus into practice. Everyone is called to give glory to God by working well, loving his or her family and friends, and serving those in need. Knowledge helps a person judge rightly and keep to the path of justice.

Piety is the gift of the Holy Spirit that accentuates the Christian's sense of connection with God the Father through Jesus Christ. In practice, it leads us to a greater awareness that we are infinitely loved by God as his children. An immediate ramification of sensing the infinite love of God is the realization that everything works out for the best and nothing simply ends in tragedy. People are drawn to Christ when his disciples clearly demonstrate that they are unconditionally loved by God, as recent Popes have done so well at World Youth Days.

Fear of the Lord, which is mentioned often throughout the Old and the New Testaments, is the gift of the Holy Spirit characterized by a fear of separating oneself from God. It does not consist in apprehension over God's punishment or his disfavor toward us; rather, it is a fear born out of so great a love that the disciple of Christ dreads the thought of displeasing the one who has so loved us first. Christian witness, which consists in the charity of Christ, finds its inspirational force in this gift. An outcome of fear of the Lord is beautifully expressed in habitual piety and kindness to others since love for God and neighbor is what gives God most glory. This good example is usually expressed in the body language of selfless love, a kind attitude, friendly demeanor, and genuine joy. Nothing is more inspiring than the example of one who loves Jesus Christ with concrete deeds to show it.

Children of the Father in the Son

The Sacrament of Confirmation, which more closely unites us with Jesus Christ, the Son of God, brings us into a more intimate union with the Father. United to the Son, we are now loved by the same Spirit by which the Father loves the Son. In both the baptized and the confirmed Christian, "God has sent the Spirit of his Son into our hearts, crying, 'Abba! Father!'"[13] Every Christian is a child of God by living in God the Son—in other words, we are children *through* the Son, *not in addition to* the Son.

The effects of the Sacraments are God's work in us, but they must also include a willing struggle to follow Christ and do his will. It would be a serious misunderstanding of Confirmation to think that every recipient is on a spiritual autopilot that circumvents a sincere willingness and personal effort to conform to Our Lord's

13. Gal 4:6; cf. Rom 8:15.

will. For example, when St.Thomas More was imprisoned for professing his faith in the authority of the Pope against the wishes of King Henry VIII, it took a while for St.Thomas to acquire a courageous demeanor in the face of execution. While spending a year in the Tower of London awaiting execution, he found himself at first afraid and fraught with self-doubt. Only after prolonged periods of prayer, meditation, and heart-wrenching cries for help, did he go bravely to his death.

Another important effect of Confirmation on the soul is the indelible mark, or character; this is the "seal" mentioned in the form of the Sacrament. Confirmation imparts a supernatural, permanent mark on the soul showing that the recipient belongs to Christ. The first indelible mark is received in Baptism, and an additional mark is acquired in Confirmation to perfect the baptismal character. In addition to associating us more fully to Christ, this mark signifies that we are enrolled in the service of Christ forever. This mark also assures us of divine protection in the trials and tribulations connected with discipleship.

This indelible mark, or character, is not just mere spiritual decoration or sacramental window dressing but rather reveals supernatural power. In Confirmation, this character signifies the fullness of the common priesthood. In practice, the seal of the common priesthood imparted by Confirmation enables every Christian to unite his or her prayers, works, joys, and sufferings with Christ's redemptive Sacrifice on the Cross as a most direct way of winning graces for others. This mark is an admission ticket, as it were, to co-redeem with Christ by joining all the diverse aspects of everyday life with Christ's Sacrifice on the Cross. The disciple of Christ who cooks, teaches, practices law, or engages in any other work—and offers up what he or she does—is united to Christ's redemptive Sacrifice. Spending oneself in doing the best possible work certainly would constitute an exercise of the common priesthood on behalf of the salvation and evangelization of others. One classic example of the exercise of a priestly soul is that of a terminally ill person who joins his or her illness with Christ's pain and suffering, offering it to God for the conversion of a family member or friend.

This exercise of a priestly soul, through the sacramental mark of Confirmation, involves a greater impetus in professing faith in Christ by both example and word. Professing and defending the faith does not mean that the Christian becomes a moral watchdog or surveillance officer but rather that he or she speaks the truth in a timely, loving way and lives according to God's will amid the most difficult circumstances and strongest temptations. God does not ask such things without providing the means to do them. The gifts of the Holy Spirit support and sustain all our work of furthering God's plan in the world so long as we "set our sails" to the wind of the Spirit.

CHAPTER 14

THE HOLY EUCHARIST, GOD'S GREATEST GIFT

The Sacrament of the Eucharist, which also refers to the celebration of Holy Mass, finds its greatest expression in the reception of Holy Communion at Mass. It is the amazing gift of Christ—administered through his Church—of bread and wine becoming the Body, Blood, Soul, and Divinity of Jesus Christ, and the faithful are able to receive him as true nourishment for their souls. History is filled with beautiful stories of conversion in the presence of the Eucharist. Blessed Nicolas Steno (Niels Stensen) spent his youth studying and became a renowned scientist in the seventeenth century. At the age of twenty-eight he converted to Catholicism while watching a Eucharistic procession on the Solemnity of the Most Holy Body and Blood of Christ ("*Corpus Christi*"); this impelled him to realize the magnificence of the Eucharist. In the twentieth century, Andre Frossard, an atheist and skeptic, entered a Church and experienced a profound mystical experience in front of the tabernacle—the ornate receptacle where the Eucharist is reserved—that converted him in an instant. While these occurrences are not the norm, there are many such accounts that speak to the power of Christ's presence in the Eucharist.

Stories of strength and perseverance given to people through the grace of Christ in this Sacrament abound. The tabernacle in the chapel inside the building that formerly housed Claretian seminarians in Barbastro, Spain is configured in the form of a picnic basket. If its history were not known, one could make the conclusion that the tabernacle was made in poor face-value artistic taste, but the image represents one of the most moving narratives of Christian martyrdom that took place during the Spanish Civil War in 1936. Fifty-one seminarians were kept in captivity under harsh physical and moral conditions by a revolutionary militia. They were at first very much afraid and demoralized amid the harsh conditions and imposed indignities, but after a period of time during their captivity, a kind, resourceful person who was assigned to bring sandwiches to the seminarians daily hid a Eucharistic host in each sandwich.

The seminarians' daily reception of Holy Communion changed their lives completely. To the consternation and frustration of the Communist authorities, fifty-one seminarians courageously paid the ultimate price as martyrs of Christ as they joyfully and serenely expressed deep gratitude to God for this grace. Such is the power of the Church's greatest treasure, the Holy Eucharist. These seminarians now form part of the ever-growing roster of canonized saints.

Source and Summit of the Christian Life

The Eucharist, along with Baptism and Confirmation, is one of the three Sacraments of Christian Initiation. In the Early Church all three of these Sacraments were administered together in one liturgical celebration. In the Western Church, these Sacraments have been separated in time but united in initiating the recipient into the Body of Christ, the Church. In the Western Church, the initiation of a child usually occurs in stages: First comes Baptism, followed by the second—either Confirmation or First Holy Communion—and then concluded by the third. (The order of Confirmation and the Eucharist is less important than receiving both; following your bishop will not lead you astray.) The initiation of an adult, even in the Western Church, is accomplished by receiving all three Sacraments in one liturgical celebration, usually at the Easter Vigil.

Baptism and Confirmation configure the recipient to Christ the Eternal High Priest so that he or she can directly and more effectively share in the Eucharist, the greatest fruit of Jesus Christ's redemption. The members of the Church are initiated into a real sharing in Jesus' Sacrifice on Calvary that is sacramentally brought to the altar by virtue of the celebration of the Liturgy of the Eucharist. Receiving Holy Communion intimately unites the faithful with Christ, "who makes us sharers in his Body and Blood to form a single body."[1]

The following analogy can help understand the relationship among Baptism, Confirmation, and the Eucharist. The effects of Baptism are like reading a musical score. Confirmation enables a person to play the chords and groups of notes. Both of these are at the service of effective participation in the Eucharistic Sacrifice and reception of Holy Communion, which is like sitting down to play actual music.

1. CCC 1331.

The Eucharist, so vital for true renewal and growth in the spiritual life, takes center stage among all the Sacraments. The Church describes it as the "fount and apex" or the "source and summit" of the Christian life.[2] As "source," the Eucharist is the wellspring of every possible grace since it is Jesus' gift of his very self. As "summit," the Eucharist is the height of what the Church has to offer, that is, Jesus Christ himself.[3] This sacramental treasure, which he entrusted to his Church, might seem too good to be true. What occurs in the Eucharistic celebration boggles the mind: The Passion of Christ is *re*-presented every time the Mass is celebrated. Though called a "memorial," the Eucharistic Sacrifice is not a mere "remembering" but a liturgical act that makes present again (re-presents) the one Sacrifice of Christ. The Eucharistic Sacrifice is a real participation in Jesus' suffering and Death on the Cross and his Resurrection—in an unbloody manner.

Even more, what was once bread and wine has truly become the Body and Blood of Christ, who desires to have such a close communion with his disciples that he invites the baptized to receive him in this humble form. Because the Eucharist involves the reality of both his redemptive self-offering that occurred on Calvary and his living presence in the sacred Host and Chalice, this Sacrament is at the heart of a Christian's spiritual life and the life of the Church. Every authentic ministry and ascetical or spiritual practice finds its reference point in the Eucharist. At the same time, the Eucharist looks forward to future glory and offers a foretaste of the joys of the heavenly banquet to come.[4]

The Eucharist in Scripture

Before turning to the celebration of the Holy Eucharist, we should examine its place in salvation history and how God prepared his people. Christians did not invent formal rites for the worship of God. In the Old Testament, God himself, through his Revelation to Moses, outlined the norms that people should follow in worshiping him. A very detailed set of laws was established that included the institution of a priesthood, the construction of a Temple, principal feasts, practices of worship, and above all the celebration of

2. LG, no. 11.
3. Cf. CCC 1324.
4. Cf. CCC 1402.

the Sabbath. From the very beginning of the Bible, we can see the importance of the Sabbath, or seventh, day; "Sabbath" is derived from the Hebrew for "rest." It is widely believed that the narration of creation as happening in seven days is meant to highlight the importance of the seventh day and the obligation to dedicate this day to divine worship.

Later, when God had formed the Israelites as his people, he made laws concerning the observance of the Sabbath in the Third Commandment:

> Remember the sabbath day, to keep it holy. Six days you shall labor, and do all your work; but the seventh day is a sabbath to the LORD your God; in it you shall not do any work, you, or your son, or your daughter, your manservant, or your maidservant, or your cattle, or the sojourner who is within your gates; for in six days the LORD made heaven and earth, the sea, and all that is in them, and rested the seventh day; therefore the LORD blessed the sabbath day and hallowed it.[5]

In this passage, we see *rest* from labor as the primary purpose of the Sabbath and *divine worship* as secondary, but soon thereafter, the Sacred Authors gave the Sabbath a dual purpose: It was a day consecrated to God. The Book of Leviticus prescribed:

> Six days shall work be done; but on the seventh day is a sabbath of solemn rest, a holy convocation; you shall do no work; it is a sabbath to the LORD in all your dwellings.[6]

Consequently, from the time of Moses, the Sabbath included the obligation to rest from labor and to offer sacrifice to God. Both requirements showed the recognition of the power of God over his entire creation and over all people. The bread of the presence—the ritual twelve loaves kept by the Jewish high priests for use as a sacrificial offering—would be renewed on the Sabbath, and specific sacrifices were to be celebrated.

If the Commandment sets apart the *seventh* day as the day of rest and worship, why do Christians celebrate the Eucharist on Sunday, that is, the *first* day of the week? Some Christians, in fact, like the Seventh Day Adventists argue that following the Third Commandment requires Saturday to be the day of Sabbath. Yet, from the beginning of the Church, the Eucharist was celebrated on Sunday.

5. Ex 20:8–11.

6. Lv 23:3.

Sacred Tradition has always held the *first day* of the week as a commemoration of the Resurrection of Our Lord, which introduced this notable change in the practice of divine worship. By worshiping on Sunday, we celebrate the completion of the first creation *and the new creation* in Christ signified by the Resurrection of Jesus, which occurred on a Sunday. God's command on the first day of creation, "Let there be light,"[7] has taken on a double meaning when Christ revealed himself, "the light of the world; he who follows me... will have the light of life."[8] All of creation is "re-created," and the baptized are "re-born"[9] in Christ. As the *Catechism* teaches, for Christians, observance of Sunday worship replaces that of the Sabbath. It fulfills the "spiritual truth" of the Sabbath and announces our "eternal rest in God."[10] The celebration of Sunday observes the "moral Commandment" to offer God public and regular worship.[11] The Third Commandment, then, applies to the obligation to observe Sunday as the day of rest and worship.

In addition to setting aside a day consecrated to God, he also prepared his people for the Eucharist in particular. The history of Israel recorded in the Old Testament is called "salvation history" because through the people and events of Israel, God worked to prepare his people (and the world) for the coming of the Messiah who would redeem them. He gradually taught his people all they needed to know for their salvation. We saw this preparation already for Baptism and Confirmation, and it is no less so for the Eucharist.

In the Old Covenant, bread and wine were the first fruits of the earth to be offered to God in thanksgiving for his many blessings. The oldest prefigurement of the Eucharistic Sacrifice is intimately associated with King Melchizedek; Abraham, upon encountering him, asked him for a blessing. In conjunction with the requested blessing, The Book of Genesis reveals that Melchizedek offered sacrifices in the form of bread and wine.[12] The Psalmist adds that Melchizedek was a priest.[13] Here, with the Father of the Israelite people, the matter of the Eucharist is offered by a priest as sacrifice.

---

7. Gn 1:3.
8. Jn 8:12.
9. Cf. Jn 3:3.
10. CCC 2175.
11. Cf. CCC 2176.
12. Cf. Gn 14:18.
13. Cf. Ps 110:4.

Another significant prefigurement of the Eucharist occurred while Moses led the Israelites to the Promised Land through the desert. He requested that God give his hungry people food. In response to his prayer of petition, God provided them a bread-like substance called *manna*, which appeared on the grounds of their campsite the next morning.[14] This historical event has deep symbolic meaning. The journey through the arid terrain where the chosen people were experiencing relentless hunger represents any person embarking on the journey of life, famished for strength and grace to arrive at the Promised Land of everlasting life. The manna that kept them going prefigures the power of the Bread of God called the Holy Eucharist, which provides the spiritual energy to reach eternal happiness.

Christ revealed that this manna in the desert was a foretaste of what he would offer his disciples. Those following Jesus asked for a sign, like the one given when Moses gave them "bread from heaven."[15] In his profoundly moving Eucharistic discourse, recorded by St. John in his Gospel, Jesus explained to the people that it was not Moses but the Father who sends the true bread from heaven, "for the bread of God is that which comes down from heaven, and gives life to the world."[16] The people then ardently asked Jesus to give them this amazing bread, to which Jesus answered, "I am the bread of life; he who comes to me shall not hunger, and he who believes in me shall never thirst."[17] These words, "the bread of God... which comes down from heaven," aptly explain the essence of the Eucharistic celebration. When the words of consecration are pronounced, the bread becomes Jesus, the Son, the Bread of God, who comes to us from heaven. It gives life to the world on many counts, especially because it brings the redemptive Sacrifice of Christ to the present moment. Though all the Sacraments draw their power from the merits of Jesus' redemption, the Eucharist is the only Sacrament completely and directly identified with Jesus' Sacrifice on the Cross and his Resurrection.

The Passover feast most clearly prefigures the Eucharistic Sacrifice, and it was on the feast of Passover that the Last Supper took place. At Passover, presented in Chapter 6, a lamb is offered and

14. Cf. Dt 8:3.
15. Jn 6:32.
16. Jn 6:33.
17. Jn 6:35.

consumed together with unleavened bread in commemoration of the Israelites' liberation from the oppression of the merciless Egyptians when death "passed over" the people of Israel during the tenth plague in Egypt. The bread in that first Passover meal was unleavened because the Jewish people needed to eat the bread in haste in their rushed effort to escape the clutches of the hostile Egyptians. The true Passover occurred when Jesus overcame sin by dying on the Cross: Jesus' Sacrifice of himself established a passage into everlasting life. Jesus' redemptive offering on the Cross was anticipated when he ate the Passover meal with his disciples the night before he died. After offering his Body and Blood at the Passover banquet of the Last Supper, the Apostles consumed the true Passover, or "Paschal Lamb," under the appearance bread and wine. Christ instructed his Apostles, "Do this in remembrance of me."[18]

This confluence of events speaks to the timelessness of the Mass, that is, the way in which, because Christ is God, the Eucharistic Sacrifice exists across all stretches of time and space. The Hebrew Passover prepares for the Last Supper, which both memorialized what God had done for Israel in the past and prepared for what God would do on the Cross. Christ, celebrating the Passover with his Apostles, instituted Our Lord's Supper as a memorial of his Passion even before those events take place. This memorial continues to serve as a participation in those events so long ago in a faraway place while at the same time looking forward to the eternal banquet in heaven. Perhaps in no other way do we see more clearly how God works with us using a plan he has had for all time. At no other moment are we as connected to the "eternal now" of God.

The teachings derived from salvation history are not limited to the Old Testament, for during his life Jesus offers many insights and teachings in preparation for the Eucharist. The very first public miracle Jesus worked involved changing water into wine at the Wedding Feast at Cana. This conversion of water into wine points to the change of wine into the Blood of Christ in the Eucharist, but it also prefigures something more significant. This marriage celebration was a preview to Christ's "mystical marriage" with his Bride, the Church. Marriage is one of the foremost symbols God uses for his relationship with his people. God entered into the covenant with Israel like a bridegroom with his bride. When the Hebrews went after idols and

18. Lk 22:19.

forsook God, the prophets called them God's "faithless" and "adulterous" bride.[19] The Bible begins and ends with a wedding, spanning from Eve being created as "a helper fit for" Adam[20] to the Wedding Feast of the Lamb in the Book of Revelation.[21] When Jesus was asked why his disciples do not fast like those of St. John the Baptist, he asked, "Can the wedding guests fast while the bridegroom is with them?"[22] Through his complete self-immolation, Jesus Christ established his Church as his Bride when he laid down his life for her. This truth was reinforced when Jesus declared from his Cross, "It is finished"[23]—or using a literal translation from the Latin, "It is consummated." Our Lord, by converting water into wine at the Wedding Feast at Cana, demonstrated the connection between the Eucharist and the mystical marriage of the Lamb with his Church.

Most explicitly, Jesus prepared for the celebration of the Eucharist in what is called his "Bread of Life Discourse" recorded in St. John's Gospel. This passage includes Jesus' remark that the Father provides the true "bread from heaven" from a few pages ago. As Jesus reached the culmination of this sermon before the people at the synagogue, he finally and repeatedly told them they must "eat" his body and "drink" his blood:[24] "For my flesh is food indeed, and my blood is drink indeed."[25] Many of his disciples took offense and turned away from Jesus after this shocking statement, saying, "This is a hard saying."[26]

To have the necessary trust that somehow a person can eat the flesh of Christ and drink his blood without any aberrations with respect to human dignity requires strong faith. If they had trusted Our Lord, his former disciples should have realized that Jesus would never command anything impossible or in violation of the natural law. St. Peter himself did not *understand* but *trusted*. When Jesus asked the Twelve if they, too, would now abandon him, St. Peter in total sincerity replied, "Lord, to whom shall we go? You have the words of eternal life."[27] He had already come to believe that Jesus

19. Cf. Hos 2:2.
20. Cf. Gn 2:18.
21. Cf. Rev 19:6–9
22. Mk 2:19; cf. Lk 5:34.
23. Jn 19:30.
24. Cf. Jn 6:53–58.
25. Jn 6:55.
26. Jn 6:60.
27. Jn 6:68.

is the Anointed One of God—the Messiah—and had faith that, in time, he would understand.

Meal and Sacrifice

The "Lord's Supper" is another term that aptly describes the Holy Eucharist since this extraordinary Sacrament was instituted within the context of an evening meal. It was the most special of meals because the food served was a heavenly food consisting of nothing less than Our Lord's Body, Blood, Soul, and Divinity under the appearance of bread and wine. "The breaking of the bread"[28] is a term to describe the Eucharist, recalling when Jesus broke bread during the celebration of this first Eucharistic Sacrifice on the evening of Holy Thursday. This phrase is not meant to simply state the obvious; the Jewish observance of the Passover meal entrusted the ceremonial task of breaking the bread to the head of the house, who presided over the meal. Celebrating the Passover with his disciples, Jesus was, of course, the presider. At the breaking of the bread, Jesus pronounced, "This is my body."[29] At the blessing of the cup he states, "This cup ... is the new covenant in my blood."[30] Jesus presided over this supernatural dinner gathering as he offered his Body and Blood as heavenly food in anticipation of his Passion and Death on the Cross.

The image of a shared, communal meal is certainly an important one for this Sacrament. The celebration of the Liturgy of the Eucharist, like sharing a meal with friends, ought to create a greater sense of fellowship and communion with others. The image of a meal aids our understanding, but as a symbol it does not represent the full meaning of the Mass since the Last Supper was so much more than the sharing of food with friends. Recall that part of the observance of the Old Testament Sabbath involved making sacrifice to God.

Beginning with the Last Supper, every Mass is a memorial re-presentation of Jesus' Crucifixion, Death, and Resurrection. Other titles that describe this sacrificial memorial include the Holy Sacrifice of the Mass, the Sacrifice of Praise,[31] and the Spiritual Sacrifice.[32]

---

28. Lk 24:30.
29. Lk 22:19.
30. Lk 22:20.
31. RMiss, The Order of Mass: Eucharistic Prayer I, no.85.
32. Ibid., Easter Time: Saturday in the Second Week of Easter, Prayer over the Offerings.

The Mass does offer a "horizontal" experience of communion among those present, but it is much more profound than a regular gathering at a meal precisely because of its "vertical" dimension as a Sacrifice to God the Father by Christ his Son in the Holy Spirit. It must always be kept in mind that the Liturgy of the Eucharist makes present the one and only redemptive Sacrifice Jesus made of himself on the Cross. This one Sacrifice enters into our present moment whenever the bishop or priest recites the words of consecration: "This is my Body..../This is the chalice of my Blood."[33]

Included in the institution of the Eucharist at the Last Supper is Jesus' command that this singular event, whereby Jesus is both the Eternal High Priest and sacrificial victim, be continued in his Church until the end of time: "Do this in remembrance of me."[34]

The Structure of the Mass

It is truly remarkable that this memorial of the Passion and Death of Jesus Christ, first celebrated at the Last Supper, continues all over the world to this present day. Although throughout the ages there has been significant development in the prayers and gestures in the Mass, its essential structure has not changed. This can be verified by the earliest record of the format of the Eucharistic celebration spelled out by St. Justin around AD 155.[35] A modern reader would clearly recognize the structure of the Mass related by one of the earliest Christian writers.[36] The Church has, through the millennia, faithfully administered this Sacrament.

The basic structure surrounding the Eucharistic Sacrifice consists of two parts: the Liturgy of the Word and the Liturgy of the Eucharist. In the Early Church, the Mass was divided into the same two parts, often called the Table of the Word and the Table of the Eucharist. The earliest Christians clearly showed deep veneration

33. Ibid., The Order of Mass, no. 89.

34. Lk 22:19.

35. Cf. St. Justin Martyr, "The First Apology," in ANF, vol 1: "On the day called Sunday, all who live in cities or in the country gather together to one place, and the memoirs of the apostles or the writings of the prophets are read.... The president verbally instructs, and exhorts to the imitation of these good things. Then we all rise together and pray, and... bread and wine and water are brought, and the president in like manner offers prayers and thanksgivings... and the people assent, saying Amen; and there is a distribution to each... and to those who are absent a portion is sent by the deacons. And they who are well to do... give what each thinks fit; and what is collected... takes care of all who are in need."

36. Cf. CCC 1345.

for both the Word of God in Scripture and the Word of God made present in the Eucharist. They would come to Mass to be nourished by these two sources of spiritual food—Sacred Scripture and the Holy Eucharist—hence the use of "table."

Christ himself "presides" over the liturgy. As the *Catechism* teaches, "He is high priest of the New Covenant; it is he himself who presides invisibly over every Eucharistic celebration."[37] For this reason, a bishop or priest is the minister of this Sacrament. The ordained minister is the visible sign of the sacred reality that Christ himself presides, while the bishop or priest stands *in persona Christi capitis* ("in the Person of Christ the Head").

From time immemorial, the Mass began with readings from the Old Testament since they foreshadow and prepare for the coming of Christ. On Sundays and many feasts, a reading from one of the New Testament Epistles or the Acts of the Apostles is also included. These readings, along with a recitation from one of the Psalms, culminate in the reading of the Gospel, which narrates the life of Christ and transmits his teachings and works. As signs of reverence, the congregation stands during the reading of the Gospel, and the deacon or priest kisses the contents of the Gospel. The Gospel is followed by a homily and the Profession of Faith, or Creed. Then in the Universal Prayer, or the Prayer of the Faithful, "the people pour out their petitions... for the needs of the whole Church and for the salvation of the whole world."[38] The Mass, as a Sacrifice, is offered with these intentions in mind.

The second half of the Mass is called the Liturgy of the Eucharist. This begins with the Preparation of the Gifts: bread and wine, which also represent the offering of the faithful, with emphasis on their work and suffering. The lay faithful, in fulfillment of their priestly mission, offer up their daily works, joys, and sufferings with Christ at Mass. The minister then prays the Prayer over the Offerings as the bread and wine are presented (offered) to God to be consecrated. Next comes the Preface, which consists of profound words of thanksgiving and praise for God's blessings demonstrated by his works of creation, salvation, and sanctification.

The sacramental signs of the Eucharistic are bread made from wheat and wine made from grapes; these are the matter of the Sac-

37. CCC 1348.

38. RMiss, Chapter II: The Structure of the Mass, Its Elements, and Its Parts, no.55.

rament of the Eucharist. This is what Christ himself used, but like all things he did, there is more to be learned. The process of making bread points to the Sacrifice of the Mass: The wheat must be ground down and pulverized into flour, and the grapes must be crushed to extract juice. Both the wheat and the grapes undergo a kind of "death" to themselves to become bread and wine. Moreover, the wheat flour is transformed (baked) to become bread, and the grape juice is transformed (fermented) to become wine. These visible changes of wheat into bread and grapes into wine are a symbolic prefigurement of the invisible changes of bread and wine into the Body and Blood of Christ.

The use of wheat bread and grape wine is necessary for the celebration of the Eucharist. Bread made from, for example, corn or barley cannot be substituted for wheat; neither can wine made from, for example, plums or pomegranates take the place of grapes. It is fitting that the matter of the Eucharist is bread and wine, as both are commonly used for nourishment. The image of bread instantaneously prompts the idea of basic food. By the same token, wine is a standard beverage at a meal or a banquet. Bread provides energy and strength, whereas wine quenches thirst and brings good cheer: "[The Lord] bring forth food from the earth, / and wine to gladden the heart of man."[39]

Since Jesus expressly stated in the Bread of Life discourse that his Body and Blood are the food and drink of his disciples, it makes sense that we nourish ourselves with his Body and Blood under the properties of bread and wine.

The heart of the liturgical celebration is the Eucharistic Prayer. The Eucharistic Prayer includes prayers of petition and thanksgiving and pleas for forgiveness of sin. It crescendoes toward its high point during the *epiclesis* wherein the minister petitions the Father:

> Make holy, therefore, these gifts, we pray,
> by sending down your Spirit upon them like the dewfall,
> so that they may become for us
> the Body and Blood of our Lord Jesus Christ.[40]

Following the *epiclesis*, the Liturgy of the Eucharist reaches its high point at the moment of consecration whereby Jesus Christ, the Eternal High Priest, brings the mystery of his self-immolation

39. Ps 104:14–15.

40. RMiss, The Order of Mass, no. 101.

to the present moment. The words of consecration spoken by the minister occasions the change from bread and wine into the Body, Blood, Soul, and Divinity of Jesus Christ.

The words of consecration are the form of the Sacrament of the Eucharist. They are the very words of Christ at the Last Supper recorded in Sacred Scripture:

> This is my body which is given for you. Do this in remembrance of me....This cup which is poured out for you is the new covenant in my blood.[41]

After the minister had pronounced the form over the matter, the bread and wine have not changed in appearance; nonetheless, they have truly *become* the Body and Blood of Jesus. This is called "transubstantiation," which is derived from the Latin *trans* ("across") and *substantia* ("substance") because the *substance* has changed, not the *appearance*. The words of consecration, articulated by the bishop or priest, prompt the Holy Spirit to turn the bread and wine into the Body and Blood of Jesus Christ. He instituted all the Sacraments, but to highlight the supreme importance of the Eucharist, we have scriptural record of Jesus actually celebrating it.

The *anamnesis*, or memorial, that follows the consecration, recalls the Passion, Resurrection, and Ascension of Jesus Christ. This part of the Mass refers to the power of his Sacrifice on the Cross to bring salvation to the world. Petitions for the Church, the Pope, the bishop, and the whole People of God form part of the Eucharistic Prayer. Prayers of intercession are not limited to those living on earth but include the deceased as well, who are alive in Christ.

The Communion Rite then begins with the *Lord's Prayer*, or "Our Father," and the faithful asking for mercy from the Lamb of God. Then the reception of Holy Communion is preceded by the words first addressed to Jesus by the centurion:

> Lord, I am not worthy
> that you should enter under my roof,
> but only say the word
> and my soul shall be healed.[42]

The priest concludes the Eucharistic Sacrifice by receiving the Body and Blood of Christ. The faithful are then invited to receive Jesus Christ in Holy Communion. This is a most intimate encounter

41. Lk 22:19–20.

42. RMiss, The Order of Mass, no. 132; cf. Mt 8:8.

with the Risen Christ, who is really and sacramentally present in the Eucharistic species. All are then dismissed to take the love and joy of Christ into the world.

The Real Presence

Our Christian faith assures us that Christ makes himself present in a number of ways:

> Christ is always present in His Church, especially in her liturgical celebrations. He is present in the sacrifice of the Mass, not only in the person of His minister, "the same now offering, through the ministry of priests, who formerly offered himself on the cross,"[43] but especially under the Eucharistic species. By His power He is present in the sacraments, so that when a man baptizes it is really Christ Himself who baptizes.[44] He is present in His word, since it is He Himself who speaks when the holy scriptures are read in the Church. He is present, lastly, when the Church prays and sings, for He promised: "Where two or three are gathered together in my name, there am I in the midst of them."[45]

Nothing can compare with the Real Presence of Jesus Christ—Body, Blood, Soul, and Divinity—in the sacred Host and Chalice after the consecration. These Eucharistic species are called the "Blessed Sacrament" since Christ is just as much there as he was in his sojourn on earth over 2000 years ago.

As mentioned earlier, this substantial change from bread and wine into the Body and Blood of Jesus is called transubstantiation. It is the will of God that the words of consecration occasion the divine power of the Holy Spirit to makes this miraculous change while keeping the appearances of bread and wine intact. Believing in this truth requires a significant amount of faith since before the consecration, there is bread and wine that looks, feels, and tastes like bread and wine; after the consecration, however, there is *no longer* bread and wine, although it still looks, feels, and tastes like bread and wine. As with all mysteries of faith, humility and clear reasoning is needed to "see with the eyes of faith." For instance, if God can create something out of nothing, he can certainly bring about this mysterious change in the bread and wine whereby Jesus becomes

43. Ecumenical Council of Trent, Session XXII, Doctrine on the Holy Sacrifice of the Mass, ch. 2.
44. Cf. St. Augustine, *Tractatus in Ioannem*, Book VI, no. 7.
45. SC, no. 7; Mt 18:20.

substantially present. Here, we have a visible reality (the appearance of bread and wine) of a sacred reality (the Body and Blood of our Lord). As St. Thomas Aquinas expressed it in his great Eucharistic hymn *Tantum Ergo*, "Faith for all defects supplying / Where the feeble senses fail."[46]

The Real Presence of Our Lord in the sacred Host and Chalice is the Catholic Church's greatest treasure since we have the same Jesus who lived with the Blessed Virgin Mary and St. Joseph and who lived with and taught his Apostles directly. It is exactly the same Jesus who preached and worked astounding miracles to the point of bringing people back to life. It is quite mind-boggling that any believer—or human being, for that matter—has such complete access to Jesus. To actually deal with Jesus as a friend, faith in the Real Presence is necessary since the properties of bread and wine remain after their substance has been replaced by the full presence of the Risen Christ.

So great a treasure is the Real Presence of Jesus Christ that the sacred Host is often kept after Mass, or "reserved," in the tabernacle for distribution to those who could not be present at Mass—the sick, the homebound, the incarcerated, etc.—and for prayer. A tabernacle is an ornate cabinet often covered in gold or other precious materials; it is always located in a prominent place. Precisely because Jesus Christ is really present, Catholics have the custom to genuflect or bow before the tabernacle.

The custom whereby people spend time in silent prayer in the presence of the Blessed Sacrament is called Eucharistic Adoration. A person might spend as little as fifteen minutes in Eucharistic Adoration, but the usual period of Eucharistic Adoration is one hour;[47] hence, it is often called a Holy Hour. Christ's humble waiting in the tabernacle of every Catholic church is a powerful invitation from him to spend time in prayer before his Real Presence in the Eucharistic species. St. John Paul II summarized these ideas well:

> The Church and the world have a great need of eucharistic worship. Jesus waits for us in this sacrament of love. Let us be generous with our time in going to meet Him in adoration and in con-

46. St. Thomas Aquinas, "*Tantum Ergo* / Sing My Tongue," in HBP, 283.
47. Cf. Mt 26:40.

> templation that is full of faith and ready to make reparation for the great faults and crimes of the world by our adoration never cease.[48]

Jesus waits for every person—waiting to strengthen, forgive, convert, and console. The only plausible explanation for this display of affection and selfless service is that Jesus is truly the Incarnation of infinite love. As St. Josemaria Escriva observed after countless hours in Eucharistic Adoration:

> The humility of Jesus: in Bethlehem, in Nazareth, on Calvary. But more humiliation and more self-abasement still in the Sacred Host: more than in the stable, more than in Nazareth, more than on the Cross.
>
> That is why I must love the Mass so much.[49]

Reception of Holy Communion

What can be more worthy of eliciting praise and thanksgiving than the fact that we can receive Jesus as our real food when we receive Holy Communion at Mass? Christ's Real Presence in the Eucharist represents the fullness of God's blessings that could ever possibly be lavished on anyone who accepts this gift. The immediate, natural reaction to such largesse should be thanksgiving. There exists absolutely no better blessing than to have Jesus Christ all to oneself at the moment of receiving the Eucharist. In a real sense, the person who has received Holy Communion, for some minutes, can be described as a living tabernacle. The fact that Christ is truly present in the Blessed Sacrament and that we can receive him in Holy Communion should elicit deep gratitude.

Again, we see the confluence of "meal" and "sacrifice." For example, the altar on which the Eucharistic Sacrifice is celebrated has a double significance. First, it represents the sacrificial aspect of the Eucharist since sacrifices are offered on an altar. Second, the altar conveys the meaning of a meal since a table is the customary place for eating together. Thus, the altar signifies that the Eucharist is both a sacrificial offering and spiritual nourishment. The altar will always serve as a sign of Christ's presence in his redemptive Sacrifice and his Real Presence in our heavenly food under the appearance of bread and wine.

---

48. St. John Paul II, Apostolic Letter on the Mystery and Worship of the Eucharist *Dominicæ Cenæ* (February 24, 1980), no. 3.

49. St. Josemaria Escriva, *The Way* (Princeton, NJ: Scepter Publishers, 1992), no. 533.

Though no material object can sufficiently correspond to the exalted dignity of the Eucharist, the cleanliness of the altar cloth and the beauty of the sacred vessels should reflect the grandeur of and love for the Eucharist. Beautiful liturgical objects are meant to elicit a greater devotion among the participants at Mass and recipients of Communion. The celebrant of the Eucharist will even kiss the altar at the beginning and conclusion of Mass. But all these material objects and gestures are at the service of elevating our internal dispositions. The first sign of respect for the inestimable value of the Blessed Sacrament is the reception of Holy Communion with the proper interior conditions and dispositions. No one is *worthy* to receive Holy Communion, but everyone has great need for the Eucharist because we are all flawed sinners. Nevertheless, being in a state of grave sin or not being in full communion with the Church would preclude a person from receiving Holy Communion. The proper recipient of the Eucharist, then, is a baptized Catholic who is not in a state of grave sin, that is, one who is in the "state of grace."

The Church's teachings about who can or cannot receive the Eucharist is sometimes misunderstood. It is not an expression of elitism or being holier-than-thou. Quite the opposite! In the words of Pope Francis, "The Eucharist, although it is the fullness of sacramental life, is not a prize for the perfect but a powerful medicine and nourishment for the weak."[50]

The Eucharist is given to us in "Holy Communion" because it is a true communion with Christ and his Church. Receiving the Eucharist presumes that the person agrees with and adheres to the teaching of Christ's Church. In a sense, for a person who is not *in communion* to receive Holy Communion would be a false act. It would be like taking a pledge with no intention of acting on it or signing a contract with no intention of fulfilling it. Lack of sacramental communion through Baptism or mortal sin would mean the recipient would not share in the communion that the reception of Holy Communion represents.

There are still many graces to be gained from attending Mass, even if a person cannot receive the Eucharist. Such a person still receives the benefit of hearing the Word of God proclaimed, instruction through preaching, participation in the most perfect form of

50. EG, no. 47.

prayer in the Church, and praying to God in front of the Real Presence of Christ.

No one is *barred* from receiving the Eucharist; nothing prevents anybody who desires to receive the Eucharist from obtaining the proper conditions. Everyone who (1) is in the state of grace, (2) is in communion with the Church, and (3) has fasted at least one hour is most welcome to receive Holy Communion. In the case of a Catholic who is contrite for mortal sin, recourse to the Sacrament of Penance and Reconciliation restores him or her to the state of grace. In the case of a non-Catholic, a profession of belief in the Catholic faith (plus, for a non-Christian, the reception of Baptism) brings him or her into full communion with the Church. These requirements do not make anyone more or less deserving than anyone else for Holy Communion. Given the infinite divide between the dignity of Christ in the Eucharist and wounded human nature, no human person—except the Blessed Virgin Mary by means of her Immaculate Conception, presented in Chapter 6—is worthy. The proper dispositions do not, therefore, remove our unworthiness but rather express respect and reverence for what is being received and give the capacity for personal benefit.

In addition to receiving Holy Communion, it is a sign of faith, love, and appreciation to dress appropriately for Mass. Obviously, high esteem and profound respect for the Church's liturgy does not require wearing something as formal as a tuxedo or an evening gown; appropriate attire might be what would be worn to a job interview, to attend a wedding, or to host a special guest. Excessively casual or shabby clothing detracts from the dignity and proper tone of this most exalted event of Jesus Christ coming down from heaven to be with us. A guest at a wedding reception would insult the couple and the importance of their commitment by showing up in shabby clothing. Similarly, our appreciation for the Real Presence of Christ in the Eucharist is shown in the attire we adopt. Financial means should be considered but not be used as an excuse; in some of the poorest eras and regions of the world, Catholic families have and still do reserve their "Sunday best" for going to church.

A contemplative disposition is another important component of preparing to receive Holy Communion. Great benefit is derived from the Mass when the bishop or priest and the faithful pray with energy and enthusiasm. This can be more of a challenge for people raised in the Church for whom the liturgy has become a familiar routine; such a Catholic might find it easy to drift into being more of a passive observer. But as the old adage goes, "You get out of the Mass what you put into it." Both the ordained and the lay faithful should reflect on what they are saying and to whom they are speaking. This participation reaches a crescendo with the reception of Holy Communion. Interior acts of faith, hope, and love serve as a more immediate preparation for reception of the Eucharist.

Intense prayer should also continue after Holy Communion, while Jesus is most interiorly present. It is a precious moment of intimacy with Our Lord who infinitely loves us. Eucharistic piety also involves making time for thanksgiving for the grace and privilege of having received the Risen Christ. This time of thanksgiving might include prayers for family members, friends, the sick, people stricken by war and poverty, and other matters that we want to bring to Our Lord's attention at this most intimate moment.

Perfect Prayer

Prayer will be presented in more detail in Chapter 20, but it is important to know here that prayer is often categorized according to four forms: *adoration*, or praise, of God; *thanksgiving* for all of God's blessings; *atonement*, or contrition to God for one's sins or the sins of others; and *petition*, or requests for God's favor.[51] The Eucharistic Sacrifice addresses God the Father with all four of these forms of prayer. Each form is engaged in the Mass—each is accomplished perfectly because it is accomplished through the perfect Sacrifice of Christ the Eternal High Priest.

How can our prayers, repeated each time the Mass is celebrated, participate so intimately in Christ's self-offering to God the Father? Recall that the memorial of Christ's Passion and Death is not a mere remembrance but actually a *re*-presentation of those events that took place so long ago in a land far away. The celebration of the Eucharist is the same living Sacrifice of Jesus' self-emptying on the Cross that has burst into the present moment. The Church clearly teaches that the Eucharistic Sacrifice is not an additional Sacrifice but rather the one redemptive Sacrifice re-presented on the liturgical altar. Because of the timeless nature of Christ's Sacrifice, its re-presentation in the

51. Cf. CCC 2626–2643.

Eucharist is a means of literally uniting our prayers to his perfect act of praise, thanksgiving, atonement, and petition.

There are many instances in the Mass that take the form of adoration; the Church has composed some of the most beautiful praises of God as parts for the Mass. Regardless of these many opportunities to adore God at Mass, the greatest act of homage to God the Father is Jesus' obedience as he offered himself on the Cross. At Mass, the faithful share in this perfect adoration of Jesus Christ, who is both Eternal High Priest and sacrificial victim. What better form of praise can there be than to praise God the Father through Jesus' redemptive Sacrifice?

Another key objective of the Mass, as often expressed in the texts of the liturgy, is to give thanksgiving to God the Father for his work of creation. Eucharist is derived from the Greek *eukharistia*, which means "thanksgiving." According to Hebrew custom, when God's blessings were especially apparent during a meal, the participants would give heartfelt thanks to him. The meal was a powerful reminder of God's blessings manifested through created things, especially common ones like bread and wine. God's generosity is radically demonstrated in redeeming and sanctifying us through the Sacrifice of his Son, made present in the Eucharistic Sacrifice. In the sacred liturgy, the Church gives thanks to God for his numerous blessings by uniting herself to Jesus Christ in thanksgiving through his perfect Sacrifice.

Because Christ's Sacrifice on the Cross has made atonement for the sin of Adam and all personal sins throughout history, the Mass is the perfect prayer to express contrition for sin. We can unite our sorrow over our sins and the sins of the world to Christ's work of perfect atonement.

Since no type of prayer can come close to rivaling the power of the Eucharist, the most effective supernatural means to ask for favors is during the Mass, hence the custom of offering Mass for the repose of a particular soul, for peace and justice, for the evangelization of peoples, etc. The Mass is the surest way of accelerating the purification process, if needed, after death. Petitioning for the conversion of oneself and of others also finds its perfect setting at the Eucharistic table.

Though the Mass is the Sacrifice of Jesus who is the priest and victim at the same time, the same Eucharistic Sacrifice allows for the members of his Mystical Body to share in that self-offering. Our work, joys, sufferings, and relationships can all be joined to Christ's Sacrifice. Though the Mass is the *one* Sacrifice of Christ offered in a sacramental way, an *unlimited* number of the baptized can be part of that self-immolation. Prayers, work, and sufferings can be joined to Christ on his Cross through the Eucharistic Sacrifice: God gave us this Sacrifice in the form of the Eucharistic celebration so that everyone can become part of Jesus' redemptive Sacrifice. In the Mass the faithful can adore, thank the Father, make reparation, and petition God through nothing less than Jesus' self-Sacrifice to the Father on our behalf.

Effects of Holy Eucharist

The term used to express reception of the Body and Blood of Jesus is "Holy Communion" because receiving the Eucharist involves an intimate, holy communion with Jesus Christ. Jesus revealed in his Eucharistic discourse, "He who eats my flesh and drinks my blood abides in me, and I in him."[52] In addition to this very personal encounter, the reception of Holy Communion leaves the recipient more immersed in the life of Christ. To fulfill the New Commandment of Love with the very love of Christ, the Eucharist is necessary. The Eucharist has the power to transform a person into "another Christ" to the degree that his or her dispositions allow for it. Throughout the history of the Church, every saint has had deep Eucharistic piety, which was the secret to his or her holiness. Anyone who exudes great joy and charity most likely receives Holy Communion with exquisite faith and love.

So closely does Jesus Christ want to be united with his disciples that his Real Presence is consumed as food. Even though it must initially enter our bodies like any other food, the Eucharist is meant to be nourishment for the soul. One way to understand the workings of Jesus' Real Presence in the Eucharist under the appearance of bread and wine is to observe what food does for the body. Nourishment has various roles in serving the welfare of the human body. Food gives energy to work, serve the needs of others, and converse with them. Actual bodily growth counts on a proper diet incorporated into the various parts of the body. Health and avoidance of sickness is another vital effect of proper nourishment: Food is the immediate

52. Jn 6:56.

source of energy, growth, and repair for the body. On the spiritual level, Eucharistic food affects the soul in similar ways. Communion fosters the energy of charity, the growth in the life of Christ, and the avoidance of sin together with spiritual healing. These constitute the chief effects of the Eucharist.

There is one very basic difference between natural and spiritual food: Whereas natural food is incorporated into the body, heavenly food incorporates the human person into the divine food, Jesus Christ. As Our Lord revealed to St. Augustine on his path to conversion:

> I am the food of grown men, grow, and thou shalt feed upon Me; nor shalt thou convert Me, like the food of thy flesh into thee, but thou shalt be converted into Me.[53]

By receiving the Eucharist, we are transformed into the life of Christ whereby, little by little, we take on his virtues. The recipient of Holy Communion *becomes Eucharistic* since he or she reflects a greater presence of Christ.

As the Eucharist unites us to Jesus Christ, it purifies the soul from the sins of the past and, at the same time, gives strength to avoid sins in the future. As charity grows, venial sins are wiped away since expressions of selfishness are drowned out by an abundance of charity. As charity grows and venial sins are removed, the recipient is preserved from committing mortal sin. This growing friendship with Christ makes the likelihood of committing grave sin less and less. The reception of Holy Communion does not *automatically* prevent a person from committing grave sin, as history has tragically demonstrated, because Our Lord never hinders the exercise of free will. But if the recipient is well disposed and desires to be transformed in Christ, the Eucharist will leave the person strengthened to grow in holiness, which is totally incompatible with grave sin. Many people have reported that frequent reception of Holy Communion has liberated them from sinful habits and strengthened them in a new way.

The Holy Eucharist is also called the "Sacrament of Unity" with the Church, the Mystical Body of Christ. Through Baptism, Jesus Christ, the head of the Mystical Body, extends his supernatural life to all members of the Church. This intimacy with Christ strengthens unity among the faithful for the simple reason that the bonds of charity among its members are fortified. It is no mere accident that

53. CSA, Book VII.

those sincerely centered on this most exalted Sacrament have a great love for the Pope; the bishops, priests, and deacons; those in the consecrated life; and all the faithful of the Church. This union with Christ is also typically marked by love for the Church's teachings and Sacraments. The recipient of the Eucharist, despite the shortcomings of the individual members of the Church, deeply appreciates every aspect of the Church's life: her teachings, means of sanctification, and service of leadership.

The reception of Jesus in his sacramental, Real Presence is not just an intimate participation in the greatest fruit of the Eucharistic Sacrifice—it also provides grace to evangelize others. "The bread of God," as Jesus taught, "gives life to the world."[54] Now the mere presence of the Eucharistic Sacrifice and the Real Presence of Jesus in our churches and chapels gives life to the world. The main reason is obvious: The Light of the World promised that every disciple "who follows me ... will have the light of life."[55]

Nevertheless, there is corollary to the meaning of Christ as both the Light *and* the Life of the World. The Eucharist gives life to the world through Jesus' disciples, who become transmitters of the life of Christ as they fulfill their prophetic and kingly missions. As the Eucharist transforms the disciple of Christ, a disciple becomes more of a light attracting others to God, repentance, and building up the Kingdom of God. Mass is derived from the Latin dismissal at the end of Mass: "*Ite, missa est,*" which means: "Go; she has been sent." The faithful are sent into the world to evangelize and fulfill the threefold mission of Christ as priest, prophet, and king.

Along these lines, it is worth recalling that Jesus washed his Apostles' feet during the Last Supper. Most recollections of the Last Supper focus on the institution of the Eucharist—and rightly so!—nevertheless, these two events are closely related. Throughout the Gospel, Jesus makes it abundantly clear that he has special affection and compassion for the poor and the indigent. It stands to reason that Eucharistic piety leads to a greater sensitivity toward those who suffer whether physically, morally, or psychologically. Putting on Christ means that we put on his compassion, mercy, and spirit of service. The Eucharist provides the fuel not only to notice but also to desire to help those going through painful trials or who find

54. Jn 6:33.
55. Jn 8:12.

their lives in turmoil. The ability to metaphorically wash feet comes from the spiritually high-energy food that we call the Eucharist. This capacity for radical and selfless service is one of the effects of receiving Holy Communion. St. Teresa of Calcutta, lovingly called Mother Teresa, is an image of heroic self-giving for both the Church and the world; she would spend hours in front of the Blessed Sacrament to be refueled with the love of Jesus.

The Eucharist is also a sign of the glory that awaits us in heaven. Jesus, hidden under the appearance of bread and wine, will be seen face to face and no longer through the shadows of faith. Union with Christ through receiving and praying before the Eucharist is a preview of the face-to-face contemplation of God in heaven. Though receiving Holy Communion and praying before the Blessed Sacrament is a grace so precious that it has no price, it still gives a tiny hint of the inconceivable joy of the everlasting life to come. What was first prefigured at the Wedding Feast at Cana will become the eternal Wedding Feast of the Lamb in heaven.

A person does not need to be a great Pope or to live the heroically missionary life of St. Teresa of Calcutta to be transformed by the Eucharist. Our Lord's humble gift of himself to us as food under the appearance of bread and wine demonstrates how accessible he wants to be to all of us. Blessed Carlo Acutis was no more than a teenage Web site designer and gamer who died at the young age of fifteen. He lived a beautiful life of charity, using his savings to buy sleeping bags for the homeless, and at night he brought them hot drinks. He had a profound devotion to the Eucharist. Using his Web design skills, he created a website to catalog stories of Eucharistic miracles. The Eucharist, he said, was his "highway to heaven."[56] Carlo was declared "Blessed"—a step on the way to being declared a saint—in 2020.

People who allow the graces of the Eucharist to transform them effectively renew the world, like Blessed Carlo Acutis did. It is the power of Eucharistic Communion that leaves an increased presence of Christ in the Christian, empowering him or her to testify that Jesus is the Way and the Truth and the Life.

---

56. Cf. Ephrem Kunnappally, *Highway to Heaven: A Spiritual Journey Through the Life of Blessed Carlo Acutis* (Kozhikode, Kerala, India: Pavanatma Publishers Pvt., Ltd., 2020).

Obligation to Attend Sunday Mass

The obligation for Catholics to attend Holy Mass on Sundays and certain other feast days is rooted, as already noted, in the Third Commandment to keep the Sabbath holy. This was first presented in Chapter 2 and expounded on earlier in this chapter. Together with the celebration of Mass on the Lord's Day, the custom of celebrating Feast Days quickly grew up, assigning days to important events in the life of Our Lord and the saints. The Christian calendar is punctuated by the important mysteries of the faith and Feast Days of the Blessed Virgin Mary, the angels, and the saints. Sunday, however, stands in a class by itself because it commemorates the Resurrection of Jesus Christ.

In addition to fulfilling the Third Commandment, the Sunday obligation underlines the importance of the Eucharistic Sacrifice, the sacramental re-presentation of Jesus Christ's redemptive Sacrifice on the Cross, which makes present the one Sacrifice of Christ and celebrates his Resurrection from the dead. The Mass is called "the *Holy Sacrifice,* because it makes present the one sacrifice of Christ the Savior and includes the Church's offering."[57] In her maternal care for the faithful, the Church makes attendance at Sunday Mass obligatory because of the tremendous spiritual benefits derived for those who participate.

Though there are many temptations to *not* attend Mass, the Sunday obligation should not be approached as a burden. Sunday is the day on which the Church celebrates Our Lord's work of redemption. The center and high point of a Christian's life is participation in the liturgical celebration of the Paschal Mystery. As the Council Fathers of Vatican II taught, "The liturgy is the summit toward which the activity of the Church is directed; at the same time it is the font from which all her power flows."[58] We have already seen the many graces that can be obtained through the liturgical participation in the Eucharistic Sacrifice and the reception of Holy Communion, its powerful effect on the moral life to instill love for others as well as closer union with Christ. As the *Catechism* teaches, "It is this mystery of Christ that the Church proclaims and celebrates in her

---

57. CCC 1330.

58. SC, no. 10.

liturgy so that the faithful may live from it and bear witness to it in the world."[59]

The *Code of Canon Law* first regulates the importance of Sunday in the Christian life and, second, mandates the obligation of attending Mass and refraining from servile work on Sunday. Holy Days of Obligation, on the other hand, are days on which the Church commemorates the important events in the life of Christ and his Mother or other important mysteries of the faith. The Church has established these Holy Days of Obligation to recall the love of God the Father through his Son Jesus Christ with the close cooperation of the Blessed Virgin Mary, his Mother. Not only are these events called to mind, but they also serve as an example for us to follow. These days serve as occasions for the Church to teach the faithful about the most important mysteries of the faith.

The Blessed Virgin Mary, the Mother of Jesus Christ and Our Mother, is an example of faith and a model of Christian discipleship. By the grace of God, she was "preserved free from all stain of original sin"[60]—the "Immaculate Conception"—and remained sinless throughout her life.[61] As a fruit of the redemption earned by her Son, she was taken body and soul to heaven at the moment of her death (the Assumption).[62] These two aspects of the remarkable life of the Blessed Virgin Mary, in addition to a third as the Mother of God, are Holy Days of Obligation.

The Solemnity of Mary, the Holy Mother of God, is in honor of her role as the Mother of Jesus, the Incarnate Word of God (see Chapter 6); it sheds light on her title as the Queen of Heaven and Earth. Some people are surprised by the idea that heaven has a queen, but this title has deep biblical roots. In the Kingdom of David in the Old Testament, it was not the king's wife that had royal honors, but the king's *mother*. The "Queen Mother" is also frequently represented as an advocate for the people before the king. When Bathsheba came to her son, King Solomon, with a request on behalf of the people, he replied, "Make your request, my mother; for I will not refuse you.[63] The Blessed Virgin Mary, the Mother of Jesus, is

59. CCC 1068.
60. ID.
61. Cf.CCC 491–493.
62. Cf.CCC 966.
63. 1 Kgs 2:20.

confidently invoked by Christians who trust in her as Queen of Heaven and Earth to be our intercessor before our King.

In addition to every "Sunday... as the primordial holy day of obligation," canon law lists ten Holy Days of Obligation:

> The following days must also be observed: the Nativity of our Lord Jesus Christ [Christmas], the Epiphany, the Ascension, the Body and Blood of Christ, Holy Mary the Mother of God, her Immaculate Conception, her Assumption, Saint Joseph, Saint Peter and Saint Paul the Apostles, and All Saints.[64]

However, the *Code of Canon Law* also permits the bishops' conferences of individual countries to remove the obligation from certain Holy Days or to transfer their observance to a Sunday. This allows for the possibility that the observance of a Holy Day of Obligation would create too much of a burden on the faithful in that country. For example, in the United States of America, there are six Holy Days of Obligation:

- "January 1, the solemnity of Mary, Mother of God.
- "Thursday of the Sixth Week of Easter, the solemnity of the Ascension.
- "August 15, the solemnity of the Assumption of the Blessed Virgin Mary.
- "November 1, the solemnity of All Saints.
- "December 8, the solemnity of the Immaculate Conception.
- "December 25, the solemnity of the Nativity of Our Lord Jesus Christ [Christmas]."[65]

This means the bishops of the United States have transferred the Epiphany and the Body and Blood of Christ [Corpus Christi] to the closest Sunday and have removed the obligation of St. Joseph and Sts. Peter and Paul. In most US dioceses, the Ascension has also been transferred to the following Sunday. Catholics are encouraged—although not obligated—to attend Mass and rest from labor on these days.

Some people are surprised to see Easter not listed as a Holy Day of Obligation; since it is always on a Sunday, it already car-

64. CIC, can. 1246 §1.

65. "Canon 1246, §2—Holy Days of Obligation" (Washington, DC: National Conference of Catholic Bishops, November 17, 1992).

ries the obligation. But Easter is far from just any other Sunday! Easter is the celebration par excellence of the Resurrection of Jesus Christ from the dead and the high point of the liturgical year. So important a feast is Easter that receiving the Eucharist during Easter Time—the fifty days from Easter to Pentecost—is required as one of the Precepts of the Church: "You shall receive the sacrament of the Eucharist at least during the Easter season."[66] While many Catholics receive Holy Communion every Sunday, many others refrain from receiving. There are good reasons not to receive Communion at Mass, including being in a state of mortal sin or failing to fast at least one hour. Here it is honorable and virtuous to refrain. (A person who has grave sin should receive the Sacrament of Penance and Reconciliation right away.) On Easter, though, it is strongly encouraged that the faithful devoutly receive Holy Communion.

Fulfillment of the precept to attend Mass is a grave obligation. A person fully cognizant of the serious obligation to attend Mass on a Sunday or Holy Day of Obligation but chose to skip it might well have committed a mortal sin. Even if that person is not in a state of grace or otherwise able to receive Holy Communion, he or she would still be expected to come to church and participate in the liturgy to fulfill this obligation of Catholic life.

Sickness, the immediate need to help someone in an emergency, and other similar circumstances can dispense a person from attending Mass on Sunday or a Holy Day of Obligation. But picking up an extra shift at work, attending a basketball tournament, being on vacation, or having homework to do are not grave, or serious, reasons. If work, school, sports, or other issues preclude the possibility of attending Mass on Sunday or a Holy Day of Obligation, that person should speak with the boss, professor, coach, or person in charge; it is also a good idea to talk with the pastor about ways to fulfill the obligation, perhaps by attending Mass at a different time or at another parish church. It is more important to worship God in his Church than to participate in a sporting event or to work a particular shift.

Organizing a person's life around the obligation to attend Mass can usually be done. This information is at our fingertips. In much of the world, an urban parish church usually offers several Mass times from Saturday to Sunday evening and different parish churches to

66. CCC 2042.

attend. A rural area, even when camping or on vacation, should offer a parish church nearby or on the way to or from a destination. The Church, being such a wonderfully solicitous Mother, wants all her children to draw full benefit from the exposure to the Word of God, direct participation in the Eucharistic Sacrifice, and reception of the Body and Blood of Christ. Let us also keep in mind that throughout history, Christians have gone to great pains and even suffered martyrdom in order to attend Mass. These duties should never be seen as burdens but as occasions to entrust ourselves to God's loving care.

Sunday Rest

Attending a Sunday Mass that "is anticipated on the preceding Saturday"[67]—that is, Saturday evening—is always an option, as it certainly fulfills the Sunday precept. However, the remaining requirement remains: setting aside time for rest to make sure the meaning of the Day of the Lord is not lost.

From the beginning of salvation history, the Lord's Day included rest from normal daily occupations.[68] There are several reasons for this: Resting from labor facilitates the worship of God by eliminating much expenditure of energy and many distractions. Resting from labor allows for recuperation and makes time for other activities that enrich the human spirit, like deepening family ties and friendship. Resting from labor is a reminder that life is not ultimately about cleaning the house, making money, or advancing in a career. Resting from labor turns attention to the real value of life—the praise of God, family and community, service, contemplation, etc.—realigning focus to higher and more important values that make life worth living and express our eternal nature. Finally, resting from labor is a reminder that despite our labor, we are always in the hands of our loving Father.

While this type of rest can and should be embraced at moments throughout the week, setting aside a block of time bears more fruit because it tempers the will. Embracing the requirement to rest is, of course, itself an act of the will, but obedience to God always bears fruit in the soul and liberates us from the worry that we "should be doing something." Rather than putting a burden on us, many people could really stand to think about the Lord's Day as "permission" to

67. RMiss, Universal Norms on the Liturgical Year and the Calendar, no. 56.
68. Cf. Mt 11:28.

rest. Jesus proclaimed the true meaning of the Lord's Day: "The sabbath was made for man, not man for the sabbath."[69] Setting aside time for rest gives our other activities their proper priority.

In the Western world, with its emphasis on activity and productivity, the idea of taking an entire day off every week can sometimes sound impossible—but another great effect of following the Third Commandment is that it will produce greater organization of the rest of life. Many people intend to rest on Sunday *only* after they will have sorted out the rest of the week and caught up on their work. From a Christian perspective, the exact opposite is true. A simple example can demonstrate this: Imagine you have an important event coming up—tickets to watch a game with a friend and thousands of fans or plans to host a large dinner party with your spouse. Knowing that the day of the event is not available, you would be sure to get everything else done ahead of time: Your report will get written, the bathroom will get cleaned, and all your travel or purchasing plans will be completed the night before. You will plan for the day of the event to be "unproductive." The same holds true for Sunday rest. Once a person fully commits to taking Sunday "off the table" for labor, much of the rest of the week falls into place. The wrong approach is to "get life organized" and then start assigning time for rest on Sunday; rather, reserving Sunday for rest causes the rest of life to become more organized.

Of course, Sunday rest should not be absolutized. Jesus himself often came into conflict with the Pharisees over their excessive legalization of the Sabbath rest.[70] Work required for the welfare and safety of the person him- or herself and for the common good is permissible on Sunday. Some of these lines of work, though not exhaustive, fall into that category: health care workers, restaurant workers, police officers, firefighters, pharmacists, and fuel station attendants. Additionally, "work" done out of charity rather than servility is not only allowed but encouraged. Giving Sunday over to caring of others is praiseworthy. Jesus himself declared that the care of the sick comes before the Sabbath.[71] Such necessary or laudable work, however, does not eliminate the requirement to attend Mass. Labor that habitually impedes attendance at Sunday (and Saturday evening) Mass must be curtailed. Part of being a witness to the value

69. Mk 2:27.

70. Cf. Mt 12:1–8.

71. Cf. Lk 13:10–16; 14:1–5; Jn 5:9–10.

of the Gospel is that Catholics insist with their employers on the importance of attending Mass. It is an important witness for colleagues, friends, and family members to see that God comes before anything else. Part of the New Evangelization of re-Christianizing society needs to include restoring the observation of Sunday and Holy Days of Obligation as the Lord's Day.

Centering Our Life on the Eucharist

Given the overwhelming reality of containing the entire spiritual treasure of the Church, it is impossible to fully describe and comprehend the Holy Eucharist. The Real Presence of Christ received in Holy Communion includes every possible grace and blessing; it is up to the recipient to harness as much of this grace as possible. The principal effect of the Eucharist is to transform the recipient of the Body and Blood of Christ into "another Christ." In the wake of these powerful effects, many Christians throughout history have made heroic sacrifices to attend Mass and receive Holy Communion. There are scores of edifying stories of deep faith and love for the Eucharist among people living under squalid human conditions; just the stories from the twentieth-century Nazi concentration camps and Soviet Gulags could edify a person's soul. Both priests and lay Catholics have gone to great lengths to obtain bread and wine for the Mass in dangerous circumstances.

If a person is looking to understand the Catholic faith, to grow in virtue, or to better know who Jesus is, there is no better place to begin than by regularly attending Sunday Mass. Even if such a person is unable to receive Holy Communion, regular participation in the Mass will aid understanding, strengthen moral fortitude, and increase love of God and neighbor. When unable to receive the Eucharist, it is highly encouraged to pray an "Act of Spiritual Communion" that expresses the soul's desire to receive Holy Communion, showing the utmost respect for the reality of the Eucharist. Many people have given words to this desire; one of the more popular is from St. Alphonsus Liguori:

> My Jesus, I believe that You are truly present in the Most Holy Sacrament. I love You above all things, and I desire to receive You into my soul. Since I cannot at this moment receive You sacramentally, come at least spiritually into my heart. I embrace You as being

> already there and unite myself wholly to You. Never permit me to be separated from You. Amen.[72]

The Eucharist is a Sacrament of hope and consolation for a confused, broken world. As St. John Paul II reflected in the twilight of his pontificate, the Eucharist is the main pillar of the New Evangelization. It is thus urgent that the modern disciple be wholeheartedly centered on the Holy Eucharist in order to make Christ real in an age pining for the joy and hope of Christ. As Pope Francis taught, evangelization comes out of the overflow of our union with Christ through the Eucharist and the Word of God:

> The work of evangelization enriches the mind and the heart; it opens up spiritual horizons; it makes us more and more sensitive to the workings of the Holy Spirit, and it takes us beyond our limited spiritual constructs.[73]

72. St. Alphonsus Liguori, *Prayer of Spiritual Communion*.
73. EG, no. 272.

CHAPTER 15

RECONCILIATION AND RENEWAL

We have discussed the Sacraments of Christian Initiation that bring us new life in Christ:

- *Baptism,* by which an individual is reborn or initiated into the life of Jesus.
- *Confirmation,* which perfects that birth into the life in Christ by introducing the recipient to the role of becoming a witness and proclaimer of the faith.
- The *Eucharist,* by which the disciple grows in union with Christ.

Though the guilt of Original Sin is forgiven in Baptism, it does not remove the *effects* of Original Sin; our wounded human nature remains, what St. Paul called "earthen vessels."[1] Within that vessel there is the beauty of Christ's presence and the indwelling of the Holy Spirit. Despite a participation in the life of Christ, however, any Christian, through sins of weakness or simple pride, can reject this close relationship of being a child of God. Because of these endemic weaknesses, which never leave a person, it is to be expected (but never justified) that everyone will fall into sin somewhere along the line.

These tendencies manifest themselves in pride, laziness, anger, greed, envy, gluttony, and lust. It is impossible to always avoid sins of weakness caused by inordinate appetites and passions, and only with considerable struggle can a person begin to dominate these various weaknesses. Though self-mastery can grow through grace and acquired virtue, it can never be so complete that personal weakness vanishes. The pursuit of holiness is a struggle of a lifetime.

Since so many weaknesses and temptations hold such a strong grip on every human being, Jesus, in his merciful extravagance, instituted two Sacraments of Healing.[2] One of them is the Sacrament of

1. 2 Cor 4:7.
2. Cf. CCC 1421.

Penance and Reconciliation, which removes sin every time there is repentance. The other, the topic of the next chapter, is the Anointing of the Sick, which bestows strength on any person afflicted by serious illness that could at least remotely lead to death. Unlike Baptism and Confirmation, performed only once and leaving an indelible mark on the soul, the Sacraments of Healing are repeated throughout life as a person works for greater communion with God and a closer relationship with Jesus Christ.

The Need for Healing

Sin has multiple effects. First, every sin is an offense against God, the source of all goodness who loves us with an infinite love. Sin also wounds the sinner. Sin is not a mere unethical mishap but a thought, word, or action that leaves the human heart debilitated; Christians' sins also wound the entire Church, Christ's Mystical Body. Every Christian is connected with all the others since they all form part of the Communion of Saints. This Mystical Body of Christ can be affected positively by deeds of faith and love or adversely by sins. "If one member suffers, all suffer together."[3] It is fitting, therefore, that this Sacrament has as one of its names "Reconciliation" since the repentant sinner's severed or strained relationship with Jesus Christ and his Church is restored. Through this Sacrament a person asks for both mercy and healing to remedy the harm caused by sin.

Rejecting sin and embracing the New Commandment of Love always requires internal transformation. Another name for Penance is the "Sacrament of Conversion" since by this Sacrament, Christ provokes a conversion of heart. Conversion consists in recognizing one's own sin and the subsequent impulse to turn away from it. The name "Sacrament of Repentance" emphasizes the grace of repentance—which is given alongside the grace of penitence. These interior sentiments are expressed in contrition (sorrow) for sin and purpose of amendment. This is truly a Sacrament of Healing since it pertains to the restoration of health to the soul.

The "Sacrament of Confession" is a frequently used name that refers to the action of the recipient, that is, the self-accusation of personal sins, an essential part of the Sacrament. Only through the acknowledgment and accusation of sin can there be full repentance

3. 1 Cor 12:26.

and true reconciliation with Jesus Christ and his Church. As the penitent confesses personal sins, true contrition and sorrow is often awakened for having rejected the love of Jesus Christ.

This same Sacrament is called the "Sacrament of Forgiveness" since the confession of sins invariably elicits a response of merciful forgiveness. In his abundant mercy, Jesus will eagerly forgive anyone who exhibits contrition for sins. This name signifies God's perpetual open-door policy in forgiving us of any type of sin at all times. When it comes to this Sacrament, Jesus is open for business twenty-four hours a day, seven days a week. As Jesus revealed, "There is joy before the angels of God over one sinner who repents."[4]

The gravity of the sin is of no consequence to God, so long as there is true repentance. This message was given anew by Jesus through St. Faustina Kowalska, a Polish nun and mystic in the early twentieth century. Jesus revealed to her his great desire to offer forgiveness to repentant sinners. From these visits to St. Faustina, the Catholic Church has fostered a devotion to "Divine Mercy." Jesus urged St. Faustina: "Let no soul fear to draw near to Me, even though its sins be as scarlet."[5] Jesus is not waiting for us to confess so that he can condemn us; he waits so that he might offer his infinite mercy and forgiveness:

> My Heart overflows with great mercy for souls, and especially for poor sinners. If only they could understand that I am the best of Fathers to them and that it is for them that the Blood and Water flowed from My Heart as from a fount overflowing with mercy.[6]

Reconciliation in the New Testament

The mercy of Jesus Christ was first revealed in a material way while he walked the earth. Throughout the Gospel, the sick are often recipients of Jesus' merciful healing power. Most of Jesus' miracles involve healing sick, debilitated people. The Gospel narratives reveal that Jesus' specialty is to heal the sick, console the suffering, and to ward off the Evil One. This whole range of diverse sicknesses found in the Gospel serve as symbols of infirmity of soul through sin. Jesus, who healed physical ailments, will heal the wounds of the soul as

4. Lk 15:10.
5. DSFK, no.699, 10.
6. Ibid., no.367, 114.

the divine Physician, particularly through the Sacrament of Penance and Reconciliation.

Jesus himself highlights the connection to be drawn. The first miracle of Jesus recorded in the Gospel of St. Mark is the healing of a leper. Leprosy, as presented in Chapter 11 of this book, is a perfect analogy for the inner effects of sin on the soul. Coming to Jesus the suffering man said, "If you will, you can make me clean." Jesus, "moved with pity" responded, "I will; be clean."[7] After this, St. Mark related another healing when some good men lowered their paralyzed friend through the roof of a house where Jesus was. In this act of love for their friend, Jesus, seeing their faith, looked down at the paralytic and said, "Your sins are forgiven."[8] Some religious leaders took offense at this because only God can forgive sins. Jesus then asked them, "Which is easier, to say… 'Your sins are forgiven,' or to say, 'Rise, take up your pallet and walk'?"[9] To demonstrate his own authority to forgive sin, he orders the paralyzed man to rise up and walk.[10] In these and other miracles, the Gospels relate the healing mission of Jesus for both body and soul.

To encounter this healing forgiveness requires repentance and a change of heart. St. John the Baptist prepared for the Messiah by preaching repentance. Jesus began his public life inviting everyone to repentance and belief in the Gospel. Repentance is Our Lord's first admonition of his public life since the immediate obstacle to a relationship with Jesus Christ is sin. Any form of selfishness always poses a barrier between ourselves and Jesus Christ, the Incarnation of self-giving love. Belief in the Gospel, more than an academic assent to Christ's teachings, consists in embracing all that Jesus did and taught. To conform to the heart of Jesus, purification from sin is the necessary starting point. The whole public life of Jesus is comprised of moving narratives of repentance from sin and the pursuit of holiness in imitation of the Master.

In fact, in Jesus' public life virtually all the people he met needed serious repentance. Many of them eventually became saints, but not before they had reconciled with God and resolved to avoid sinning. The Apostle St. Matthew, before meeting Our Lord, was widely

7. Mk 1:40–41.

8. Mk 2:5.

9. Mk 2:9.

10. Mk 2:11.

known as a public sinner given his line of work as a tax collector. A tax collector in the time of Christ would have sold out his own people, being loyal to the occupiers; they made money by taking extra from their fellow citizens with the backing of the powerful empire oppressing God's chosen people. St. Matthew's profound change of heart contrasts with the indignation of the self-righteous Pharisees upon witnessing his festive celebration with his wayward friends. This is how Jesus made it abundantly clear that his ardent desire is, under no uncertain terms, to call sinners to the joy of repentance: "Those who are well have no need of a physician, but those who are sick; I have not come to call the righteous, but sinners to repentance."[11]

St. Peter, Head of the Apostles, is another clear example of both the need for and power of contrition for sins committed and the deep resolve to follow Christ more closely. St. Peter would provide leadership in the challenging, dangerous enterprise of the first evangelization. Even after faithfully following Our Lord, when Christ had to suffer, St. Peter grew scared and three times vehemently denied that he had any relationship or connection with Jesus Christ. On a natural level, the Church was not off to a good start with the first Pope denying any allegiance to the Church's founder! In a very moving scene of reconciliation, Jesus forgave and healed St. Peter,[12] who went on to suffer his own death rather than deny Our Lord again.

The preliminary step to these conversions—and to all the conversions recorded in the Gospels—is a friendly encounter with Jesus Christ. Through friendly exchanges, the different people contemplate Jesus' goodness and mercy in his affectionate eyes, loving words, and sentiments of deep compassion. Repentance over sinful lifestyles is not driven by a dry consideration of ethical wrongdoing but by a desire for a relationship with Jesus Christ. None of the people in the Gospels converted a compelling ethical instruction or an argument over a moral issue, but rather they gazed into the face of Jesus Christ and conversed with him. These affectionate encounters led to acknowledgment and sorrow over sin and a newfound commitment to follow Jesus faithfully.

None of Jesus' relationships is initiated by exhortations to external acts of self-denial and religious observances but rather by gentle

11. Lk 5:31–32; cf. Mt 9:12–13, Mk 2:17.
12. Cf. Jn 21:15–19.

invitations to a change of heart through sorrow for sin and commitment to discipleship. For a spirit of penance to be a springboard for conversion, it must emerge from within the intimacy of the human heart. True piety and ascetical practice must, therefore, presuppose repentance and a desire for union with Christ. Then Jesus can say, as he said to the woman caught in adultery, "Go, and do not sin again."[13] The famous penitential Psalm 51 reveals that God's favorite act of penance is "a broken and contrite heart"[14] since the humble, penitent heart provides the proper staging area for true love for God.

Furthermore, conversion from sin is not merely an isolated incident of sorrow for a single action that offends God. The repentance God wants is, in Greek, *metanoia;*[15] this word is difficult to translate with total precision. It is a profound sorrow for sin that leads to a serious rejection of all sin coupled with an ardent desire to genuinely walk with Christ. Almost all the people in the Gospels are model penitents who expressed profound sorrow for sin and commitment to embracing Christ's teaching. Their interior conversions were so deep that many of them eventually died as martyrs for the faith. The spirit of penance Jesus required of his first disciples still holds for the contemporary disciple as the standard of true Christian living.

In line with these stories of repentance, the initiation of virtually all conversions throughout the ages begins with a personal encounter with Christ's love through a good example by someone, an interior illumination, or exposure to the life of a holy person. Many have experienced profound changes of heart and desires for spiritual reform by an encounter with a saint.

At a papal audience with St. John Paul II, a woman introduced her husband to the Pope, disclosing that her husband was not practicing his faith. The Holy Father looked at him with much love and verbally lamented how sad it must be to be separated from Jesus Christ. The person in question found the first opportunity to receive the Sacrament of Penance and Reconciliation after many years of being away from it.

---

13. Jn 8:11.
14. Ps 51:17.
15. Cf. Mt 3:8, 11; 9:13; Mk 1:4; 2:17; Lk 3:3, 8; 5:32; 15:7; 24:47; Acts 5:31; 11:18; 13:24; 19:4; 20:21; 26:20; Rom 2:4; 2 Cor 7:9 ff.; 2 Tm 2:25; Heb 6:1, 6; 12:17; 2 Pt 3:9.

The Prodigal Son

Jesus' moving Parable of the Prodigal Son [16] is the ideal paradigm for repentance and interior healing from the ravages of sin and the boundless forgiveness of our loving Father. Read according to the moral sense of Scripture (see Chapter 1), this parable is packed with lessons on the nature of sin, human freedom, and the indescribable mercy lavished on every repentant person. The parable unfolds with the younger of two sons demanding his inheritance and leaving his father in pursuit of a wasteful life of sensual pleasure. He uses his greatest gift, which is his free will, for self-indulgence and a life of dissipation.

This lavish lifestyle eventually drains the prodigal son's money, leaving him destitute and miserable. He lost his freedom, joy, and dignity because he was chained to lustful pleasures. His debauched life is symbolic of sin, which falsely promises satisfaction, but fleeting pleasures ultimately lead to disillusionment and dissatisfaction. Alienation from God and rejection of his overtures of love through the pursuit of illicit self-gratification leaves a human person morally and spiritually bankrupt. The effects of sin generally enslave a person to inordinate passions of anger, lust, and avarice — to name a few. These idolatries of selfishness are diametrically opposed to love for both God and neighbor. They greatly diminish freedom for self-giving love and a life of real happiness.

In a moment of intense sadness and borderline despair, the Gospel reveals, "He came to himself,"[17] recalling the goodness of his father and the contentment that everyone enjoyed at home. Recalling his father's goodness sparked a change of heart. He reflected on how wonderful it was in those times gone by when he lived with his father and had food in abundance. He realized that in his present state of separation from his father, he was lacking even the food of the pigs he had been hired to feed. He wanted to recover that joy of being in his father's house, so he planned to make a profound apology to securing a menial position in his father's household. He resolved to return home and declare: "Father, I have sinned against heaven and before you; I am no longer worthy to be called your son;

16. Lk 15:11–32.

17. Lk 15:17.

treat me as one of your hired servants."[18] In this planned declaration, he intended to acknowledge his guilt and seek reconciliation.

The prodigal son, however, underestimated the love of his father. The parable clearly implies that each day the father was peering off into the distance for a sign of his son's return. "While he was yet at a distance,"[19] the father saw his son, was filled with compassion, and rushed out to joyfully embrace him. The contrite son repeated his prepared self-accusation, "Father, I have sinned against heaven and before you; I am no longer worthy to be called your son."[20] What does a person expect in such a moment? In our own life we might expect recrimination and judgment. The prodigal son was prepared to accept servitude as a mercy. His father, however, immediately rejoiced, covered his son in the finest robe, put rings on his fingers, and ordered that the fatted calf be killed so that they could celebrate his son's return. "My son was dead, and is alive again; he was lost, and is found."[21]

The son made the startling discovery that his father had so much love for him that he never made even the slightest reference to the deeds of his sinful past but was ecstatic over his son's unexpected return. Not only did his father refrain from any mention of his son's wrongdoing, but he threw a huge party. The father showed not the slightest amount of resentment over his son's disgraceful, irresponsible deeds. Instead of the typical reaction expected from the parent of a wayward son, the father rewarded his son's contrition and repentance with an extravagant feast because the son's contrite heart had sprung him back to life.

Before this joyful occasion, the father was overcome with sorrow, feeling that his son was dead. As the prodigal son's life of dissipation reveals the effects of the life of sin, his "death" was not a physical death but a worse kind. The son was morally and spiritually dead and, consequently, gripped with a punishing despair caused by his culpable alienation from his father. He had come back to life, which is intimately linked to coming to his senses, repenting of his misdeeds, and returning to his father's house.

18. Lk 15:18–19.

19. Lk 15:20.

20. Lk 15:21.

21. Lk 15:24.

Every time a penitent approaches the Sacrament of Penance and Reconciliation, this joyful celebration is realized. Though it may lack the external drama described in this parable, spiritually there can be the same joy. The father of the prodigal son, who equally symbolizes God the Father and Jesus Christ, the Son of God, rejoices in forgiving every person who shows contrition for sin. It almost seems too good to be true that our God became man and died on his Cross so that we can be liberated from our sins any time we express sorrow, especially in Confession. The rich food, joyful dancing, and welcoming reception plays out in an interior way every time we make a good confession. People who nervously or even fearfully push themselves to make a good confession regularly come out elated and brimming with hope. This Sacrament, no matter how great the severity of sin, recuperates the loss of dignity, freedom, and joy.

In fact, former hardcore sinners have led saintly lives precisely because of the love and mercy lavished on them through their experience of this Sacrament of Forgiveness. The Parable of the Prodigal Son makes it patently obvious that God loves each one of us as a perfect Father who revels in forgiving his children and giving them endless chances for a fresh start. The infinite love of God for every person is made visible in the humanity of Jesus Christ, whose mission is to reveal God's love for us and eradicate sin. Therefore, in the Sacrament of Penance and Reconciliation, the recipient especially sees God's most salient perfection of mercy and compassion.

Why Do I Need a Priest?

Given the abundant mercy of God and his unfailing desire to forgive his children, many people wonder why there needs to be a formal Sacrament: "Why do I need to go tell some priest what I've done wrong? Can't I simply confess to God and be forgiven?" It must be acknowledged that the Sacrament of Penance and Reconciliation is not absolutely necessary for remission of *every* sin since forgiveness can be found in acts of contrition expressed in remorse and purpose of amendment outside of Confession. Recall, for example, from Chapter 14 that receiving Holy Communion can absolve a person from at least venial sins.

When it comes to grave sin, however, God must directly intervene to restore that person from the state of mortal sin to the state of grace. In the physical realm, it depends on the severity of the sickness whether medicine and medical intervention is needed or whether the body on its own can get over a minor infirmity. The response to a common cold is certainly different than to an aggressive cancer; the cold will go away with a bit of rest and proper nourishment, whereas cancer requires serious medical intervention. For mortal sin, therefore, which prevents a person from receiving Holy Communion, Jesus needs to intervene directly to remove that sin through the reception of Penance.

No one can singlehandedly restore a severed relationship with God nor heal oneself of the effects caused by his or her iniquities. Though the Sadducees in the story of the paralytic[22] were misguided, they were not wrong: Only God can forgive sins. The Gospels reveal that Jesus directly heals physical diseases and on his own authority; this is only possible because Jesus is divine. But as with the Eucharist, where the bishop or priest acts *in persona Christi*, in his infinite wisdom and mercy God has willed that forgiveness of sin could be administered through his Apostles and their successors, who are empowered to directly forgive sins in his name. Jesus gave this power to his bishops—who share it with their coworkers, the priests—since he wanted easy, merciful access to an immediate removal of sin.

It was Jesus who made reparation for every sin and won graces that could forgive all sins and transform every person into a saint, but it has pleased God to apply these graces through his Church through the actions of Jesus' ordained ministers. The proper minister of the Sacrament of Penance and Reconciliation, then, is a bishop or priest. By virtue of the sacred power transmitted through the Sacrament of Holy Orders, bishops and priests have the power to forgive sins in the name of Jesus Christ. This Sacrament was officially instituted on the night of Christ's Resurrection, which is the greatest sign of his victory over sin and the Evil One. He gave his Apostles the power to forgive sins: "If you forgive the sins of any, they are forgiven; if you retain the sins of any, they are retained."[23] Jesus' Apostles, in turn, handed on this authority and power to forgive sins to their successors, the bishops, who have handed it on to successive bishops to the present day. Any time someone wants forgiveness of personal sins, all that is needed is a sign of contrition

22. Mt 9:1–8; Mk 2:1–12; Lk 5:18–26.

23. Jn 20:23.

and accusation of sin before a bishop or priest who, in turn, absolves him or her of sin in the name of Jesus.

No bishop or priest wields the power to absolve sins in the name of Christ without discretion; it is exercised after making a determination about whether there is sufficient repentance and a firm amendment to change. The minister cannot arbitrarily withhold absolution from sin, but he must evaluate whether the penitent has the necessary contrition to be forgiven. If someone were to confess to habitually stealing large sums of money, show no remorse, and make it clear he or she has no intention to stop, then absolution would not be given due to lack of repentance. As always, the disposition of the recipient is essential to the Sacrament.

There is another reason for approaching Confession for the forgiveness of sin: Being a Sacrament, it offers special graces and healing. Sin is not just an ethical mistake or an academic digression from a proper moral choice. Every sin leaves the person damaged, heart and soul. In fact, a sin offends God simply because it harms his greatest creation: the human person. The remedy for maladies caused by sin requires divine healing that springs from the Sacrament of Penance and Reconciliation.

But why is sacramental confession before a bishop or priest necessary? Spiritual and moral wounds affect not only the individual Christian personally but also his or her relationships with others and with the Church as a whole. There is, therefore, a need to be reconciled not only with God but also with his Body, the Church. In fact, reconciling with God *involves* reconciling with Christ's Church; the Head of the Church cannot be separated from his Mystical Body. An offense against Christ through violation of his Commandments is automatically an offense against his Church. The bishop, as head of the local Church, is the minister of the Sacrament of Penance and Reconciliation. He represents not only Christ but also the Church, to whom the penitent must confess his or her guilt. Since the priests are coworkers in the ministry of their bishop, they are delegated by their bishop to hear confessions.

For someone approaching the Sacrament of Penance and Reconciliation, the minister should not be imagined as a harsh critic, lying in wait to dole out judgment. The minister is a sacramental sign of all the different images of Jesus that we find in the Gospel. Jesus Christ is the Good Shepherd who eagerly seeks out his lost sheep and knows each one by name.[24] The minister's mission is to heal spiritual and moral infirmities caused by sin. The Good Samaritan is another image of Jesus Christ, who binds the wounds of the penitent and helps him or her recover health.[25] The minister is called to be a sign of the merciful Heart of Jesus.[26] The minister is expected to pray and do personal penance for their penitents. He represents Christ identified with the father of the prodigal son, rejoicing at the recovery of his lost child.

Last, given the lofty grandeur of this particular ministry of reconciliation and the special access the bishop or priest has to the intimacy of consciences, he is gravely obligated to keep absolute secrecy about what transpires in Confession. In the confessional, the recipient speaks not *to* him but *through* him to God. If he violates what is called "the sacramental seal,""the seal of the confessional," or "the seal of confession," severe penalties are imposed upon him: "It is a crime for a confessor in any way to betray a penitent by word or in any other manner or for any reason."[27]

The seal of the confessional is necessary in establishing the full confidence for the recipient to come clean without the least bit of concern over a possible disclosure by the minister. Without this clear obligation to secrecy, many people would simply never go to Confession, especially in the case of grave sin. Absolute confidentiality must be maintained. This secrecy must be so strictly kept that the priest can never use that information to influence the opinions of others, even in a court of law. Every bishop or priest realizes he is the minister of a sacred and treasured Sacrament.

Development of the Sacrament of Penance and Reconciliation

To understand the role of the minister in the Sacrament of Penance and Reconciliation, it might be helpful to consider the development of this Sacrament over time. From its very inception, Penance has always been recognized as a sure avenue for the forgiveness of sin; nevertheless, many features of its celebration and reception have undergone profound developments without changes to its essen-

24. Cf. Ps 23; Jn 10:1–21.

25. Cf. Lk 10:29–37.

26. Cf. Ps 103; Hos 11:1–12.

27. CCC 2490; quoting CIC, can. 983 § 1.

tial elements. During the early years of Christianity, only penitents who had committed very serious sins like idolatry, adultery, murder, and apostasy would have recourse to this Sacrament. The recipients, because of their grave sins, would be barred from receiving the Eucharist and required to do public penance before receiving absolution.

During early persecutions, for example, there was a difficult controversy over how to reconcile with Christians who had lapsed by renouncing Christ to avoid torture. They had committed a grave sin, and some of the faithful—particularly those who had themselves faced torture at the hands of the Romans—felt the lapsed Christians should be permanently excommunicated, no matter how sincere their sorrow and desire to continue following Christ was. The bishops of the early centuries knew they had both the "power to bind" and the "power to loose"[28] and determined that Christians who had lapsed but were now truly repentant could return to full communion after a period of public penance. Seeking forgiveness for a mortal sin required a serious commitment to years of prayer, penance, and contrite reflection on the sins committed.

The following incident illustrates how the Sacrament of Penance and Reconciliation was received in the Early Church. St. Ambrose, Archbishop of Milan, excommunicated Emperor Theodosius and demanded that he do public penance for having slaughtered 700 villagers in Thessalonica. The emperor took reprisals against the Christians. St. Ambrose barred the emperor from entering the church and receiving Holy Communion. Theodosius, wearing the clothes of a penitent, prostrated himself in the form of a cross outside of the church's entrance before every Sunday Mass. After eight months of penance and public prayer, St. Ambrose pardoned the emperor and lifted the excommunication.

Over time, however, public confessions were replaced with private confessions, and Penance became more accessible to the faithful, not limited merely to grave sin. Pope St. Leo the Great prohibited public confessions and insisted they be private. Though *confessions* were now private, the Church did not put a stop to public *penance*, which only revealed that a person was making expiation while the specific sin remained a private matter.

28. Cf. Jn 20:23.

In the Early Church, it was not customary among Christians to have recourse to the Sacrament of Penance and Reconciliation for venial (less serious) sin. She taught, and still teaches, that these lesser, more common sins can be removed by normal ascetical practices, an act of contrition, or the reception of Holy Communion. Although it is not absolutely necessary to receive Penance if a person is not aware of mortal sin, as the *Catechism* teaches:

> Confession of everyday faults (venial sins) is nevertheless strongly recommended by the Church.[29] Indeed the regular confession of our venial sins helps us form our conscience, fight against evil tendencies, let ourselves be healed by Christ and progress in the life of the Spirit. By receiving more frequently through this sacrament the gift of the Father's mercy, we are spurred to be merciful as he is merciful.[30]

Over time the Church grew in its appreciation for the role that regular Confession plays in a Christian's growth in holiness.

The Sacrament of Penance and Reconciliation, using an image from the early Fathers of the Church, is like a lifesaving plank after a shipwreck. The message of Jesus' mercy is all about getting another opportunity to make amends and begin again. Penance unleashes a reservoir of gratuitous mercy. As the administration of Penance has been refined through the ages, its appreciation has also been greatly enhanced. Its accessibility has made it clear that sacramental Confession is indeed an invaluable treasure. Today, it is not uncommon for people to receive Confession frequently and to view the Sacrament not only as a means of restoring communion after serious sin but also as a font of grace to grow in holiness. Frequent reception of Penance provides graces to overcome habitual venial sins, to grow in charity, and to trust more fully in Jesus' mercy and love.

Necessary Conditions for Confession

For the proper and valid celebration of the Sacrament of Penance and Reconciliation, two essential requirements are necessary. The matter of Penance is the recipient's right dispositions and proper actions. These penitential dispositions and actions are sorrow for sins personally committed, self-accusation of these offenses against God's Law, and a willingness to make satisfaction for those sins—

29. Cf. Ecumenical Council of Trent: DS 1680; CIC can. 988 § 2.
30. CCC 1458; cf. Lk 6:36.

contrition, confession, and penance. The form of Penance involves Christ's forgiveness through the words of the minister, who provides the absolution from sin in the name of Christ: "I absolve you from your sins, / in the name of the Father, and of the Son, and of the Holy Spirit."[31]

The most important penitential disposition for the Sacrament of Penance and Reconciliation is *contrition*: the virtue of sorrow for having committed sin. The internal sorrow over sinful thoughts, words, or deeds must also be supernatural, that is, it must be connected to a person's relationship with God and the state of his or her soul. It cannot simply arise out of a sense of disillusionment over a poor performance; a feeling of natural shame or embarrassment due to the loss of a good reputation; or some other emotional, self-centered response. The contrition necessary for Penance is a sorrow over having offended God—not the pain of having a lowered self-esteem.

There is a distinction between two levels of contrition: Contrition is *perfect* when the sadness and grief is born purely out of love for God, and contrition is *imperfect* when it is prompted by fear of eternal damnation, the pains of purgatory, or the ugliness of being stained by sin. Although both are inspired by supernatural motives, imperfect contrition is not prompted by total love of God. Contrition—whether perfect or imperfect—is always the work of the Holy Spirit, who enlightens the mind and moves the will to desire forgiveness.

It is important, though, not to over-scrutinize how perfect our contrition is in a way that would prevent us from going to the Sacrament of Confession. Growth in holiness is a journey, and staying away from the Sacrament of Healing would be like not visiting a doctor until a disease is cured.

When it comes to contrition, true sorrow is lacking unless it is coupled with a firm purpose of amendment and a commitment to make satisfaction for sins committed. A person who fully intends to commit the same sin again or has no intention of repairing any of the harm done clearly is not truly sorry. Contrition in the Sacrament of Penance and Reconciliation is like the remorse necessary for natural reconciliation between people.

---

31. *The Order of Penance*. The Order for Reconciling Individual Penitents (Washington, DC: United States Conference of Catholic Bishops, 2023), no. 46.

An example of this natural reconciliation is children playing baseball in a backyard surrounded by houses. They were told to play in the spacious, local park to avoid damaging houses. They play in the backyard anyway, and someone hits a foul ball through a bedroom window. The batter is profoundly sorry because she did not heed the directive to play in the park. She rings the doorbell and apologizes profusely with tears in her eyes and clearly admits she was at fault for breaking the window. She makes a plea for forgiveness, commits never to play baseball in the backyard again, and promises to pay for a new window.

The sentiments displayed by this batter correspond to the contrition needed for Confession. If there is no contrition that at least implicitly has those three properties, the Sacrament is ineffective. How can a person seek forgiveness who is eager to find the next chance to insult that person again? How can a person be truly remorseful if there is no willingness to pay back the value of what was stolen? For the most part, what applies in demonstrating repentance in human relationships applies just as well to reconciling oneself with God. If a person fully intends to commit the same acts again, then he or she cannot be truly sorrowful over committing them the first time.

This does not mean that falling into the same sin again invalidates the reception of Penance. A person can have a firm determination not to commit the same sins again but lack the will to overcome a bad habit, particularly regarding habitual venial sins. This should not prevent a person from going again to Confession because this Sacrament can strengthen a person to overcome even the most difficult sins.

For true contrition to be properly stirred up, the penitent should, in preparation for receiving the Sacrament, make an examination of conscience; it is helpful to use the Ten Commandments and the Beatitudes as guides. In fact, all of Jesus' deeds and teachings serve as a perfect light for an examination of conscience.

An examination of conscience must first reflect on whether any grave sins have been committed since the last confession, but the recipient must be careful not to reduce the focus of an examination of conscience to only serious infractions of the divine Law. The goal of the Christian life is to grow in charity in union with Christ. Many people find that sins of commission—acting lustfully, being dishonest, and the like—are easier to see than sins of omission—lacking temperance, failing to help someone in need, and the like. In many instances recipients neglect evaluating the life of charity toward God and neighbor almost as if this virtue were inconsequential. It is also good to arrive at the motives and causes for anger, arrogance, resentments, etc., and to examine the spirit of prayer and penance.

Since contrition is the essential ingredient for obtaining forgiveness of sin, the penitent must acknowledge culpability for sin through self-accusation, and so confession of sin is the second essential part of the matter of this Sacrament. In human affairs, when someone seeks pardon, the person in question must admit and acknowledge guilt in causing offense to the injured party. The actual declaration of wrongdoing fosters remorse and contrition. We see this moving plea for forgiveness when the prodigal son states that he has sinned against heaven and earth and is no longer worthy to be called a son. Transparent accusation of sin in many instances becomes a person's finest hour.

If in the state of mortal sin, what is required to secure reconciliation with God is the explicit accusation of all mortal sin—in kind and number—and any pertinent circumstances that affect the gravity of the sin. This confession of sin corresponds to the process of asking an offended party for pardon. For instance, if a person is guilty of both verbal insults and stealing money from someone, it certainly would not make sense to seek forgiveness for the insults and ignore the robbery. If there is going to be true sorrow for all grave sin, then there must be the appropriate accusation of virtually all those serious sins. If the recipient were to purposely hide a grave sin from the minister in his or her confession, the imparted absolution would be rendered totally ineffective. In fact, the false self-accuser commits a sacrilege against the Sacrament of Penance and needs now to confess making a sacrilegious confession in addition to all the mortal sins—in kind and number—of the previous bad confession.

Considering the Sacrament as a Sacrament of Healing, such a situation can also be likened to going to a physician with a serious illness but intentionally keeping it secret. Implicit withholding of information from the doctor in the case of grave infirmity causes the person to become even sicker for lack of appropriate medical attention. As a doctor cannot cure an illness left undisclosed, Our

Lord cannot forgive a sin that is not contritely acknowledged. One important difference is that God already knows every person's heart and the state of every soul, so withholding a sin in a confession does not hide it from God.

This aspect of the Sacrament, that one must verbally admit to faults and weaknesses, which can be embarrassing, is probably the main cause of avoiding the confessional. Who wants to admit out loud the things he or she is most ashamed of? But all experienced penitents realize the actual confession of sin, no matter how serious, produces interior cleansing, unburdening of guilt, and a newfound sense of peace. Though it is never pleasant to make oneself so vulnerable in the presence of another person, sacramental Confession produces a deep sense of liberation and interior serenity. Some have gone so far as to say that it is the most liberating and satisfying catharsis ever experienced, even if amid repentant tears.

This experience, of course, has a natural counterpart. It is in the nature of the human person to experience shame and guilt over serious sin. On one hand there is a strong desire to keep an embarrassing sin hidden and, at the same time, there is a burning need to release the guilt through complete transparency with someone trustworthy. Grave sin causes a loss of hope and a low, even despairing, self-esteem that can be counteracted through an honest disclosure of wrongdoing. Relief can come from simply talking with a good friend or a counselor. The confession of sin and psychological counseling are quite different in their purpose and scope, but they do share some important traits. In both the Sacrament of Penance and personal counseling, the common baseline is total transparency articulated with a full disclosure of fears, traumas, shameful actions, and interior sentiments. When a person seeks to bare his or her heart and soul, the healing process is set in motion on a natural level. When this sincere, honest self-accusation is raised to a sacramental level, however, the healing is much more profound.

For one thing, no one can forgive a person except the one who has been offended. If we feel truly sorry for offending God, Christ himself comes to forgive us in the Sacrament of Penance and Reconciliation. The release of shameful guilt—coupled with the knowledge that Jesus Christ not only loves us but wants us for discipleship—gives recipients new leases on life. In addition to the assurance of God's forgiveness, the Sacrament also imparts special graces that no natural source can provide. All this explains why people who go back to confession, even after a long time away from it, begin to go often because of this sense of peace and encouragement to make a fresh start.

One time, a newly ordained priest—before he had heard any confessions—erroneously thought that self-accusation of sin served as the primary means of reparation and a deterrent from sinning again, especially given the recipients' feelings of shame. After hearing some confessions, the same priest became enlightened as to why forgiveness of sin takes place in this particular format and why Jesus did not simply urge penitents to confess directly to God without a human intermediary. He realized that Jesus knew exactly what he was doing when he instituted the Sacrament of Penance and Reconciliation in this sort of fashion. The priest noted that as each penitent unburdened him- or herself with accusations of shameful transgressions, there came tremendous relief; however, interior peace was greatly enhanced as the recipient—through confession, conversation, and absolution—became more cognizant that God loves him or her. Through the Sacrament, the confession of sin occasioned a new beginning. The release of this buried guilt produced, in many instances, deep conversions driven by an awareness of God's unconditional love. If the minister reflects the merciful heart of Jesus, the recipient can acquire a whole new lease on life. After a short time of hearing confessions, this priest discovered that it was the most merciful and medicinal way of pardoning sins.

Sorrow for guilt and confession of sin are indispensable but do not fully fulfill the necessary dispositions of the penitent. The penitent, amid contrition and willingness to come clean with personal sins, must also have a firm willingness to repair the damage incurred by the sins. For example, if a penitent has stolen something, her or she must make restitution. If a person's good name has been harmed, the penitent must make an effort to restore it. If a penitent has injured someone, he or she must make compensation for those injuries. God is infinitely merciful, which does not detract from his infinite justice. In most cases, the sin committed cannot be repaired through a form of material restitution, and the minister will "impose a penance." Penances often consist of a certain prayer or some time devoted to meditation, the offering of a donation, performance of a work of mercy, a service to neighbor, fasting, etc. The imposed penance, though in many instances minuscule, is meant to meet a bit of the requirements of justice. The penitent fulfills the requirement of atonement for sin by willingly accepting the penance the priest gives.

Effects of the Sacrament of Penance and Reconciliation

The effects of the Sacrament of Penance and Reconciliation are one of the Church's "best kept" open secrets. It brings the recipient back into a state of grace and restores his or her friendship with Jesus Christ. In many instances, it engulfs the heart with peace, serenity, and joy. In the case of mortal sin, the punishment of eternal damnation is abrogated. This renewed life in Christ can be called a "spiritual resurrection."

Another personal benefit of going to frequent Confession is that it serves as an anticipation and dress rehearsal for the Particular Judgment required of every person after death. It gives the recipient the chance to rectify and improve moral conduct and the spiritual life before being called out of this present life. A person can truly grow morally and spiritually by means of habitually sincere confessions of personal sins.

Since Penance reconciles the recipient to Jesus Christ, the penitent is reconciled to the Church as well. Part of this reconciliation with the Church involves an infusion of grace that redounds throughout the entire Church since every member of the Church is connected spiritually as organs and cells of a body.[32] This tenet of faith indicates that just as personal sin inflicts damage to the Mystical Body, so growth in holiness benefits this same Mystical Body. The more the Church's faithful seek forgiveness through the Sacrament of Penance, the more the wounds on the Mystical Body caused by sin are healed. This truth of the Catholic faith, though a mystery, can be partially understood with the common example of a bodily illness that affects the whole person. Even with a local infection or the extraction of a tooth, the whole body suffers as it feels weak and fatigued. When the infection or the wounded gums are healed, the whole body feels much better.

Given the importance of this Sacrament, the Church requires, "You shall confess your sins at least once a year."[33] Anyone who is

32. 1 Cor 12:12–31.

33. CCC 2042.

conscious of mortal sin should not receive Holy Communion until he or she has gone to Confession. Children who have knowledge of right and wrong and some control over their actions—which usually comes around age seven—also ought to receive their "First Confession" before receiving their First Holy Communion.

Whether conscious of serious sin or not, it is highly recommended that every Christian receive this Sacrament of mercy often. Sin does not only cause harm to a neighbor but also entails self-inflicted damage. It is important to remain mindful that contrition and confession of sinful wrongdoing and the reception of absolution do not take away the human inclination to sin and the enhanced weaknesses caused by sin. The recipient, even after receiving absolution, must struggle to live specific virtues that are meant to reverse the corresponding sins and weaknesses. This purification process of replacing sins with virtues or overcoming sinful habits is no easy endeavor. These struggles to reach full recovery and spiritual renewal form part of making satisfaction. Even though sacramental Confession is a wonderful start, there must be serious ascetical follow-up since Confession, though strengthening, does not instantaneously remove the inclination left by sinful actions and habits.

A good confession is certainly a huge help in initiating a life of virtue and holiness but does not take away a penitent's arduous struggle to live a Christian life. Habitually watching inappropriate movies or images that demean the human body and awaken lust can reverse that trend. Recovery of lost moral and spiritual ground will involve substantial prayer, acts of self-denial, and more frequent deeds of charity toward others. It would be naive to believe that Confession replaces the need to go through a spiritual recovery period. Jesus Christ, who is the Incarnation of mercy, will invariably respond to deeds of reparation by lavishing the repentant sinner with many graces. Ultimately, the effort to counteract the weaknesses left by sin ends up transforming the recipient into someone very close to Christ. These transformations have marked the lives of saints who, in many cases, had been serious sinners.

As mentioned earlier, though not strictly necessary, it is helpful to confess venial sins on a regular basis. Frequent confession of venial sin helps form a conscience to be sensitive and objective. It also helps overcome sinful tendencies and allows Christ to heal moral deficiencies more thoroughly. Through this wonderful Sacrament of healing, little by little, virtues replace sins and defects. Not only is sin forgiven, but much grace is given to grow in a life of holiness. It is no accident that the saints availed themselves of frequent confession. It is the personal experience of many that periodic confession accomplishes the following: Spouses become more united to each other, parents show more patience and love for their children, and children grow in respect for their parents. In general, good penitents become more understanding and compassionate toward the weaknesses and sins of others.

The Sacrament of Penance, like Baptism and all the others, is not a magic bullet. Union with God involves a steady change of heart by virtue of the work of grace and a desire to grow in holiness. Through the gift of grace, the Holy Spirit prompts the heart to reject sin and resolve to become a better disciple of Jesus Christ. The Holy Spirit recreates every Christian heart to serves as the energy source for a holy life. The prompting of divine grace in concert with a positive response to that grace are the basic components of the conversion process.

The Sacrament of Penance and Reconciliation specializes in healing the heart and giving peace to the soul. This interior refreshment spills into family relationships and ultimately contributes to the common good of society. The practical reason why Confession is an effective public service rests on the recipient's expectation to confess personal sins of selfishness that in many instances involve the family, the workplace, and social relations. People who frequent confession become more honest, fair, and charitable in their dealings with family, coworkers, and society. Lay Christians who receive this Sacrament better fulfill the role of the lay faithful to transform the world according to the plan of God.

CHAPTER 16

THE ANOINTING OF THE SICK

The Anointing of the Sick is the other Sacrament of Healing, one that is centered on the physically ill and the dying.

> The Sacrament of Anointing of the Sick has as its purpose the conferral of a special grace on the Christian experiencing the difficulties inherent in the condition of grave illness or old age.[1]

When someone is experiencing a serious illness, it is not uncommon that the person becomes fearful, anxious, and at times despairing. In that situation, Our Lord has instituted this Sacrament to combat those weaknesses and temptations that more readily come with serious infirmity.

In the Gospels, the sick are very prominent figures and the chief beneficiaries of Our Lord's healing power. The infirm in the Gospel narratives and throughout the history of Christianity play many key roles in manifesting the richness of Jesus Christ's compassion and mercy. By his teachings and actions, Christ reveals an obvious preference for the sick. Throughout the history of Christianity, the suffering and downtrodden have always served as a medium to showcase the love of Christ and the strength of his grace. Given the special circumstances of a seriously sick person, for good reason, Jesus instituted a Sacrament especially tailored to meet people's needs in situations of illness and possible imminent death. While the healing of the sick by Jesus is certainly an analogy for the ultimate healing from sin, this does not take away from the literal sense of Christ's compassion for those suffering.

The vast amount of time Jesus spent healing the sick demonstrates the importance of this Sacrament. This priority given to the infirm in the Early Church is captured by the Apostle St. James:

> Is any among you sick? Let him call for the elders of the church, and let them pray over him, anointing him with oil in the name of the Lord; and the prayer of faith will save the sick man, and the Lord will raise him up; and if he has committed sins, he will be forgiven.[2]

---

1. CCC 1527.
2. Jas 5:14–15.

In this passage, physical and spiritual healing are united, as indeed they are in the Sacrament. The Church's earliest tradition of anointing the sick is a clear testimony that she has always faithfully administered this Sacrament.

Those with serious illnesses or advanced in age are the prime candidates for the specific graces of the Anointing of the Sick.

Administering the Anointing of the Sick

From the earliest times, bishops and priests would visit the sick and the dying to administer the Anointing of the Sick, what has sometimes been called "Extreme Unction."

As the name implies, anointing with oil is the material element of the Anointing of the Sick. Jesus gave power to his Apostles to heal the sick by means of anointing:

> [Jesus] called to him the twelve, and began to send them out two by two.... So they went out and preached that men should repent. And they... anointed with oil many that were sick and healed them.[3]

After Jesus' Resurrection from the dead, he again instructed his disciples to anoint the sick with oil: "In my name... they will lay their hands on the sick, and they will recover."[4]

The element and actions necessary for the celebration of this Sacrament is the application of olive oil on the forehead and hands of the sick person. Alongside the Oil of Catechumens and Sacred Chrism, this "Oil of the Sick" is blessed by the bishop at the Chrism Mass. The application of the Oil of the Sick with the words of the Sacrament are preceded by laying hands on the head of the sick person.

The Oil of the Sick is the matter of the Sacrament of the Anointing of the Sick. This is preceded by the laying on of hands, in imitation of how Jesus cured the sick during his public ministry. The minister of this Sacrament is either a bishop or priest since the Anointing of the Sick requires the celebrant to act in the name and person of Christ.[5] The form of the Sacrament is the prayer of the priest:

3. Mk 6:7, 12–13.
4. Mk 16:17–18.
5. Cf. CIC, can. 1003 § 1.

> Through this holy anointing, by his most loving mercy, may the Lord assist you by the grace of the Holy Spirit so that freed from your sins he may save you and raise you up.

The Last Things

This Sacrament is meant not only to counteract the possible negative effects of an illness but also to unite the recipient to the Cross of Jesus. Our Lord especially calls the sick and the suffering to have a special relationship with him on his Cross and to unite their suffering with his. This can be extremely difficult during the pain and anxiety of illness or old age. The grace of the Anointing of the Sick helps the recipient to capitalize on the special condition of weakness and the humbling vulnerability for greater conformity to Jesus' teachings on humility and charity. The dividends, as it were, are extremely high for every person who identifies him- or herself with Christ's sufferings, and the sick and suffering enjoy a special place in the heart of Christ.

To fully benefit from this Sacrament—indeed, to suffer well—a recipient must have a proper understanding of the end of physical life as not the *end* but the *beginning* of a new, better life with God. The Book of Wisdom reveals that the beginning of all wisdom is knowing that this life is temporary and that what we do now will transform us for an eternal life that is to come.[6] Only after realizing this can we understand our lives. To suffer well requires faith, especially when suffering is joined to the possibility of death. It should be helpful, then, before discussing the effects of the Anointing of the Sick, to review the Church's teaching on the "Last Things": judgment, heaven, purgatory, and hell. This knowledge is important because we cannot know how to live our lives unless we understand the destination we hope to reach.

Particular Judgment

One of the painful consequences caused by sin's entrance into the world is the sad inevitability of death. Death, as clearly revealed in the Book of Genesis, was not part of God's original plan for our first parents. In fact, before they sinned, they were in what is called the state of innocence; this means that, according to the initial plan, they were immune from sickness and death. They would have been

6. Cf. Wis 9.

spared the anguish of the dying process, usually through illness and old age, if it were not for their Original Sin. Upon rejecting God's only command, together with ignoring the consequent punishment and death, the first man and woman ushered sin into the world. The violation of this Commandment brought hardship and death on every human person. No human person has been or will be exempted from this stain of Original Sin and its ensuing consequences—except the Blessed Virgin Mary by means of her Immaculate Conception, presented in Chapter 6.

In theological and philosophical terms, at the moment of death, the soul separates from the body. While all living things have a spirit, or "life force," that leaves them at the point of physical death, the human person's composition transcends that of all purely physical beings—every human being has a soul that is both immaterial and eternal. There is a radical difference between the soul of a dog or a flower and that of a human being. Though the physical components are made of the same raw material, the capacities of the respective souls are essentially different. The human soul not only possesses the animating characteristics enjoyed by plants and animals but also strictly spiritual activity. In addition to the power of growth, movement, and sensation, a human person can know the truth and make free choices to pursue goods.

The abilities to know and love, which stem from the gifts of an intellect and a free will, are properties of an immortal soul (cf. Chapter 4); therefore, at the moment of human death, the soul does not simply vanish with the death of the body but lives on without the body. The human being, after this separation, is incomplete because this type of soul, although spiritual, is made to animate a body. After death, the person lives on as a bodiless soul. For this reason, we pray in the Mass that at the moment of death, "For your faithful, Lord, / life is changed not ended / and... an eternal dwelling is made ready for them in heaven."[7] For a while, the soul will live independently of the body until it is rejoined with its body at the resurrection on the Last Day.

Death brings an inherent suffering because by nature everyone ardently desires to live. Since we only die once without the experience of someone returning to describe what death and the afterlife

7. RMiss, The Order of Mass, Preface I for the Dead (The Hope of Resurrection in Christ), no. 78.

are like, the imminence of this eventuality brings with itself a natural anxiety and apprehension. The Anointing of the Sick, therefore, fulfills a real need. Sickness brings about certain states of mind that usually are not anticipated in times of health and youth. Amid a serious infirmity there is that common and, at times, novel experience of weakness and inadequacy. Under these conditions of fragility and vulnerability, a person has a chance to contemplate the swift passing of human life. This state of mind can bring about deep sadness, fear, anxiety, and despair, especially in the case of a terminal illness. Despite resistance and incredulity, every person must come to terms with the reality of imminent mortality. This experience is not meant to cultivate dread or despair; it should, rather, inspire personal conversion, a deeper contemplation of the life of Christ, and transformation in Christ. It is the experience of priests and ministers of care who visit the seriously ill that the sick in many cases grow in holiness and reveal the face of Christ.

The topic of death naturally segues into the question concerning the situation of the soul and body, now separated. First, there is a type of "registration" or "checking in" at the "eternal lobby" where metaphorically speaking the divine Judge, Jesus Christ, will conduct a type of interview. This meeting is traditionally called the "Particular Judgment." This Judgment occurs right after death since the time for merit and spiritual growth will have come to a close with our last breath. Only during our short sojourn here on earth can we gain graces that would contribute to our salvation and personal growth in holiness. By the same token, only in our life on this earth can we regress in our moral life and fall back in our journey to God through sinful choices and actions.

Since the chance to earn merit or blame ends at death, only in this life can we reform and repent. Only while alive can we intensify our relationship with Christ and grow in Christian virtue. When Our Lord calls us out of this world, it will no longer be possible to either regress or progress in our quest to follow Christ; the state of our final disposition remains fixed. At the moment of death, the divine and merciful Judge, Jesus Christ, makes his verdict regarding our eternal destination.

What will be covered in the Particular Judgment is certainly not a mystery, nor should it come as a surprise. Throughout the New Testament, the loud and clear message is that Our Lord will judge every person according to his or her works, measured by our love for others.[8] Jesus, who is the Incarnation of mercy, will be our Judge. He has explicitly mentioned the questions that will be addressed to us at the time of judgment: He will review our works of charity, which include both corporal and spiritual works of mercy. Included in the deeds of charity is its driving force of contemplative union with Jesus Christ by means of the Word of God and the Holy Eucharist. Treatment of family and friends as well as the sick and the underprivileged will fall under Jesus' merciful scrutiny. In the face of this exit interview, we want to be prepared with a life replete with acts of self-giving love specified by the traditional corporal and spiritual works of mercy.

Although Jesus' descriptions of judgment are focused on growth in charity, this does not make morality or sinfulness a side note of no importance. Recall that in Chapter 4 on the moral life, sin is at root a selfishness that turns the soul away from God and harms the neighbor; it cuts a person off from a loving relationship with God. Pursuing the moral life, on the other hand, turns a person toward God and offers the correct choices for better loving God and neighbor. Striving to live a moral life through mastery over disordered passions is like working out the body to be fit for doing the deeds of love that Jesus expects of us. As St. Peter reveals, "Love covers a multitude of sins."[9] Acts of love should be the goal of life in spite of personal weakness.

Once the soul undergoes this Particular Judgment, its eternal destiny is determined. There are two possible destinations that are permanent and one temporary. These two definitive possibilities consist either of eternal happiness in heaven or never-ending woe in hell. Those who are saved through the pursuit of holiness and repentance without being fully purified enter into a state of purification called purgatory. After the necessary purgation in purgatory has been completed, the soul acquires the capacity to contemplate God in heaven.

Those who die in the state of God's grace and have no need of further purification in the afterlife will no longer see God through the light of faith but directly, face to face; this is called the Beatific

8. Cf. Mt 25:31–46.

9. 1 Pt 4:8.

Vision. Until "the resurrection of the dead"[10] on the last day, the soul alone possesses this indescribable, everlasting happiness. This eternal bliss cannot be imagined as St. Paul revealed under the inspiration of the Holy Spirit: "No eye has seen, nor ear heard, / nor the heart of man conceived, / what God has prepared for those who love him."[11] Human beings can only imagine what they have perceived, and St. Paul makes it abundantly clear that the human mind and imagination have no frame of reference for how fabulous heaven is.

From the perspective of heaven—as the celebrated phrase Jesus addressed to a rich young man reveals—"No one is good but God alone,"[12] takes on a clear meaning. Although all of creation is good, only God is goodness itself. This utterance does not simply mean that no created thing is good but rather that God is the one and only universal good. God is the only good that can fully satisfy the desires of the human heart; every other good is a partial good because it yields a fleeting or passing happiness. Following the line of St. Paul's thought, our most gratifying thrill, satisfaction, or success falls woefully short in comparison to the ineffable contentment of the Beatific Vision. The intense euphoria of winning a trophy, marrying the love of your life, or perfecting a career does not come close to the glory of heaven.

The rewards of heaven are not meant to be limited to some class of elite. Our Lord loves every person unconditionally without limit, and he wants to handsomely reward all who have responded to his innumerable overtures of love. Like a good earthly father who shows his love for his children by giving them gifts, God the Father will pull out all the stops for those who have accepted his friendship. It is the nature of love to want others to be happy; moreover, our all-powerful, all-loving God wants to reward his children with perfect happiness. God's glory is to bestow everlasting life on those who will accept that gift. Perhaps the classic example of a person madly in love with the sweetheart of his or her dreams sheds a bit of light on God's attitude toward his loved ones. Such a person spares no sacrifice in showing great fondness with expensive gifts and lavish entertainment; in fact, there is an ardent need to demonstrate profound, intense love with a ceaseless barrage of loving gestures. Why would an infinitely loving God be any different, let alone outdone

10. RMiss, The Order of Mass, no. 18.

11. 1 Cor 2:9.

12. Mk 10:18.

in generosity by human love? The affection and kindness among friends and family is a reflection of divine love.

Even though heaven is beyond human comprehension, there are some hints from earthly existence about the joys that await those who answer God's call of love. One indescribable source of joy in heaven is to be with loved ones forever without the painful, sorrowful prospect of death. The fear of separation will be something of the past that will never again be a remote possibility. We cannot imagine the euphoric happiness that will come from seeing a loved one in a perfectly beautiful state, radiant with joy. Family members and friends will eternally be at their very best in terms of love, affection, and joy. We will experience the great joy of finally being able to love others as we ought without vulnerability or fear. There will be no selfish defects, mood swings, or a "bad day." Our desires of love and happiness will be eternally and totally fulfilled without any remote chance of boredom or tedium.

The first cause of happiness, though, will be the Beatific Vision of God, the Blessed Trinity. Every good that could possibly be experienced is preeminently present in God, who is all-good. In addition to this direct vision of and union with God, the blessed in heaven will gaze on Jesus in his humanity and his holy Mother, St. Joseph, the angels, and all the saints. Once the soul has reached the proper threshold of holiness, it can now see God and the supernatural world directly. Like all graces, the Beatific Vision is the ultimate gratuitous gift since it involves a direct union with and possession of God. The aim of the Church is to lead all men and women to heavenly glory.

As we contemplate heaven through the use of Scripture passages and our reasoning powers, we understand a glimmer of heaven as our overarching goal. Part of this close look at heaven should include the price tag that made this reward possible and accessible to everyone. It took the Crucifixion and Death of Jesus Christ to make the necessary atonement for everlasting life available to all who are faithful. Before the redemption, the heavenly doors were closed until the exorbitant admission payment was made by Jesus' supreme Sacrifice on the Cross. The backdrop of heaven is the Passion and Death of Jesus on the Cross, for which we will be able to eternally express our gratitude.

God is lavish in mercy, and heaven is his reward for everyone who repents of even grave sin; however, many people who die must wait to see God face to face. God's infinite mercy includes his limitless justice. His justice and mercy require both reparation and the necessary purification from the effects of sin for the reward of eternal happiness. Although sin is totally forgiven in the Sacrament of Baptism—and again in the Sacrament of Penance and Reconciliation—the necessity remains for reparation and further purification to reach the holiness needed to see God face to face in heaven. These lingering effects are called "temporal punishment," and if any remains after death, the soul must suffer a purification in purgatory.

Recall the concept of satisfaction from Chapter 15. The same desire to make satisfaction that accompanies the reception of the Sacrament of Penance and Reconciliation can help explain the need for purification after death. The penalty for mortal sin is eternal punishment. Whenever a mortal sin is forgiven in Confession, so is the eternal punishment that is owed for that grave sin; nevertheless, although the forgiven penitent would not incur eternal condemnation, there still remains the obligation for reparation of the sins already forgiven. Using the same story of the batter who broke a window, lacking the money to make a full restitution on that day would not erase the responsibility to work until the debt had been paid in full.

In addition to the need for reparation, all forgiven sin, except in the case of an extraordinarily profound act of repentance, still leaves in its wake inclinations to sin again. These weaknesses and tendencies to sin are only overcome by the practice of corresponding virtue and penitential purification. Every sin leaves the person in a more weakened state that is overcome by both the grace of the Sacraments and personal struggle to pursue virtue. It is a common experience that Confession removes culpability but does not dispense with the need for purification. A person can chip away at the temporal punishment that remains after sin is forgiven through prayer and by bearing his or her cross[13] in union with Christ's Cross.

Although temporal punishment and purification can be fulfilled in this present life, whatever remains to be done at the point of death must still occur before attaining heaven. This happens in purgatory. The ultimate purpose of this purification before and after

13. Cf. Lk 9:23–24.

death is to put a person in a condition to be able to see God face to face. Since God is unadulterated, infinite, self-giving love, a person can enjoy a face-to-face contemplation of God only by habitually loving God with his or her whole heart and strength. He is absolutely selfless. There cannot be even the slightest trace of selfishness in God. A person's soul must be on a similar "loving wavelength" to see God. The soul, though finite, must reach the necessary threshold of self-giving love to directly contemplate God and for the grace of the Beatific Vision to have its intended effect. It should not be surprising if the majority of people who are saved still need further purification to acquire the conditions to enjoy heaven. As Jesus revealed in the Beatitudes, "Blessed are the pure in heart, for they shall see God."[14] Through God's merciful forgiveness, all sorts of hardened sinners are saved before the end, but not necessarily with the time they need to purify their hearts for this joy. Usually, to get to that high level of selfless love, intense purification needs to occur both here and in the afterlife.

Of course, we cannot and should not try to discern how God will judge each person who passes out of this world. Since God's knowledge of the human heart is perfect, only God can judge the human heart. It may be safe to think, though, that a great saint's whole life replete with heroic deeds of faith and charity stands a much better chance of receiving an immediate heavenly reward over someone who expresses imperfect contrition on his or her death bed. The one who repents at the eleventh hour will receive everlasting life but probably only after going through a purification process.

The Holy Souls in purgatory awaiting heavenly paradise are often called the "poor souls" because purification of temporal punishments involves suffering. Even in this life, accepting suffering with patience and faith leads to purification. Suffering softens the human heart so that it repents of selfishness, relies more on the grace of God, and grows in love for others. Embracing one's cross will always serve as a transformation into a deeper life in Christ. The purifying "fire," which consists of a privation of seeing God, puts the soul in the condition to see God.

One insight into purgatory is that suffering is always caused by an absence of a needed or desired good. For example, a person with a headache lacks perfect health to some degree. A person overcome

14. Mt 5:8.

with sorrow and grief experiences the absence of a loved one or the loss of some valuable good. A person who senses failure lacks the ability to achieve an accomplishment. Possible examples are legion. These examples concern goods that are partial, meaning that they do not exhaust the fullness of goodness. God is the only universal fullness of goodness; every other good is partial. If the absence of these finite goods can cause so much turmoil, we cannot fathom the pain produced by the deprivation of the one who is all-good. Nevertheless, the suffering of purgatory is tempered by the joyful hope of seeing God face to face.

Another unique aspect of the Holy Souls' condition in purgatory is their inability to merit on their own, as was the case in earthly life. The time for growth in holiness, atonement, and reparation ends with death. Once the soul has separated from the body, there is no possibility for any meritorious movement toward the goal of holiness; neither is it possible to incur more sins and penalties. The Holy Souls in purgatory cannot "offer up" their suffering in a way that will shorten its duration. For this reason, the Church has always strongly urged her faithful to pray for the souls in purgatory and to offer their own earthly suffering on behalf of the dead. Although the Holy Souls in purgatory cannot help themselves, the Church on earth can certainly help decrease their suffering through her prayers. Only the prayers of the Church on earth and in heaven can win indulgences for either a decrease—or even a total dispensation—of the required purification.

This is the source of the Church's often misunderstood practice of offering "indulgences." As St. Paul VI taught, reflected in the *Catechism*:

> An indulgence is the remission before God of the temporal punishment due sins already forgiven as far as their guilt is concerned, which the follower of Christ with the proper dispositions and under certain determined conditions acquires through the intervention of the Church which, as minister of the Redemption, authoritatively dispenses and applies the treasury of the satisfaction won by Christ and the saints.[15]

In other words, the self-offering of Jesus Christ and the works of his saints in a certain sense "paid more" than was necessary, which leaves a "treasury" in heaven that the Church can "dispense." With

15. St. Paul VI, Apostolic Constitution Whereby the Revision of Sacred Indulgences Is Promulgated *Indulgentiarum Doctrina* (January 1, 1967), norm 1; cf. CCC 1471.

certain dispositions and specified actions or prayers, the Church offers an "indulgence" from this treasury of grace that "counts" for more than they would otherwise be "worth." The Church has the authority through a power entrusted by its founder, Jesus Christ, to administer these indulgences. A "plenary" indulgence removes all temporal punishment due to sin. A "partial" indulgence takes away part of the punishment due to sin. These indulgences can be applied to the person him- or herself, another person or people living on earth, or to one or more the Holy Souls in purgatory.

Certain prayers offer indulgences. For example, during the Year of St. Joseph (2021), Pope Francis declared a plenary indulgence for a variety of actions, including a husband and wife praying the Rosary together and participation in a retreat that includes a meditation on St. Joseph. A plenary indulgence must also include sacramental Confession, prayer for the intentions of the Pope, and a detachment from sin. Many indulgences in the past also required almsgiving, which is the source of the notion of "buying my way" into heaven. Though some unscrupulous members of the Church in history took advantage of this practice, the exchange of money attached to indulgences was always meant to demonstrate a corporal work of mercy, not a purchase of remission of sin.

Though it can be an upsetting topic of discussion—to say the least—nobody can just dismiss or ignore the reality of hell. Jesus clearly taught about the possibility of eternal punishment several times in his teachings.[16] It would be wrong to reject this specific item of his message simply because, at first glance, God's loving mercy appears to be incompatible with everlasting condemnation. Jesus' frank Revelations of the existence of eternal punishment have led the Church from her outset to teach that hell exists. The Church specifies that this punishment corresponds to sins involving a total, unrepented severance in friendship with God through a grave violation of his Commandments.

How can the reality of eternal punishment square with an infinitely merciful, loving God? The answer to this is the same as why a merciful, loving God would allow Adam and Eve to fall in the first place: because God gave the human person free will. Just as the ability to sin was a possible outcome of the gift of freedom, so

16. Looking at just one of the Gospels, for example, cf. Mt 5:22, 29-30; 7:13; 8:8; 10:28; 12:32; 18:9; 25:46.

damnation must remain an option for a person to be free. God never coerces a person to embrace his will; it is an exercise in freedom. Love of God and neighbor is intimately bound up with freedom because only a free person can authentically love. Personal freedom can be misused through a rejection of God's Commandments.

If there were rewards for choosing to do evil, then the gift of freedom would be totally compromised—particularly if evil were chosen with full knowledge. Freedom can only be fully present when there are consequences to actions. With freedom comes responsibility for the results of those actions, and with responsibility comes accountability. If, despite the innumerable chances God gives for repentance, a person remains adamant in refusing God's love and invitations to repentance, then eternal alienation from God awaits that soul.

This is not what God desires. Sacred Scripture shows in an overwhelming way how ardently God desires the salvation of every human being: "God our Savior… desires all men to be saved and to come to the knowledge of the truth."[17] In fact, the only reason he created human beings in the first place was to enjoy everlasting life for eternity. The most eloquent, dramatic display of God's will to save us is Jesus Christ's Death on the Cross. This supreme Sacrifice speaks volumes about Jesus' desperate efforts to prevent everyone from being consigned to the pains of hell. Jesus' entire life is a radical expression of God's will to win back the sinner for the sake of everlasting happiness. In a certain sense, the entire Gospel can be summarized by the Parable of the Prodigal Son (cf. Chapter 15) since it shows in a poignant way the indescribable joy of a father over his son's repentance and return. As much as the father wanted his son back, he did not force him to come back since love is all about respecting freedom, even at the peril of its tragic abuse.

Keeping in mind the lengths to which God has gone to make salvation available to all, rather than being "banished" to hell, the unrepentant sinner self-imposes eternal misery upon him- or herself. Perhaps an example can shed some light on this tragic possibility. There are people who are unhappy and miserable because they cultivate hateful resentment without considering the prospect of changing those dispositions. God is not imposing despair and sadness on those people; their toxic sentiments are self-induced,

---

17. 1 Tm 2:4.

natural consequences. Such a person chooses to wallow in resentment, hatred, and envy, automatically producing a state of misery that could be avoided and overcome.

Grave sins like murder, marital infidelity, and injustice toward the weak and downtrodden already bring about a hell in this present life. Without any effort to repent, this earthly travail will continue into the next life. A person needs to look no farther than a news feed to find evidence of the fact that horrific evil and anguish are directly linked to a willful rejection of God and his Laws. These past and present horrors show clearly that hell is man-made and freely chosen despite God's incessant invitations to reconciliation.

It is impossible to grasp the full extent of the sufferings that define the pains of hell. We can get a glimpse of eternal punishment through the same analogy used earlier for purgatory. Human suffering accompanies a privation of natural goods like health, the presence of a loved one, food, rest, and success. All these goods are derived from the overflowing goodness of God. Unlike purgatory, where the soul can look forward to its eventual fulfillment, the essence of eternal damnation consists in the permanent absence of the universal good, God himself, from whom absolutely every good comes. This eternal absence of God—and any remote chance of moral and spiritual healing—leaves the soul totally deprived of any ray of hope or vestige of joy.

Another frightening aspect of the place of the damned is that it is populated by the Devil and his demons. In addition to being surrounded by these personal doers of evil, the human population shares the common denominator of unmitigated hate and despair. There is no happiness, peace, or solace since the discordant society of the damned is marked by mutual envy and resentment.

In the Garden of Gethsemane, Jesus sweated blood[18] over the terrible consequences for those who reject his loving overtures, especially expressed by his redemptive Sacrifice. Jesus Christ revealed the horrors of hell by offering his suffering and Death on the Cross as a preventive measure to save all souls from eternal damnation. Through his redemption, Jesus won the needed graces for all repentant changed hearts that accept his love and mercy. A person who rebuffs these countless invitations to salvation and everlasting life, however, chooses eternal damnation.

18. Lk 22:44.

It can be frightening to contemplate the outcome of hell, but it should not be the cause of fear or despair. It should, rather, be a reminder to pursue a life in Christ, to put more trust in his merciful love, and to live a life of gratitude for all that God has given us. If we are tempted to despair at the thought of hell, we should turn to Christ in praise and thanksgiving for all that he suffered for our salvation. The simple prayer that Jesus revealed to St. Faustina to accompany the image of his Divine Mercy (see Chapter 15) is, "Jesus, I trust in you."[19]

The possibility of total withdrawal from God in the face of his infinite goodness should also serve as a stimulus to help family and friends to come to Christ. The modern evangelizer finds him- or herself in a spiritual tug of war between the forces of good and evil. The outcome of this struggle against the demonic deceptions of evil will result in victory for those closely united to Jesus Christ.

Effects of the Anointing of the Sick

The goal of every Christian is to undergo a good death and enter into eternal happiness, which has no frame of reference in our earthly life. For every person who has died, a new and perfectly happy life awaits him or her, provided that person renounced sin and was committed to living God's Commandments. The imminence and certainty of death are an impetus to make best use of the gift of life. Death, in many cases, comes suddenly; this should spur us on to be prepared at any time.[20] Being vigilant and alert does not imply an anxiety or dread of the end but rather urges a person to have a sporting spirit that fills each day with love for God and others.

Since our days are literally numbered, our future death becomes a "reality check" to prioritize what is truly important and not to squander the unrepeatable opportunities to live the Gospel message. A priest tells the story of going on a routine sick call to anoint a young man who had a serious illness but looked like he was on his way to recovery. After he had received the Sacrament, he resolved to take his Christian life much more seriously from that moment on, but his life was cut short when he died unexpectedly just minutes after the Anointing of the Sick. The time for conversion is always now—today.

19. DSFK, xx.
20. Cf. Mt 25:1–13.

Every Christian at every stage of life is called to have faith in Christ and to view death as the entrance to everlasting life, but this can be a great challenge when the prospect is near. Facing the pain of illness with patience and the prospect of death with peace requires faith born of grace. Our Lord strongly desires to strengthen people with the lights of faith and hope when they are in conditions of weakness, affliction, and pain or faced with the danger of death. Some people might use a serious infirmity to revolt against God and be angry with him. Feelings of vulnerability and fear can also serve as an occasion for the Devil to instill a false sense of hopelessness and rejection by God. One of the Devil's more commonplace tricks is to remind us of our past sins and tempt us to despair. These negative reactions are not inevitable or inescapable. The sufferings caused by sickness can and should bring about a profound interior renewal accompanied by a much deeper friendship with Christ. Countless bishops and priests have experienced how the Anointing of the Sick truly brings strength and consolation to the recipient.

Just like all the other Sacraments, the Anointing of the Sick is not exclusively spiritual because the human person is not exclusively spiritual, and Jesus came to redeem the whole human person. Redemption consists of healing the soul of its sinfulness and eventually glorifying the body. Our Lord's public healings of the sick and dying serve as an instructive measure to illustrate the spiritual effects of his redemptive graces on the soul, but the body also participates in the sanctification of the soul and will be glorified at the resurrection on the last day. For this reason, by healing the soul, the Anointing of the Sick in many instances heals the body as well. It is Jesus Christ who spiritually heals the sick person and not infrequently brings remedy to bodily infirmity.

Though physical healing can accompany the Anointing of the Sick, it is not the primary end. The grace of the redemption enables every person to overcome sickness and death through growth in holiness. Through this Sacrament, the weakness of the body and soul lead to a greater intimacy with Christ as a witness of Christ's holiness. One of the reasons that Our Lord permits this special time of suffering through illness is so the person can accelerate in becoming Christlike. A very holy woman who was stricken with a terminal illness felt that she was eminently blessed by God. She wanted to make good use of her remaining time in this world by embracing her cross. She even said that she had to capitalize on all the opportunities to offer her suffering to Christ on behalf of her family and friends because in heaven she would never again be called to Christ's Cross. With this special call to his Cross and the grace derived from the Anointing of the Sick, she experienced a special access to the strength of grace and to Christ's heart.

The primary effect of the Anointing of the Sick consists in uniting a sick person to the Cross of Christ. This Sacrament helps the recipient draw meaning from suffering and connect it to Jesus' sufferings. It gives interior peace and courage not only to cope with the illness but to embrace it with faith and love for Jesus. Under the stressful conditions of suffering, the Evil One sees one of his last opportunities to tempt the infirm person to despair or anger on account of the illness. This sacramental anointing is, therefore, designed to overcome these temptations to withdraw from God and bring the soul courage and peace. Given the positive experience people have with this Sacrament, they are often eager to receive it again when the need arises.

If there is at least implicit imperfect contrition, the Anointing of the Sick is also a means of the forgiveness of sin when sacramental Confession is not possible. As with Penance and Reconciliation, another effect of this Sacrament is a greater healing for the whole Church on account of the intimate connection among the members of Christ's Mystical Body. Last, if death is imminent, it helps the recipient of the anointing to look forward to the next life.

Last Judgment

Christian Tradition teaches that the world as we know it will come to an end. No one knows when this will occur: "Of that day and hour no one knows, not even the angels of heaven."[21] But we know that the Church is on a journey and pilgrimage toward her heavenly destination until the end of time. The Church's sojourn on earth will be marked by many dips and turns, persecutions, sins of her members, and the ongoing struggle to advance the Kingdom of God in this world. Once the world ends, the Church will become glorified and exist for eternity in heaven.

The Catholic faith clearly holds that Jesus—who came to this world amid poverty, humility, and silence—will return in glory:

21. Mt 24:36.

"They will see the Son of man coming on the clouds of heaven with power and great glory."[22] This reappearance of Christ in splendor defines his Second Coming. In his first entrance into the world, he came as the Redeemer and Savior who manifested himself as a Suffering Servant. Once his plan of redemption has been fulfilled, he will come to judge every human being who has ever lived. Some people will still be part of the living population. Hence, we profess in the Creed, "He will come again in glory / to judge the living and the dead."[23]

The Second Coming of Christ will bring the Last Judgment. The second Judgment is necessary because every person's Particular Judgment will not have included all the effects of his or her good and evil actions on others until the end of the world. At the Last Judgment, Christ will reveal all the ramifications that everyone's good and evil actions have had on the world.

For example, the inestimable good that has come—and has yet to come—out of the lives of the saints will be completely seen. The saints never cease to affect people in future eras and faraway places. How many souls have been instructed by hearing the Epistles of St. Paul, been moved to conversion by learning about the life of St. Francis of Assisi, or grown in prayer by reading the writings of St. Teresa of Avila? By the same token, the evil that resulted from every sinful act will also be exposed at the Final Judgment. Nothing will be hidden when the Light of the World returns as Judge.

The resurrection of the body will follow the Last Judgment. Until that moment, the soul of every human being whose earthly life has ended—except the Blessed Virgin Mary, who was assumed body and soul into heaven, presented in Chapter 14—will have existed separated from its body. At the Final Judgment, the souls of the just will receive a glorified body that will share in the joyful bliss of heaven. On the other hand, the souls of the damned will also be reunited with their bodies and will suffer for all eternity.

Our faith tells us that everyone who has obtained salvation will live forever with his or her resurrected body. This glorified body will enjoy perpetual health and beauty. Eternity will be filled with the consolation of the presence of loved ones in their glorified, beautified state. There will be no possibility of defects and character flaws,

22. Mt 24:30–31.

23. RMiss, The Order of Mass, no. 18.

let alone sins. All will be at their kindest and most loving, experiencing an overflow of unending joy.

This new world, called the "heavenly Jerusalem," is ruled by Jesus Christ and marked by perennial joy and everlasting life:

> He will wipe away every tear from their eyes, and death shall be no more, neither shall there be mourning nor crying nor pain any more, for the former things have passed away.[24]

Though still cloaked in mystery, this promise fills every Christian with joyful expectation. The new heaven and new earth will occasion a perfect union and harmony for the whole human race. In fact, the purpose of the Church is to bring about unity and solidarity among all people through the grace of Jesus Christ's redemption.

These eternal truths revealed by God give us hope that the trials of the present life are meant to pass away. We realize that suffering, illness, and the perils of nature will pass. The disciple of Christ awaits in joyful suspense for an ideal world, enlightened by the beauty and goodness of God, in which there will dwell a perfectly loving people with the unimaginable bliss of a glorified body.

The World Needs Healing

Both of the Sacraments of Healing—Penance and Reconciliation and the Anointing of the Sick—not only prepare us for the life to come but also, more immediately, bring God's kingdom to earth. In our present world of suffering, there is an urgent need that people be reintroduced to Christ in these Sacraments of Healing. The moral health and the common good of society ultimately depend on repentance and spiritual healing. The Sacrament of Penance heals the wounds of sin and replaces them with virtue. The Sacrament of the Anointing of the Sick especially drives home the point that every person enjoys an exalted dignity; moreover, this Sacrament promotes the common good by focusing attention on the transcendent worth of every human person, especially the weak and most vulnerable, the sick and those in danger of death.

24. Rev 21:4.

CHAPTER 17

MARRIAGE AND SPOUSAL LOVE

Having covered the Sacraments of Christian Initiation and the Sacraments of Healing, we now turn to the two Sacraments at the Service of Communion: Matrimony and Holy Orders. Marriage and the Sacrament of Matrimony—at the heart of God's Revelation about himself and the center of human life—will be the subject of the next two chapters.

Given its fundamental importance to the dignity of the person and the many challenges that marriage faces in our day, this topic spans two chapters.

THE BASIS FOR MARRIAGE

The formalization of the love between a man and a woman, who become each other's wife or husband, is a dimension of natural law deeply rooted in human nature. The norm of a mutual, exclusive commitment between the sexes has been present virtually in every civilization, tribe, or cultural milieu throughout the ages. Although the process and rituals for marriage can differ radically from culture to culture, the common thread is the promotion, celebration, and recognition of marriage within a society. From the dawn of humanity to the present, it has been incompatible with the demands of human dignity for a man and a woman to simply cohabitate, treating one another as disposable. The proper setting for sexual expression and intimate friendship is a committed, lifelong relationship formalized before God, the couple's families, and society.

The exalted dignity of marriage was established at the dawn of creation with the first man and woman. God created man and woman in an intimate union with each other[1] and called them to live this union.[2] There is imprinted in the respective male and female expression of human nature a powerful tendency to enjoy physical, emotional, and psychological fulfillment from each other. Equal but different, unique but complementary, the two sexes are drawn to

1. Cf. Gn 1:27.
2. Cf. Gn 2:28.

each other to give themselves to each other in a permanent union. Males and females are divinely designed so that a man and a woman can grow to love each other so much that they will dedicate their entire lives to each other. God wills and blesses this drive for sexual and emotional union, accompanied by a close friendship.

The desire of a man and a woman for an intimate union on a physical, psychological, and spiritual level is meant to be lived within the bulwark of marriage. When a man and a woman fall in love, they set the stage for a commitment to wholehearted, exclusive fidelity to each other. This intense, all-absorbing fondness that a man and a woman can have for one another calls for a permanent, exclusive union. Thus, the chief characteristic of marriage is a lifelong bond exclusively between one man and one woman.

There is a very good reason that this multifaceted attraction is most intense between a man and a woman during childbearing years: This mutual, biological, and psychological complementarity is at the service of bearing and raising children. In the wide historical and societal diversity of wedding ceremonies, most tend to be religious in nature since there is an implicit sacredness to this relationship that produces new life. Marriage, therefore, is the normal and proper setting for bearing and raising children. The idea that the dignity of the spouses and the rearing of children can be just as easily served without a permanent union is a relatively modern concept.

The *Catechism* defines authentic marriage:

> The matrimonial covenant, by which a man and a woman establish between themselves a partnership of the whole of life, is by its nature ordered toward the good of the spouses in the procreation and education of offspring.[3]

Discussions of Catholic marriage focus on preserving these two intertwined purposes: the "good of the spouses" and the "procreation and education of offspring." This chapter will focus on the "good of the spouses," the total gift of self each spouse is meant to make to the other; this is also called the "unitive" purpose of marriage. The next chapter will focus on marriage in its openness to and obligations toward the gift of new life; this is also called the "procreative" purpose of marriage. The unitive and procreative purpose of marriage can never be separated in practice but only in theory, so there will be some expected overlap between the two chapters.

3. CCC 1601; quoting CIC, can. 1055 § 1; cf. GS, no. 48 § 1.

Marriage as a Lifelong Covenant

Though marriage has been held in high regard by virtually every society, its dignity was significantly enhanced by God's Revelation of the Ten Commandments, which established both adultery and covetousness as contrary to his plan for the dignity of the human person.[4] As in other areas of salvation history, what was first revealed in the Old Law was later perfected by Christ. Jesus restored the sacred bond of marriage according to the original divine plan, revealed in the Book of Genesis, which had been weakened in practice by the Israelite people; but Christ also went further, elevating marriage to the level of a Sacrament and opening the door to graces that bolster and sustain a healthy marriage and family life.

Scripture begins with marriage. As was presented in Chapter 3, Scripture relates the creation of the world in two narratives. The First Creation Account is a poem, succinctly yet beautifully relating the creation of the entire material order categorized according to seven days. On the sixth day, God created the human person according to two sexes: "God created man in his own image, in the image of God he created him; male and female he created them."[5] Both the man and the woman were created in God's image with equal dignity and humanity.

Then begins the Second Creation Account, augmenting the first with more of a story. In this account the man was created first. "God said, 'It is not good that the man should be alone,'"[6] but looking around at all the rest of creation, Adam sadly could not find a suitable partner: None of the animals would suffice. God then created the woman out of Adam's flesh, and upon seeing Eve, Adam rejoiced: "This at last is bone of my bones and flesh of my flesh."[7] The animals had all been inferior; Eve alone, created in God's image as much as Adam, was a suitable partner for Adam. This Second Creation Account adds to the First, demonstrating the relationship for which Adam and Eve are made: "Therefore a man leaves his father and his mother and cleaves to his wife, and they become one

4. Cf. Ex 20:13, 17.
5. Gn 1:27.
6. Gn 2:18.
7. Gn 2:23.

flesh."[8] From this original orientation toward relationship comes all the relational qualities of human beings in the world.

The creation narratives in Genesis reveal that God is the author of marriage, which is a natural consequence of the attraction and complementarity between the two sexes. In his institution of marriage, God specified that marriage would be marked by an intimate, permanent union between a man and a woman. The celebrated phrase "one flesh" used in Genesis wonderfully summarizes the nature of marriage. The notion of "one flesh" signifies that the bond between a husband and a wife is unbreakable. God makes it abundantly clear that no one is at liberty to break this bond, which he himself has established.[9]

The union of two people into one flesh means the love between a man and a woman in marriage supersedes every other type of human relationship. This is revealed in Genesis: "A man leaves his father and his mother and cleaves to his wife."[10] This scriptural admonition does not advocate alienation from parents but rather that spousal love is ordained by God to be in a class unto itself. Spousal love takes priority over any other human love, even the closest of human relationships like the love of a child for a mother and father. Given the nature of this highest form of love, this marital relationship is meant to last for life and stand the test of time and adversity.

Because this relationship is so "hardwired" into the nature of the human person, it was most directly harmed by the Fall of our first parents. As was presented in Chapter 3, the first relationship to suffer on account of the Fall was between God and his children, witnessed in the way that Adam and Eve try to hide from God's loving gaze.[11] The second relationship to suffer was between the man and the woman. After Adam and Eve gave in to the temptation of prideful disobedience, God weighed in and disclosed the future consequences of their sin on their marriage: "Your desire shall be for your husband, and he shall rule over you."[12] These words speak to both the man and the woman on the future difficulties of

8. Gn 2:24.

9. Cf. Mt 19:6: "They are no longer two but one flesh. What therefore God has joined together, let not man put asunder."

10. Gn 2:24.

11. Cf. Gn 3:8.

12. Gn 3:16.

their life together. The relationship that began with a mutual gift of self between equals is now marred by disorder and a struggle for domination. These words reveal our challenge of marital unity and growth in mutual love. What should be our gratifying, loving relationship of intimate, common life is so often marred by tensions and resentment.

Another consequence of the Fall was that the marital relationship would be marred by a tendency to lust and the physical objectification of the other. "The man and his wife [had been] both naked, and were not ashamed,"[13] but they lost this intimate relationship of trust. After the Fall they tried to conceal themselves from each other: "They knew that they were naked; and they sewed fig leaves together and made themselves aprons."[14] This reveals the sense of lost innocence manifested by a new awareness of mutual lust, triggered by the sight of each other. Before Original Sin nakedness neither awakened lust nor detracted from their pure love for each other. Because of this first and fateful sin, the will, the intellect, and the passions derived from human nature are inclined to sinful selfishness. These effects of Original Sin can especially flare up in interactions between a husband and a wife as they are tempted to look at each other as objects of self-gratification rather than subjects worthy of love and sacrifice.

Despite the serious challenges of our fallen nature, the union of a husband and a wife remained, as with most cultures, a sacred institution in the Old Covenant. The patriarchs of the Israelites, however, did not fully appreciate marriage. Even the heroes of the chosen people had multiple wives and seemed to ignore God's requirements for the marriage covenant. In the Old Testament we often find Israelites following their neighbors' pagan customs, especially concubinage and polygamy. As God continued to guide and form them, he revealed in the Ten Commandments what marriage required.

The Fourth Commandment, which will be treated more fully in Chapter 18, enjoins, "Honor your father and your mother."[15] It is significant that, after the first three Commandments about the love of God, the very next relates to stability in family life. The Sixth Commandment speaks to the permanence and fidelity of marriage:

---

13. Gn 2:25.

14. Gn 3:7.

15. CCC, Part Three Section Two; Ex 20:12.

"You shall not commit adultery."[16] In the Ninth Commandment, God forbids even the objectification of lust: "You shall not covet your neighbor's wife."[17] Three of the seven Commandments ordered toward love of neighbor are focused on marriage and family.

These Commandments encompass a wide range of moral teachings on Christian marriage; they also evince the authentic nature of human sexuality as revealed by God. The Sixth and the Ninth Commandments, in particular, teach us that human sexuality can only find its true meaning and full expression in the inner sanctum of marriage. We are called to a vocation of chastity, which the *Catechism* defines as "the inner unity of man in his bodily and spiritual being."[18] These Commandments warn against lust or carnal concupiscence; however, the Old Law could not completely inspire the permanent fidelity between spouses originally established by God; simply knowing does not equate to doing. Since the original plan seemed untenable in many instances and marital infidelity was so rampant, Moses modified God's original stipulations about marriage and gave a special dispensation for divorce.

In spite of Moses' permission for a husband to divorce his wife, marriage continued to be seen as a sacred institution that strongly discouraged divorce. The prophets taught that marriage was a true covenant established by God from the very beginning, and a covenant bond was permanent and indissoluble. Permanence is the nature of a *covenant*—as opposed to a *contract*, which can be dissolved.

Throughout the Old Testament there was a strong awareness that marriage is permanent. This is illustrated very clearly by the poetic allegory of marital love in the Song of Songs. "Set me as a seal upon your heart, / as a seal upon your arm; / for love is strong as death."[19] Though many marriages failed to meet the ideal set by God, the instructions transmitted to the chosen people highly lauded faithful, strong marriages.

Due to the ongoing presence of the inborn selfishness of our wounded human nature, however, a husband and a wife must struggle to grow in love for each other and ultimately preserve their

16. CCC, Section Two; Ex 20:14.
17. CCC, Section Two; Ex 20:17.
18. CCC 2337.
19. Sg 8:6.

marriage. Under the influence of evil, a husband may very well have strong tendencies to be abusive to his wife by dominating her, squelching her freedom and dignity. A wife, in turn, can be torn between a retaliating bid for power and the passive abandon of her dignity. Within marriage a man and a woman can also see each other as objects of lust, failing to love each other as persons made in the image of God. Even key figures in the history of the chosen people had marriages that failed to meet the standard of the original plan that God mandated to our first parents.

Among many examples were King David and his son, King Solomon, who were serious violators of the Commandment of lifelong fidelity to only one woman. David even committed adultery with another man's wife, which earned him a strong rebuke and punishment from God.[20] Solomon, who was known for his prodigious wisdom, ignored any semblance of fidelity to his marriage covenant and justified having numerous wives, which led to his moral downfall.[21] Most Israelite kings did not remotely consider the indissoluble bond of marriage; what is clear from the Old Testament, nonetheless, is that laws and exhortations alone cannot sustain the integrity of marriage.

In the modern world the vulnerability of the institution of marriage is especially apparent. If the hemorrhage of selfishness is not staunched, a marriage will metaphorically bleed to death. The reality of so many failed marriages points to the fact that something is not working; this challenge for the preservation of marriage has been a reality from the dawn of human history. It is not right to conclude from this that the very idea of marriage is misguided or that lifelong relationships are impossible. Without exception, God never makes mistakes; this also obviously applies to marriage. The problems that accompany marriage is not with the institution but with the parties who all have a fallen nature. Husbands and wives who strive to purify their souls and to control and heal their inordinate selfish tendencies can have a successful marriage.

Since no man or woman is immune to the wounds left by the stain of Original Sin, a marriage marked by a loving harmony is virtually impossible without the divine intervention of grace. Because of the weakened human condition, restoration of marriage to its

20. Cf. 2 Sm 11–12.

21. Cf. 1 Kgs 11.

original model cannot be accomplished by human effort. Especially with respect to the married state, the grace of God is called on to counteract Original Sin's damaging effects. Without the aid of grace, it is anything but easy to remain faithful and to grow in affection for one another. The endemic challenges to enduring fidelity require divine intervention, especially in our time, when divorce is such a common recourse. Despite the similar difficulties we find between the Old Testament and today, the many components of the Old Law served as preparation for Jesus Christ's restoration of marriage. With the graces won by Jesus Christ's redemptive Sacrifice on the Cross, wounded, fallen human nature is strengthened and elevated to reflect the life of Christ.

The New Covenant in Christ, like so many key moments in salvation history, begins with the announcement of a child. While in the Old Testament the news typically comes to the father, in the New Covenant the message was given to the Blessed Virgin Mary: She would conceive a child by the power of God.[22] The angel appeared later to St. Joseph, assuring him that he should take Mary into his house and raise the child, Jesus.[23] When the Son of God came into the world, he did not simply drop down from heaven but was born of a Mother and raised in a family. God cannot be clearer about the importance of marriage and family; his Son was born into a family and educated and formed by a Mother and a father.

Throughout his mission on earth, Jesus frequently displayed a particular goal of reestablishing the role of marriage according to God's plan. The first miracle of Jesus' public ministry occurred within the context of a wedding.[24] His intervention at Cana inaugurated the restoration of marriage according to God's original plan, and his presence at Cana clearly illustrated that Jesus wants to make his home in every marriage. As Jesus turned water into wine to preserve and enhance the marriage feast, he elevated the life of the spouses so that they reflect his light and life. The special feature of the Sacrament of Matrimony is Christ's active presence by means of the sacramental graces bestowed on the couple. His role in every sacramental marriage consists in strengthening the husband and the wife with the grace to love each other as Jesus loves.

22. Cf. Lk 1:30–33.

23. Cf. Mk 1:18–21.

24. Cf. Jn 2:1–12.

Though the Law of Moses was perhaps the best marriage law of its time, it still allowed for divorce and was frequently abused. This was particularly devastating to women, as it was the husband who could petition for divorce. Jesus' most explicit defense of God's original plan for marriage occurred when some Pharisees, typically trying to trip Jesus up, asked him, "Is it lawful to divorce one's wife for any cause?"[25] Jesus responded by quoting Scripture:

> "Have you not read that he who made them from the beginning made them male and female, and said, 'For this reason a man shall leave his father and mother and be joined to his wife, and the two shall become one flesh'? . . . For your hardness of heart Moses allowed you to divorce your wives, but from the beginning it was not so.[26]

Jesus made it abundantly clear that marriage is indissoluble in an absolute sense and that divorce was not in God's plan. He abolished Moses' concession to divorce in his next breath: "Whoever divorces his wife, except for unchastity, and marries another, commits adultery."[27]

Jesus did not stop with restoring to marriage its original intentions at creation. Jesus, as always, went further and elevated marriage to the level of a Sacrament, instituting it as a sacramental sign of a sacred reality. Already in the Old Testament, the natural institution of marriage fulfilled this role. God's faithfulness to his covenant was an analogy for the fidelity of spouses; the prophets frequently equated God's covenant with his people to the sacredness of marriage: "As the bridegroom rejoices over the bride, / so shall your God rejoice over you."[28] Through their teachings and exhortations, the prophets explain that God calls his people to permanent fidelity, just like the marital bond between a husband and a wife. God promised that his people would be lavishly blessed if they would stay faithful to him. Just as a man and a woman form a covenant of fidelity for life, with an exclusive love for each other, God had to be Israel's exclusive object of adoration and worship.

Along the same lines, the frequent *lack* of faithfulness by the chosen people was often compared to marital infidelity. When they strayed from God's Commandments and worshiped pagan gods, the

25. Mt 19:3.
26. Mt 19:4–5, 8; cf. Mk 10:11–12; Lk 16:18.
27. Mt 19:8–9.
28. Is 62:5.

prophets likened this conduct to prostitution and adultery, which separates the sexual act from spousal fidelity: "Can a maiden forget her ornaments, / or a bride her attire? /Yet my people have forgotten me / days without number."[29] Most dramatically, God instructed the prophet Hosea to "preach" with his life by play-acting the role of God with an unfaithful spouse, his chosen people: "Take to yourself a wife of harlotry… for the land commits great harlotry by forsaking the LORD."[30]

Despite the Israelite people's infidelity, God remained faithful. In fact, God's attitude reveals a moving kindness, tenderness, and spirit of forgiveness. The Old Covenant, which reflected a marriage covenant, was meant to be permanent and faithful. This analogy reveals both the love of God and the original purpose of marriage: "I hate divorce, says the LORD."[31]

All these Old Testament prophecies set the stage for Jesus Christ to elevate marriage to the level of a Sacrament. Christ, the Son of God, is the Bridegroom of his Church, his Bride. In all four of the Gospel accounts, Jesus either refers to himself as or is called the "Bridegroom."[32] Since the days of the Apostles, this analogy has illuminated both Christ's love for his Church and the sacred nature of human marriage.

This perfected marital love is attested by the inspired words of St. Paul to spouses: "Be subject to one another out of reverence for Christ."[33] This is what Pope Francis called "the foundation of the family… the couple's mutual gift of self"[34] intended by God from the beginning. In Christ, though, spouses are called to an even higher standard: "Husbands, love your wives, as Christ loved the church and gave himself up for her, that he might sanctify her."[35] This richly instructive verse goes way beyond the Old Law; St. Paul equates the love between spouses to Christ's love for every person, dramatically made manifest in his Crucifixion and Death on the Cross. This means that the love between spouses should be marked

29. Jer 2:32.

30. Hos 1:2.

31. Mal 2:16.

32. Cf. Mt 9:15; Mk 2:19–10; Lk 5:34–35; Jn 3:29.

33. Eph 5:21.

34. Pope Francis, *Address to Participants in the Plenary Assembly of the Pontifical Council for the Family* (October 25, 2013), no. 2.

35. Eph 5:25–26.

by a continuous spirit of sacrifice and joyful affection in serving each other's needs. The Sacrament of Matrimony does so much more than just help spouses maintain their commitment to unity and lifelong fidelity; the grace of this Sacrament is designed to enable a husband and a wife to love each other with the heart of Jesus Christ.

The difficult challenges in persevering in marriage for life might prompt good people to believe that marital fidelity is an ideal standard that is virtually impossible to reach. Rates of divorce seem to corroborate this. Our Lord certainly understood the reason for Moses' relaxation of the strict moral obligation to maintain the unity and dissolubility of marriage. By reaffirming the true purpose of marriage, though, Jesus did not simply restate the Law—he provided the means to fulfill the Law. One of the fruits of Jesus' suffering and Death on the Cross are the special graces that Matrimony transmits to married couples. By virtue of his Incarnation and redemptive Sacrifice on the Cross, Jesus merited the necessary graces to sustain the effort to cultivate and preserve a marriage. With the grace of Matrimony bestowed by Christ, spouses are amply fortified by Christ's assistance throughout their marriage.

The sad reality, of course, is that even sacramental marriages frequently fail. What we must remember here is that the grace of the Sacraments is not "magic" and does not exempt the recipients from personal struggle and the pursuit of virtue. God's grace never imposes itself against human will. The spouses must cooperate with the graces of the Sacrament and grow closer to Christ in their marriage. If a husband and a wife are intent on following Jesus, their marriage will grow and become increasingly solidified.

The Virtue of Chastity

Before turning to the celebration of the Sacrament of Matrimony, it will be helpful to review the Church's teachings on human sexuality. In order to cooperate with Christ's grace in marriage, spouses need to have a correct understanding of human sexuality and what is required to be faithful to and respectful of each other.

Respect for the dignity of a spouse in the face of temptation requires the self-control of *chastity*. The goal of chastity before and after marriage is challenging, more so in a culture not directed toward helping people to achieve it—but with a firm commitment and the help of God's grace, it can be accomplished and bring great joy. If a person trains him- or herself in chastity and grows in self-mastery, then he or she will have a fuller possession of him- or herself, thus being in a better position to give the gift of self to a spouse in marriage.

A person who lives the virtue of chastity will also have a better marital relationship because he or she is able to look at a spouse with respect, ready to lay down his or her life as St. Paul urges[36] rather than treating a spouse as on object of personal gratification—sexual, emotional, or otherwise. Such a person is more likely to remain faithful because virtue and self-esteem help withstand even unexpected, great temptations. Couples who enter into marriage without remaining chaste or who marry outside of the Church—but who still strive to cooperate with God's grace—can grow stronger together. However—as we saw in a similar way when looking at the possibility of salvation without the graces of Baptism in Chapter 12—lacking the graces of the Sacrament of Matrimony makes a loving, life-giving marriage all the harder and uncertain.

The Catholic Church is accused of many things regarding her teachings on human sexuality, usually that the teaching is repressive of sexual expression. Far from being repressive and regressive, the Church celebrates the God-given human sexual expression. But like any other gift, it has to be used in the proper context. The gift of a violin can lead to beautiful expressions of music that bring people together, but it would be a misuse of that gift to play loud, piercing notes while someone is trying to sleep in an adjacent room.

Like all of the Church's moral teachings, the goal is to deepen our respect for human dignity and liberate the human spirit from bondage. Pope Benedict XVI acknowledged that Christianity in practice has sometimes been rightly accused of being "opposed to the body." He pointed out, however, that the contemporary tendency of "exalting the body" has reduced sex to "a commodity, a mere 'thing' to be bought and sold, or rather, man himself becomes a commodity." Human sexuality becomes a form of using people and exploitation. "Here we are actually dealing with a debasement of the human body."[37] Promiscuity diminishes the person and turns people into things; self-mastery serves human dignity and liberates people.

36. Cf. Eph 5:21.

37. Pope Benedict XVI, Encyclical Letter on Christian Love *Deus Caritas Est* (December 25, 2005), no. 5.

This distortion of human sexuality as a "commodity" seems ubiquitous in the media, which tend to convey the message that expressions of human sexuality are not intimate, spiritual, or sacred aspects of marriage but mere outlets for physical and emotional needs and desires. Premarital, extramarital, casual, and adulterous relationships are often presented as acceptable modes of behavior. Movies, advertisements, music, fashion, and other media outlets incessantly but deceptively proclaim that self-indulgence—not self-sacrifice—is the key to human happiness.

Many otherwise excellent movies include gratuitous scenes portraying nudity with little to no relevance to the films' overall themes. Many television series portray otherwise intelligent, successful, and charming men and women with loose morals and a total lack of self-control as an example of acceptable or even exemplary behavior, not to mention those shows that include semipornographic scenes with no other purpose than to titillate. The base sexualized nature of modern entertainment goes beyond visual media. Many songs contain lyrics that are explicitly demeaning and offensive, particularly to women. Many fashions, instead of emphasizing the dignity of the person through elegant dress, transmit the false message that the wearer is primarily an object of sensual gratification—and some of these fashions have reached even the youngest and most innocent children. Watching a ball game can even occasion commercials designed to arouse the passions. In fact, most media seems content with the idea that human sexuality is a mere commodity for gratification, as witnessed by the old adage, "Sex sells."

On the other hand, the Church teaches that human dignity forbids the objectification of another person's body. The selfish pursuit of physical gratification is itself demeaning.

The Church calls people to chastity not because human sexuality is inherently "dirty" or "sinful"; she is not "prudish" or "frigid." On the contrary, "Chastity means the integration of sexuality within the person. It includes an apprenticeship in self-mastery."[38] The self-control required by the Sixth and Ninth Commandments is directed toward the genuine expression of Christian love, expressed in a true, selfless love of God and neighbor. Chastity enables every person to love another person as an end in him- or herself and never as an object of use. Through this virtue, a person is empowered to seek

38. CCC 2395.

the good of another for his or her own sake. Chastity recognizes that sexuality cannot be separated from love and that true love requires an exclusive devotion. This means that sexual pleasure cannot be an end in itself; instead, it must be a vehicle to communicate the total gift of self to another person.

Confusion exists because many people confuse chastity with celibacy or virginity; in other words, avoiding sexual expressions with all people. Indeed, celibacy and virginity are two expressions of chastity; both demonstrate the qualities listed in the *Catechism*: integration and self-mastery. These qualities, however, are necessary in every vocation. A person who is not married lives chastely by refraining from sexual activity. Such a person thus integrates his or her sexuality, expressing itself in a self-mastery that enables true love of God and neighbor, according to the example of Christ. A married husband and wife are equally called to *live chastity*. By respecting each other's human dignity, remaining faithful, and not treating each other as an object of self-gratification, a married couple integrate their own sexuality, expressing it in self-mastery, which enables *them* to truly love God and neighbor.

In this regard chastity is connected to *temperance*—one of the four Cardinal Virtues—"which seeks to permeate the passions and appetites of the senses with reason."[39] God has placed certain natural inclinations within us toward the pleasure of the senses; we are inclined to "feel good." Among the strongest passions are our desires for food and drink and sexual expression. These are instinctive acts required for our individual survival and for the preservation of the human race; a person who fails to eat or drink will die; married couples who fail to express their love sexually will not have children to raise, and the human race will become extinct. Human passions serve a good, positive purpose, but acting on them inordinately is destructive. Eating the wrong foods, in the wrong manner, or to excess is destructive to the body and soul; medical advice to eat healthy, eat in moderation, and get physical exercise is not "repressive." Sexual expressions, similarly, are a great good, but they can be misused with the wrong person, in the wrong manner, or if no longer controlled by the will.

The practice of the virtue of temperance submits human passions to human reason, which prevents the passions from control-

39. CCC 2341.

ling a person. Chastity is the exercise of temperance with respect to sexuality. The virtue of chastity, then, is not lived by repressing a person's sexual inclinations; rather, it controls the sexual passions to ensure they are exercised and expressed properly. Catholic morality does not view sexual pleasure as evil—far from it!—but as a good, beautiful gift from God, a gift that serves a true, complete, committed, and self-giving love between a man and a woman. God included this gift in human nature.

Chastity can help every person become less self-centered and more other-centered. A chaste person is not enslaved to desires and passions, freeing him or her to be able to give the gift of self and to serve others. A chaste person is better able to look at another person as the beautiful, unique person that he or she is rather than as an object of pleasure or a conquest. Living chastity makes it easier to look to the good of others, making a person more free to love as Christ loves.

Chastity is a call for not only those in the married state but also all people in every relationship, as the *Catechism* so aptly teaches:

> Chastity is expressed notably in *friendship with one's neighbor*. Whether it develops between persons of the same or opposite sex, friendship represents a great good for all. It leads to spiritual communion.[40]

The virtue of chastity contributes to truer, deeper friendships! Genuine friendship requires an ability to form a relationship based on love for who the other person is, not what we can get from him or her.[41] Through pure, chaste, self-giving love, we imitate the love of God's self-giving. The more we love in this way, the more we begin to resemble God because we live by the example of Christ.

In the Beatitudes Christ revealed, "Blessed are the pure in heart, for they shall see God."[42] The virtue of chastity, then, pertains not only to what acts we do or refrain from doing with the body but also the related struggle for purity of mind and heart. It calls for purity in thought, intention, love for others, and commitment to living the faith. Thus, the Ninth Commandment forbids even desiring another's spouse, let alone acting on it. Jesus, always revealing

---

40. CCC 2347.
41. Cf. Philip D. Halfacre, *Genuine Friendship* (Downers Grove, IL: Midwest Theological Forum, 2010), 54–55.
42. Mt 5:8.

the perfection of the Law, taught, "Every one who looks at a woman lustfully has already committed adultery with her in his heart."[43]

The practice of chastity—and temperance in general—is a lifelong endeavor. Growth in virtue requires ongoing effort since everyone has a fallen nature. Lustful temptation can be especially intense amid personal difficulties; peer pressure and a hedonistic culture certainly intensify temptations to sins of impurity. As with all the moral virtues, the work of self-mastery never ends since these disordered inclinations never leave. God's graces, especially through the Sacraments, coupled with our personal struggles gradually forms us in the heart of Christ.

Looking specifically at Matrimony, a life lived in pursuit of personal gratification is not good preparation for marriage, which is blessed and joyful to the extent that the spouses love one another with the sacrificial love of Christ. This requires formation in chastity.

Formation in Chastity

As challenging as Christian morality may appear in the modern world, the inner recesses of the human heart desire the holy purity taught by Jesus Christ. Many people, despite so much propaganda to the contrary, experience that growing in chastity is not only possible but also a joyful, liberating virtue. A person leading a chaste life has a greater sense of his or her dignity, develops stronger friendships, experiences greater freedom to love in sacrificial service to others, is inclined to have a deep relationship with Christ, and is better able to contemplate God's goodness and beauty in every person. Effective ways to grow in chastity include fostering a life of piety and Christian virtue, using media prudently, exercising modesty in dress, developing sensible norms for dating, praying, and practicing certain spiritual devotions.

A firm commitment to Christ and a sincere desire to make Christ the center of one's life is the first step in leading a chaste life. Such a person will naturally want to remove those obstacles that impair a relationship with him and compromise moral integrity. Given the many temptations and pressures that exist, it is extremely difficult to honestly pursue chastity without a firm commitment to follow Christ.

---

43. Mt 5:28.

Bad habits, a weak commitment to Christ, and a lackluster love for God and neighbor can make difficulties in growth in the virtue of chastity seem insurmountable. Exhorting his disciples to avoid occasions of sin, Christ taught that everyone should act decisively; for example, "If your right eye causes you to sin, pluck it out and throw it away."[44] Christ used very graphic imagery to reveal that we must aggressively rid ourselves of anything that leads us into sin.

Passivity and ambiguity of purpose can cause major falls in sexual morality. Unless a person has explicitly and seriously decided to reflect Christ's love and his teachings in his or her life, the chances for impure conduct are high. Modern culture is overwhelmingly not in service of chastity, and sexual passions, particularly among younger people, are strongly ordered toward pleasure. These two factors combine to form a strong current; rowing against it requires an active, clear intention and a good execution in cooperation with God's grace. A person who has made a wholehearted decision to live by Christ's teachings is less likely to be caught by the surprise of overwhelming temptation. He or she will be on guard to avoid situations and occasions to behave unchastely. God will always give the necessary grace to help overcome temptations, to avoid occasions of sin, and to grow in virtue.

Prudent use of media is critical to guarding purity. Provocative images on the Internet, on television, in magazines, in movies, in literature, and in conversation can be tempting. Christ revealed the vital importance of the custody of the eyes to grow in and maintain purity.[45] A person who is genuinely serious about the virtue of chastity should avoid looking at things designed to arouse the passions. Consuming media that portray immoral or anti-Christian behavior and are designed to lead a person into temptation is incompatible with the Christian life.

Modesty in dress is an often overlooked virtue to cultivate. Many fashions do not emphasize elegance, which ultimately reinforces the dignity of the person; instead, immodest attire conveys that a person is defined mainly by his or her sexual appeal. Although this is true for everybody, this seems to be especially true of women, who are encouraged to show off the sexually enticing features of their bodies rather than to enhance their personal dignity. Such fashion deceives

44. Mt 5:29.
45. Cf. ibid.

people into believing that the human body is primarily an object of lustful desire rather than a unity with the soul in a human person, deserving of respect and love. It also diminishes *self*-respect, drawing attention to the body as an object for the pleasure of others. A person's choice in clothing should reflect and enhance the dignity and inestimable value of the human person. It should communicate that he or she expects to be respected by others.

In addition to dress, the virtue of modesty is expressed in how a person conducts him- or herself in conversation, in thought, and in what he or she sees and hears. Modesty demands discretion, requires remaining silent at times, keeps a healthy reserve, or declines to consume certain media, especially in circumstances when the dignity of the human person might be degraded. A modest person might not laugh at a joke that degrades human dignity or listen to and encourage gossip about other people. Modesty warns against an unhealthy curiosity, especially in the area of human sexuality.

In addition to a firm commitment and the fostering of virtue, spiritual measures are indispensible to protecting chastity. These are a natural outgrowth of a commitment to Christ. A person who has Christ at the center of his or her life will be given graces to follow his teachings. The virtue of chastity requires not only the exercise of the will but also a good relationship with God, characterized by habitual recourse to prayer, self-denial, acts of penance, and the Sacraments of Penance and the Eucharist. A nightly examination of conscience serves to foster a humble recognition of sins committed together with efforts to avoid occasions of sin; this helps overcome temptations. These and other spiritual measures are sources of grace that give a person the disposition and strength to live a Christian life.

Devotion to the Blessed Virgin Mary is a powerful means to grow in chastity. The Mother of God—who is our Mother as well—will not fail in helping her children liberate themselves from whatever is contrary to the love of her Son, Jesus Christ.

Upon achieving the age and maturity to start dating, common-sense norms should already be established by every adolescent in conjunction with his or her family. Many people want to maintain an exclusive, long-term relationship almost from their first dates, but "going steady" for a long time when marriage is not imminent can make the practice of chastity quite difficult.

Long-term, exclusive relationships have little value in the early teenage years, but they should be generally discouraged even in later teenage years, which leading into the early twenties, are characterized by rapid development that are very critical to personal formation as an adult. Being tied to an exclusive relationship precludes other types of relationships that might provide insights into what a person might want in a future spouse. Exclusive dating also tends to limit a person's activities because couples tend to engage in courtship, and new experiences tend to be limited to one other person's interests, which narrows a person's socialization and activities precisely at a time when these should most be broadened. Until a young man or woman is ready to consider marriage, it is better to be "just friends" with people of the opposite sex. One way to do this is to organize group dates, which have the advantage of limiting "alone time" to avoid situations where temptations are more likely to arise.

When a couple chooses to form a more exclusive dating relationship, it is good to consider it temporary and short-lived. If they think and feel that it might be leading to marriage, then it can proceed along that line. Every steady relationship should be viewed as remote marriage preparation, not as an open-ended imitation of an engagement. Long-term, exclusive relationships without imminent hope of marriage often present growing temptations to sexual expressions. Such a relationship can also distort a person's understanding of what a true commitment entails if he or she begins to experience too close a bond within something impermanent.

When the right partner is at last discovered, the possibility of an imminent marriage can provide good incentive for the couple to live chastely. The virtue of chastity fosters a deeper friendship, which will make the wedding day and subsequent married life all the more special. People looking toward marriage should realize that sexual restraint in dating and in their engagement promotes a deeper friendship, which fosters an exciting romance. Serious observation of chastity in a dating relationship will also strengthen the couple's capacity for fidelity in marriage.

Theology of the Body

Much of the modern Church's language about the role of human sexuality—indeed much of what has already been presented in this chapter—is the fruit of the writings and public lectures of St. John

Paul II. During his pontificate, he explained the beauty of marital relations through his deep insights into the original meaning of marriage as revealed in the Book of Genesis. Through his profound meditation on the dignity of man and woman, the saintly Pope saw with great clarity that a person must always be given love for his or her own sake and never become an object of use. These considerations formed the underpinnings of his teachings on chastity and human sexuality called the *theology of the body*.

In his catechesis, St. John Paul II taught that the union between a husband and a wife reveals the image of God. The "communion of persons" that typifies the union between a man and a woman in marriage reflects the community of persons of the Blessed Trinity:

> Man became the "image and likeness" of God not only through his own humanity, but also through the *communion of persons* which man and woman form right from the beginning. The function of the image is to reflect the one who is the model, to reproduce its own prototype. Man becomes the image of God not so much in the moment of solitude as in the moment of communion.[46]

By revealing the Trinity, Jesus revealed that the image of God in every human person includes the communion of love enjoyed by the three Persons of the Trinity. Thus, human potential is only fully realized in a sincere gift of self. For most people, the most fundamental and primary way of making this sincere gift is through the married state, especially in the Sacrament of Matrimony.

On other occasions St. John Paul II explained that not only the relationship between spouses but the *marital act* reveals God's plan for the expression of their total gift of self in an act of spousal love. The marital act is the "language of the body" that communicates spousal unity and expresses the commitment to serve and love each other for life. Since man and woman possess body and soul, the physical, one-flesh union must always reflect the spiritual union expressed in the faithful and total commitment within the marital covenant. The intimacy shared between a husband and a wife reiterates what was stated verbally with the "language of the body": a dedicated, sacrificial love, which Christ intended to be continually present in their hearts and minds. In this way the true meaning of the marital act expresses an enduring, exclusive, faithful, and sacrificial love. In this manner the marital act is a renewal of the mar-

46. CPIG; emphasis ours.

riage covenant analogous to the way that the Eucharistic Sacrifice is a renewal of the New Covenant established by Christ through his total self-giving on the Cross.

This "language of the body," which is expressive of the total gift of self, is a useful way of looking at the practices Church teachings discourages such as divorce, contraception, cohabitation, masturbation, fornication, homosexual acts, and pornography. Each of these acts—in one way or another—hinders the "total gift of self" and inserts a falsehood into the "language of the body." The next section will include some of these behaviors with regard to the exclusivity of the marital act, leaving for the next chapter those that more directly threaten marriage and family.

Sins Against Chastity

The *Catechism* teaches that the marital act "is morally legitimate only when a definitive community of life between a man and a woman has been established."[47] Marriage is undermined by increasingly commonplace practices: couples living together and availing themselves of sexual expressions with no intention of ever marrying. "Free unions" often include the rejection of marriage as an institution; cohabitating couples practice a kind of "trial marriage," ostensibly with the purpose of "getting to know each other" as a test of compatibility. Some include reasons as banal as saving money. As the *Catechism* teaches, however: "Human love does not tolerate 'trial marriages.' It demands a total and definitive gift of persons to one another."[48]

Sexual expressions outside of the context of marriage cannot be an expression of true love. A gift of self the creates a "unity of the two" can be neither total nor mutual outside of a permanent, exclusive bond. When making marriage vows, whatever form they take across societies and historical eras, each of the spouses promises to give him- or herself totally and exclusively to the other. Sex outside of this bond is deceitful, a misuse of sexuality, and the objectification of one's own and / or another's body. Separated from marriage, the marital act ceases to express—and, in fact, blatantly contradicts—its true meaning. In the "language of the body," the marital act is meant to reflect a complete union of persons. Absent a true self-giving love,

47. CCC 2391.

48. Ibid.

a lifelong commitment in marriage, the marital act and all sexual expressions are a lie: They signify a union that does not exist. Therefore, the Sixth and Ninth Commandments forbid acts that belong to marriage when they occur outside of that sacred union.

A disturbing modern trend, especially among teenagers, is the belief that while sexual intercourse is forbidden outside of marriage, other acts such as passionate kissing and petting are permissible. These behaviors sometimes occur even among casual friends who are not dating and among young people who claim a commitment to abstinence and virginity. It is not just the marital act that must be reserved for marriage, however; the truth is that *all sexual expressions*, with their accompanying pleasure, are meant for the loving embrace of a husband and a wife. The misuse of these actions treat human sexuality as a commodity and the human body as an object of gratification rather than as ordered toward a union of total, self-giving love.

Classroom and conference discussions about chastity with adolescents inevitably elicit the question, "How far can we go before it is a sin?" The assumptions behind this question indicate a misunderstanding of chastity being a joyful affirmation of liberation to truly love. Imagine a similar question, "How badly can I treat my friend before it is a sin?" The absurdity of this latter question sheds light on the mistaken assumptions about the gift of human sexuality.

When it comes to premarital sex, sometimes called "fornication," the Church's moral teachings prohibit not only the marital act but any sexual expressions designed to elicit sexual pleasure outside of marriage; this includes passionate kissing and sexual petting. There are absolutely no circumstances or considerations that would justify these sexual activities outside of marriage. They are not justified even if the relationship is exclusive, even if the partners truly love and care for each other, or even if they are engaged and / or already "feel married." All sexual expressions are "foreplay"—naturally designed to lead to the marital act—and are closely connected to marital intimacy. Prudence insists that people avoid any situations, discussions, or actions that may lead to temptations toward sexual expressions.

If the question, "How far can we go?" insists on an answer, it is this: Performing any act by its very nature designed to cause sexual stimulation or arousal is going too far. These acts include passionate kissing and sexual touches of body parts. It is also true that sexual arousal can occur without a moral act, that is, not intended and not accompanied by an overt sexual act. Becoming aware of sexual stimulation or arousal by either partner should serve as a warning signal to exercise self-restraint and take measures to avoid lustful behavior. Derived from Jesus' teachings, the *Catechism* teaches that any deliberate lustful thought, desire, or action is sinful.[49] Sexual expressions, which bring about sensual pleasure, must be at the service of the total self-gift within the marriage.

In light of the teachings of Christ, chastity includes not only the physical actions of a person but also his or her thoughts and desires. Impure thoughts and desires are, of course, virtually inevitable, particularly for adolescents undergoing hormonal and bodily changes. But *harboring* impure thoughts is a sin against chastity. In the Sermon on the Mount, Jesus taught that it was not enough for a person to avoid adultery, but that even a lustful look or desirous thought of adultery was a sin:

> You have heard that it was said, "You shall not commit adultery." But I say to you that every one who looks at a woman lustfully has already committed adultery with her in his heart.[50]

It can be difficult to understand how "thinking" something, which "doesn't hurt anyone," can be evil. In raising Christian morality to a higher level, Jesus taught that evil action proceeds from the thoughts that come from the heart. The best response is to curtail, or "mortify," impure thoughts and desires before they take root.

The moral question regarding impure thoughts and desires is not about how often random, unintended ideas pop into a person's mind but rather how he or she handles these transitory thoughts. Recognizing a temptation and quickly pushing it aside, offering all sexual desires to God coupled with a brief prayer for the grace to resist them, is a good moral choice and not sinful. It helps to have built up strength in many natural virtues such as chastity, fortitude, and temperance. Instead giving consent to and dwelling on impure thoughts, willfully entertaining them, having an implicit desire to go along with these flights of fantasy for even a short while, and perhaps even allowing the mind to be aroused by them constitutes the evil of impure thoughts and desires. Such a person has weak-

---

49. Cf. CCC 2351: "Lust is disordered desire for or inordinate enjoyment of sexual pleasure. Sexual pleasure is morally disordered when sought for itself, isolated from its procreative and unitive purposes"; cf. Mt 5:28.

50. Mt 5:27–28.

ened in virtue, becoming more susceptible to dwelling on impure thoughts and more likely to act on them. All sin requires an act of the will, as described in Chapter 5, so the question of sinfulness hinges on *consenting* to these thoughts or not. Even many saints were tormented by unintended thoughts of impurity, with the Devil even presenting images before their eyes. Their holiness was shown in rejecting temptations.

What Christ revealed in his rejection of lust is the esteem by which human dignity should be held. He taught this most clearly in the quote on the previous page: Looking at a woman with lust was to commit adultery with her. Another way of looking at this is the objectification of the woman involved, using her as an object of physical self-gratification, is identical to even *considering* her an object. Anyone who indulges in impure thoughts and desires weakens his or her respect for the human person by dwelling on his or her own gratification by the other. The content of such thoughts might be different between men and women, but the root selfishness is the same. Thus, the standard to which Christ calls us begins with aligning our will to his New Commandment of Love—"that you love one another; even as I have loved you"[51]—of seeing every person as a being who is worthy of unconditional love.

The struggle with impure thoughts merits one more mention of the media. A person seeking to grow in chastity should never willfully entertain nor *be entertained* by the thoughts or desires presented for consumption in certain media. Romance has always made for good storytelling, but it is sensible and necessary to avoid sexually provocative images or discussions, either consumed directly or at the theater, in magazines, or on the Internet. Applying appropriate means to keep custody of the eyes and mind is a virtuous practice that serves to avoid near occasions of sin and being overcome by passions. Capitalizing on an inclination toward sensuality, the Devil is always on the lookout for ways to tempt people to sin.

The teaching against impure thoughts and desires strikes at the root of two practices that are particularly acceptable today: pornography and masturbation. It is typically thought that viewing pornography and / or masturbating are nothing more than "healthy expressions of human sexuality" and that to overcome such urges is "repressive." The Church, however, teaches quite the opposite. Both

51. Jn 13:34.

pornography and masturbation weaken a person's moral character, cause that person to objectify and demean his or her own or another's body, and ultimately make him or her a slave to passions that can no longer be controlled. The enjoyment of sexual pleasure is part of God's plan connected with the self-giving expressed in sexual expressions and the marital act within marriage.

More recently, psychologists and neurologists have discovered that repeated use of pornography and / or acts of masturbation can result in *physical* addiction as well due to the impact on neurochemistry when a person repeatedly engages in these actions. Not only the spirit but also the body and the mind are altered by repeated use of pornography and masturbation, leaving a person wounded and lacking in self-mastery. Lives have been damaged and families destroyed by addiction to pornography, particularly as it becomes so much easier to find and consume; custody of the eyes has never been more necessary given the options available.

By masturbating a person misuses his or her God-given sexuality by focusing this gift only on him- or herself, which completely separates sexuality from its purpose. Every act of self-stimulation or self-satisfaction is morally wrong because the authentic expression of human sexuality is innately "*other*-centered" and "*new-life*-centered"; it is not "*self*-centered," disconnected from spousal love. This is why the *Catechism* teaches, "Masturbation is an intrinsically and gravely disordered action."[52] Its practice tends to become habitual and can lead to sexual obsession and a greater proclivity to run away from the challenges and problems of real life. Once a person has become habitually prone to this type of behavior, oftentimes he or she can only overcome this habit with God's abundant grace coupled with strenuous effort, frequent reception of the Sacraments of Penance and the Eucharist, prayer, and acts of penance.

When arousal takes place unwittingly it lacks the freedom of a truly moral act, as described in Chapter 5. Occasionally, particularly with young men, an erotic dream can result in sexual stimulation and even satisfaction. As long as these acts are neither consented to nor entertained, there is no culpability.

Another point of contention between the Church's teaching on human sexuality and modern cultural attitudes is the Church's con-

52. CCC 2352; quoting PH, no. 9.

sistent position that "homosexual acts are intrinsically disordered."[53] Criticism of the Church's teaching most often comes from two directions: First, there is the aforementioned claim, with regard to masturbation and pornography, that what people need in order to feel good about their own sexuality is total abandon to engage in whatever actions they want, whenever they want, with whomever they want. The Church teaches that this attitude is an *attack* on the good of the person and human dignity and offers enslavement and exploitation—not liberation. Simply *having* a sexual attraction does not require acting on it. The Church requires the same chastity of a person with a same-sex attraction than of any unmarried person, who must refrain from sexual expressions, or any married person, who must remain faithful to his or her spouse. The teaching on homosexual acts is consistent with the entire body of Church teachings on the dignity of human sexuality and its proper expression within marriage.

Second, however, is the claim that the teaching against homosexual *acts* is a veiled hatred or fear of the homosexual *person*. This, too, is false. As in any organization, the Church might have homophobic members who are guilty of hatred of and prejudice against homosexual people, but these outliers do not hold the formal position; in fact, the Church calls such people to conversion through ongoing formation. The Church has produced beautiful writings on the dignity of every homosexual person and repeatedly taught that the *inclination* is not the sin. All sin requires an act of the will, as described in Chapter 5, so no impure thought is sinful in itself. The Church makes no judgment on what causes some people to be attracted to members of the same sex; from a moral perspective, it makes no difference whether the inclination is determined by genetics, psychology, environmental conditioning, or other influences. Independent of the cause, only acting on a homosexual inclination—with full knowledge and full use of the will—is gravely sinful.[54]

Based on what has already been presented, especially about the theology of the body, homosexual acts must be unnatural in and of themselves and contrary to the married state established by God. God created a man and a woman to be sexually attracted to each other for the purpose of a marital relationship of life-giving love.

53. CCC 2357; quoting PH, no. 8.

54. Cf. CCC 2537.

Given the complementarity of the sexes and the direct, intimate connection between the marital act and new life, attraction between members of the opposite sex is derived from human nature. Therefore, any same-sex inclinations are outside of God's plan of sexual complementarity that leads to the conception of new life.

The intrinsic connection between the marital act and new life will be discussed in greater detail in the next chapter; this chapter is focusing on chastity, human dignity, and the relationship of mutual respect that exists between spouses. An important part of this mutual respect is to fully acknowledge and accept the sexual identity of the other (as well as one's own sexual identity). God created men and women with natural sexual differences. A person's sex describes not only the constitution of his or her body but also his or her very identity. Sexuality affects every person at the most elemental level of personhood. Inscribed in a person's sexual identity is a profound complementarity to the opposite sex. In addition to ensuring the continuation of the human race, sexual attraction between a man and a woman includes a personal calling to a community of love. Men and women, made in God's image, have been inscribed with the vocation of love and communion. Homosexual acts, lacking in the complementarity of sexes—"male and female he created them"[55]—cannot achieve the authentic "language of the body": The "creation of man consists in the creation of the unity of two beings."[56]

This is not to say that homosexual couples are incapable of great friendship and mutual support on a deep emotional level. Opponents of the Church's stance on homosexual activity often accuse the Church of "condemning" homosexuals to a "life of loneliness." This accusation reveals a hyper-sexualized understanding of the human person, wrongly suggesting that a relationship with sexual expressions is the *only* relevant human relationship. In reality, self-gift can be experienced in a multitude of ways. Chastity, as noted above, *increases* friendship. As we shall see in Chapter 19 on the Sacrament of Holy Orders, a gift of self that is *chaste* and even *celibate* can be a greater act of love when it is freer of selfish intentions. A life without sexual gratification is a life wholly worth living and filled with opportunities for authentic, deep communion with others.

55. Gn 1:27.
56. CPIG.

Just like every person, people with same-sex attraction are called by Christ to live a life of chastity. Spiritual direction, prayer, and frequent recourse to the Sacraments are indispensable aids for *everyone* to live in accordance with his or her Christian vocation. The *Catechism* strongly encourages those with same-sex inclinations to personal holiness.[57] The Church recognizes that many people in society have same-sex inclinations, and with much pastoral concern, the *Catechism* addresses their particular situation and the need for God's love, along with guidance for living a moral life focused on Jesus Christ.

> By the virtues of self-mastery that teach [homosexual persons] their inner freedom, at times by the support of disinterested friendship, by prayer and sacramental grace, they can and should gradually and resolutely approach Christian perfection.[58]

At the same time, the Church has steadfastly opposed all unjust discrimination against those with homosexual inclinations along with acknowledging the difficulties faced by homosexual persons:

> The Church seeks to enable every person to live out the universal call to holiness. Persons with a homosexual inclination ought to receive every aid and encouragement to embrace this call personally and fully. This will unavoidably involve much struggle and self-mastery, for following Jesus always means following the way of the Cross.... The Sacraments of the Eucharist and of Penance are essential sources of consolation and aid on this path.[59]

The Sacrament Itself

With a better understanding of marriage as a total gift of self, meant to foster unity and partnership between a man and a woman, along with an overview of some of the evil activities that threaten the ability to withstand the challenges to the sanctity of marriage, we can now turn to the celebration of the Sacrament of Matrimony itself.

As St. Paul revealed to the Ephesians, spouses ought to "be subject to one another out of reverence for Christ."[60] The universal image of spousal love is the Crucifix, which represents Christ's

57. Cf. CCC 2359.

58. Ibid.

59. United States Conference of Catholic Bishops, *Ministry to Persons with a Homosexual Inclination: Guidelines for Pastoral Care* (November 14, 2006), 13.

60. Eph 5:21.

suffering and Death for every person. The commitment of spouses should be characterized, therefore, by unconditional love and mutual self-giving. That is certainly a tall order, only possible with the added supernatural help provided by the Sacrament of Matrimony. As the celebrated preacher and writer Venerable Fulton Sheen offered in his book *Three to Get Married*: "It takes three to make love in hearts—The Lover, the Beloved, and Love."[61] That special Third Person involved with every Christian marriage is Jesus Christ, represented by the symbol of the Cross.

Conjugal love (literally, the love that yokes people together) involves a physical, emotional, psychological, and spiritual unity at the deepest level. For this one-flesh unity to truly be present, there must exist the baseline of an unbreakable bond. This indissoluble relationship should serve as a powerful incentive not only to maintain but to grow in the commitment of total self-giving. The prayer "that they might no longer be two, but one flesh"[62] pertains not only to physical union but also goes way beyond it to include emotional and spiritual union. There is an intimate unity of spirit forged by a friendship so profound that each party identifies with the needs of the other; each one sees the other as another self.

Given modern challenges to marriage, it may seem utopian to expect a marriage to stay intact in a fast-paced society. With so many factors militating against a faithful, lasting marriage, there is an ongoing temptation to move on when the thrill of falling in love has ebbed. There can be a prevailing self-seeking attitude and an excessive attachment to personal fulfillment in marrying a particular person rather than an eagerness to promote that same person's welfare and happiness. Too many people place as a condition for perseverance in a marriage an ongoing personal satisfaction and delight in the other's company. Once the euphoria of a courtship or being newly wedded has worn off and mutual shortfalls become more apparent, people are erroneously tempted to think the marriage must be flawed. Outside of the ambit of the Gospel message, there is not much of a cultural sense that the spouses must pull out all the stops to make their marriage last.

This totality of faithful, sacrificial love requires that the union between a man and a woman be permanent and unbreakable

61. Ven. Fulton J. Sheen, *Three To Get Married* (New York: Appleton-Century-Crofts, Inc., 1951), ii.

62. RMiss, Ritual Masses: V. For the Celebration of Marriage, Nuptial Blessing.

regardless of prevailing circumstances. The marital covenant of fidelity and lifelong permanence includes openness to life since children and their rearing is one of the purposes of marriage. The unbreakable bond of fidelity and love between spouses extends also to the greatest fruit of their love: their children. This community of love is by no means meant to be static, let alone stagnant, but is meant to grow with the progression of years.

Because union with Christ forms the human heart to love as he loved, marital friendship grows to the extent that each spouse loves the other out of devotion and dedication to Jesus. The presence of Christ ensures that the love between spouses is perfected and intensified. This begins with a sacramental marriage—with its graces—based on a lifelong commitment, which is preserved and nurtured by the healing Sacrament of Penance and Reconciliation and the nourishing Sacrament of the Eucharist. Christ has redeemed and elevated marriage; he also makes it a possibility.

The commitment that a husband and a wife make to each other is so central to marriage that the spouses are not simply the *recipients* of the Sacrament—as with, for example, Baptism or Confirmation—they are the *ministers* as well! The spouses administer the Sacrament to each other by their presence and mutual consent to marry. Specifically, the matter (object or action) and form (words) are identified with the couple: The *matter* of Matrimony is the man and the woman themselves. The *form* of Matrimony is the matrimonial formula consisting in their words of consent (the promises, popularly called the "vows") to a lifelong, exclusive, and faithful conjugal love.

The Sacrament of Matrimony is conferred when the spouses freely consent to a faithful, exclusive communion with each other for the rest of their lives. The spouses are called to mirror God's fidelity to his people and Christ's total self-giving to his Church. Mutual consent is at the heart of the Sacrament of Matrimony; this consent is an act of the will given in formal this expression: "I, [Name], take you, [Name], to be my wife."… "I, [Name], take you, [Name], to be my husband."[63] Their consent binds the husband and the wife to each other for life since they spiritually and morally become one flesh. This spiritual union will be reinforced when their marriage is consummated by the marital act.

---

63. OCM, The Celebration of Matrimony: The Consent, no. 62.

If any of the principal conditions of Matrimony are missing from the consent, that marriage covenant would be invalid. If the spouses commit themselves to each other out of fear or coercion rather than as a free and deliberate choice, there would be no real marriage. If one partner intentionally withholds crucial information that would immediately alter the other's consent, this, too, would invalidate the union. The consent must also involve the decision and desire to remain faithful to one's spouse for life as an absolute condition for validity. A valid marriage must also include the disposition to be open to new life. If a couple marry with the express goal of never having children, that marriage would be rendered invalid.

Another key feature of marriage is the capacity to have marital relations since the marital act is the "language of the body" that mutually communicates a total gift of self and manifests openness to life. This does not mean that any psychological or physical illness that occurred during the marriage that would prevent the possibility for sexual relations would retroactively make the covenant invalid. Nor does it mean that people who are sterile by accident or birth or people who are past childbearing age cannot have a sacramental marriage. In the first case, a valid marriage has already (presumably) taken place, and the couple are bearing life's struggles as "one flesh." In the second case, the couple's wills are not *closed* to life; the option is simply not available to them. But if one partner were physically or psychologically incapable of consummating the marriage it would nullify the vows and thereby the Sacrament.

If the couple represents the recipient, minister, matter, and form of a valid ceremony, why get married in a church building rather than on a beach, in one of their parents' backyard, or at a courthouse? Who needs an ordained minster of the Church?

The Sacrament of Matrimony depends on the marriage being blessed by an ordained minister of the Church: a bishop, priest, or deacon. Matrimony is a true covenant not only between the spouses but also with the Church. The bishop, priest, or deacon, as already presented, does not *administer* the Sacrament, this is true, but he does serve as the Church's official *witness* and gives God's blessing to the couple's union. Part of the service of the ordained minister is to ensure that the requirements for marriage have been fulfilled, for example, making sure the consent of each engaged person to be a husband or a wife is being given freely. Matrimony is so important for the Church and the couple that a marriage not explicitly acknowledged and blessed by the Church would be considered invalid.

The presence of the minister of the Church demonstrates that the Sacrament of Matrimony is intimately linked to the Church and her mission on earth. The bishop, priest, or deacon gives public recognition that the marriage in question is a true sign of Christ's love for his Church; in addition, there are pastoral considerations for the presence of an ordained minister. The Church, as a good Mother, wants her married children to enjoy all the benefits that can be obtained through the Sacrament of Matrimony. Given our wounded human nature, every marriage will always have its difficulties, and fidelity to this covenant can never be assured without the help of divine grace. The sacramental graces are designed to help the spouses stay faithful throughout their lives. Matrimonial graces are both at the service of fidelity and foster a steady growth in mutual love and affection.

The Sacrament of Matrimony should be celebrated, unless there is a serious reason otherwise, in a church building because it is a liturgical act with specific gestures and rites. Moreover, celebrating in a church is a sign that the newlywed couple are members of the Church and a public declaration that they live in the married state, which is a distinct vocation recognized by the Church. A Catholic wedding also signifies that, as members of the Church, the newlywed couple acquire certain rights and responsibilities, especially the pastoral support of the Church and their children having access to the Sacraments, specifically the right to have their children baptized in the Church to begin their own share in eternal life.

It is most fitting, though not necessary, that Catholics be married within the celebration of the Mass. It is appropriate to celebrate spousal communion among the faithful in the context of the Eucharistic Sacrifice and the reception of Holy Communion. As with each Sacrament, there is a connection between Matrimony and the Eucharist: Christian marriage is a sign of Christ's love for his Church, and the Eucharist is the celebration of the mystical marriage between Christ and his Church.

In the context of a marriage, reception of the Eucharist becomes especially meaningful as the recipients become one with Christ as they enter the one-flesh union. The Eucharist, received in Holy

Communion, enhances not only union with Christ but also the union between spouses.

The Sacrament of Matrimony is the source of ongoing grace to grow in love and bear the hardships of marital and family life. The engaged couple should prepare for and arrive at their wedding celebration with the best possible spiritual dispositions. The better the dispositions, the greater the capacity to receive graces from this special Sacrament. Purification of heart and soul through the Sacrament of Penance and Reconciliation is highly recommended to take full advantage of the sacramental graces of Matrimony, so it is common, shortly before the wedding day, to make a good confession. This practically puts the newlywed husband and wife in better conditions to love each other in a more giving way. The graces of Matrimony have a greater influence on the future spouses when they allow the graces of Penance and the Eucharist to remove the roadblocks of selfishness and better dispose each spouse to a life of charity.

Confession prior to marriage is particularly necessary for engaged couples entering marriage without living the chastity proper to unmarried people. For example, engaged couples who live together or engage in sexual expressions hinder their openness to God's graces offered by the Sacrament of Matrimony. It is not that Our Lord withholds his graces; rather, the wrong dispositions impede the workings of grace, as presented in Chapter 11. It is in the interests of an engaged couple to put their best foot forward in preparation for a loving, lifelong marriage. Many cohabitating couples who desire a sacramental marriage in the Church have chosen to live separately and forego further sexual expressions in preparation for their marriage, opening themselves to receive the fullest possible benefit of God's graces. The Sacraments of Penance and the Eucharist are giant, effective helps in this endeavor.

In a sense, the couple are proving to each other that they are so madly in love with each other that they are willing to renounce sexual expressions, which are proper to marriage, until they are married. Many people who are seeking to be joined in marriage act as if they were already married; too often their sexual activity leads to spiritual inactivity. Such sexual expressions hinder the normal growth of a loving, close friendship, robbing the future engaged couple, in a beautiful and noble way, of the experience of the "language of the body" of their mutual gift of self as the consummation of the Sacrament of Matrimony. The marital act profoundly signifies a union to which the spouses are called—by God—to a new kind of love that fittingly corresponds to the reality of the married state.

When unmarried couples use sexual expressions before they have hardly had the chance to get to know each other, they can easily eclipse nonsexual facets of dating. The physical focus of their relationship is disproportionately large. Many marriages have failed due to an underdeveloped friendship and mutual affection. Couples who are considering marriage have a vested interest in living the chastity proper to unmarried people since this virtue liberates the couple to grow in true love for each other as persons and not as occasions of sensual gratification.

Effects of the Sacrament of Matrimony

The first effect of the Sacrament of Matrimony is that a true bond is formed between the spouses that is permanent and irreplaceable for life, as the Church's minister prays: "that they might no longer be two, but one flesh, / and ... must never be divided."[64] The Church describes this bond as "indissoluble." By virtue of Matrimony, the couple is consecrated to Christ in their marital duties toward each other and parental duties regarding their children. When the husband and wife consent to give themselves to each other in faithful and mutual self-giving, a bond emerges that is sealed by God himself. It is a matter of divine Law that the marriage bond is unbreakable: "What therefore God has joined together, let not man put asunder."[65] Once a marriage is concluded by the physical consummation of the marital act, no authority on earth can break that bond. Not even the Church has the power to dissolve the marital bond once their marriage is consummated.[66]

The Sacrament of Matrimony bestows special graces on the husband and the wife that help them in preserving and strengthening their bond. Their love is reinforced by grace, and consequently their union with each other is fortified even more. This sacramental grace also assists the man and the woman in their growth in union and

64. RMiss, Ritual Masses: V. For the Celebration of Marriage, Nuptial Blessing.

65. Mk 10:9.

66. Cf. CIC, can. 1141: "A ratified and consummated marriage cannot be dissolved by any human power or for any reason other than death."

friendship with Jesus Christ. Forming the marital covenant through this mutual consent of total self-giving can occasion an intimate encounter with Jesus Christ throughout the marriage. The presence of Jesus within the marriage bond helps the couple bear the crosses that come with a marital relationship and the effort of raising children. Matrimonial grace helps the couple exercise patience with each other and fosters a spirit of forgiveness toward the other's weaknesses and defects. Christ helps the couple be subject to one another joyfully and strive to serve each other's needs generously. This Sacrament provides the help needed to live Jesus' New Commandment of Love—"that you love one another; even as I have loved you"[67]—by loving with his very heart. This welcomed presence of Jesus Christ is enhanced when the couples avail themselves of the Sacraments of Penance and the Eucharist.

Even under the best conditions, married couples will encounter many challenges and hardships. Difficulties take on countless forms, many of which cannot be anticipated. Adjusting to differences in temperament, coping with each other's flaws and weaknesses, caring for unexpected illnesses, exercising patience with psychological issues, and communicating about financial problems are but some of the actions that spouses have to take. The formation and education of children is another significant area of stress and anxiety, especially in modern culture. These crosses, which in many instances are the order of the day, require grace from God. The graces of Matrimony will provide the necessary strength to cope and to grow through all adversities that impact a marriage. The Church desperately wants to give her children this effective help in bearing their inevitable hardships.

Matrimony is a wonderful source of much needed grace not only to protect the marriage but also to improve it. A common observation by deacons and priests during marriage preparation is that marital dysfunction can be greatly lessened when the spouses cooperate with the graces of Matrimony. This cooperation with grace involves both a husband and a wife making a genuine effort to follow Christ. Spouses who attend Mass regularly, go to Confession regularly, converse with Christ daily in prayer, and accept their crosses daily are likely to have a good marriage. On the other hand, couples who are not close to the Church hinder the blessings and

67. Jn 13:34.

graces of Matrimony, sometimes to the point of having little effect, thereby increasing the chances for marital failure. Simply having a "church wedding" does not guarantee that the spouses will cooperate with God's graces or be committed to a life with Christ in his Church. As the popular adage goes, "A wedding is for a day; a marriage is for a lifetime."

To receive the full benefit of the graces of Matrimony, an engaged couple need to develop the proper dispositions through good formation, both "remote" and "immediate" preparation.

To help with this remote preparation, the Church encourages, protects, and cultivates marital fidelity, especially given the pressures of societies that not only accept but recommend divorce as a way of dealing with problems, offering little encouragement to resolve difficulties. The throw-away culture, which especially includes struggling marriages, has seriously damaged a healthy, proper understanding of this exalted institution. Good Christian upbringing—with the good example of a faithful mother and a faithful father—more than anything positively contributes to future marriages. Nothing in this regard can rival parents who are totally committed to their union by the enduring witness of sacrificial love and heartfelt affection.

Another very important aspect of remote preparation for marriage consists in being brought up in the Catholic faith. From their earliest years, children should grow in their relationship with Christ and observe the sacredness of the marriage bond as well as the permanence of their parents' fidelity to Jesus Christ and to each other. Joy and affection within the family enjoys its finest hour when its driving force is the love of Christ. This positive experience of living in a Christian home naturally carries over into the children's future marriages. If both a husband and a wife are striving to make Christ the center of their lives, they will grow leaps and bounds in their love for each other. This habitual effort to conform their personal lives to the life of Christ will move the couple to discover and rediscover ways to make each other happy.

Not everyone is blessed to grow up with the example of a faithful marriage, and this seems increasingly true as time passes. The good news is that marriage, like any other challenging pursuit, can be helped by good role models but does not absolutely depend on them. People raised by divorced parents or by a parent who was abandoned can be more likely to doubt that a faithful, lifelong marriage is possible. People whose families failed to provide a good example of a faithful, sacrificial marriage should not be discouraged—rather, they should recognize the need to rely all the more to the power of graces offered in the Sacrament of Marriage.

All couples who seek marriage in the Church undergo immediate preparation with a deacon or priest; in some circumstances the deacon or priest might appoint a catechist or married couple to lead this preparation. This immediate preparation explains the nature of marriage, the Sacrament of Matrimony, and the Church's teachings and expectations related to these subjects. This preparation should strongly urge cohabiting engaged couples or those who engage in sexual expressions to live chastity as it is proper to unmarried people out of love; this helps ensure that their married love is deeper than physical and emotional attraction.

CHAPTER 18

MARRIAGE AND FAMILY

The previous chapter focused on the Sixth and Ninth Commandments as they relate to chastity and expressions of human sexuality as acts of total, mutual self-gift within marriage. Even before Christ elevated marriage to the level of a Sacrament, natural marriage was sacred from the time of creation. Not only does marriage unite two people in love so intimately that they become one flesh, but it is also the foundation of the most fundamental building block of human society—the family.

Catholic social teaching, as presented in Chapter 10, holds the family as the basic unit of all society. Civilization itself springs from the social nature of the human person, expressed first in the fact that everyone comes into the world as a result of the coming together of people. "The family," Pope Francis taught, "is the fundamental cell of society, where we learn to live with others despite our differences and to belong to one another."[1] All social relationships spring from the family, and because of the Fall of Adam and Eve, by extension all human relationships are now weakened in their capacity to form authentic communion.

Looking at the Ten Commandments, God clearly places importance on family life. The Fourth Commandment, "Honor your father and your mother,"[2] is the first of the Commandments directed toward love of neighbor—after God comes family. The Church has often pointed out that the breakdown of the family is most negatively impacting society. A healthy family environment ultimately contributes good citizens, while the opposite situation has left many people psychologically and emotionally wounded. Despite all the challenges, despite all that families must battle nowadays to stay together, and despite those who argue that family makeup is irrelevant to human thriving, a loving, united family is still possible with the help of God's grace, particularly when begun by receiving the Sacrament of Matrimony.

1. EG, no.66.
2. CCC, Part Three, Section Two; Ex 20:12.

Marital Union Ordered Toward Family

One key aspect to the sacredness of marriage in all societies is its close connection to bringing children into the world; marriage is suited not only to the propagation of new life but also to the creation of the proper environment for rearing the human person. The best, most salutary setting for the education and formation of children essentially involves the active presence of both a mother and a father. Any institution that promotes and serves the human person enjoys an exalted dignity, and nothing can give a greater endorsement to human dignity than the loving friendship between a mother and father for each other and their children.

Millennia of recorded history and evidence from prehistory attest that a human being's upbringing and moral and physical support find its ideal setting within the context of a family. A newborn entering the world is best served in terms of protection, physical development, and education under the care and supervision of a loving mother and father in a stable relationship. The vital importance of the family for the well-being of the human person explains why the Fourth Commandment takes pride of place among the Commandments relating to human relationships.

In salvation history a husband and a wife are consistently introduced as key figures in bearing and raising children. The parents of Isaac, Jacob, Samuel, Samson, and St. John the Baptist all had an important part to play in forming and educating their respective children for their distinct missions. The Son of God himself took on human nature and came into this world through a family, revealed first to the Blessed Virgin Mary, his Mother; he spent most of his years on earth living in a family, with his mother and father.[3] This reveals a powerful message of the exalted dignity and importance of the family. In the Early Church a father, a mother, and their children were considered a "domestic church." Because of the virulent persecutions of Christianity and the subsequent absence of church buildings, the family was the unit of the universal Church. In the early Christians' homes, the Eucharist was celebrated, and people received religious instruction. Within the intimacy of family life, the Christian faith was transmitted.

3. Cf. Lk 2:51.

As in the nascent Church, a modern-day married couple with their children is a domestic church. Within a family children practice Catholic traditions and learn basic tenets of their faith. Through the instruction and example of their parents, children celebrate the Sacraments by going to Confession, attending Mass, attending weddings, etc. Out of the experience of family life, serving the needs of others becomes a top priority. The Christian home is the first school of prayer, service, and charity:[4] It is where we learn how to make sacrifices for each other out of love and to contribute our labor to the common good. As Pope Francis said, "In a world often marked by selfishness, a large family is a school of solidarity and sharing; and this attitude is to the benefit of society as a whole."[5] Within the family the love of Christ finds a permanent home.

In this fallen world no family can maintain this perfect harmony without conflict or disruption. Every person comes from a family that is flawed in some ways, and too many are from truly difficult family situations. Only the Holy Family—Jesus together with his Mother Mary and St. Joseph—was perfect. Acknowledging the eventuality of shortcoming is no cause to reject God's beautiful plan for a healthy family. As in many other cases, physical health offers a good analogy. Every living person benefits from at least a minimum level of good health, yet not every person is healthy. Some people ignore their health, and others have poor health thrust on them through no fault of their own. Everyone seeking better physical health needs to know what will improve his or her situation: What kind of nutrition? How much exercise? What foods to avoid? What does "good health" look like? The same goes for the challenges of a healthy family life; to strive for a happy, healthy home, we need to know what it looks like and the means to achieve it.

The Church's extensive, loving teachings on marriage and human sexuality offer a wonderful road map for healthy, happy marriages. It is precisely when these guidelines are rejected or ignored that untold problems arise in marriage, in family life, and ultimately throughout every human society.

---

4. Cf. St. John Paul II, Apostolic Exhortation on the Role of the Christian Family in the Modern World *Familiaris Consortio* (November 22, 1981), no. 36; Second Ecumenical Council of the Vatican, Declaration on Christian Education *Gravissimum Educationis* (October 28, 1965), no. 3.

5. NNFA.

Since every human being depends first on his or her parents for physical, emotional, and moral health, there are many important ramifications derived from the Commandment, "Honor your father and your mother."[6] This chapter will first present the duties of parents and children and how God's plan for the family is reflected in society. Then this chapter will return to the study of the Sixth and Ninth Commandments, discussed in some detail in the previous chapter, focusing on how these relate not only to the couple in marriage but also to the family.

Honor Your Father and Your Mother

Every human being shares in our social nature. An essential aspect of the divine image in the human person that everyone carries within his or her intimate self is the inclination to love others and to seek their good. By virtue of the natural law, the closer the relationship, the greater the duty to love. We must love first those closest to us by reason of family ties, especially in the case of spouses, parents, and siblings. By reason of marriage, then, a husband and wife must show their greatest, most intense love for each other. Linked to their spousal love is the very close bond parents have with their children, the fruit of their intimate love for each other. Because every person's existence, in cooperation with God's creative power, is a direct consequence of his or her parents' love, children must honor, obey, respect, and love their mother and father as representatives of God's authority over them.

There are several places in the Old Testament where the Fourth Commandment is repeated. In the Book of Exodus, when God revealed the Law to Moses, he proclaimed: "Honor your father and your mother, that your days may be long in the land which the Lord your God gives you."[7] The formula was later repeated by Moses in the Book of Deuteronomy:

> Honor your father and your mother, as the Lord your God commanded you; that your days may be prolonged, and that it may go well with you, in the land which the Lord your God gives you.[8]

Besides the formula itself, the Old Testament is filled with exhortations and considerations concerning the obligations to honor

6. CCC, Part Three Section Two; Ex 20:12.

7. Ex 20:12.

8. Dt 5:16.

fathers and mothers. God promised many blessings for those who respectfully love, serve, and revere their parents. The idea behind the powerful encouragement to truly love father and mother is that human life, a priceless gift, comes from them. No matter how solicitous and grateful children are, they can never repay their parents for the gift of life and upbringing.

Though the Commandment is directed at honoring parents, the parents first have obligations toward their children. St. Paul profoundly summarizes the duties of good Christian parents: "Fathers, do not provoke your children to anger, but bring them up in the discipline and instruction of the Lord."[9] These words exhort parents to love their children with the love of Jesus Christ. This love involves not only kindness, mercy, and affection but also fortitude and courage in imparting discipline in their education and formation.

"Do not provoke your children to anger"; this conveys the message that parents must try to earn and maintain the respect of their children. Raising children is neither the extreme of laxity in leadership and guidance nor the other extreme of abusive tyranny. Children belong absolutely to God, and God has entrusted those children to the care of their parents. Every human child is a child of God, redeemed by Jesus Christ, and must be treated as such. Abuse—emotional, physical, psychological, or otherwise—is totally incompatible with Christian parenting. While infants, children, and even adolescents are not adults, Christian charity requires that parents treat them with the age- and maturity-related respect owed to children of God. If there is genuine concern and desire to truly help them, children will quickly perceive that discipline and guidance spring from deep love.

Discipline is a crucial component in raising children to become good citizens as well as disciples of Christ. Most children reach the age of reason by about seven years of age, so developing the capacity for true self-control requires consistent discipline that, in turn, paves the way for virtuous actions. As in most facets of human development, formation in the proper use of freedom, self-control, and a sense of responsibility rests in large part on the parents' success in instilling discipline. Insensitivity to the needs of others, habitual laziness and idleness, and an inability to fulfill tasks reasonably betrays in many instances a lack of parental discipline. These atti-

---

9. Eph 6:4.

tudes are reflective of the attitude parents have taken toward their own responsibilities.

There is a special urgency for parents to genuinely fulfill their roles as a mother and a father and avoid the common pitfall of limiting themselves to simply being "friends" with their children. The modern world has brought a generalized fear of exercising "tough love" when it comes to forming children in a spirit of sacrifice typified by hard work, good manners, selflessness, and temperance in creature comforts. The virtue of generosity as a way of sharing and advancing the Kingdom of God always presupposes the conscientious sense of responsibility that comes out of discipline.

A helpful analogy exists between the role of good parents and the relationship between God and his children. As the Book of Deuteronomy reveals, "Know then in your heart that, as a man disciplines his son, the LORD your God disciplines you."[10] The Epistle to the Hebrews reveals the role of discipline in the formation and education of children by highlighting how and why God disciplines:

> My son, do not regard lightly the discipline of the Lord,
> nor lose courage when you are punished by him.
> For the Lord disciplines him whom he loves,
> and chastises every son whom he receives.[11]

Discipline is an act of love whereby one person forms another in what is known to be for that person's good. The Sacred Author of Hebrews continues, "For the moment all discipline seems painful rather than pleasant; later it yields the peaceful fruit of righteousness to those who have been trained by it."[12] Consistent, rational discipline directed toward the child's good might not always win happiness in the moment, but in the end it will produce a happier child and adult.

In addition to overseeing the physical well-being of their children, parents have a serious obligation to form and educate their sons and daughters in the Catholic faith. As the child grows, every child should be instructed in the *Catechism* and in the lives of the saints, enjoy regular reception of the Sacraments, and learn how to cultivate friendship with Jesus Christ and other people. A key component of Christian upbringing involves training in charity, kindness,

10. Dt 8:5.

11. Heb 12:5–6.

12. Heb 12:11.

compassion, and service. For instance, all children should contribute to the upkeep of the house, share their possessions with others, and learn how to care for anyone who is suffering, beginning with members of their own family. Especially in a consumerist culture, it is very important for parents to train and form their children to be happy with what is necessary to lead a simple, ordered life. If the child accumulates many possessions, that same child can easily become self-centered and distracted from other people and from God. A Catholic education is much more than learning the facts and information about the Catholic faith, so parents cannot simply pass this job off to their Catholic school or a religious education instructor at their parish. As the adage goes, "Charity begins at home"; children are primarily shaped by their family environment. It should be easy to see that these virtues are much easier to instill when children are blessed with brothers and sisters, though any child can and must learn these virtues from his or her parents.

Children, owing their care and personal formation to their parents, must not only honor their parents but are also expected to obey them. "Respect for parents," teaches the *Catechism* ...

> derives from gratitude toward those who, by the gift of life, their love and their work, have brought their children into the world and enabled them to grow in stature, wisdom, and grace.[13]

In principle, parents have a divinely bestowed authority over their offspring. Independent of their character flaws, the natural law reinforced by the Fourth Commandment requires that children honor, respect, and obey their parents in all that is not sinful.

Despite this duty of children, it is important that parents earn the respect of their children by being effective role models in the Christian life. Habitual anger, impatience, irritability, and many other defects cause parents to lose their moral authority. Parents effectively direct and guide their children not primarily by their verbal commands but chiefly by their good examples. Behind the lives of many contemporary saints are the holy lives of their parents.

Even when a parent does not act in an honorable way—or directions are immoral and not to be obeyed—his or her position as parent requires respect. Even children in difficult situations have an obligation to honor their parents with charity and support without condoning their wrongdoing. A child is not only expected to honor

---

13. CCC 2215.

and obey his or her parents but also all the reasonable directions of grandparents, aunts and uncles, caretakers, teachers, civil authority and other adults to whom they have been entrusted, except in cases where the authority is acting immorally.[14]

Unitive and Procreative Nature of Marriage

The Fourth Commandment demonstrates the importance of the family in God's plan for human happiness, but the Sixth and Ninth Commandments, both of which guarantee that sexual relations are exclusive to marriage, are also at the service of preserving the family. Preserving the union of the spouses is the first, most fundamental protection of not only the dignity of the spouses but also the family unit. Before looking at some sins that commonly threaten the good of family life, it will be helpful to review the two purposes of marriage introduced in the previous chapter: unitive and procreative.

For any sexual expression between spouses to be morally good, it must fully respect both the unitive and procreative aspects of sexual union. This is the fundamental truth that governs every moral question involving marriage and sexuality. To act in a manner that denies or denigrates either of these two purposes degrades the dignity and the meaning of the marital act itself. The Church uses the word *unitive* to describe the marital act as an act of mutual, total self-giving love, and she uses the word *procreative* to describe the openness to the possibility of conception from the marital act.

The unitive purpose of marriage was the focus of the previous chapter. Marriage is first a good since each spouse "cannot fully find himself except through a sincere gift of himself."[15] This loving, lifelong gift is expressed physically in the marital act, which is a renewal of the covenant of marriage that created this permanent, exclusive, one-flesh union. For marital relations to maintain their true meaning, a habitual spirit of loving sacrifice must be continually present in the relationship between a husband and a wife. If the spouses lack kindness, affection, and a spirit of total self-giving and sacrificial service for each other, then their shared intimacy begins to lose its meaning. If a truly sacrificial love is present, then the marital

14. Cf. CCC 2217.
15. GS, no. 24.

act is an expression of charity and a means of growing in holiness and true joy.

Procreation refers to the conception of a new human person, who is the direct consequence of marital relations. In the natural order the reproductive organs found in life forms are for the purpose of reproducing the species. For human beings—endowed with an intellect, will, and self-awareness—this component of procreation takes on a spiritual meaning as well. Animals that reproduce sexually act only according to instinct, while a human man and a human woman give expression to their love and willingly cooperate with God in his creation of a new, uniquely willed person. At the moment of conception, God infuses a soul, creating a new human being; God and the spouses are, as it were, partners in bringing every new human being into the world. Conjugal love and the marital act are a participation in a great mystery that results directly in the creation of new life. The united couple chooses to cooperate with God in the creation of a human person who is made in the image and likeness of both the parents and of God. Thus, the union of a husband and a wife becomes a sacred act blessed by God.

Modern society often depicts children as a burden to be avoided or minimized. The Church teaches, "Children are really the supreme gift of marriage and contribute very substantially to the welfare of their parents."[16] The unitive purpose cannot be relegated to secondary importance as if the spouses were nothing more than "breeding machines." Ignoring the procreative purpose of marriage objectifies one or both of the spouses:

> The true practice of conjugal love, and the whole meaning of the family life which results from it, have this aim: that the couple be ready with stout hearts to cooperate with the love of the Creator and the Savior. Who through them will enlarge and enrich His own family day by day.[17]

The teaching of the Church with regard to human sexuality and marriage seeks to protect not only individual purity and the strength of the marriage but also the holiness of the family and, by extension, all human societies.

---

16. GS, no.50.
17. Ibid.

LIFELONG

One grave threat to healthy families is a lack of fidelity in marriage. Any act that directly violates the marriage covenant—either failing in fidelity to the permanent, exclusive nature of marital love or misuse of one or both purposes of the marital act—is gravely evil. Adultery, explicitly prohibited by the Sixth Commandment, is never justifiable under any circumstances. Adultery not only violates the true meaning of the conjugal act, but it also radically betrays the marital commitment and covenant made before God. Such a person commits a grave injustice against his or her spouse who, in justice, deserves unfailing fidelity. Adultery is gravely evil in part because infidelity causes severe emotional and psychological damage to the offended party, from whose emotional wounds is it exceedingly difficult to fully recover. Adultery not only harms the union of the spouses but also leaves deep and permanent emotional scars on the children, especially during their sensitive formative years when a significant part of their human development depends on their security and knowledge of their parents' loving union.

Many acts of adultery lead to divorce, the ultimate break in the covenant of matrimony, but other divorces are precipitated by far less disruptive reasons. Some people enter marriages with simply unrealistic expectations and fail to uphold their commitments out of boredom when the "honeymoon is over." But the decision to separate or divorce is incompatible with marriage as a lifelong commitment to faithful and self-sacrificing love.

Even prior to acts against the marriage covenant, just accepting the possibility of divorce as an option diminishes conjugal love, possibly making it disappear. A spouse who holds on to the possibility of divorce is not making a true gift of self and is, in a sense, refusing to complete the bond of unity by withholding part of him- or herself. Marriage was established by God with the creation of the first man and woman and raised to the level of a Sacrament by Jesus Christ. These conditions for marriage are not a whimsical divine caprice; rather, they correspond to the social nature of the human person. The very idea that the marriage covenant is not permanent can prevent any couple from enjoying the proper bond of unity.

There are exceptional situations in which couples should separate. Separation is warranted if a spouse is dangerously abusive, physically violent, or causes severe psychological problems within the family. In some cases separation can serve as an impetus to help a spouse come to his or her senses, especially when substance abuse or marital infidelity is involved. Separation, though in some cases necessary for the protection or pursuit of a greater good, should serve only as a last resort. This does not mean the spouses can marry again: Separation cannot break the marriage covenant. The couple remain married while living apart and are expected to practice chastity, which includes physical fidelity to one another. As God reveals often in his covenant with his chosen people, infidelity on the part of one spouse is not license for the other to be unfaithful, and it is Christ's nature to be faithful to us: "If we are faithless, he remains faithful—for he cannot deny himself."[18] The faithfulness of the Bridegroom to his Bride, the Church, is the model for spousal fidelity.

If a spouse remarries after a separation, this new situation is adulterous. (This describes an "attempt" to marry since the spouse is still really married in the eyes of the Church and Our Lord.) Such a person would not normally be in a condition to receive the Sacraments until the situation is remedied. The pastors of the Church still reach out to divorced Catholics and invite them to pray, attend Mass, contribute to the support of the Church, listen to the Word of God, and bring their children up in the Catholic faith. It is important to give everyone hope that his or her situation can be resolved. The Church ardently desires that couples who are divorced and remarried find their path back to full communion with the Church and with God.

The Church does grant some couples an *annulment*: a declaration that the marriage bond never happened in the first place. This does not mean blessings did not result from the supposed marriage: the gift of children, loving moments, comforts in hardship, and many others. It is a declaration that something was lacking to prohibit the marital union, for example, if one or both of the couple could not give full consent or did not understand that marriage is a lifelong commitment. The Church alone has the divine authority to determine whether or not a marriage was valid. An annulment is not the same as a divorce at all! A divorce is a human attempt to rupture a true marriage bond.

18. 2 Tm 2:13.

One of the requirements for marriage is a commitment to lifelong fidelity with one spouse, which presupposes the proper use of reason to make a permanent commitment of fidelity. There would likewise be grounds for nullity if one person was deceived regarding a serious issue that, had it been known, would have dissuaded him or her from the marriage; for example, if one spouse concealed the intent to never have children, true consent would be lacking. If there was deception regarding the established conditions, the Church would most likely declare that marriage null. Obtaining an annulment is certainly not a "Catholic version of divorce" but rather a judicial determination of whether the necessary conditions for validity were present at the time of the marriage. Remember the consent of the spouses is both the matter and the form of the Sacrament of Matrimony, so lack of knowledge or consent invalidates the union.

It may seem at first that divorce is harmful only to the unitive purpose of marriage, but a key aspect to the near-universal institution of marriage is its close connection to bringing children into the world. Not only is the purpose of marriage the propagation of new life but providing an environment for rearing children. The best, most salutary setting for education and formation of children essentially involves the active presence of both a mother and a father in a stable, loving relationship. Nothing can give a greater endorsement to human dignity than the loving friendship union of a mother and a father both for each other and for their children.

In addition to uniting the spouses in a true communion of love, Our Lord's teachings on the permanence of marriage have tremendous importance for the emotional, psychological, and spiritual health of children. Intimately linked to marital fidelity is one of the essential purposes of marriage: the formation and education of children. Both boys and girls need guidance and love from both a father and a mother. The physical, moral, and psychological well-being of children rests on the clearly faithful love between a husband and a wife. The unity of a mother and a father give security and a sense of self-worth to their children. The faithful love, commitment, and dedication of the spouses to each other presents to the children a clear reflection of the love of God for each person. A child's point of reference regarding God's love for him or her is the parents' love for each other and their children.

In many cases children who have witnessed instability between their mother and father experience anxiety and fear because they never received the focused love and attention so necessary for healthy emotional development and moral maturity. It is not uncommon for children to engage in self-destructive behaviors like drug abuse and sexual promiscuity if they lacked the loving support and attention of both a mother and a father. A dysfunctional upbringing in no way consigns a child to character flaws or psychological fragility; rather, it makes character formation and emotional stability more of a struggle. Divorce can leave terrible emotional and psychological scars that render the spouses and their children emotionally, psychologically, and morally worse off. A person who initiates a divorce after having committed to an enduring, exclusive marriage betrays him- or herself, the spouse, the children, and society as well.

Children need an ongoing sense of security and stability manifested by the parents' love and fidelity toward each other. The greatest contribution for the moral, spiritual, and even physical integrity of society overall comes from intact marriages. The health of every society is always rooted in morally and spiritually healthy families. When the institution of marriage is protected and promoted, all societies benefit.

The importance of intact marriages and the struggle to maintain them should inspire people preparing for marriage to do everything they can to ensure success. They should seek self-mastery through education in chastity and embrace all the graces Christ has to offer in the Sacraments, especially Matrimony.

LIFE-GIVING

Another threat to the stability of family life is the availability and prevalence of artificial birth control. Many people—Catholic and non-Catholic alike—find this claim surprising. Artificial birth control has become such an accepted part of modern life that until a person is presented with the contrary opinion, he or she might find it ridiculous that the Church even has teachings about this. The Church does not forbid the use of artificial birth control because she is reactionary or "behind the times." As with the other sins against marriage, artificial birth control is harmful because it diminishes or even destroys the plan for marriage to be a total, mutual gift of self. It inserts a lie into the "language of the body."

God, who is Love,[19] created men and women out of love. "Love," which is God, signifies a self-giving love or quest to bestow good on someone else. By revealing the Blessed Trinity, Jesus reveals that men and women are images of God precisely because they have the capacity for self-giving love. Thus, the general vocation for men and women is a calling to a self-giving love expressed in family life, work, and friendship. The divinely instituted setting for this self-giving love is marriage, whereby a man and a woman give themselves totally to each other.

This relationship between a wife and a husband is an image of God not only as *one* God but also as a *Trinity* of divine Persons. God the Father and God the Son are totally united to each other by a personified bond of love called the Holy Spirit. Analogously, a husband and a wife give their whole selves to each other, and their love brings about a new person, the fruit of their total self-giving love. Every child enhances the bond of marriage since they are not only husband and wife but also mother and father of their daughters and sons.

Given the two properties of Matrimony — the good of the spouses and the good of the children — a natural feature of marriage is openness to having children and educating them. If the couple is blessed with progeny, they are a great gift to the marriage. As Pope Francis said:

> You have come with the most beautiful fruit of your love. Motherhood and fatherhood are a gift of God.... Each of your children is a unique creature that will never be duplicated in the history of humanity.... We are astounded by how great a miracle a child is! A child changes your life![20]

A couple that intend, however, to permanently thwart conception to avoid having children contradict the nature and purpose of marriage. But even the occasional use of artificial birth control threatens both the unitive and procreative nature of marriage.

The promise, "I take you to be my wife / husband,"[21] and the consummation of the covenant of the marriage is a total commitment and openness to a future together. Each time the couple comes together in the marital act, their "language of the body" repeats that

19. 1 Jn 4:8, 16.

20. NNFA.

21. OCM, The Celebration of Matrimony: The Consent, no. 62.

same promise. For this physical expression to be truthful, it must contain the same commitment and openness; otherwise, the parties, instead of expressing their complete devotion and dedication to each other through sexual union, turn each other into objects of use. They say, instead, "I give you everything except...." They desire pleasure from each other, but they do not entrust their whole selves to each other. They want some of the pleasure while avoiding the responsibility that might result from the marital act, so sexual expressions become selfish rather than self-giving.

Such selfishness will over time erode the closeness of the couple. The harm to the unity of the spouses occurs even if artificial birth control is only used occasionally. Analogous to spoken language, it is not much comfort if a spouse is prone to "only sometimes" telling lies. Every lie can destroy trust, even one told in the "language of the body." Consciously or not, the use of artificial birth control weakens and can ultimately destroy the bond of unity between the spouses.

The marital act is designed to communicate total self-giving, of which openness to procreation is an integral part. The intentional withholding of fertility and the refusal to accept a spouse in his or her totality through the use of artificial birth control places limitations on this gift of self and degrades the image of God. St. John Paul II made it abundantly clear that artificial birth control "contradicts the full truth of the sexual act as the proper expression of conjugal love."[22] The significance of total self-giving inherent in the marital act is lost by the use of artificial birth control.

Some of the methods employed by artificial birth control to prevent new life can also act as *abortifacients*: drugs or devices that can hinder fertilization, prevent a fertilized egg from attaching itself to the lining of the womb, or expel a fertilized egg that has already attached itself to the lining. These include the intrauterine device (IUD), birth control pill, and the morning-after pill.

Direct sterilization is a permanent form of artificial birth control that involves a surgical procedure to render future conception biologically impossible. Surgical modifications of either the male or female generative organs violates the sacredness of the human body and is a sin against the openness to life in marriage; thus, it is gravely evil. The *Catechism* teaches: "Legitimate intentions on the

22. St. John Paul II, Encyclical Letter on the Value and Inviolability of Human Life *Evangelium Vitæ* (March 25, 1995), no. 13.

part of the spouses do not justify recourse to morally unacceptable means (for example, direct sterilization or contraception)."[23] As noted earlier, the marital act was created by God and is intended to express a complete gift of self, which presupposes the integrity of the unitive and procreative aspects.

Many people believe a misrepresentation or even a ridiculous caricature of the Church's teachings: They wrongly think the Church expects every couple to leave their family size to chance or to have as many children as physically possible. While, yes, the Church unequivocally maintains large families are a blessing from God,[24] she also knows there are many legitimate reasons to limit family size or to space children. God has given married couples knowledge of the wife's fertility cycle so that they can cooperate with God in having children, spacing births, or deciding not to have more children by abstaining from the marital act when a pregnancy could occur. This body of this scientific knowledge is called Natural Family Planning (NFP), which is compatible with the openness to life in the nature of marriage. The spirit behind being open to life is that the marital act communicates the total gift of self, including openness to life.

Refraining from the marital act during those days when conception would most likely occur neither alters the act of total self-giving nor hinders the union between spouses. On the contrary, when used with the proper intentions, the practice of temporary abstinence in marriage can be a gift of self-sacrifice and can increase the communication and love shared between a husband and a wife. In the case of marital relations when artificial birth control is used, the gift of fertility is intentionally withheld. When refraining from the marital act, each spouse acknowledges that if a child is not intended, both the husband and the wife make a sacrifice for the other rather than turn each other into objects to be used. This can enhance their mutual respect and inspire awe at the workings of each other's body, strengthening their marriage bond rather than weakening it.

Considerations of responsible parenthood include physical, economic, psychological, and social conditions. This is exercised either by the generous decision to raise a large family or by the decision, made with respect to the moral law, to avoid a new birth for the time being or even for the foreseeable future. NFP, however, is far from

23. CCC 2399.
24. Cf. NNFA.

"Catholic birth control." Refusing to accept the procreative purpose of marriage can still harm the couple in other ways, even if they are using a licit method to avoid having children. Marriage is by its nature productive of new life in partnership with God to create a family. If a married couple reject this responsibility completely or limit their number of children without good reason, then they refuse their gift, and their union can suffer. Commonly cited poor reasons not to have children are selfish, materialistic, or express a lack of faith and trust in God. Even if avoiding a new birth begins as a shared goal, persisting with the wrong intentions can weaken the spouses' ability to be generous with each other and harm the marriage.

God has a plan for every couple, which for those in the married state, includes openness to children. He does not force his will on anybody, but he wants the couple to freely and generously cooperate with his plan. Sometimes this means joyfully accepting the gift of new life even when it was not part of their plans. Children are always a source of joy when they are born out of the parents' love for each other. The Church, following the testimony of Sacred Scripture,[25] has traditionally viewed large families as a sign of God's blessing and the generosity of the parents.

For other couples, faith in God's plan for them might mean that their desire for children is unfulfilled due to biological conditions that make conception impossible. Infertility, like unexpected pregnancy, is a chance to grow in faith, trusting that God has a plan. If God does not bless a couple with biological children, it is anything but a failure; it indicates that God wants something more from this couple, and there are many options. One beautiful option is adopting children. This kind of generosity is a needed service to children who are not blessed with a home or a loving mother and father. An option for a couple that does not feel called to adopt is devoting time in a host of other ways: spending more time in prayer without the normal and expected distractions of family life, helping relatives who are overwhelmed with their families, and helping the sick, the elderly, the incarcerated, those who need education, and others on the margins of society.

Couples who are working with medical professionals to help them conceive must avoid certain practices that are contrary to the

25. Cf. Ps 127:3–5.

purposes of marriage. Some of these, such as *in vitro* fertilization, were presented in Chapter 10 as evils against the dignity of life. Other common practices such as artificial insemination and surrogate pregnancy also harm the unitive property of marriage as well as the dignity of the marriage bed by disconnecting new life from marital union. The dignity of human life requires that the conception of new life be the fruit of the physical expression of marital love and not a biological procedure performed in a laboratory.

The separation of procreation from the marital act poses other moral difficulties. The usual means for obtaining sperm for some procedures is masturbation, which is a misuse of human sexuality and a sin against chastity. Additionally, the practice of utilizing nonspousal sperm, egg donors, or surrogate mothers is morally objectionable since procreation involves someone who is not one of the spouses. This makes procreation the fruit of, in a certain sense, biological adultery.

Laboratory means of procreation, even when employed for the good and natural desire for children, does not show proper respect for the child, either. A child is not a unit of property that is owed to the couple but what the *Catechism* calls "the 'supreme gift of marriage.'" The *Catechism* continues, there is no...

> alleged "right to a child."... Only the child possesses genuine rights: the right "to be the fruit of the specific act of the conjugal love of his parents," and "the right to be respected as a person from the moment of his conception."[26]

None of this should be misunderstood to say a new child is never wanted. Every child—whether resulting from a loving marital union, a laboratory setting, or any other environment—is a gift uniquely willed by God, sharing having the same human dignity as all other people. In truth, it is this human dignity the Church fights to protect.

In the 1960s, in the midst of the development, increasing use, and acceptance of hormonal artificial birth control, St. Paul VI wrote *Humanæ Vitæ*, rejecting its use as immoral.[27] He predicted that widespread use of artificial birth control would cause an increase in marital infidelity, moral laxity, and harm the dignity of women

26. CCC 2378; quoting Congregation for the Doctrine of the Faith, Instruction on Respect for Human Life in Its Origin and on the Dignity of Procreation *Donum Vitæ* (February 22, 1987), part II, no. 8.

27. St. Paul VI, Encyclical Letter on the Regulation of Birth *Humanæ Vitæ* (July 25, 1968).

in particular. Over the following decades, attacks on the proper use of human sexuality and the dignity of human life reached alarming levels. Laws were passed around the world permitting the destruction of unborn life, and the divorce rate—as well as incidents of out-of-wedlock pregnancies, sexual promiscuity, and sexually transmitted infections—have skyrocketed. Indeed, many modern immoral practices—genetic engineering, *in vitro* fertilization, assisted suicide, euthanasia, embryonic stem-cell research, cloning, and others—are at least indirectly related to the ubiquity of artificial birth control. Artificial birth control weakens the respect between spouses in marriage, encouraging a "consumerist" view of both sexual activity and children. Artificial birth control also increases the abortion rate: When children are viewed as an unnecessary and unwanted "side effect" of sexual relations, then a failure of artificial birth control is all too often corrected by abortion. This "contraceptive mentality" has done much to devalue the sanctity of human life.

On the other hand, there is a large and growing body of evidence that couples who use NFP have stronger, healthier, lasting marriages. Many couples who stop using artificial birth control report an increase in their intimacy and enjoy their marriage more. Large families almost always sacrifice some material luxuries, but they gain much more when they are the haven of charity and friendship a family is meant to be.

Good Marriages

In view of the last two chapters, marriage and family are two of the premier concerns for the modern Church since both are intimately involved with the dignity of the human person (both the spouses and the children). Protecting the sanctity of marriage and the gift of new life requires an attitude toward human sexuality that runs counter to worldly ideas and depictions. Human sexuality is not merely an instinct as it is for animals, a physical itch to be scratched. Human sexuality involves psychological aspects and is subject to the intellect and will; therefore, a person can control and direct it. The only true forum for virtuous sexual expression is when the "language of the body" communicates total self-giving in marriage. The marital act is a personal, loving "meeting" between a husband and a wife, reaffirming their total dedication to each other.

During her 2000-year history, the Church has dealt with numerous false attitudes toward human sexuality. These can be generally separated into two categories: a *puritanical* approach and a trivialized, or *self-centered*, approach that denies the sacredness and dignity of human sexuality.

The puritanical approach considers all human sexual passions and attractions to be evil, borne of base inclinations. This approach holds any expression of human sexuality distasteful and an occasion of sin. At best, it views the marital act as necessary for procreation but inherently sinful. Some taking this approach have gone so far as to denounce marriage itself as evil. While large groups that hold these views mostly belong to a bygone age, strains of this approach can be found in the modern world.

The self-centered approach, in radical opposition to the puritanical point of view, holds human sexuality is designed primarily for self-gratification. This approach ignores all sense of mystery and respect from sexual expressions, giving way to self-indulgence. Human sexuality is discussed irreverently, openly, and casually, and sexual expressions themselves are sought and carried out just as irreverently, openly, and casually, failing to respect their sacredness. Many taking this approach have little or no shame and guilt in living such a lifestyle, discarding and replacing sexual partners often and easily. Rather than manifesting an act of self-giving, sexual expressions become acts of selfishness. A growing number of people hold these views in the modern world.

The Catholic understanding of human sexuality stands in opposition to both of these extremes. The Church teaches that all of God's creation reflects his infinite love and is, therefore, inherently good. Human sexuality is natural, and the love shown by sexual expressions within marriage is a special expression of God's goodness and thus is inherently sacred. The marital act is made holy when it reflects God's self-giving love that is open to life, a physical expression of profound personal love between a husband and a wife.

Begetting and raising children are not the only purposes of marriage; the other purpose of marriage is the joy and fulfillment of the spouses through their mutual self-giving. If spouses are truly dedicated to each other's good, both a husband and a wife will see their marriage as a wonderful blessing and gift. This mutual self-giving makes the other an ongoing priority. It is not uncommon for couples who have been married for decades to declare how much they are in love with each other. In one instance, a gentleman married for many years boasted about how much he loved his wife and that in his eyes she rivaled the beauty of a twenty year old. A long, happy marriage is not the product of luck or of finding the "perfect person"; both parties must work very hard to sustain and improve their marriages. If a couple commits their marriage to God's plan and invites Christ into their marriage, particularly through the Sacrament of Matrimony, then every struggle the couple endures, with the help of God's grace, strengthens their bond, increases their love, and offers a more secure and healthy environment for their children. This little society of charity and joy ripples out goodness for larger societies as well.

As an outgrowth of the family, the success of all societies is based on the success of the family. Just as every organ of the body is crucial to the functioning of the whole body, so does the health of individual families contribute to the functioning of the "body" of society. It is in everybody's self-interest for all members of society to make a concerted effort to promote the well-being of the family. In this way the well-being of society will be promoted.

In many modern cultures there is a significant absence of Christ, which results in much disillusionment, sadness, and despair. It is the hope of the Church that the family—a mother, a father, and their children—makes incarnate in a very attractive and convincing way the treasure of the Gospel message. Due to the close natural ties between parents and their children, every household should be an oasis of happiness and charity. For this vision to become a reality, every family member must have a strong relationship with Jesus Christ. The practice of family prayer, especially the Rosary, and frequent recourse to the Sacraments of Penance and the Eucharist help to maintain an atmosphere of love. Both parents and children should have as a priority and goal the imitation of Christ's affection, kindness, and spirit of service toward those closest to them.

CHAPTER 19

HOLY ORDERS

Together with Matrimony, the other Sacrament at the Service of Communion is the Sacrament of Holy Orders. The recipients of these two Sacraments are consecrated to Christ in service to the needs of his people. Every Christian who has received the Sacrament of Matrimony or Holy Orders has a vocation to "lay down his life"[1] for the good of others in imitation of Jesus Christ. Both Sacraments are essentially ordered toward making a sincere gift of self. Matrimony consecrates a man and a woman to give themselves to each other with the charity of Christ and to bear and raise children for the Kingdom of God, whereas Holy Orders consecrates a man to preach and dispense grace in the name of Jesus Christ in service to the members of the Church.

THE OLD TESTAMENT PRIESTHOOD PREFIGURES THE PRIESTHOOD OF CHRIST

Some form of priestly activity has comprised the social fabric of every human person and society throughout the ages. Religious ceremonies have been a common feature of human existence. Though many rites have involved worship of idols and the practice of superstition, they all share the common theme: sacrifices offered on behalf of the people by a priestly representative. In the many pagan rituals of diverse peoples, the priest represented the people before a deity or deities. Priests, on behalf of the people, acted to placate their false gods with sacrifices to avoid droughts, ensure good harvests, cure illnesses, and other common concerns.

The presence of some kind of priests in every society reveals a natural religious impulse in human nature; moreover, in a remote way, this mediation between the people and their deities ultimately points to Christ's Eternal High Priesthood. Christ on his Cross offered the definitive priestly act when—as priest, sacrificial victim, and altar—he reconciled all of humanity to God the Father.

1. Jn 15:13.

The priesthood of Christ, like all the other elements of the New Covenant, was prefigured in the Old Testament. The Israelite people were collectively a kingdom of priests, a chosen people set apart to worship the one true God with prayer and sacrifices. As God revealed to his people through Moses, "You shall be my own possession among all peoples; for all the earth is mine, and you shall be to me a kingdom of priests and a holy nation."[2] Despite their common priesthood among the Twelve Tribes of Israel, God designated the Tribe of Levi to function as his priests.

The Old Testament priests taught the Word of God, exhorted the people to be faithful to God's Law, and offered sacrifices to God. Many rituals were prescribed for the Old Testament priests, from the garments they wore to the ceremonies that consecrated them and anointed them to serve as priests. Though holy and called by God, this priesthood could not sanctify or save the Israelite people. They had to repeat endless sacrifices that, though pleasing to God, were not redemptive and therefore insufficient. The Old Testament priests fulfilled the Old Law but can also be seen as a prefigurement of the definitive priesthood of Jesus Christ and his perfect, redemptive, sufficient Sacrifice, which saved not only the Israelite people but also all peoples.

Even before the institution of the Tribe of Levi as priests, the priesthood of Christ is first prefigured in the Book of Genesis by the appearance of Melchizedek. After Abraham had experienced a victory over his foes, "Melchizedek king of Salem" and "priest of God Most High" appeared and bestowed on Abraham his blessing along with gifts of "bread and wine."[3] This mysterious person has no known genealogy and functioned as a priest before the time of Israel. There are no groups of priests associated with Melchizedek; he is unique and the only priest of his kind that appears in the Old Testament.

In this way, Melchizedek accurately symbolizes the Eternal High Priesthood of Jesus Christ.[4] Like Melchizedek, Jesus has mysterious origins (no biological human father) and celebrated a Sacrifice—the Eucharistic Sacrifice at his Last Supper using bread and wine. Since Jesus is not descended from the Tribe of Levi, his priesthood has

2. Ex 19:5–6.

3. Gn 14:18–20.

4. Cf. Heb 5:6, 10; 6:20; 7:1, 10–11, 15, 17.

no connection with that Old Testament priestly tribe and totally transcends it.

Institution of the Priesthood

The New Covenant has one Eternal High Priest, Jesus Christ, who offered himself for the salvation of the whole world. Unlike the multiple sacrifices of the Old Covenant, in the New Covenant there is one redemptive Sacrifice whose effects and merits apply to everybody. Through the celebration of the Sacraments, the redemptive Sacrifice of Christ is made present every time sacramental graces are imparted. The effects of his redemption are specially bestowed in the Holy Sacrifice of the Eucharist and in the reception of Holy Communion. As presented in Chapter 14, the Mass does not *repeat* the one Sacrifice of Christ like the Old Testament sacrifices had to be repeated; instead, the Mass *re-presents* the one Sacrifice of Jesus Christ on his Cross. In a similar way the one priesthood of Christ is exercised through his ministers who possess the power to *re-present* his Sacrifice in the celebration of the Sacraments, especially in the Eucharist. It is Jesus Christ who is the priest: the true minister acting through his ordained ministers. Our Lord is truly present, sacramentally, in his priests.

The ministry of Jesus Christ through his priests began when he made present his own Eternal High Priesthood through his Apostles and their successors, the bishops. The Apostles were not simply close collaborators with Christ—not mere helpers—they were his actual representatives on earth who exercised Christ's triple mission of priest, prophet, and king. They were the template of exercising Christ's new priesthood, which will remain until the end of time. The Eternal High Priesthood of Christ, entrusted to his Apostles, was in turn communicated to succeeding generations of bishops. Through the Apostles Christ ensured that the sanctifying power of his priesthood endured in his Church.

The power to exercise Christ's priesthood was given to the Apostles in various ways at different moments. There are two instances, however, that stand out most clearly: at the Last Supper and after Christ's Resurrection. The first clear transmission of Christ's priestly power occurred when Jesus instituted the Eucharist at the Last Supper. Christ's words—"This is my body," and, "This cup … is the new covenant in my blood"[5]—instituted the Sacrament of the Eucharist, but when he added, "Do this in remembrance of me,"[6] he gave his Apostles a sacred charge by giving them a share in his priesthood. Our Lord was not telling the Apostles to call to mind a special memory but rather that they should repeat just what he did. Since the Eucharist will remain until the end of the world, they appointed successors to do the same.

Amid Jesus' priestly prayer at the conclusion of this unforgettable evening, he consecrated the Apostles into his Eternal High Priesthood a second time—this time to the office of teaching and preaching the Gospel. Addressing his Father, Jesus prayed:

> Sanctify them in the truth; thy word is truth. As thou didst send me into the world, so I have sent them into the world. And for their sake I consecrate myself, that they also may be consecrated in truth.[7]

Jesus prayed for their capacity to preach and interpret the Gospel, which is the perfection of truth. He consecrated his Apostles to the mission of bringing the whole world to the truth of the Gospel message. This endeavor, too, will last until the end of time, so the Apostles and their successors, the bishops, have the task of preserving the Deposit of Faith and applying it to every culture and time.

After his Resurrection Jesus gave his Apostles explicit authority and power to forgive sins as if they were Christ himself: "Receive the Holy Spirit. If you forgive the sins of any, they are forgiven; if you retain the sins of any, they are retained."[8] Christ gave them both the power to forgive sins and the authority and obligation to determine whether an individual has manifested the appropriate repentance for forgiveness. If a penitent shows some purpose of amendment, every bishop or priest will give absolution.

In these actions Christ instituted the New Testament priesthood that carries on his redemptive work in the Church. He imparted to his Apostles his power to offer the Eucharist, forgive sins, and preach the Gospel. In this priesthood the Church is visibly reminded of the spiritual reality that it is Christ himself who is the source of truth and grace.

5. Lk 22:19–20.
6. Lk 22:19.
7. Jn 17:17–19.
8. Jn 20:22–23.

Two Ways of Participation in the Priesthood of Christ

The priesthood conferred on the Apostles by Christ is continuing in his Church until the end of time. Already in the New Testament, in the Acts of the Apostles, the Sacred Authors record that the Apostles of the Church conferred the authority Christ gave them to other helpers to continue their ministry. But the presence of an ordained priesthood in the Church should not cause anyone to think of lay Catholics as second-class citizens or that bishops, for all the honor due to them for their sacrifice and ministry, are some kind of royalty. Like the Israelite people in the Old Testament, the people of the new Israel, the Church, "are a chosen race, a royal priesthood, a holy nation, God's own people."[9] The "one mediator between God and men, the man Christ Jesus,"[10] has "made us a kingdom, priests to his God and Father."[11] Every Christian is called through Baptism to share in Christ's triple office of priest, prophet, and king; these three missions of the lay faithful were presented in Chapter 12 on the Sacrament of Baptism. By virtue of Baptism every Christian exercises the common priesthood and becomes a conduit of grace by uniting his or her sacrifices to Jesus' redemptive Sacrifice. As the *Catechism* teaches, "The common priesthood of all the faithful participate, 'each in its own proper way, in the one priesthood of Christ.'"[12]

The common priesthood of the faithful, linked to Baptism and Confirmation, is distinct from the ministerial priesthood, which is given in Holy Orders.[13] This structure was prefigured in the Old Testament by the Israelites' common priesthood being manifested in a particular way by the Tribe of Levi. The ministerial priesthood, while essentially distinct from the common priesthood, is also intimately connected to it. It could be said that the common priesthood and ministerial priesthood complement each other. The common priesthood enables every Christian to benefit from the graces merited by Christ's redemption and therefore share in the life of Christ; on the other hand, the ministerial priesthood possesses a sacred power to act in the place and name of Jesus Christ in serving the spiritual

9. 1 Pt 2:9; cf. Ex 19:5–6.
10. 1 Tm 2:5
11. Rev 1:6.
12. CCC 1547; quoting LG, no. 10 § 2.
13. Cf. ibid.

needs of all the baptized. For this reason there is a separate Sacrament for this singular participation in the priesthood of Christ.

Effective evangelization requires the functioning of both shares in Christ's priesthood. The everyday work of God in the world is through the family and the normal activities of lay Christians. It would make no sense to have the ministerial priesthood if there were no faithful to serve; likewise, without the ministerial priesthood, the lay faithful would be greatly hindered in the pursuit of holiness and the work of evangelization. The purpose of the ministerial priesthood is to serve the common priesthood.

For the proper exercise of their common priesthood, both those in religious life and lay Catholics depend on ordained ministers for instruction in the Word of God and the administration of the Sacraments. Through the ministerial priesthood the Church is energized and builds up the holiness of all her members. The call of the baptized to bring Christ into the heart of the modern world can only be fulfilled if they receive the Sacraments and hear the Gospel preached by ordained ministers. Bishops, priests, and deacons have the mission to inspire, teach, and sanctify lay Christians through preaching and celebrating the Sacraments.

One example of the connection between the common priesthood and the ministerial priesthood is shown in people who have returned to the Sacrament of Penance and Reconciliation and started to attend Mass frequently. A return to the Sacraments is a sign of friendship with Christ and greater love for others. By good example and habitual charity, these people model the Christian life to their families and friends. As a result of the priestly service of Penance and the Eucharist, these lay Catholics more and more live up to Jesus' vision of being "light of the world" and "salt of the earth"[14] at home, at work, at school, and at every social gathering. These people have the vocation to engage in temporal affairs and order them according to the plan of God,[15] as presented in Chapter 10. The domain of the ministerial priesthood is the altar, the confessional, and the hospital. The ordained minister is a conduit of grace for the faithful, and lay Christians are the usual vehicle of evangelization of secular structures. They chip away at consecrating the world to Christ by first loving as Christ loved and then attracting others to the sacramental

14. Mt 5:13–14.

15. LG, no. 31.

life of the Church. Both forms of priesthood form an organic whole in the work of evangelization.

Recipient of Holy Orders

The proper recipient of the Sacrament of Holy Orders is a baptized and confirmed Catholic man. Though not necessary for validity, there are many qualities that make for a good candidate. A good sign of a priestly calling is the reality of growing love for Jesus through contemplation of his Word, a deep devotion to the Holy Eucharist, and a desire to share Jesus with others. A candidate should also be excited about serving the sacramental needs of the people and being a witness of the heart of Christ. It is important that a candidate have a deep love for Jesus and the Sacraments as well as a robust spiritual life. The driving incentive embracing the priesthood should be union with and imitation of Christ, which is crucial to spreading the Gospel to many others. A candidate's main aspiration should be to serve the Church by replicating the heart and mercy of Christ before his people. This includes effectively nourishing the faithful with the Word of God and the Sacraments. Every diocese has a screening process and a long period of discernment before a man receives Holy Orders. In the end, however, the proper candidate is one who has been called by Christ to that vocation and whose calling has been confirmed by his bishop. The bishop will certainly scrutinize any man seeking ordination, but it is not his human qualities that make him a candidate; it is his calling from God.

The reasons the Church has maintained that only men can be validly ordained do not even remotely imply any superiority of men over women. The Church steadfastly teaches, as expressed in the *Catechism*, "Man and woman have been *created*, which is to say, *willed* by God... in perfect equality as human persons."[16] The most fundamental reason for the all-male priesthood is that Jesus only called men for this role. Despite his great admiration for women and their prominent roles in his earthly ministry—starting with his own Mother, the Blessed Virgin Mary—Jesus did not include women among the Twelve. Though the Apostles governed the Church in Jesus' absence and structured the Sacraments, and though women played key roles in spreading Christ's Church with the Apostles, they never invited women to the ministerial priesthood. In this regard the

16. CCC 369.

Church follow Christ's and the Apostles' example, not changing any of the essentials that pertain to doctrine and Sacraments.

Some people argue that Jesus only chose men because he was acting according to the biases of first-century Judaism. "Times change," goes this objection, and it is time to overcome this supposed prejudice in the Church. While human traditions do change over time, the Church is not at liberty to alter anything that Our Lord himself established; to depart from Christ is to depart from the truth of the Gospel. More importantly, the accusation is false. The Gospels reveal Jesus consistently breaking the norms and prejudices of his day, particularly with regard to his treatment of women. He scandalized his own people [17] by healing women, praising their virtue, speaking with them, maintaining close friendships with them, sharing theological discussions with them, and even revealing to them his identity as the Messiah. Many of Christ's actions were designed to recognize the dignity of women in society such as when he criticized the unjust, one-sided practice of divorce in the Mosaic Law,[18] defended the woman caught in adultery,[19] and had a deep theological discussion with a Samaritan woman at the well.[20] As God Jesus behaved in a completely sovereign fashion. Looking at his entire life and teachings, no one could accuse Jesus of doing things just to please people. It is safe to conclude that his choice to choose only men for his Apostles was intentional.

The Church obediently accepts Our Lord's decision to only ordain men, but she has still long reflected on the reasons why. These reasons have nothing to do with a woman's imagined lack of capacity to "do the job." One of the reasons most central to the role of the priesthood itself is the fact that, being a Sacrament, Holy Orders is a visible sign of a sacred reality. Acting *in persona Christi*, the bishop, priest, or deacon is a sign that it is Christ who is, in fact, the true minister of the Sacrament. As an immediate sacramental sign of Christ, the Eternal High Priest, the priest resembles Jesus Christ, who took on human nature as a male.[21]

As to why it is important for the visible sign of Christ to be male, some might ask, "Isn't every Christian, in some fashion, a witness

17. Cf. Jn 4:27.
18. Cf. Mt 19:8.
19. Cf. Jn 8.
20. Cf. Jn 4.
21. EG, no. 104.

to Christ?" This is true, of course, but being male is significant to the task of officially acting *in persona Christi* in a sacramental way. Recall that with all the Sacraments, the material sign aptly stands for what it does; for example, Baptism cleanses with water, and the Eucharist nourishes with bread and wine. Being male, the priest is an apt sign of the deeper symbolism of Christ, who is the Bridegroom of the Church;[22] the Church, his Bride,[23] corresponds to the fact that, in the beginning, "male and female he created them."[24] Given Christ's role as the Savior who lays down his life for every member of his Church, his relationship with his Church is that of a Bridegroom and his Bride. For that rich, beautiful symbolism to be maintained, the priesthood remains male. If it were a matter of holiness or worthiness for this exalted calling, it would be reasonable to assume the Blessed Virgin Mary would have been the first one called to the priesthood.

It is worth repeating this in no way diminishes the role of women in Christianity, the plan of Salvation, or the life of the Church. The Blessed Virgin Mary, the Mother of Jesus, is herself a model for all Christians. It was through her "yes" that salvation came to the world. Every covenant in the Old Testament was made between God and a man, but the New Covenant of salvation for the entire world was first announced by an angel to the Blessed Virgin Mary. She is the "woman"[25] first revealed in the Book of Genesis[26] when God promised a savior that would redeem humanity from the Fall. From the Gospels to the Acts of the Apostles up to the present day, the work and witness of women has been integral to the growth and function of the Church. Sts. Felicity, Perpetua, Agatha, Lucy, Agnes, Cecilia, and Anastasia are mentioned by name in the Eucharistic Prayer at Mass.[27] Sts. Catherine of Siena, Teresa of Avila, Therese of Lisieux, and Hildegard of Bingen are all Doctors of the Church whose writings had a tremendous impact on explaining and spreading of the Gospel. Countless women have helped bring the salvation of Christ to others.

22. Cf. Lk 5:35.
23. Cf. Eph 5:27.
24. Gn 1:27.
25. Jn 2:4.
26. Cf. Gn 3:15.
27. Cf. RMiss, The Order of Mass: Eucharistic Prayer I, no. 96.

The question of male or female priests is not about "rights" because nobody has a right to a calling from God. Nor is it a question of a career, like deciding to pursue the priesthood like a job. It involves a call from God just as Jesus first called the Twelve. There is nothing more incompatible with a vocation to Holy Orders than a desire to climb the Church's career ladder. No one should pursue this calling to make a mark on the Church or the world, gain notoriety, provide a social service, or any other selfish motive. Like the Twelve Apostles, it is a calling from Christ. A man does not so much choose to receive Holy Orders as he responds "yes" to the call of God to receive this Sacrament.

A life in the ordained ministry is often not an easy "yes" to give. A man is truly asked to "lay down his life for his friends"[28] when he becomes a bishop, priest, or deacon. One sign of this sacrifice is that a bishop commits himself to living celibacy for the sake of the Kingdom of God; in addition, a priest in the Western Church lives celibacy. A married man may be ordained a deacon, but once ordained, a deacon may not marry. (This rule for a deacon also holds for a priest in the Eastern Churches.) This divinely inspired discipline of celibacy, revealed in the Gospels and in St. Paul's Epistles,[29] is not required for the validity of Holy Orders or even for the exercise of Church ministry, but this discipline has been accepted and long practiced in the service of the Church.

Priestly celibacy is certainly a sacrifice—a man must sacrifice the great joy of being a husband and a father—but it should not be considered a mere deprivation to be endured. It is a positive action, not a negative one. Being without the usual encumbrances of a wife and family enables a celibate minister to give himself directly and wholeheartedly to Christ and to give his undivided attention to the People of God. While this availability for pastoral service is a practical consequence, it is not the essential reason. Celibacy reinforces the meaning of Holy Orders in a man who acts in the place of Christ the Bridegroom by loving the Church as his Bride. The celibacy of Jesus Christ is a sign that he is exclusively focused on the will and glory of his Father; it communicates the clear message that he laid down his life for all people in a total way. Just as a married man prioritizes his spouse and children, so the celibate priest signals his priority is the Bride of Christ.

28. Jn 15:13.

29. Cf. Mt 19:12; 1 Cor 7:32–34.

Although perhaps not immediately obvious, Jesus' institution of the Sacrament of Matrimony can better explain the practice of celibacy for the Kingdom of God. This is so much more than simply being unmarried! Spousal love is the premier metaphor for God's covenant with his people, and marriage is the model for every Christian vocation as each uniquely willed person, who "cannot fully find himself except through a sincere gift of himself";[30] this was presented in Chapter 10. Celibacy for the sake of the kingdom cannot be a mere "no" to marriage and marital intimacy; it must be a profound "yes" to another, deeper vocation to self-gift.

A married person grows in holiness and love of God through love for and service to a spouse and family. A direct relationship to Jesus Christ, without the intermediary of a spouse and children, can bring about a more intense love and, as the Church notes, an even greater capacity for service. Christ confers his graces on spouses to love one another as he loves; therefore, direct union with Christ through a renunciation of marriage can yield a more focused love of God and universal love for others. Matrimony is a sign of Jesus' faithful, unconditional love for every person, especially every member of his Mystical Body, the Church. Laying down one's life for the good of another[31] always has this "spousal" character. Women in religious life, who live celibacy for the sake of the kingdom, are images of the Bride of Christ. They are witnesses to the "yes" that the Bride wholeheartedly returns to her Bridegroom. Like a celibate bishop, priest, or deacon, a religious woman has a heart for everyone, seeing the image of Christ her Spouse in every person.

As was the case in the Early Church, a lay Christian can live the gift of celibacy for the Kingdom of God so that he or she can focus more directly on a closer relationship with Christ and provide a more universal, intense love for others. A person who chooses to remain single and celibate is able to use his or her freedom in greater service to a parish, diocese, community, and extended family. Like all lay Christians, he or she works for the salvation of the world from within; like all who are celibate for the kingdom, his or her life offers a greater capacity for service.

Celibacy for the sake of the kingdom also, analogously to marriage, produces new life. Those living celibacy in union with Christ

30. GS, no.24; cf. 2 Cor 5:15.

31. Cf. Jn 15:13.

are called to be spiritual fathers and mothers. If a person's life does not bear the fruit of new life, then it is not fulfilling its true purpose. As Pope Francis explained in plain language:

> You see, when I perceive negative behavior in ministers of the church or in consecrated men or women, the first thing that comes to mind is: "Here's an unfruitful bachelor" or "Here's a spinster." They are neither fathers nor mothers, in the sense that they have not been able to give spiritual life.[32]

Another comparative perspective between celibacy for the sake of the kingdom and the married state is an exclusivity of love. In Matrimony, for the sake of Christ, the spouses commit themselves totally to each other as an image of the love between Christ and his Church, so a married person renounces all others in favor of wholehearted dedication to one spouse. By the same token, a person who lives celibacy gives up the possibility of an earthly spousal love in favor of an undivided focus on Christ through prayer and a life marked by charity.

Finally, celibacy for the sake of the Kingdom of God is a great witness to the dignity of every unique human person. In many past and present-day societies, the worth of a person is wrongly based on his or her spouse and / or children; this is particularly true of a woman. To be unmarried might be seen as a humiliation, and a widow has historically fared very poorly. To be childless might be seen as a curse. Celibacy for the sake of the kingdom welcomes this condition, which gives explicit witness to the fact that every person is uniquely loved by God. Nobody needs an earthly spouse or a biological child to "earn" his or her dignity and worth; rather, every person has great dignity just by virtue of his or her very existence as a human person and a child of God. Understanding his or her own human dignity, a person who lives celibacy is freer to look selflessly on others, seeing the fullness of his or her unique dignity.

Three Degrees of Holy Orders

The *Catechism* defines this Sacrament:

> Holy Orders is the sacrament through which the mission entrusted by Christ to his apostles continues to be exercised in the Church

32. Pope Francis; quoted in Rev. Antonio Spadaro, "Interview with Pope Francis," in *L'Osservatore Romano* (September 21, 2013).

> until the end of time: thus it is the sacrament of apostolic ministry. It includes three degrees: episcopate, presbyterate, and diaconate.[33]

The "diaconate" is the order of deacons, the "presbyterate" is the order of priests, and the "episcopate" is the order of bishops.

The word "order"[34] reflects a particular social, political, or economic system, for example, when describing a person of a higher "social order." The ancient Roman process of incorporation into an order of civic officials was called "ordination." Although the use of "Holy Orders" is reserved to deacons, priests, and bishops, there are other "orders" in the Church: the order of catechumens, the order of virgins, the Franciscan Order and other monastic orders, and several others. In the Early Church, enrollment into any order involved prayers of consecration and blessing. But in the modern era, "ordination" almost exclusively refers to Holy Orders.

By the Sacrament of Holy Orders, a man is incorporated into the order of deacons, priests, or bishops. He does not enter these orders by popular vote or someone offering him the job; rather, he receives a sacred power through a sacramental celebration. This sacred power can only come directly from Jesus Christ and cannot be conferred by anyone else. Even in the Early Church, when it was the custom in some places for the people to elect their bishop, their choice had to be either confirmed by God—through ordination—or not. The election did not make a bishop; the sacramental grace of Christ did.

The third degree of Holy Orders is the episcopacy, or bishops. Every bishop receives the "fullness" of Holy Orders. His sacred power can be traced back to the Twelve Apostles and ultimately to Jesus Christ: His Apostles handed on their authority to the first bishops, who handed it on to other bishops, who handed it on to others.... This unbroken line of ordained bishops is called Apostolic Succession. The Apostles were given sacred power directly from Jesus Christ to rule, teach, and sanctify in his name and in place of him. This power was given to the Apostles through a special outpouring of the Holy Spirit and has ever since been handed on to successive bishops in an unbroken line. Upon the reception of Holy Orders, the bishop receives an indelible mark, or character, that confers full participation in Jesus Christ's Eternal High Priesthood.

33. CCC 1536.

34. Cf. Heb 5:6; 7:11; Ps 110:4.

By virtue of his ordination, a bishop is part of the College of Bishops, which forms a hierarchical communion with Christ the Eternal High Priest. One sign of this communion among bishops can be seen at his ordination, where several bishops are usually present. The Pope is the unique sign of unity and communion among the bishops, and for that reason "the Supreme Pontiff freely appoints bishops."[35]

The bishop of a diocese is Christ's vicar, or official representative, who has jurisdiction over the faithful there. Since he belongs to the College of Bishops, every bishop must also oversee the governance of the universal Church underneath the authority of the Pope. A bishop's leadership is the distinguishing feature of his direct connection to the Twelve Apostles and the possession of the fullness of Holy Orders.

The second degree of Holy Orders is the presbyterate, or priests. For the bishops to fulfill their mission in a more thorough, effective way, Our Lord has given them the order of priests. A bishop can ordain priests, who are "coworkers" with their bishop, so every priest's ministry is an extension of his bishop's pastoral ministry as shepherd of the people entrusted to him. The Sacrament of Holy Orders is necessary for the priesthood since a priest, like a bishop, acts in the name and place of Christ, albeit with a partial sharing in the Eternal High Priesthood of Christ. A priest has the power to celebrate all the Sacraments except Holy Orders. He can absolve sins in Penance, witness marriages in Matrimony, and celebrate the others through an indelible mark, or character, received in Holy Orders; the concept of an indelible mark was presented in Chapter 11.

Because of his sacramental subordination to his bishop, a priest depends on his bishop to exercise his priestly ministry. One sign of this dependence is at a priestly ordination: The newly ordained priest expresses an oath of obedience to his bishop. A diocesan priest is assigned to a parish to preach the Gospel in the name of Christ and to celebrate the Sacraments in the Person of Christ. This close reliance on his bishop for authorization to exercise his priestly ministry is a sign of every priest's participation in the Eternal High Priesthood of Christ. Priests, therefore, share directly in the mission originally entrusted to the Apostles.

35. CIC, can. 377 § 1.

The Sacrament of Holy Orders binds every priest with every other priest in communion with their bishops. One sign of this college of priests is at a priestly ordination: A fraternal embrace of peace signifies every priest's loving relationship with his bishop as a coworker, brother, and son. Priests are extensions of their bishops' service to their dioceses. Every bishop relies heavily on his priests for the simple reason that he could not even come close to fulfilling all the duties that would best spiritually serve and nourish the faithful.

The heart of the priestly mission is to celebrate the Eucharistic Sacrifice, through which the faithful unite their works and sufferings to Christ's Sacrifice on the Cross. During the Eucharistic Liturgy a priest offers the prayers and sacrifices of the faithful to God the Father through Jesus Christ. Connected to celebrating Mass is the distribution of Holy Communion, the Bread of God, to the congregation, the sick, and the homebound. A key component to the priest's role in Mass consists in preaching the Gospel in such a way that it is both instructive and applicable to everyday life.

A priest draws his spiritual energy and charity for his people from the celebration of Holy Mass and reception of the Eucharist. Saintly priests like Sts. John Paul II and John Vianney demonstrate that a priest should never be content with simply presiding over sacramental celebrations but rather seriously aspire to live what they represent and do sacramentally. Following in the footsteps of great evangelizers, every priest should give priority to saying Mass daily and spending time before the Blessed Sacrament, especially before Mass. Only through the effort of making his spiritual life an absolute priority can a priest be an effective evangelizer who attracts others to Christ.

Another essential part of the priestly vocation is that he be a vehicle for spiritual healing, especially through the Sacrament of Penance and Reconciliation. Christ, through Holy Orders, gave every priest the power to forgive sins in the name of Jesus Christ. In Confession a priest is especially obligated to manifest Jesus' compassion and mercy. Hence, it is of crucial importance that every ordained priest emulate as best he can the loving and merciful heart of the Eternal High Priest, Jesus Christ.

The first degree of Holy Orders is the diaconate, or deacons. Every deacon is ordained to a ministry of service rather than to the priesthood; in fact, "deacon" comes from the Greek *diakonia*, meaning "service." Jesus Christ, the Eternal High Priest, is a Suffering Servant for the redemption of the world.[36] In the Sacrament of Holy Orders, every deacon receives an indelible mark, or character, that marks and configures him to Christ for the ministry of service. Ordination configures every deacon to Christ the Servant. A deacon cannot celebrate Mass or give absolution in Confession, but he can facilitate the sacramental ministries of the bishops and priests.

A deacon especially serves his bishop in various parts of the Eucharistic Liturgy. A deacon proclaims the Gospel, preaches, and distributes Holy Communion. He is also an ordinary minister of Baptism and can witness marriages in Matrimony. Many deacons also prepare recipients for Baptism, Matrimony, and Confirmation. They oversee different works of charity, especially the distribution of Holy Communion to the sick, homebound, and incarcerated.

Deacons were active in the Early Church, but in the Western Church, over the passage of time, their ministry waned; however, their ministry was rejuvenated and refocused in the second half of the twentieth century. While *transitional* deacons have always existed as a step toward priestly ordination, nowadays in many regions of the Western world, *permanent* deacons are a great boon as ministers to the faithful. Every deacon bolsters his bishop's ministry of service through liturgical celebrations and works of charity.

Celebration of Holy Orders

Each of the three orders requires the celebration of Holy Orders in ascending order; nobody can skip an order. A bishop does not accumulate sacramental characters through the repetition of Holy Orders, but rather grows to a greater fullness in his configuration to Christ the Eternal High Priest.

Since the first people to receive the fullness of Christ's priesthood were his Apostles, they were also given the power to hand on Christ's priestly power to their successors. The ability to ordain is a poignant manifestation of Christ's fulfilled desire to hand on his priestly powers to his Apostles and their successors. This priestly power is expressed by a bishop during the laying on of hands.

36. 1 Pt 2:24: "He himself bore our sins in his body on the tree.... By his wounds you have been healed." Cf. Is 52:13—53:12.

Like all the Sacraments, the liturgical celebration of Holy Orders is rich in symbolism. The various rites reveal the effects and meaning of Holy Orders. The celebration begins with the presentation of the candidate, and he is examined for his worthiness. One of the most meaningful moments is when the recipient lays prostrate before the altar while the congregation sings the Litany of the Saints, asking the members of the Church in heaven to intercede for him.

In the ordination of a priest, he is given a paten and chalice used at Mass, which signify his important role of offering the Eucharistic Sacrifice to God the Father on behalf of the faithful. In the ordination of a deacon, he is given the Book of the Gospels, which signifies his mission to proclaim and preach the Gospel.

Another significant part of the ordination of a priest is an anointing of the palms of the recipient's hands with Sacred Chrism. This is the same Holy Oil used in Baptism and Confirmation; it was presented in Chapter 12. His hands, which will be used to celebrate the Sacraments, are consecrated to show his conforming to Christ the Eternal High Priest.

Given the deep significance of anointing with oil, a bishop is anointed on the head as a sign of the fullness of the priesthood. In the celebration of the Sacrament of Holy Orders, a bishop is again given the Book of the Gospels as a sign that his ministry primarily consists in preaching the Word of God and instructing people in the faith. He is the principal preacher of the Word of God and teacher of the Catholic faith in his diocese. In the same celebration, he receives a ring as a sign of his fidelity to the Church like Christ the Bridegroom is committed to his Bride, the same Church. A miter is placed on his head as a sign of his ruling authority in the name of Jesus Christ. He then receives a crozier—a staff resembling a shepherd's crook—signifying his role as shepherd of the People of God under his care. All these signs and actions signify that the bishop is a successor of the Apostles.

In both the Old and New Testaments, the laying on of hands signifies a transmission of power and the handing on of authority. Moses, the great prophet and Lawgiver, conferred his power on Joshua to replace him by laying his hands on Joshua's head.[37] St. Paul revealed that he had handed on the power of Christ when he laid his own hands on St. Timothy:

---

37. Cf. Nm 27:22–23.

> I remind you to rekindle the gift of God that is within you through the laying on of my hands; for God did not give us a spirit of timidity but a spirit of power and love and self-control.[38]

The Apostles laid hands on a group of men, ordaining them deacons, to assist them in their ministry. The recipients of this first deaconate ordination were "set before the apostles, and they prayed and laid their hands upon them."[39]

The laying on of hands, which has been practiced since early in the Old Testament, is the matter of the Sacrament of Holy Orders, and the form is the prayer of consecration over the recipient's head. A deacon is consecrated to service, and a priest is consecrated into the Eternal High Priesthood of Jesus Christ.

Through a special grace of the Holy Spirit, the ordained can represent and act in the place of Christ the Eternal High Priest as a mediator between God and his people. His power and authority draw from the indelible mark left by the Sacrament of Holy Orders. This configuration to Christ the Eternal High Priest is not subject to change: A priest, for example, is a priest forever.

In Persona Christi Capitis

Deacons are consecrated in Holy Orders to service: *in persona Christi servus*—"in the Person of Christ the Servant." This section will focus on priests and bishops, who are consecrated in Holy Orders to a *priestly* ministry in the Person of Christ the Head.

Jesus Christ is Head of his Church as the Good Shepherd of all the faithful. Jesus is also the teacher *par excellence* of the truth that brings freedom, hope, joy, and salvation. His teachings can bring out the very best in every human person. Jesus is not just a historical Person from the past; he is alive and with us in his Church. He is present most especially in the Eucharist—in his Body, Blood, Soul, and Divinity—waiting to be with us, but he is also present through the ministry of his bishops and priests, who teach, sanctify, and lead his people to everlasting life. He is the one and same Christ who acts through all his ordained ministers. It is Christ who heals through Confession; it is Christ who offers himself for all people in the Sacrifice of the Eucharist; it is Christ who imparts the sacred power

38. 2 Tm 1:6–7.

39. Acts 6:6.

of Holy Orders. Regardless of the oratorical skills of a particular human minister, it is Christ who preaches and instructs. Regardless of the holiness or sins of a particular human minister, it is Christ who touches hearts and souls through sacramental graces. When a bishop or priest celebrates Mass, hears a confession, or administers any other Sacrament, Christ is the true minister.

One striking instance where the faithful can witness a bishop or priest acting *in persona Christi capitis*—"in the Person of Christ the Head"—is during the consecration at Mass. When the bread and wine are changed into Jesus' Body and Blood, we hear, "This is *my* Body," and, "This is the chalice of *my* Blood."[40] Christ himself is speaking through his minister. The bishop or priest does not say, "This is *Jesus'* Body," or, "This is the chalice of *Christ's* Blood," as if he were giving someone else's gift to the faithful. Jesus himself, working though his priestly minister, changes the bread and wine into his own Body and Blood.

An ordained minister does not only represent Christ to his people but also represents the Church before God. The priest is an image of Jesus, who both revealed the Father to the world and stood in our place as an offering to the Father. Like Christ, the bishop or priest, from one perspective, is a mediator of Christ to his Church; from another perspective he is a mediator of the Church to our heavenly Father.

Obviously, no human person is worthy or entitled to receive such honor and responsibility to act in Christ's place. The power to exercise the priestly ministry, therefore, depends not on worthiness, holiness, or any natural ability. A recipient of Holy Orders must have at least the implicit intention to administer the Sacraments according to the mind of the Church, using the form and matter established by Christ and specified by his Church.

The certainty of sacramental graces is one of the great gifts of a ministerial priesthood acting *in persona Christi capitis*. The faith of the People of God does not depend on the ordained minister; rather, their faith rests on the fact that Jesus himself is the true minister of each Sacrament. A bishop's homily might not be engaging; a priest might sing off-key, and he might even cheat at bingo, but so long as he celebrates the rites prescribed by the Church, the faithful can be confident, for example, that Christ has come to them in his

40. RMiss, The Order of Mass, no. 89; emphasis ours.

Body and his Blood at Mass and that God has forgiven their sins in Confession.

Though the personal qualities of a particular bishop or priest have no bearing on the efficacy of the Sacraments, his holiness is nonetheless of utmost importance. The more an ordained minister exhibits fatherly virtues in his personal life—compassion, courage, clarity in doctrine, a spirit of service, etc.—the more others experience the heart of Christ. Because the priest is an image of Jesus Christ and the Fatherhood of God, he cannot be satisfied with just administering Sacraments but must also witness Christ in his personal conduct. As Jesus taught his disciples, "By this all men will know that you are my disciples, if you have love for one another."[41] The more the heart of the priest is conformed to the merciful heart of Jesus, the more his people will experience the light of Jesus Christ. There are countless beautiful conversion stories that begin with the personal holiness of a priest.

Considering the spectacular power granted to a bishop or priest to act *in persona Christi capitis*, there is a mighty responsibility to strive to lead a saintly life. No matter how much a particular bishop or priest struggles to imitate Jesus, he should always try to narrow the gap between what he does in his capacity to celebrate the Sacraments and how he follows Christ personally. This special power to act *in persona Christi capitis* in no way guarantees that he will be holy: He must cooperate with God's grace and struggle to conform his life to the teachings of Christ, just like every other Christian.

When Priests Fall Short

Some bishops and priests, tragically, have irreparably betrayed their holy vocations. Given the role of priestly minister in his sacramental ministry and to be an image of Christ to others, their scandals have both shaken the faithful and even driven some to leave communion with the Church. Decades spent suppressing the disclosure of abuse by a few have inflicted a terrible stain on the whole priesthood and the whole Church. Beyond the immediate physical and psychological toll on the victims, another tragic result of these terrible sins has caused a loss of moral credibility and esteem for the Church and the priesthood. This dark chapter in the modern history of the Church is certainly not a reflection on the priesthood

41. Jn 13:35.

of Christ, just as marital infidelity is not a reflection on the Sacrament of Matrimony.

Nevertheless, invoking one of the insightful teachings of St. Augustine, Our Lord's merciful power can bring good out of even the worst evils.[42] In response to this sad reality, many priests, especially younger priests, are inspired by St. Paul: "Do not be overcome by evil, but overcome evil with good."[43] They are increasingly determined to cooperate with God's grace to grow in holiness, witnessing the love of Jesus in every dimension of their lives. They know the Sacraments do not magically transform people, and Holy Orders is no exception. Every priest, too, must work for a discipleship marked by a robust prayer life centered on the Eucharist, frequent recourse to Confession, and habitual effort to imitate Jesus' unconditional love predicated upon a heroic charity.

While the history of the Church contains far too many instances of sinful and scandalous behavior, in contrast, her history is also replete with examples of extraordinary, holy priests. The patron saint of parish priests, St. John Vianney, would hear confessions up to sixteen hours every day in his small village church. He spent hours in front of the Blessed Sacrament in deep prayer, practiced rigorous penance, and lived heroic poverty to win the conversion of his parish. His ministry influenced people way beyond the confines of the sixty-family village; people from all over France and Europe came and often waited days to go to Confession with him. Though they had their own distinct callings, Sts. John Paul II, Pius of Pietrelcina (lovingly known as Padre Pio), John Bosco, and countless others reflected the heart of Christ and consequently had a profound evangelical influence throughout the world. Like St. John Vianney, each spent a tremendous time in prayer, bore heavy crosses throughout their lives, and were known by their exquisite charity toward people.

Because the priestly ministry is sacred, it is urgent that every priest seriously struggle to cooperate with God's grace to grow in holiness as best he can. Only in this way can he draw his people to Christ as he acts in the name of Christ. It is also essential that the lay faithful pray for priests. As St. John Vianney once said, "There are no bad priests, only priests for whom there has not been enough

42. Cf. CoG, Book XI, ch. 9

43. Rom 12:21.

prayer."[44] As the Church is blessed with holy priests, the New Evangelization becomes less of a dream and more of a reality.

44. Terry Boldin, "Prayers for Priests," in *Monthly Prayer Request for Priests—Milwaukee* (June 2022), *www.mprp-milwaukee.org/prayers-for-priests*.

CHAPTER 20

CONVERSATION WITH GOD

Any work that gives an overview of the Catholic faith with all its beliefs, Sacraments, and moral teachings must include clear guidance in establishing a personal relationship with the central character: Jesus Christ. Without a spirituality strongly rooted in habitual dialogue with Our Lord, the study of the Catholic faith becomes just an academic discipline, albeit a very lofty one. The purpose of studying the faith is not only to grow in factual knowledge of God—the Father, the Son, and the Holy Spirit—but also to have a personal relationship with each divine Person. This bond between God and every member of his Church occurs through a deep friendship with Jesus Christ, who is the gateway to the Father and the Holy Spirit, who are totally transcendent and invisible. The process of forging a friendship with the Father and the Holy Spirit through the Son involves regular prayer.

"Prayer is an uprising of the mind to God or a petitioning of God for what is fitting."[1] Prayer consists in elevating the mind and heart to God either with express words or sentiments of affection and love. Though it may seem that we initiate contact with God, in reality, we always respond to God, who first pursues a relationship with us. The interior human impulse to speak with God is a response to Christ knocking on the door of the human heart, awaiting an answer through the gift of grace.

Prayer involves every aspect of the human person, including physical gestures, posture, recitation, singing, and periods of silence. The source of prayer, prompted by the grace of God, is the innermost part of the human person, which is represented by the heart. Prayer, therefore, is ineffective without the engagement of the heart. In every human relationship the animating force of any meaningful dialogue is not audible verbiage devoid of heartfelt meaning but a person's desire to share his or her inner self. This same idea most definitely applies to the spiritual life, which should never consist of empty forms or lackluster exercises of pious expressions. The par-

---

1. St. John of Damascus, *De Fide Orthodoxa: An Exact Exposition of the Orthodox Faith*, Book III, ch. 24.

ticipation of the human heart is such an indispensable component of prayer that, according to the *Catechism*, Scripture refers to the heart "more than a thousand times."[2] The human heart is so deep that only God and the person him- or herself can actually know its desires, sentiments, dispositions, and aspirations. The heart is where a person and God encounter and communicate with one another, in many cases even without words.

Christian prayer is not a groveling supplication before a wrathful, capricious superpower like Zeus of ancient Greece. Nor is it the obliteration of self like in so many Eastern mystical religions. Christian prayer is a loving dialogue between a child and his or her divine Father.

Christian prayer follows a Trinitarian pattern. We speak to God the Father through God the Son by the power of God the Holy Spirit. In the course of a person's prayer, there should be not only an acknowledgment of the Father, the Son, and the Holy Spirit but also a true friendship with each divine Person. This capacity for friendship with the three Persons of the Trinity is derived from the grace of Baptism. For this reason, Catholic prayer so often begins by tracing a cross on the body while praying the *Sign of the Cross*: "In the Name of the Father, and of the Son, and of the Holy Spirit."[3] The *Sign of the Cross*, in its own right, is a prayer.

Lack of experience with prayer should never stop anyone from starting. In fact, it is only with a humble spirit, admitting that *we do not know* how to pray, that we can succeed in praying. Humility is essential: No one is capable of prayer without the aid of God's grace. As he revealed in the Gospel, Jesus Christ will only accept a prayer or request made with a humble demeanor.[4] "A broken and contrite heart"[5] is always the medium through which we can effectively converse with Jesus.

The Prayer of Jesus

Since prayer is dialogue with God, there can be no better example than God himself, the Word made flesh. There has never been a more perfect life of prayer than that of Jesus Christ. And Jesus

2. CCC 2562.
3. "Sign of the Cross," in HBP, 59.
4. Cf. Mt 7:21.
5. Ps 51:17.

taught his disciples to pray by his example, parables, and express instructions. In his humanity Jesus first learned to pray at the feet of his Mother and father, the Blessed Virgin Mary and St. Joseph. In his divinity Jesus enjoys perfect communion with the Father, in which relationship we are joined by Baptism into Christ. Our prayer progresses to the degree that it conforms to Christ's prayer.

It is quite noticeable from Jesus' example that he prays in earnest before key events of his public ministry. Before initiating his public life, he retreated into the wilderness to devote his time exclusively to prayer.[6] He did not select his Twelve Apostles until he had spent an entire night immersed in prayer. The raising of Lazarus from the dead—the most significant miracle before his Resurrection—was preceded by prayer.[7] One of Jesus' favorite venues for serious meditation and prayer of petition was to go "up on the mountain to pray":[8] a place of silence, which is ideal for a more focused conversation with God. A quiet mountaintop also symbolizes heaven. Jesus' habitual pursuit of solitude drives home his union with the Father and his ardent desire to identify with his will. On several occasions Jesus spent entire nights immersed in prayer. Our sharing in the prayer of Jesus means not being satisfied with simple, cursory prayer that is over in a short time.

The contents of Jesus' prayer were the needs of every person past, present, and future since this was the whole reason for his Incarnation. Jesus petitions for the needs of every human person—each one called to be redeemed. The Gospels record some of the conversations Jesus had with his Father; sentiments of gratitude and desires to give his Father glory and embrace the Father's will are some of the features of Christ's prayer. Jesus' last words, as he was hanging on the Cross, are a moving testimony of his total obedience and docility to his Father's will: "Father, into thy hands I commit my spirit!"[9] His loud cry is a dramatic *tour de force* of his solidarity with all the troubles, sufferings, and sins of humanity—coupled with his desire to liberate every person from the afflictions of sin.

In addition to his example, Jesus also taught about prayer. Three parables are particularly wonderful for understanding prayer accord-

6. Cf. Lk 4:1–13.

7. Cf. Jn 11:41–42.

8. Mk 6:46.

9. Lk 23:46.

ing to the mind of Jesus Christ. In the first parable a person asks his friend, who is already in bed for the night, for bread to feed a visitor. Their friendship was not enough to impel the friend to get up to give him bread; however, the person's dogged pestering wears down his friend to inconvenience himself and provide what is requested.[10] God, of course, does not feel literally pestered, but by analogy this parable reveals that effective prayer requires repeated petitions despite the lack of immediate results.

In the second parable, the Parable of the Widow and the Unrighteous Judge, a widow bothers a godless judge so persistently that she secures a legitimate, just decision.[11] This lesson is similar to the first parable's but with a more poignant emphasis on the power of insistent perseverance. Our Lord again makes it crystal clear that dedication to petitioning drives home the power of prayer in the face of apparently insurmountable obstacles. Since this judge has no sense of justice or human compassion, it requires unrelenting nagging to cause him to act with justice: "Though I neither fear God nor regard man, yet because this widow bothers me, I will vindicate her."[12] Countless saints have extended the Kingdom of God in the face of overwhelming odds and untold suffering by continuous prayer, driven by the conviction that God would invariably answer with a marvelous outcome.

In the third parable, the Parable of the Pharisee and the Publican, both a Pharisee and a tax collector open up to God, revealing their inner thoughts and dispositions.[13] The Pharisee has a good life, fulfilling the requirements of a religious person. He boasts of his spiritual and moral accomplishments in comparison to those who fall short: "God, I thank thee that I am not like other men, extortioners, unjust, adulterers, or even like this tax collector."[14] This prayer is rejected by Jesus since it certainly does not lead to the true love of God manifested in mercy and compassion for others, especially for those alienated from God. A prayer that excludes a humble, contrite heart is simply not pleasing to God. The Pharisee is completely unaware of his personal fault and approaches God full of himself rather than humbly hoping to be filled by God.

10. Cf. Lk 11:5–8.

11. Cf. Lk 18:2–5.

12. Lk 18:5.

13. Cf. Lk 18:10–14.

14. Lk 18:11.

A prayer to elicit a positive response from God must always be inspired by the humility expressed in the tax collector's simple prayer: "God, be merciful to me a sinner!"[15] The tax collector's humble prayer for God's mercy and forgiveness is a universal model for prayer. Jesus concluded this parable:

> I tell you, this man went down to his house justified rather than the other; for every one who exalts himself will be humbled, but he who humbles himself will be exalted.[16]

When discussing prayer Jesus established necessary conditions for fruitful prayer. He spoke about the need to resolve any enmity or resentments with a friend, brother, or sister. Before approaching the altar for worship, it is indispensable to be reconciled with anyone who is a source of enmity: "First be reconciled to your brother, and then come and offer your gift."[17] Jesus spoke about the need to love all people unconditionally, including those who have caused injury, as another prerequisite for effective prayer. He urged his disciples to pray with good intentions so that their prayer would be exclusively directed to God's glory; for instance, any inordinate desire to impress others with shows of piety or to bargain with God for favors is incompatible with true prayer. True conversation with Jesus Christ requires purity of heart, a spirit of forgiveness, and a desire to always embrace God's will. These sentiments involve a constant conversion of heart and spirit of repentance.

Jesus also spoke about the need to pray from the heart and not to mindlessly repeat a bunch of empty, pious words: "In praying do not heap up empty phrases."[18] To pray "from the heart" does not mean to be overwhelmed by emotion or sentimentalism; rather, it means that, in prayer, a person should mean what he or she is saying and at the same time seek union with Jesus Christ. Prayer must be personal and not simply a series of phrases dryly addressed to God. In fact, Jesus encouraged his disciples to pray with confidence and daring to God, our loving and merciful Father. God will listen to a prayer that reflects the desire to grow in humility, purity, and unconditional love for others. The reason for the heavy stress on purity of heart is that the ultimate answer to prayer comes in the

15. Lk 18:13.
16. Lk 18:14.
17. Mt 5:24.
18. Mt 6:7.

form of a more intimate union with God the Father through Jesus Christ by the power of the Holy Spirit.

Jesus also encouraged his Apostles to make their petitions to the Father in his name. "Whatever you ask in prayer, believe that you have received it, and it will be yours."[19] This does not mean that God is a genie or a concierge, providing every request or caprice. Desires expressed in prayer will be met if they serve the good and true happiness of the petitioner. This might entail a specific material outcome but not necessarily so. The end goal of prayer is our true good—union with God—therefore, these words of Christ imply the pursuit of holiness. While we might ask anything of God, a person of faith will trust that God has heard the prayer and that, whatever the outcome, it will result in a more perfect and complete identification with God's will.

Even in the case of a great miracle—the healing of a physical ailment or the expulsion of a demon—it is clear that effective prayer must be inspired by faith. Through reflection on the Gospels, the human response of faith to God's invitation is clearly needed for prayer to be answered. Before working a miracle, Jesus, without fail, asked for a certain prerequisite threshold of faith. In fact, after Jesus worked a miracle, he gave attribution to the person's attitude of faith more than to his own divine powers.[20]

Another necessary condition to secure a good outcome in prayer is habitual union with God through Jesus Christ. Jesus presented the paradigm of this union with God in his Parable of the Vine and the Branches.[21] The way a branch is united to the vine—so much so that it is an actual extension of it—symbolizes how we should be united to Jesus Christ. This intimate union with Christ is the setting for a positive response to every petition for holiness and the fruits of evangelization. "If you abide in me, and my words abide in you, ask whatever you will, and it shall be done for you."[22]

Faith in prayer, though, must be accompanied by faith in God's plan. An old adage states that God has only three answers to prayer: "Yes,""Not yet," and, "I have a better idea." Perfect prayer is distinguished by total conformation to God's will. The prayer of the

19. Mk 11:24.
20. Cf. Mt 9:22; Mk 10:52; and many others.
21. Cf. Jn 15:1–11.
22. Jn 15:7.

Blessed Virgin Mary in response to the archangel's Annunciation that she was called to be the Mother of the Savior is the perfect act of faith since it expresses her total identification with God's will: "Behold, I am the handmaid of the Lord; let it be to me according to your word."[23] Her ardent desire to do God's will and firm trust that she would be the Mother of the Son of God strike at the heart of the ideal dispositions for prayer, expressed in her humility and total self-giving to God's will for her. Mary models these same sentiments in her last recorded words, addressed to the workers at the Wedding Feast at Cana: "Do whatever he tells you."[24] Her petition resulted in the miraculous conversion of water into wine only after the workers had filled the containers—no small sacrifice—full of water. This reveals that prayer must be marked by an inner attitude of generous self-giving in fulfilling God's will.

The *Canticle of the Blessed Virgin Mary* is also a perfect teaching on prayer. It begins:

> My soul magnifies the Lord,
> and my spirit rejoices in God my Savior,
> for he has regarded the low estate of his handmaiden.[25]

Having been given the unprecedented honor of becoming the Mother of the Redeemer, the Blessed Virgin Mary gave the glory to God understanding that it is he, not she, who performs his marvelous plan.

Jesus himself offered a dramatic example of total identification with the Father's will in the Garden of Gethsemane on the night of his arrest. From the depths of his human heart, Jesus prayed, "Father, if thou art willing, remove this cup from me."[26] Every action of Jesus is an example for his disciples, and here he taught us to pray for what we desire. What is most instructive about this request is how Jesus concluded: "Nevertheless not my will, but thine, be done."[27] Jesus persevered, offering this prayer three times to the Father. He then obediently followed the plan of his Father and willingly took up his Cross. Like every prayer of Jesus, this prayer highlights the purpose of prayer as the path to uniting one's human will with the divine will. This should not lead us to think God is a taskmaster

23. Lk 1:38.
24. Jn 2:5.
25. Lk 1:47–48.
26. Lk 22:42; cf. Mt 26:39.
27. Ibid.

doling out orders. Faith in God's providence means trusting that he desires our good and whatever he has in mind, even if it is difficult, is designed for our benefit.

ABBA, FATHER[28]

A salient characteristic of Jesus' conversation with God is that he directly addresses God as his Father. Throughout his conversation with God as man, he spontaneously addresses his Father not in a formal way but with the typical familiarity with which a son addresses his father. Jesus not only presents himself to us as a model for prayer, but also invites each one of us to actually participate in his prayer addressed to his Father.

A key moment for the Apostles' instruction in prayer occurred when Jesus, amid his own prayer, caught their attention. Though the Apostles already knew how to pray from their upbringing in the Jewish faith, they nevertheless asked Jesus with those celebrated words: "Lord, teach us to pray."[29] Jesus' response revolutionized prayer; he instructed them to deal with God not just as the Supreme Being and Creator but as a true Father.[30] By telling his disciples to call God "Father," he conveyed the clear message that his disciples' relationship to God is that of a child to his or her father. In this special teaching moment, Jesus revealed the consoling truth that God loves every person with literally infinite fatherly affection and compassion. We are called to imitate Jesus in fostering that relationship of a child with God.

The prayer Jesus taught his Apostles, the *Lord's Prayer* or *Our Father*, is the "most perfect of prayers";[31] it summarizes the spiritual and moral sentiments that can be converted into prayer. Many saints and theologians have written lengthy meditations on its wealth of instruction, including St. Teresa of Avila, St. Thomas Aquinas, and C. S. Lewis. According to the ancient Christian writer and theologian Tertullian, "In the *[Lord's] Prayer* is comprised an epitome of the whole Gospel."[32] St. Thomas Aquinas stated that everything we need to ask for is stated in the *Lord's Prayer*; moreover, the requests

28. Cf. Mk 14:36; Rom 8:15; Gal 4:6.
29. Lk 11:1.
30. Cf. Lk 11:2–13.
31. STh II-II, Book 83, art. 9.
32. Tertullian, "*De Oratione*," ch. 1; in ANF, vol. 3.

are placed in their proper sequence by priority.[33] When we recite the *Lord's Prayer*, it is helpful to remember that its Author is the absolute model for prayer. Precisely because Jesus Christ recommended that we use the words "Our Father" for prayer strikes at the heart of the Gospel message, so it serves as a principal prayer during the Church's worship, especially in the Eucharistic Liturgy and the Liturgy of the Hours. As Pope Francis emphasized, "This is not one of many Christian prayers, but *the prayer of the children of God*.... When we pray the 'Our Father,' we pray as Jesus prayed."[34]

The address "Our Father" is the first consideration of the *Lord's Prayer*; it recognizes God as our infinitely loving Father. When God revealed himself to Moses, he did not explicitly reveal himself as the Father but as the Supreme Being. Jesus Christ fully revealed that we have a new relationship with God: We are not merely creatures but daughters and sons of the Father. This constitutes one of the most consoling truths of the Gospel. All prayer should have God's fatherly love as a baseline. Calling on "Our Father" is a key fruit of the redemption that enables us to be reborn as children of God in Jesus Christ.

The profound, consoling truth that God is our Father should move us toward two dispositions. First, every Christian should try to reflect God the Father's love and kindness. The Father's loving kindness is perfectly expressed and revealed in the humanity of Jesus. Having God as our Father in union with Christ is an invitation to cooperate with his grace, struggling to conform our attitudes to the sentiments of mercy and affection incarnated by Christ, who "reflects the glory of God."[35] Being a child of God is totally at odds with a mean spirit toward our neighbor.

Second, every Christian should foster a loving trust in God's merciful providence toward his children. God wants what is best for us and does not will our suffering; rather, he wants to purify and sanctify our lives through a more intimate union with Christ. God wants us to reach a high degree of joy, which consists in living a full life in Christ. For this reason St. Paul revealed, "In everything God works for good with those who love him."[36] Jesus also taught his

33. Cf. STh II-II, Book 83, art. 9.
34. Pope Francis, *General Audience* (March 14, 2018).
35. Heb 1:3.
36. Rom 8:28.

disciples about the Father in the Parable of the Prodigal Son, which was presented in Chapter 15. Every child of God who falls short of perfection—or even fails miserably—knows God the Father is waiting and watching with a loving embrace for his or her return.

Not only does Jesus teach his disciples to call God "Father" but, more specifically, "*our* Father."[37] It is not "my Father" who art in heaven. First, "our" expresses the invitation of Jesus to be children of God the Father in union with God the Son. Additionally, "our" highlights the communion that God desires among his children, within the Mystical Body of Christ, with the implicit desire to overcome all divisions. Addressing God as "*our* Father," we view every person as a son or daughter of God the Father, which is how we pray for unity, first among all the baptized and ultimately for the entire human race. "Our Father" expresses a desire to bring everyone into Jesus Christ's light and life.

The words "who art in heaven,"[38] which immediately follow "Our Father," does not refer to God's abode but a mode of being. God completely transcends both time and space, so he cannot be located geographically or spatially. Associating God with heaven stresses not a place but rather his infinite majesty and transcendence. "Heaven" also emphasizes that eternal life with God is the ultimate goal of every prayer.

Seven petitions follow "who art in heaven." The first three petitions articulate a desire to praise and give glory to God, clamoring for help to be totally identified with God's will. They are a humble cry for personal holiness since this is essentially the will of God. The last four petitions cry out for nourishment, forgiveness, and the help to avoid sin. These seven requests, instructed by the Messiah, include what is truly necessary for spiritual perfection and happiness. The desires expressed in the *Lord's Prayer* can be perfectly fulfilled by cooperating with the graces merited by Jesus' redemption on the Cross.

The first petition, "Hallowed be thy name,"[39] can be understood as, "Blessed is your name," or, "May your name be blessed." First, this is a way of expressing thanksgiving and adoration in appreciation of God the Father's unbounding goodness and mercy. Second,

37. Mt 6:9; emphasis ours.

38. Ibid.

39. Ibid.

we are asking that his name be holy within us: that we be holy in his eyes. This phrase recognizes that God is calling us to multiply his love and mercy in our daily life. We honor the name of God by leading holy lives; on the other hand, we can denigrate the name of God through a sinful life. Finally, this phrase includes the petition that his name be holy in those who do not yet know God. We do not pray that God's name be *made* holy—he is already holiness itself—rather that his name be *recognized* as holy both in us and in everyone around the world.

The next petition, "Thy kingdom come,"[40] is a plea that the Gospel spread to more people and transform the world according to his plan. Jesus made crystal clear that the Gospel is for everyone. The Kingdom of God is marked by the character traits of Jesus, which include joy, peace, happiness, truth, love, and freedom. The spread of his kingdom always begins within the heart of one disciple of Christ. This phrase, so loaded with meaning, comprises a request for intimate union with Jesus Christ as a means of bringing his light and life to others. True evangelization consists of an overflow of the life of Christ from person to person; sharing in the life of Christ defines the Kingdom of God. For this reason Jesus teaches that his spiritual kingdom lies within the heart of the human person and is not a geographic kingdom.

At the same time, the spreading of the Gospel transforms the world. As St. Augustine taught, to the extent that Christians live according to the Kingdom of God on earth, they bring the Kingdom of God *to* earth.[41] As presented in Chapters 9 and 10, "The laity, by their very vocation, seek the kingdom of God by engaging in temporal affairs and by ordering them according to the plan of God."[42] "Thy kingdom come," means right now, in our world; moreover, we desire and acknowledge that this will only fully occur when Christ establishes his kingdom forever at the end of time.

"Thy will be done,"[43] concludes the petitions for personal holiness. The will of God is shown to be identified with holiness as clearly revealed in one of the oldest writings of the New Testament when St. Paul reveals: "This is the will of God, your sanctification."[44]

40. Mt 6:10.
41. Cf. CoG, Book I, ch. 36.
42. LG, no. 31.
43. Cf. CoG, Book I, ch. 36.
44. 1 Thes 4:3.

Elsewhere Scripture reveals that Jesus "learned obedience through what he suffered"[45] in his life on earth, and he taught us to pray that we, too, might be obedient to the Father's will in all things. As Jesus also taught, through doing the will of the Father, a person enters the Kingdom of God.[46] But the disciples were not taught to pray, "Thy will be done *in me,*" as if their prayer were to focus only on their personal holiness, but, "Thy will be done *on earth,*" that is, everywhere. They were taught to desire and request the transformation of the entire world, highlighting again the Christian desire that all people come to holiness in Christ.

The petition, "Give us this day our daily bread,"[47] embraces both material and spiritual needs. These words imply thanksgiving and acknowledgment that all blessings come from God's generous bounty. Asking for what we need counteracts any sense of entitlement or a short-sided attitude toward the many manifestations of God's love. We also ask for God's greatest of all possible gifts, which is the "bread of life."[48] This spiritual nourishment, also called the "bread of God,"[49] transcends any other possible blessing. We want to give thanks and request that this gift continue to come our way for the rest our lives.

These petition, "Forgive us our debts, / As we also have forgiven our debtors,"[50] initiates petitions connected to counteracting our inclination to sin. We ask Our Lord for his forgiveness for countless sins committed, both mortal and venial. Though our sins were washed away at Baptism, our inherent weaknesses lead us to easily fall back into sin. Given every Christian's high frequency of violations of God's Commandments, we are in constant need of God's merciful forgiveness.

Receiving divine forgiveness is contingent on our own spirit of forgiveness toward others. Jesus showed us through his own interactions with morally flawed people that the quality and effectiveness of our prayer depends on the recognition of our sinfulness and need for God's mercy. This abundance of mercy is certainly for the taking

45. Heb 5:8.
46. Cf. Mt 7:21–22.
47. Mt 6:11.
48. Jn 6:35, 48.
49. Jn 6:33.
50. Mt 6:12; or, as translated in RMiss, The Order of Mass, no. 124: "Forgive us our trespasses, / as we forgive those who trespass against us."

as long as we have a habitual spirit of forgiveness toward anyone who may have slighted or injured us. If we have any kind of resentment toward anyone, the grace of Our Lord's forgiveness is impeded by this hardness of heart. A sign of appreciation for and openness to Our Lord's magnanimous willingness to pardon our offenses is our eagerness to forgive anyone who may hurt us in any way. The beautiful habit of forgiveness strikes at the heart of Jesus' teachings and is therefore an indispensable condition for effective prayer: "Be merciful, even as your Father is merciful."[51]

The petition, "Lead us not into temptation,"[52] is simply a humble request for strength to overcome the temptation to sin. A literal translation of the original Greek might read, "Do not allow us to enter into temptation," or, "Do not let us yield to temptation." Without doubt Our Lord would never *lead* us into temptation, but we need his help and strength to resist the temptations of the Devil and the weaknesses of our wounded nature. God's grace helps us discern the near occasions of sin and bestows on us the means to avoid them. God permits temptation since it helps us know our weaknesses better and, consequently, helps us increasingly depend on his help. God will never let us be tempted beyond our strength; however, only through humble prayer can we overcome temptations due to human weakness and the wiles of the Evil One.

The final petition, "Deliver us from evil,"[53] concludes the *Lord's Prayer*. We ask to be liberated from evil—not only for ourselves but also for the whole People of God. This petition concerns the Devil himself, who tries to undermine our efforts to follow Christ. In light of the steady onslaught of the Evil One on all disciples of Christ, we are in constant need of God's grace. We therefore pray for liberation from past, present, and future evils. As we recite this last petition, we consider the vast amount of evil afflicting the world. We need God to fortify us against the forces of evil, which undermine God's kingdom by weakening or destroying a person's relationship with Christ. This petition is to stop evil from afflicting the entire world and its ensuing turmoil; it implies the gift of peace not only for us but also for the whole human race.

51. Lk 6:36.
52. Mt 6:13.
53. Ibid.

After all these petitions we "say 'Amen'; by this 'Amen,' which means 'So be it,' setting [our] seal to the petitions of the divinely-taught prayer."[54]

In praising and adoring God as Father, we are essentially loving all three Persons of the Blessed Trinity: the Father, the Son, and the Holy Spirit. There is no required preference among the divine Persons of the Trinity, but the Church's liturgical prayers usually follow this order: We address God the Father through God the Son under the promptings of God the Holy Spirit. This is because the humanity of Christ is the gateway to the Father by the power of the Holy Spirit. God the Son became man to reveal the love of God the Father in a human and visible way, and God the Holy Spirit prompts the Christian to always pray in the name of Jesus. Any prayer that we offer to the Father through Jesus Christ is inspired by the Holy Spirit, who is the personified bond of love between the Father and the Son. In addition to directing prayers to Jesus Christ, the disciple of Christ should follow his example and teachings by speaking directly to God the Father and God the Holy Spirit.

Forms of Prayer

Four forms of prayer were introduced in Chapter 14: *adoration*, or praise, of God; *thanksgiving* for all of God's blessings; *atonement*, or contrition to God for one's sins or the sins of others; and *petition*, or requests for God's favor.[55] This section will present them more completely.

Prayer of adoration, or praise, is a special form of prayer by which we recognize the greatness of God in acknowledgment of God's absolute dominion over all creation. As the *Catechism* defines it, "*Adoration* is the first attitude of man acknowledging that he is a creature before his Creator."[56] Prayer of adoration / praise is also an expression of love for the God who created us and bountifully fulfills all our needs. It acknowledges God has brought us into existence from nothing, and everything we have both internally and externally wonderfully expresses his infinite love for us. Adoration / praise enables a person to verbally manifest love in recognition of

54. St. Cyril of Jerusalem, "Catechetical Lectures," Lecture 23, no. 18; quoted in *Nicene and Post-Nicene Fathers, Second Series*, vol. 7 (Buffalo, NY: Christian Literature Publishing Co., 1894).

55. Cf. CCC 2626–2643.

56. CCC 2628.

God's perfection of mercy and kindness toward everyone. This form of prayer especially pleases God when it is addressed to Jesus Christ, who is both God and Savior. God the Father's greatest Revelation of infinite love and affection is the Incarnation, redemption, and Resurrection of his Son, which is how God shows that his love knows no bounds. It is important that words of praise be especially included in every Christian's prayer life.

Prayer of *thanksgiving* is an expression of our gratitude for all the benefits that God has bestowed on us; "every event and need can become an offering of thanksgiving."[57] This form is expressed by showing gratitude to God for his great gifts. St. Paul, throughout his writing, is very much aware of the blessings and graces lavished on the early Christians, so he instructs that their prayer take the form of habitually profound gratitude to God.[58] In silent recognition of so many gifts and blessings, it is a response with fervent prayers of appreciation and gratitude.

Prayer of atonement / contrition reflects sorrow for sins and should be a frequent prayer to appeal to the mercy of Jesus and ask for his forgiveness and another chance to make amends. A humble appeal for merciful pardon for sins makes this form pleasing to God. Throughout the Gospels, there are countless moving scenes depicting Jesus' lavish spirit of forgiveness. The Parables of the Prodigal Son[59] and of the Pharisee and the Publican[60] are two of the many examples of good acts of atonement / contrition for sins.

Prayer of petition is a matter of presenting needs and desires to Our Lord. Since "*every need* can become the object of petition,"[61] this form is the recognition that a person depends on God for everything, and that, as a loving Father, he gives all that is good. Since the ultimate goal of prayer is to be intimately united to the Blessed Trinity through the humanity of Jesus Christ, it is most fitting that we ask for all sorts of favors, both spiritual and material: good health, successful job performance, safety in travel, and other material outcomes. To ask God for favors acknowledges that he is the source of every temporal blessing.[62]

57. CCC 2638.

58. Cf. 1 Thes 5:18; Col 4:2.

59. Cf. Lk 15:11–32.

60. Cf. Lk 18:9–14.

61. CCC 2633.

62. Cf. Jas 1:17.

There are a few things to keep in mind when asking God for favors. First, as Christ demonstrated in the Garden of Gethsemane, a Christian must always remain identified with God's will, which is his or her good; it is not a negotiation with God. As Jesus made his heartfelt request he prayed, "Father, *if thou art willing,* remove this cup from me."[63] The most important petition is for improvement in the spiritual life. A request for growth in virtue, holiness, and communion with God will always be answered when made from the heart.

Petition should not be entirely focused on the self but on the entire human family. Petition includes intercessory prayer, which is "to pray as Jesus did":[64] for the needs of others. In communion and solidarity with others, a Christian makes the needs of other people his or her own and intercedes on their behalf before God's mercy. Among the many intentions that can fall within the ambit of intercessory prayer, the needs of the sick and the poor take special priority. It is good to specifically pray that their pain and suffering be relieved but, at the same time, that they achieve a deep encounter with Christ through his Cross. Intercession should also be made on behalf of the world, for just government, preservation from disasters, and all the human need in the world.

An important dimension of intercessory prayer clamors for the grace of conversion for people alienated from God. Jesus revealed that prayer of petition is an important vehicle to gain graces for people to fully commit themselves to following him. This conversion to discipleship, in many instances, can be traced back to a specific person praying and offering up his or her crosses for another to seriously commit to following Christ. There are examples of saints who spent much time in prayer on behalf of the conversion of people either ignorant of the gift of Christ or simply alienated from God for a variety of reasons. The model for this type of prayer is St. Monica, the mother of St. Augustine. A very typical young man, St. Augustine abandoned his mother's faith in his late teenage years. St. Monica prayed without ceasing only to have her son join a heretical sect. Without despairing, she persevered, and at the age of thirty-three her son was baptized and ordained a bishop. One of the Church's greatest theologians and saints was converted by his mother's persistent intercession.

63. Lk 22:42; emphasis ours; cf. Mt 26:39.

64. CCC 2634.

Jesus invites everyone to a radical form of love that involves praying even for enemies and those who have caused injury or been involved in persecution. The saints have been exemplary in their habitual prayer for those who have harmed and hated them. St. Maria Goretti was presented in Chapter 8; she forgave her attacker, and he converted during his prison term for having killed her.

Intercessory prayer is at the heart of devotion to the saints. The saints are models to follow in their more perfect imitation of Christ; Christ reveals himself in the lives of the saints. If the saints, however, were able to achieve such greatness on earth through their prayerful petitions, how much more so now that they are in heaven, beholding God face to face! They have a special task of interceding on our behalf to facilitate our growth in holiness and attainment of heaven with them. The saints who were so close to God through their deep spiritual life are especially inclined to interceding on people's behalf. It is not that prayer to the saints diminishes the importance given to God; rather, their union with God gives more effectiveness to every prayer.

The Blessed Virgin Mary plays a special role in the prayer life of every Christian since she always leads people to Christ. Through the work of God, she gave birth to the Son of God through her prayerful union with God's will. Each Sacrament, especially the Eucharist, ultimately finds its origin in Mary's affirmative response to the Archangel Gabriel.[65] Since Mary is the Mother of Jesus, every member of the Church is a child of Mary in Christ. God desires prayer that is addressed to Jesus through Mary. Since Jesus came to us through his Mother, it is fitting that we have recourse to him through her. Modern saints have especially shown that devotion to Mary greatly facilitates an ardent love for Jesus.

Like the wonderful Mother she is, the Blessed Virgin Mary cares for all her spiritual children through the challenges, struggles, and dangers of earthly life. Probably the most common prayer addressed to her is the *Hail Mary*, taken from the Annunciation and Visitation, greeting and praising her with the exact same words addressed to her by the Archangel Gabriel: "Hail, full of grace, the Lord is with you!"[66] We continue with St. Elizabeth's greeting: "Blessed are you

65. Cf. Lk 1:26–38.

66. Lk 1:28.

among women, and blessed is the fruit of your womb!"[67] All of Mary's daughters and sons should confidently present needs to her in hopeful expectation that she will enthusiastically help.

Every Christian should ask the Blessed Virgin Mary to be his or her advocate before Christ. Such requests can be for any good thing, especially that her Son be merciful. Human weaknesses and sins are not an obstacle for winning Mary's favor since a mother gives special attention and love to her children who suffer maladies or physical impairments. We pray that she assists with loving care until the time of death. Everyone can put total trust in this Mother and see her as a consolation in being a perfect Mother on the order of goodness and love.

Expressions of Prayer

Sometimes people think of God as distant and silent. In truth, God is always reaching out with a particular love for every person and the desire to form a relationship with him or her. God reveals himself not only through material creation but also directly through the medium of human words. God's will, his thoughts and counsels contained in the Bible, are handed on through human language. This direct communication culminates in the Incarnate Word, coming to enter into dialogue and communion with his people. Precisely because God reveals himself in this way, every person needs to both respond and develop a loving relationship with him.

A response to God's loving invitation is expressed in all sorts of ways—obedience to the moral law, efforts to improve the world according to his plan, the development of the talents and gifts he has given us, and love for neighbor. All of these are strengthened and enhanced by dialogue shared with God in prayer. Besides the four forms of prayer presented a few pages ago, there are also three expressions of prayer: vocal prayer, meditation, and contemplative prayer.

Vocal prayer consists of prayers, usually with standardized words, that a person recites, typically out loud. The *Sign of the Cross, Lord's Prayer* (*Our Father*), and *Hail Mary* are popular vocal prayers. Vocal prayer, though, must not be reduced to a mindless recitation of memorized words. As St. Teresa of Avila taught, we must know what

67. Lk 1:42.

we are saying and "to whom we speak."[68] Prayer is perfected insofar as a loving heart lies behind the expressed words and gestures.

Vocal prayer plays an important role in the life of prayer. It is the expression of prayer most conducive to uniting groups of people. There is a human need to give physical expression to spiritual dispositions since a human person has both a body and a soul. Human senses, postures, gestures, and intonations can communicate a loving reverence to God. Purposeful engagement of the senses will redound on the soul, and *vice versa*. Vocal prayer also aids when a person is tired, scared, or simply dry by offering the comfort of the words that can be spoken to God. The Psalms are a wonderful source for prayer along with the countless beautiful prayers written by the Church and her saints over the centuries.

Vocal prayer is also a good way to pray throughout the day with short expressions offered to God, asking for assistance or thanking him for his generosity. Such a short phrase—internal or external—addressed to God is called an "aspiration," and it can be a greeting, a brief expression of concern, a simple request, or a word of affection. An aspiration can be as simple as thinking, "God, be merciful to me a sinner!"[69] as the tax collector prayed; the beautiful prayer of the Miraculous Medal, "O Mary, conceived without sin, pray for us who have recourse to thee";[70] or the brief but powerful, "Jesus, I trust in you,"[71] of the Divine Mercy. Short but heartfelt aspirations are a helpful way to keep the presence of God in mind throughout the day.

"*Meditation* is a prayerful quest engaging thought, imagination, emotion, and desire."[72] Christian meditation, contrary to some popular understandings, is not a practice of clearing the mind and emptying the self. While this practice has the natural benefit of recuperation for the mind and body, it is not a proper spiritual practice. Meditation seeks not to empty the mind but to fill it by being open to the presence of God. It is an expression of prayer by which a disciple of Christ contemplates Jesus' life and teachings with the aim of listening to God. Meditation seeks to better understand God to

68. "The Way of Perfection," in ThAv, vol. I, Book II, 136.

69. Lk 18:13.

70. Joseph Glass, "Miraculous Medal," in *The Catholic Encyclopedia*, vol. 10 (New York: Robert Appleton Company, 1911).

71. DSFK, xx.

72. CCC 2723; emphasis ours.

discern his will more clearly. It might consist of a prayerful reading of Scripture, the lives or writings of the saints, or other spiritual works. Meditative reading is different than, for example, reading a story for entertainment or reading a textbook to learn facts. It might also consist of a visual component, for example, an icon of a saint or angel, a statue of the Blessed Virgin Mary, a painting of a scene from the Gospels, or most especially a crucifix.

In many instances meditation involves contemplating Jesus' words and praying to the Holy Spirit for the proper discernment on how to apply them in particular circumstances. Once God's will is more clearly perceived, whether in terms of a small resolution or a larger change of heart, prayer then transforms into a reinforced commitment to following Christ. This greater desire to follow Christ, coupled with a plan of concrete deeds, encapsulates the nature of meditation.

Meditation on the Gospel especially functions as a springboard to conform a person's life to Christ's since the Gospel's contents are the very life and words of Jesus Christ. His teachings are not ultimately meant for factual knowledge but to present the lofty standard to which every person should aspire. The lives and writings of the saints are another helpful source for meditation since they are experts on what it means to love as Christ loved. Though any venue can be compatible with meditation, nothing better serves the purpose of penetrating the Word of God than praying before the Blessed Sacrament in Eucharistic Adoration, which was presented in Chapter 14.

"*Contemplative prayer* is the simplest expression of the mystery of prayer.... Contemplation is a gaze of faith, fixed on Jesus."[73] St. Teresa of Avila described contemplation as "nothing else than a close sharing between friends."[74] It is the loving dialogue in which we sit in conversation with God or even simply sit in silence with our hearts focused on God. The pursuit of God through prayer entails sharing with Christ the joys that lift the spirit and the sorrows that weigh on the heart. The theme of the personal life is a most appropriate subject for dialogue with God. God, who loves each of his children infinitely, desires that they unburden their souls in the hope of being strengthened and assisted. Contemplation is an

73. CCC 2713, 2715; emphasis ours.

74. "The Book of Her Life," in ThAv, Book VIII, no.5, 67.

expression of prayer that can even leave words behind; St. John Vianney summarized his contemplative life with the following words: "I look at God and God looks at me."[75]

Contemplative prayer brings about a greater focus on Jesus Christ. Through God the Son a person encounters the Father and the Holy Spirit. Through an ongoing habit of contemplation, the heart and mind are totally aware of God's goodness and love. Through this intense presence of God, a person offers many acts of love and abandonment to God, our loving Father. This expression of prayer makes a Christian, little by little, more and more like Christ.

The medium for contemplative prayer involves both external and especially interior silence. Through interior silence, deeper prayer is possible. Dedicating time to converse with God is indispensable for both discernment and identification of the will of Our Lord. The Gospels reveal Jesus was often immersed in deep silence as he intensely and lovingly presented his joys, sorrows, and concerns to his Father. Given the omnipresent availability of audio and visual entertainment and the general presence of noise, it is absolutely crucial to find times and places of silence to converse with God.

Contemplative prayer requires commitment. It can analogously be compared to maintaining a human friendship: No person would want to maintain a close relationship with another by only visiting each other and conversing when they both have some free time or nothing else to do. Close friends, rather, make time to be with each other so their relationship can remain close. Contemplation builds a relationship with God in the same way. It increases intimate communion with God, making it easier to understand and follow his will. It is important to remember prayer is both God's initiative *and* his gift; contemplation is a gift of the Holy Spirit in response to fidelity and poverty of spirit, not simply the fruit of human effort.

Remembering that the fruits of prayer are a gift from God can protect a person from having wrong expectations of prayer. Many people have gone astray by assuming that contemplative prayer would have dramatic results or by expecting mystical experiences. Expecting immediate, dramatic results from prayer is a bit like expecting to lose twenty pounds overnight after walking on a treadmill once. A life of prayer is like a healthy physical lifestyle, which

75. Rev. Msgr. Francis Trochu, *The Cure d'Ars: A Shorter Biography* (Westminster, MD: Newman Press, 1955), 63.

requires maintenance and patience—particularly for a person who is out of spiritual shape!

Expecting mystical experiences can also lead a person quickly down the wrong path because it stems from vanity rather than the humility necessary for authentic prayer. The Church always urges caution and even skepticism toward claims of mystical experiences because these can have a multitude of causes, not the least of which is normal human imagination. (If a person starts to experience extraordinary things in prayer, he or she should speak with a priest or another experienced spiritual director.) A person who is growing in virtue will have a life marked by greater charity, and this assures him or her that prayer is fruitful.

It bears repeating that the Holy Spirit inspires all prayer within the deep recesses of the human heart. In fact, the *Catechism* recommends that we invoke the Holy Spirit at the beginning and end of every occupation. It also recommends "the simplest and most direct prayer . . . 'Come, Holy Spirit.'"[76]

Privileged Prayers

Since prayer is a personal dialogue with God, there are as many prayers as there are people. Analogously, in any family each child has his or her own unique relationship with the parents; the same is true with our heavenly Father. Also like in any family, there are traditions and practices that unite us. In the Church certain prayers have a privileged position in the spiritual life.

The most important prayer is the Eucharistic Liturgy—the Divine Liturgy, the Mass—"the source and summit of Christian life."[77] Liturgical prayer, without excluding any other prayer, should take priority. The Church's public worship of God in her liturgical celebrations has been forged by Sacred Scripture together with Sacred Tradition; therefore, the Holy Spirit is the inspiring, directing force behind every liturgy. As presented in Chapter 14, Christ himself offers the perfect act of praise, thanksgiving, petition, and atonement in the Holy Sacrifice of the Mass.

The Mass includes all three expressions of prayer: It is the preeminent vocal and communal prayer and an opportunity to meditate

76. CCC 2671.

77. LG, no. 11; quoted in CCC 1324.

on Sacred Scripture, the beautiful liturgical prayers, and the homily. There are also many moments of silence within the Mass for quiet contemplation, including that most intimate time after having received Holy Communion. The celebration of the Eucharist involves the whole person in mind, heart, spirit, and all bodily senses. There is music, sacred art, incense, singing, and the ringing of bells. There are different physical gestures and positions associated with the various parts of the Mass. The yearly cycle of the liturgical calendar, from the Birth of Christ at Christmas to his Resurrection at Easter, grounds us in Christ's life and the lives of his saints. There is simply no aspect of prayer that is not most perfectly expressed in the Holy Mass.

Another privileged prayer is the Liturgy of the Hours, built primarily around the Psalms. It is the official prayer of the Church. This practice of reading Scripture and the Fathers of the Church is a kind of "punctuation with prayer" seven times throughout each day. This prayer is for everyone, and it is so important that it is required of everyone in Holy Orders and almost everyone in religious life.

> It is of great advantage for the family, the domestic sanctuary of the Church... to celebrate some parts of the liturgy of the hours as occasion offers, in order to enter more deeply into the life of the Church.[78]

Another privileged prayer in the Church is the Holy Rosary. The Rosary is perhaps the single most customary prayer for both private and family prayer; it is so ubiquitous that rosary beads are often used as shorthand in movies, photographs, and other visual media to identify a person as Catholic. Like the *Lord's Prayer* (*Our Father*), both saints and Popes have written on the depth and benefits of this beautiful prayer to our Mother, the Blessed Virgin Mary. The Rosary includes both vocal prayer and meditation: the Church's most common vocal prayers—the *Profession of Faith* (Creed), the *Lord's Prayer*, the *Hail Mary*, and the *Glory Be*—are paired with meditations on the lives of Jesus and Mary. Spurred on by the spiritual tradition of the Church and private apparitions, the Rosary is a favorite prayer of Our Lady. History has given overwhelming testimony of the marvelous power of the Rosary: growth in personal

78. "General Instruction of the Liturgy of the Hours," no. 27, in International Commission on English in the Liturgy, *Liturgy of the Hours* (New York: Catholic Book Publishing Co., 1975), 36; cf. Second Ecumenical Council of the Vatican, Decree on the Apostolate of the Laity *Apostolicam Actuositatem* (November 18, 1965), no. 11.

holiness, revitalization of the life of the Church, and influence on world events.

Yet another privileged prayer is praying "in the name of Jesus." Most Catholic prayers begin "*In the name of* the Father, and of the Son, and of the Holy Spirit,"[79] but in addressing God there is also a special power in invoking the human name of Jesus; a very simple, effective way of praying is to speak to Jesus using his name. St. Paul reveals why:

> God has ... bestowed on him the name which is above every name, that at the name of Jesus every knee should bow, in heaven and on earth and under the earth, and every tongue confess that Jesus Christ is Lord, to the glory of God the Father.[80]

The name of Jesus subsumes God's total plan and work of salvation. The name of Jesus is so grace-filled that anyone who sincerely and lovingly invokes his name begins to be transformed into the very life of Christ. The influence of the Holy Spirit makes every respectful utterance of the name of Jesus so special. Without the intervention of the Holy Spirit, it is impossible to prayerfully invoke Jesus' name.[81] Given the power of his name, every disciple of Christ should pray to the Holy Spirit for the gift of prayer.

Challenges to Prayer

It is important to make time for meditation and contemplative prayer regardless of health or time constraints. Everyone committed to spending time in prayer must understand that meditation and contemplative prayer usually entail a struggle to persevere during times of spiritual tedium and dryness.

Although those in the consecrated life and in Holy Orders may be called to set aside a longer period of time for prayer than, say, a married person, this does not mean prayer requires total withdrawal from the world. All the baptized are called to be people of prayer; the workplace, school, the home, and public places can be ideal settings for prayer of various kinds. It is no accident that the greatest models of the Christian life—Jesus Christ, the Blessed Virgin Mary, and St. Joseph—maintained their common and personal lives of prayer for decades in an ordinary life of that time period.

79. RMiss, The Order of Mass, no. 1; emphasis ours.

80. Phil 2:9–11.

81. Cf. 1 Cor 12:3.

The everyday life of the Holy Family is a powerful witness to that typical effort to work, raise a family, and serve the needs of others. Being a laborer, a mother, a son, or just an "ordinary" person does not lower God's expectations for a robust prayer life. The members of the Holy Family are the greatest contemplatives of the spiritual life whose lives were marked by manual labor, the demands of family, and social life. Our Lord, together with his Mother and father, in addition to giving priority to generous amounts of time devoted to prayer, show that work itself can take the form of prayer when lovingly offered to God. Indeed, every aspect of our lives should be converted into an avenue of prayer.

It is always helpful to bear in mind that contemplative prayer requires the grace of the Holy Spirit; nevertheless, good will and personal effort is absolutely necessary to respond to God's invitation to a deeper relationship. Anybody who desires to spend time in prayer can easily be bombarded with temptations to cease praying. One common temptation is the false belief that there simply "isn't enough time" amid a hectic schedule. In many modern societies too much emphasis is placed on activities, and spending time in silence comes across as poor time management. The human tendency toward physical comfort strongly militates against the spirit of prayer since prayer usually does not result in emotional gratification or immediate consolation. Others say that their prayers are never answered, and their personal experience of sinfulness can lead to a disbelief in the power of prayer. A humble heart that neither places conditions on God nor second guesses him comprises one of the key foundations of prayer.

Another typical temptation is expressed in the oft-heard, "I get nothing out of it." For people who view success as results-oriented conditions, prayer can seem very unproductive since there are rarely noticeably, instant, tangible results; it is easy to erroneously think that the time devoted to prayer could be used "more productively." Patient, persevering prayer allows the grace of the Holy Spirit to transform a person into the light and life of Christ. When evaluating results, it is necessary to remember that the ultimate goal of prayer is to grow closer to God through knowing and doing his will. These results cannot be measured in whether a person's material desires are fulfilled but by his or her growth in charity.

Distractions are not an obstacle to prayer for a person who cooperates with God's grace and genuinely struggles to grow in his or her relationship with Jesus. In many instances, though, distractions reveal attachments to created things, inordinate fears, and worries about the future. A stream of distractions in the form of fears and worries that compete with attention to Our Lord can be an indication of a lack of faith. Becoming aware of these worries is an opportunity for such a person to abandon him- or herself into the loving arms of divine providence. Such an effort to rely on Our Lord's unfailing help amid the experience of anxiety and turmoil purifies the spiritual life. To pray well a Christian needs to be convinced of Jesus' admonition: "Apart from me you can do nothing."[82] In the last analysis, every person must hold on to Christ and stay committed to a generous prayer life despite feeling distant from and empty of spiritual sentiment.

Although every saint went through periods of painful dryness and tedium in his or her spiritual life, this experience can also be a warning sign of being lukewarm or in the state of sin. (If a person experiences a period of dryness in prayer, he or she should speak with a priest or another experienced spiritual director.) A selfish attitude of entitlement, an angry disposition, or greed for material gain can totally frustrate the effort to pray. Habitual sins of lust also make any kind of contemplative prayer virtually impossible. Since prayer is a lifting of the heart and mind to God, selfishness robs a person of the freedom to give his or her heart to God in prayer. To have the freedom to converse with God, there must be sincere repentance and a conversion of heart. Frequent recourse to the Sacrament of Penance and Reconciliation can be a great aid to prayer.

Many challenges to prayer come not from any deep-seated theological problem but spiritual laziness. Lack of effort and determination to make prayer a priority will, without a doubt, relegate the spiritual life to the realm of good desires without concrete deeds. Spiritual laziness takes the form of cutting corners in the time devoted to prayer coupled with habitual tardiness in our commitment to a set time. Daydreaming and drifting thoughts can also reveal a lack of interest and seriousness; interior listlessness presents a real barrier to the grace of the Holy Spirit. Good prayer involves a general fidelity to the time allotted for prayer and punctuality to the time

82. Jn 15:5.

established for this rendezvous with Jesus. Prayer requires vigilance and alertness in giving the mind and heart to Christ.

Finally, there is a certain discouragement at times when petitions are seemingly not heard. It is important to bear in mind that God is neither a means to an end nor a divine magic wand, doling out favors on personal whims. The goal of prayer is to give glory to God and grow in personal holiness. All petitions ultimately focus on holiness and the grace to fulfill God's will more readily. Our Lord invites everybody to trust and to certainly believe that prayer of petition will always lead to the best possible outcome, though it may not make immediate sense. Those holy men and women who have persevered and given priority to their prayer life eventually see the inestimable value of prayer as they transmit the peace and joy of Jesus Christ to others.

A person new to prayer should not worry, though, or overburden him- or herself at the start with too much. To again compare prayer with physical exercise, everyone must start with a plan that is prudent for his or her current condition. The commitment to pray can begin with as little as three *Hail Marys* before going to bed. If done faithfully and with the right spirit, the Holy Spirit will animate the heart and lead to a rich, robust life of prayer.

Prayer cannot take second place to the rest of our duties. To harness the spiritual energy of charity, prayer is absolutely crucial. Prayer serves as the meeting point between the human person and God the Father, who fully reveals himself in God the Son. The immediate objective of every Christian is to be totally one with Jesus through prayer and become salt, light, and leaven to the fallen world. To paraphrase the teachings of St. Josemaria Escriva, for the New Evangelization of society pining for Christ, prayer must certainly take the pride of place.[83]

83. Cf. St. Josemaria Escriva, *Conversations with Saint Josemaria Escriva* (New York: Scepter Publishers, 2003), no. 114.

Chapter 21
Conclusion

Importance of Faith

At the heart of Divine Revelation is God's self-communication of his love for all people. This love, fully revealed in Christ, demands a response. It invites the faithful to the obedience of faith, which involves freely accepting and submitting to the Word of God along with its implementation in every person's life.

The Blessed Virgin Mary is the perfect model of faith since she accepted and submitted to the words of the Archangel Gabriel, who announced that she would be the Mother of Jesus Christ.[1] Her act of faith was especially impressive because she adhered to God's will even as she witnessed her divine Son's suffering and Death on the Cross. Mary's acceptance of her vocation from God required a faith beyond the realm of natural reason. To accept the remarkable news that she would conceive a child, a child who "will be called the Son of the Most High,"[2] was not a natural conclusion based on a study of empirical evidence; it required supernatural faith.

Supernatural faith is based on the authority of God, who is infinite truth and, therefore, can never be wrong let alone be misleading. The response of *supernatural* faith goes beyond a *natural* faith that a person might have in the authority of another human person. This kind of natural faith relies on reason, giving credence to the reliability of a person's knowledge, understanding facts through the intellect. Assent to truths transmitted through Divine Revelation, however, requires not only the natural light of reason but also the supernatural light of faith.

Supernatural faith is both a gift and an infused virtue, affecting the mind and the will. This virtue presupposes the grace to enlighten the mind and move the heart to accept truths on the authority of God himself. Many of these truths go beyond the capacity of the human intellect. Without supernatural faith it is impossible to believe

1. Cf. Lk 1:26–38.
2. Lk 1:32.

that Jesus Christ is fully God and fully man in one divine Person; in addition, the human mind on its own could never accept the fact that Jesus Christ is present in the Eucharist under the appearance of bread and wine.

Supernatural faith is built on a growing relationship and friendship with Jesus. When Jesus revealed that eternal life would come to those who would eat his Body and drink his Blood, "many of his disciples drew back"[3] and stopped following him, saying, "This is a hard saying."[4] St. Peter, who by then was one of the closest disciples of Jesus, was just as mystified, but he had already reached the conclusion that only Jesus could provide the answer to the questions of human life. "Lord, to whom shall we go? You have the words of eternal life."[5]

It is important to note that faith is not blind knowledge, leaving reason no role to play. First, much of what God has revealed is discoverable by human reason, but because of sin the truth only becomes clearly apparent once revealed. Other aspects of Revelation are beyond human reason; these include God's inner nature and his radical love for humanity revealed in Christ. Nevertheless, there are motives of credibility regarding the entire body of revealed truth. Once revealed, the precepts are *reasonable*. And then, besides its own inner unity and rationale, one of the greatest witnesses to the truth of Revelation is the lives of those who believe it. The holiness of faithful Christians throughout the ages is a wonderful testimony to the power of the truths revealed by God. To the degree that a person abides by divine standards of morality and the mandates of charity, the beauty and magnificence of the human person emerges in any society or era. The power of Divine Revelation shines bright in some contemporary saints like Sts. Teresa of Calcutta (lovingly called Mother Teresa), John Paul II, and Josemaria Escriva. Countless people have discovered that living according to the teachings of Christ and his Church has brought greater freedom, stability, and joy.

Not to be confused with an emotion or following your "gut," the heart—that is, as presented in Chapter 1, the innermost part of the human person—can also be a way of knowing that which surpasses reason. As the Enlightenment mathematician, philosopher,

---

3. Jn 6:66.
4. Jn 6:59.
5. Jn 6:68.

and theologian Blaise Pascal once famously wrote: "The heart has reasons which reason knows not of."[6] Faith in something—someone, anything—does not usually require a fully reasoned out logic; a person simply "knows." Such instincts of faith cannot *contradict* what is reasonable, but the love of God demonstrated by the saints comes from the heart and not from a study of theological teachings. It is based on a real encounter with and experience of God.

To describe faith this way does not mean it is completely separate from reason. Though faith surpasses the power of reason, there can never be a contradiction between faith and science for the simple reason that all truth is derived from God, its source. If there appears to be a conflict between the contents of Divine Revelation and the conclusions of empirical science, there must be some flaw in the logical steps leading to that result. Sometimes it is a flaw in the scientific reasoning or how a person understands a scientific concept; other times, it is a misunderstanding of what the Church actually teaches.

Faith is a gift. Like any gift, it can be spurned and rejected or freely embraced. Without faith people cannot achieve their full happiness or potential in this life because they will never understand the God that made them or the plans he has for them. More importantly, after this life without faith a person cannot achieve salvation in the next life for the simple reason that what he or she does not know, at least implicitly, cannot be pursued. Faith is a gift that must be cultivated with perseverance and with the intention of living it. As faith is practiced, it grows and spreads to others. This well-known self-Revelation of Jesus summarizes the importance of faith: "I am the way, and the truth, and the life."[7]

Sparking an Interest

If this book has sparked at least a bit more of an intellectual interest in the Church's interpretation of Jesus' doctrinal and moral teaching, then I will have accomplished my first objective. I hope you will consult the *Catechism of the Catholic Church* as a tool in cultivating a greater desire to follow Christ and to seek happiness through holiness and relationship with God. The tenets of the Catholic faith

---

6. Blaise Pascal; quoted in Fred Kofman, *Emotions: Understanding the Basics* (Granica: Axialent Integral Evolution, 2001), ch. 21.

7. Jn 14:6.

are not simply meant to be learned like an academic discipline; rather, the elaboration of these truths is designed to help us deepen our friendship with Christ. I hope this introductory presentation of the contents of the Church's teachings provide a glimmer into the magnificent riches that can be discovered in the heart of Jesus. I hope this book has fostered a desire to follow Christ more closely, to love your neighbor more deeply, and to seek communion with Christ through the Sacraments of the Church.

In the words of Our Lord, though, a person should not light a lamp only to put it under a bushel basket![8] A lamp is put on a stand so it can light the whole house. "Let your light so shine before men."[9] One of the major obstacles to discipleship and the subsequent experience of Christian fulfillment is ignorance of Christ and his teachings and, in many instances, the acceptance of a misrepresentation or even a ridiculous caricature of the Church's moral teaching. In the wake of 2000 years of Church history, the Gospel of Christ continues to be "a sign that is spoken against."[10]

Many of the Church's moral teachings are all too often presented as hostile to the well-being of the human person. The lifelong quality of marriage that is between only two people is being relegated as just one more option for an intimate relationship. The lives of unborn children are being lost out of a misguided sense of a woman's reproductive rights. Majorities even in previously Christian regions of the world do not know the truths of Christ's Incarnation and redemption, and among those who do know, many dismiss them as totally irrelevant to everyday life.

At the same time there is a prevailing disillusionment and sadness, especially among adolescents and younger adults, about the meaning of human life, which is having tragic and even deadly consequences. It is urgent that Catholics explain, in a convincing way, the Church's defense of the value of human life and related moral issues amid a prevailing moral relativism. Given his or her close contact with people through work, family, and social life, the modern lay Christian is called on to present the teachings of the Church in a plausible way. Every one of Christ's disciples should use his or her

---

8. Cf. Mt 5:15; Mk 4:21–22.
9. Mt 5:16.
10. Lk 2:34.

abundant and varied relationships to resolve the doubts and biases peculiar to this era and society.

In the face of moral relativism, doctrinal ignorance, and religious indifference, the modern disciple of Christ can be tempted toward discouragement and disillusionment. Yet we live with great hope! These difficulties should inspire everyone to rise to the occasion to become a true modern apostle. The Gospel message did not come with the qualification that the moral and spiritual aberrations afflicting societies could stymie the advance of the kingdom. The more a person grows in true holiness and trust in Our Lord, more and more obstacles can be overcome, as Jesus revealed, "With men this is impossible, but with God all things are possible."[11] History has verified—through the faithfulness of the Church to her Founder's teachings as well as through the lives of countless holy men and women—that living and teaching the truth of Jesus Christ knows no definitive defeat. The heart of Christ is everyone's love language.

For this reason, Jesus unveiled his New Commandment of Love—"that you love one another; even as I have loved you"[12]—to teach what he has taught. As recent Popes have especially emphasized, to reveal him we must first "*see and contemplate* the real face of Christ crucified out of love for everyone."[13] If we then reflect that face of Christ into the world through joy, peace, and patience, Christ will be victorious in his disciples. These seemingly insurmountable roadblocks are a wonderful reminder of these consoling words first articulated by St. John the Apostle: "Who is it that overcomes the world but he who believes that Jesus is the Son of God?"[14]

In this sense the clock has been turned back to the first centuries of the Church's history, when the lion's share of evangelization was in the hands of lay Christians. Early Christians did not wait for people to come to church, especially when there were no physical church buildings, and in some places simply being Catholic was a capital offense. Christ's disciples of that era proactively brought the church to their family and friends because they wanted to share the Good News they had found in Christ. In fact, a process like RCIA[15]

11. Mt 19:26.

12. Jn 13:34.

13. Pope Francis, *Homily* (February 14, 2018).

14. 1 Jn 5:5.

15. Rite of Christian Initiation for Adults, a process of Christian formation for people interested in coming into full communion with the Catholic Church.

began then to equip new Christians with the tools to grow in holiness and the essential doctrinal knowledge to speak about Christ, his Sacraments, and the joyful affirmation of Christian morality. Dear reader, let us pray that we see our faith in the same spirit of those early disciples of Jesus Christ.

I will share with the reader this personal incident that I hope will illustrate the urgency to make Jesus Christ the center of our lives in order to both witness his love and teach his truth. I was speaking with a non-Catholic friend about the similarities and differences between his beliefs and Catholic teachings. My friend was quite happy being a Pentecostal Christian; nevertheless, many of his beliefs reflected a certain acceptance of the Catholic faith. After discussing the faith and answering his questions, I asked if he ever considered becoming Catholic. He reacted by immediately asking why he should become Catholic if he was happily following Christ within his own denomination. I responded that the Catholic Church has very special resources like the Sacraments and the absolutely trustworthy guidance of the Catholic Church's teaching body. He then questioned what significant difference those Sacraments made in any Christian's life. I replied that it would strongly cultivate his personal relationship with Jesus Christ. The discussion ended with his response that it was the *first time* he ever heard a Catholic talk about a personal relationship with Jesus Christ. It is my firm dream that one day Catholics *will be known* for their friendship with Jesus, bolstered by both a habitual meditation on Scripture and a robust sacramental life.

May each of us go out to share the Good News of what this friendship has given us, declaring with St. John Paul II:

> *Humanity is loved by God!* This very simple yet profound proclamation is owed to humanity by the Church. Each Christian's words and life must make this proclamation resound: God loves you, Christ came for you, Christ is for you "the Way, the Truth and the Life!"[16]

Rev. Peter V. Armenio, PhD

16. St. John Paul II, Apostolic Exhortation on the Vocation and the Mission of the Lay Faithful in the Church and the World *Christifideles Laici* (December 30, 1988), no. 34; quoting Jn 14:6.

Suggested Reading

Catechism of the Catholic Church:
This book is an instrument for communion and a norm for teaching the faith.

Pope St. John XXIII, Encyclical Letter *Mater et Magistra* (1961):
This papal encyclical is about Christianity and social progress; the title, referring to the Church, means "Mother and Teacher." It explores the call of all Christians to work toward authentic community to promote human dignity, teaching that the State must sometimes intervene in matters of health care, education, and housing.

Pope St. Paul VI, Encyclical Letter *Humanæ Vitæ* (1968):
This papal encyclical is about the regulation of birth, reaffirming the constant teaching of the Church about married love, responsible parenthood, and the rejection of artificial birth control.

Pope St. John Paul II, Apostolic Exhortation *Familiaris Consortio* (1981):
This papal exhortation is about the role of the Christian family in the modern world, and it outlines challenges to realizing that ideal.

Pope St. John Paul II, Encyclical Letter *Veritatis Splendor* (1993):
This papal encyclical is about some fundamental questions of the Church's moral teaching. It is one of the most comprehensive and philosophical works of moral theology.

Pope St. John Paul II, Encyclical Letter *Fides et Ratio* (1998):
This papal encyclical is about the relationship between faith and reason. It posits that faith and reason are not only compatible but also essential to each other.

Pope Benedict XVI, Encyclical Letter *Deus Caritas Est* (2005):
This papal encyclical is about Christian love. It treats love from a Christian perspective, focusing on God's place within all love and charity as one of the three theological virtues.

Pope Benedict XVI, Apostolic Exhortation *Verbum Domini* (2010):
This papal exhortation is about the Word of God in the life and mission of the Church. Using the Prologue of St. John's Gospel (Jn 1:1–18) as a guide, it presents God as seeking dialogue with human beings.

Pope Francis, Apostolic Exhortation *Evangelii Gaudium* (2013):
This papal exhortation is about the proclamation of the Gospel in today's world. It covers the Christian obligation to the poor and to establish and maintain just economic, political, and legal orders.

Pope Francis, Encyclical Letter *Laudato Si'* (2015):
This papal encyclical is about care for our common home. It critiques consumerism and irresponsible development, laments environmental degradation, and calls on all people to take action.

Pope Francis, Apostolic Exhortation *Amoris Lætitia* (2016):
This papal exhortation is about love in the family. It explores the contemporary challenges faced by families throughout the world,

encouraging both pastors and lay Christians to accompany and care for families and others in situations of particular need.

Pope Francis, Encyclical Letter *Fratelli Tutti* (2020):

This papal encyclical is about fraternity and social friendship. It calls for greater human solidarity and is a plea to reject war.

Documents of the Second Vatican Council (1962–1965):

—The Constitution on the Sacred Liturgy *Sacrosanctum Concilium* revised worship so that the faithful can have a clearer sense of their involvement in the Mass and other rites.

—The Decree on the Instruments of Social Communication *Inter Mirifica* calls on the faithful to give "a human and Christian spirit" to newspapers, books, movies, and other media.

—The Dogmatic Constitution on the Church *Lumen Gentium* presents the Church as a mystery, a communion of baptized believers, the People of God, the Body of Christ, and a pilgrim.

—The Decree on Ecumenism *Unitatis Redintegratio* calls all Christians to ecumenism, explaining that genuine ecumenism involves continual personal and institutional renewal.

—The Decree on Eastern Catholic Churches *Orientalium Ecclesiarum* teaches that variety within the Church does not harm her unity, calling on Eastern Catholic churches to retain their own traditions.

—The Decree on the Bishops' Pastoral Office in the Church *Christus Dominus* teaches that every bishop is expected to present Christian doctrine in modern ways, especially by exercising pastoral care jointly.

—The Decree on Priestly Formation *Optatam Totius* recommends that seminaries prepare men according to the spiritual, intellectual, and disciplinary formation necessary to become good pastors.

—The Decree on the Appropriate Renewal of the Religious Life *Perfectæ Caritatis* guides the personal and institutional renewal of people in religious life.

—The Declaration on the Relationship of the Church to Non-Christian Religions *Nostra Ætate* affirms that the Catholic Church rejects nothing that is true and holy in other religions.

—The Declaration on Christian Education *Gravissimum Educationis* affirms the right of parents to choose the type of education they want for their children, upholding the importance of Catholic schools.

—The Dogmatic Constitution on Divine Revelation *Dei Verbum* teaches that the Church depends on Scripture and Tradition as the single deposit of God's Word, commending modern Scripture scholarship.

—The Decree on the Apostolate of the Laity *Apostolicam Actuositatem* taught that lay Christians should influence their surroundings.

—The Declaration on Religious Freedom *Dignitatis Humanæ* taught that religious liberty is a right based on the dignity of every person.

—The Decree on the Ministry and Life of Priests *Presbyterorum Ordinis* taught that the primary duty of priests is to proclaim the Gospel.

—The Decree on the Church's Missionary Activity *Ad Gentes* taught that missionary activity should help the social and economic welfare of people rather than force anyone to accept the faith.

—The Pastoral Constitution on the Church in the Modern World *Gaudium et Spes* taught that the Church must talk to atheists, be oriented to peace, and aid underdeveloped nations; it also reaffirmed that marriage is not only for procreation.

THEMATIC INDEX

THE MYSTERIES OF THE ROSARY

Joyful Mysteries
- The Annunciation, 21, 415, 425
- The Visitation, 425
- The Nativity (Birth of Jesus), xiv, 11, 88, 90–91, 203, 279, 431
- The Presentation, 91–92
- The Finding of Jesus in the Temple, 92

Luminous Mysteries
- The Baptism of Christ in the Jordan, 94–95, 130, 223
- The Manifestation of Christ at the Wedding of Cana, 259–260, 276, 334, 415
- The Proclamation of the Kingdom of God, with His Call to Conversion, 97–98, 129
- The Transfiguration, 98, 102, 110, 130
- The Institution of the Eucharist, 107, 109, 205–206, 259, 261, 265, 389–390

Sorrowful Mysteries
- The Agony in the Garden, 109–110, 116
- The Scourging at the Pillar, 114
- The Crowning with Thorns, 114–115
- The Carrying of the Cross, 115–116
- The Crucifixion, 108, 113, 115–116, 118, 122, 134, 178, 261, 314, 336, 441

Glorious Mysteries
- The Resurrection, xv, 8, 29–30, 47–48, 95, 98, 103, 105, 113, 119, 121–127, 129, 131, 203, 205, 214, 219, 225, 228, 255, 257–258, 261, 265, 277, 280, 294, 304, 308, 310, 389–390, 411, 423, 431
- The Ascension, xv, 8, 48, 95, 127–128, 131, 133–134, 214, 224, 265, 279
- The Descent of the Holy Spirit, 128, 131, 134, 139, 242
- The Assumption, 278–279
- The Coronation of the Blessed Virgin Mary

The Seven Sacraments

Baptism, 26, 31, 79, 82, 105, 109, 121, 126, 135, 138, 142, 148–149, 153, 155, 205–206, 208–215, 217, 219–238, 242–246, 250, 254, 257, 269–270, 274, 285–286, 306, 315, 338, 356, 391, 395, 402–403, 410–411, 420

Confirmation, 79, 205, 208, 210–215, 224, 228, 239–251, 254, 257, 285–286, 356, 391, 402–403

The Eucharist, x, xii, 12, 29–30, 80, 106–109, 124, 129, 142, 145, 147, 153, 155, 205–206, 208–209, 212–213, 217, 222, 224, 229, 242, 244–245, 253–285, 294, 297, 312, 344, 347, 351, 354, 356, 358, 359, 361, 366, 385, 388, 389–390, 392, 393, 395, 401, 404, 407, 425, 428, 431, 438

Penance and Reconciliation, xii, 30, 79, 81, 126, 155, 205, 209–210, 212–213, 233, 245, 270, 280, 285–306, 315, 323, 325, 345, 351, 354, 356, 359, 361, 385, 392, 400–401, 434

The Anointing of the Sick, 205, 212–213, 228, 231, 286, 307–325

Matrimony, 205, 209, 212–213, 327–385, 387, 397–398, 400, 402, 407

Holy Orders, 144, 146, 201, 205, 212–215, 228, 294, 327, 353, 387–408, 431–432

The Ten Commandments

1. I am the Lord your God:
you shall not have strange gods before me, 15, 27, 33, 56
2. You shall not take the name of the Lord your God in vain, 17–18, 56
3. Remember to keep holy the Lord's Day, 29, 56, 256, 257, 277, 282
4. Honor your father and your mother, 56, 163–164, 167, 331, 365–366, 368, 371–372
5. You shall not kill, 56, 159, 167–168, 170–171, 173–176, 182, 184–185, 187
6. You shall not commit adultery, 56–57, 331–332, 349, 374
7. You shall not steal, 56, 159, 192, 197
8. You shall not bear false witness against your neighbor, 56, 71, 158, 187–190
9. You shall not covet your neighbor's wife, 56, 182, 332, 339, 341, 348, 365, 368, 372
10. You shall not covet your neighbor's goods, 56, 159, 197

Saints in This Book

Alphonsus Liguori, 283–284
Ambrose, 187, 297
Augustine, 3, 10, 49, 85, 232–234, 236, 266, 274, 407, 419, 424
Carlo Acutis (Blessed), xvii, 276
Catherine of Siena, 129, 395
Cyril of Alexandria, 100, 422
Elizabeth, 93–94, 425
Faustina Kowalska, 83, 287, 321
Francis of Assisi, 247, 324
Giuseppe Moscati, xvii, 148
Gregory of Nazianzus, 220
Ignatius of Antioch, 30
James, 98, 123
Jerome, xiv
John (Apostle and Evangelist), 30, 33, 98, 246, 258, 441
John XXIII, 162, 166
John Bosco, 407
John of Damascus, 409
John Paul II, xvii, 41, 63, 68, 104, 154, 156, 167, 186, 200, 229, 267–268, 284, 290, 345–346, 367, 379, 401, 407, 438, 442
John the Baptist, 49, 93–94, 121, 130, 223–224, 260, 288, 366
John Vianney, 401, 407, 429
Josemaria Escriva, xvii, 129, 158, 229, 268, 435, 438
Joseph, 88–93, 117, 121, 267, 279, 314, 318, 334, 367, 411, 432
Justin Martyr, 262
Maria Goretti, xvii, 136–138, 425
Mary, Blessed Virgin, 21, 29, 45, 47, 87–88, 90–94, 100, 117, 130, 134, 155–156, 212, 235, 267, 270, 277–279, 310, 324, 334, 344, 366–367, 393, 395, 411, 415, 425–429, 431–432, 437
Mary Magdalene, 123–124
Matthew, 288
Maximilian Kolbe, 136, 138
Monica, 424
Nicolas Steno (Blessed), 253
Paul (Apostle), 150, 242, 279
Paul VI, 196, 317, 382
Peter, 29, 82–83, 98, 123, 126–127, 134, 141, 145–146, 152, 242, 246, 260, 279, 289, 438
Pius of Pietrelcina (Padre Pio), 407

Teresa of Avila, 25, 324, 395, 416, 426, 428
Teresa of Calcutta (Mother Teresa), 276, 438
Therese of Lisieux, 147, 395
Thomas (Apostle), 123
Thomas Aquinas, 2, 49, 54–55, 65, 70, 117, 160, 191–193, 267, 416
Thomas More, 250

TOPICAL INDEX

A

Abortion, 70, 74, 177, 179–182, 184, 235, 379, 383
Adoration. *See* Worship, of God
Adultery, 51, 56–58, 70, 76–77, 260, 290, 297, 329, 332–333, 335–336, 339, 342, 349–350, 374–375, 382, 394, 412
Ageism, 201
Alphonsus Liguori, St., 283–284
Ambrose, St., 187, 297
Angel, 21, 40, 46, 87–90, 96, 212, 221, 277, 287, 314, 323, 334, 395, 428
Annunciation, 21, 87–88, 93, 212, 395, 415, 437
Anointing
  Baptism, 225, 228–229, 231, 237, 243, 403
  Confirmation, 243, 246
  Holy Orders, 403
  of the Sick. *See* Anointing of the Sick
  Scripture and, 89, 91, 228–229
Anointing of the Sick (Sacrament)
  effects, 212–213, 286, 307, 309, 311, 321–323, 325
  matter and form, 212, 308
  ordinary minister, 308
  recipient, 213, 307–308
  rite, 308–309
  Scripture and, 307–308
Apostle, xiii, 8, 10–13, 97–98, 104, 106–108, 110, 117, 123–124, 126–129, 131–135, 141–142, 144, 152, 205–206, 240–241, 245–246, 259, 267, 275, 279, 294, 308, 336, 389–391, 393–396, 398–400, 402–404, 411, 414, 416. *See also* James; John; Matthew; Paul; Peter; Thomas
Apostolic (mark of the Church). *See* Church, Apostolic
Apostolic Teaching, 123. *See also* Tradition
Apostolic Succession, 399
Aristotle, xii, 2, 16, 53–54, 60, 66, 191
Artificial birth control, 171, 347, 377–383, 380, 383
Ascension. *See* Jesus, Ascension
Assisted suicide, 76, 177–179, 184, 383
Atheism, 5, 86, 191, 253
Augustine, St., 3, 10, 49, 85, 232–234, 236, 266, 274, 407, 419, 424

B

Baptism (Sacrament)
  anointing. *See* Anointing, Baptism
  effects, 26, 31, 79, 105, 109, 121, 135, 138, 142, 148, 205, 210–215, 219–220, 233–238, 246, 250, 254, 285, 315, 410–411, 420
  matter and form, 208, 395
  ordinary minister, 208, 402
  recipient, 31, 153, 209–210, 231–233
  rite, 217, 224–228
  Scripture and, 149, 219–224
  threefold mission, 391
Baptism of Christ by St. John. *See* John the Baptist
Beatitudes, 60–61, 80, 168, 199, 202, 300, 316, 341
Bishop / episcopate
  college of, xi, 140, 145, 400
  council of, 9, 100, 145
  fullness of Holy Orders, 145, 245, 399–400, 402–403
  ordination of, 145, 402–404

successor to the Apostles, 9–10, 12, 126, 141, 144, 152, 245, 399–400, 403
teaching Magisterium, 13, 146
Blasphemy, 17–18, 77, 111–113

C

Calumny. *See* Slander
Carlo Acutis, Bl., xvii, 276
Catechism of the Catholic Church, ix, xi–xvii
Catherine of Siena, St., 129, 395
Catholic (mark of the Church). *See* Church, Catholic
Catholic Church. *See* Church
Catholic social teaching, 158, 161–163, 175, 190, 201, 231, 365
Chastity, 135, 137, 146, 172, 240, 332, 337–350, 352–354, 359–360, 363, 365, 375, 377, 382
Christology. *See* Jesus Christ, natures
Church
Apostolic, 149, 152–153, 156
Bride of Christ, 150, 396–397
Catholic, 151–152
degrees of communion, 153–155
founded by Christ, 129, 139–144, 154
hierarchy, 140, 155–156, 206
Holy, 150–151
inspired by the Holy Spirit, 139
Mary as Mother of. *See* Mary, Mother of the Church
One, 149–150
Pentecost and, 139–140
sign of God's love, 143
Circumstances. *See* Moral deliberation
Cohabitation, 75, 327, 347, 359, 363
Commandments, Ten
natural law, 55, 59
perfected in Christ, 57, 186, 349
revealed to Moses, 7, 15, 55, 86, 107, 368
See "Thematic Index" (p. 446) for individual Commandments
Common good, 37, 70, 82, 143, 148, 157–202, 212, 282, 306, 325, 367
Communion
Church and. See Church, One
Holy. *See* Eucharist, reception
of Saints, 143, 286
Confession. *See* Penance and Reconciliation
Confirmation (Sacrament)
anointing. *See* Anointing, Confirmation
effects, 79, 211, 213–215, 241–243, 246–251
matter and form, 243–246
ordinary minister, 208, 245–246
recipient, 244
rite, 243–246
Scripture and, 240–241, 244, 246–247
Conscience, 3, 5–6, 73–74, 77–81, 114, 147, 154, 164–165, 296, 298, 305
examination of, 199, 300, 344
Contraception, 171, 347, 380, 383. *See also* Artificial birth control
Contrition, 81, 97, 270–272, 286–287, 289–290, 292–295, 297–303, 305, 316, 323, 410, 412, 422–423
Covenant
marriage, 212, 328–337, 346–347, 356–358, 361, 372, 374–375, 378
New, 57, 86, 99, 106–107, 113, 141, 219, 219, 221, 223, 261, 263, 265, 334, 347, 388–390, 395, 397
Old, 7, 15, 55, 85, 107, 112, 161, 221, 257, 259, 331, 335–336, 389, 395
Creation
fallen, 25, 35, 42–48
Genesis and, 35–42, 167, 329

new, 25, 29–30
ordered, 35–38
revelatory, 1–4, 6–7
subject to human dominion, 39, 42–43, 45

Crucifixion. *See* Jesus Christ, Crucifixion

Cyril of Alexandria, St., 100, 422

D

Deacon / diaconate, 208, 210, 214–215, 217, 227, 263, 275, 357–358, 361, 363, 392, 394, 396–397, 399, 401–404
in persona Christi servus, 394–395, 404

Demon, 46, 98, 102, 111, 320, 414

Devil, 43–44, 46–47, 95–98, 105, 124–125, 217, 220–221, 225, 236, 320, 322, 350, 421
worship of, 28

Diaconate. *See* Deacon

Divination, 27

Divorce, 332, 334–337, 347, 362, 374–377, 383, 394

E

Elizabeth, St., 93–94, 425

Environmentalism, 201

Episcopate. *See* Bishop

Eucharist (Sacrament)
Adoration, x, 12, 147, 267–268, 428
as Sacrifice, 107, 254–255, 257–259, 261–263, 265, 268, 271–273, 275, 277, 281, 347, 358, 388–389, 401, 403–404. *See also* Mass
effects, 117, 142, 212–213, 254, 273–276, 285, 395
institution. *See* Last Supper
matter and form, 208, 264
ordinary minister, 145, 269, 390, 403
perfect prayer, 30, 272
procession, 217, 253
Real Presence, x, xii, 12, 106, 155, 266–268, 268, 270, 273, 275, 283, 404, 438
reception, 28, 80, 94, 108–109, 137, 142, 253–254, 265, 268–271, 273–274, 276–277, 280, 283, 293–294, 297–298, 305, 344, 351, 354, 356, 358–359, 361, 385, 389, 401–402, 431
recipient, 153, 209, 269–270
rite, 262–266. *See also* Mass
Scripture and, 205, 222, 255–260. *See also* Last Supper
source and summit, 205, 255
See also Mass; Last Supper; Sunday

Euthanasia, 70, 76, 177–179, 184, 383

Evangelization, xvii, 20, 108, 152, 170, 239–244, 250, 272, 283, 284, 289, 392–393, 408, 414, 419, 435, 441

Examination of conscience. *See* Conscience, examination of

F

Faith
necessity, 31
reason and, 233, 439
supernatural, ix, 4, 31, 110, 127, 156, 178, 225, 240, 381, 414, 416, 437–438

Fall
alienation and, 44, 50–51, 85, 150
effects (consequences), xv, 6, 45–48, 52, 59, 81–82, 88, 95, 214, 235–236, 285, 310, 330–331, 333, 365
Genesis and, 42–47
Original Sin and, 44–45

Father
God, xv, 7–8, 12, 18–26, 58, 86, 88–91, 94, 96, 98–103, 106, 110–112, 117, 119–121, 126–133, 137, 140, 149, 161, 182, 204, 208, 214–215, 218, 221, 224, 226, 237, 249, 258, 260, 262, 271–273, 278, 293, 298–299, 313, 378, 387, 401, 403, 405–406, 409–411, 414–415, 417–418, 420, 422–423, 429, 432, 435
of the Church, xi, xiv, 12, 123, 140, 214–215, 298, 431
Faustina Kowalska, St., 83, 287, 321
Forgiveness
in Christ, 74, 81–83, 89, 106, 109, 112, 115, 118, 125–127, 141, 155, 180, 182, 219, 224, 287, 291, 293–296, 299, 302–304, 316, 323, 336, 413, 420–421, 423
need for, 33, 49, 94, 169, 217, 264, 288, 297, 418
See also Contrition; Penance and Reconciliation
Francis of Assisi, St., 247, 324
Freedom, 52

G

Gaudium et Spes, 160, 175, 184–186, 196–197, 328, 372, 373, 397
Gender identity, 171–172
Genocide, 63, 70, 177, 184, 184
Giuseppe Moscati, St., xvii, 148
Government
laws, 64, 66, 74, 144, 164–166, 184, 196
role, 163–166
Grace
abundant, 351
free gift, 211, 244
full of (Mary), 87–88, 130, 156, 212, 425
nature and, 144, 232
Gregory of Nazianzus, St., 220

H

Happiness
false notions, 46, 53, 61, 65, 169, 171, 198, 320, 339, 355
God and, ix–x, xii–xiii, xv–xvi, 26, 42, 46, 48, 52, 60–61, 74, 77, 80, 82, 90, 95, 103, 116, 132, 155, 199, 202, 213, 258, 291, 312–315, 319, 321, 372, 414, 418–419, 439
virtue and, 54, 60
Heaven, xv, 21, 36–37, 57, 60–61, 95, 98, 105, 113, 121–122, 125, 127–129, 134, 137, 143, 150, 168, 193, 199, 202, 213–214, 219, 229, 233, 235, 255–256, 258–261, 270, 276, 278–279, 309–310, 312–318, 323–325, 334, 403, 411, 418, 425, 432
Hell, Jesus' descent into, 122
Holy
Day, 30, 279–280
Family, 89–93, 367, 433
(mark of the Church). *See* Church, Holy
Orders. *See* Holy Orders
Spirit. *See* Holy Spirit
Souls. *See* Purgatory
Thursday. *See* Last Supper
Holy Orders (Sacrament)
anointing. *See* Anointing, Holy Orders
effects, 215, 294, 391, 399–402
fullness of. *See* Bishop, fullness of Holy Orders
recipient, 214, 393–398, 405
rite, 402–404
Scripture and. *See* Last Supper
three degrees, 398–402
See also Priesthood
Holy Spirit
Baptism in the name. *See* Baptism, matter and form
Confirmation and. *See* Anointing, Confirmation
fruits of, 135, 137
gifts of, 79, 132–133, 135, 137, 143, 237, 244–249, 251
in the Church, xi, xiii, 9–12
in the Trinity, 18–20, 129–138

inspiration of Scripture, 8–9
promised by Jesus, 21, 130
Homosexual, 177, 347, 352–354
Human Person
animals and, 53
dignity, x, xvii, 4, 39, 63
fallen. See Fall, effects
free, 40, 54
Image of God, 22, 38–41
male and female, 41–42
natural rights, 165–166, 179
rational, 2, 54–55
social, 22, 41–42

I

Idolatry, 5, 15–16, 28–29, 50, 58, 161, 163, 169, 259, 291, 297, 387
Ignatius of Antioch, St., 30
Image of God. *See* Human person, image of God
Incarnation, ix, xv, 8, 24, 64, 87–88, 99–100, 102–103, 118, 130–131, 161, 172, 185, 207, 230, 241, 268, 278, 288, 305, 312, 337, 385, 411, 417, 423, 426, 440
Indelible mark. *See* Sacramental Seal
In persona Christi. *See* Priesthood
Intention. *See* Moral deliberation
In vitro fertilization, 182–184, 382–383

J

James, St., 98, 123
Jerome, St., xiv
Jesus Christ
Ascension, xv, 8, 21, 48, 95, 127–128, 131, 133–135, 204, 214, 224, 265, 279
Birth (Nativity), xiv, 11, 88, 90–91, 203, 279, 431
Crucifixion, 108, 111–113, 115–116, 118, 120, 122, 134, 178, 261, 314, 336, 354, 428, 441
Death, xv, 8, 11, 21, 47–48, 92, 95–96, 98, 102, 105, 110–111, 115, 117–119, 121–124, 126, 129, 131–132, 134, 203, 205, 214, 219, 222, 224, 235, 239, 255, 259, 261–262, 271, 293, 314, 319–321, 336–337, 355, 437
divinity, ix, 13, 18, 20, 26, 87–100, 102–103, 106, 120–121, 125, 127, 203, 210, 253, 261, 265–266, 404, 411
humanity, 26, 87–88, 98–102, 120, 125, 203, 218, 293, 314, 411, 415, 417, 422–423
love. *See* Love, God
mercy, xii–xiii, 32, 55, 81, 83, 102, 126, 151, 169, 217, 237, 287, 293, 305, 312, 321, 393, 413, 420, 423–424, 427
Messiah, 11, 49, 53, 85, 87, 89, 91, 93, 95–96, 98, 113, 118–119, 122, 131, 141, 153, 224, 229, 257, 261, 288, 394, 418
miracles, 93, 97–98, 134, 203–204, 219, 223, 259, 267, 276, 287–288, 334, 411, 414
name. *See* Name, Jesus
natures, 100, 145
Passion, 8, 11, 21, 48, 92, 95–96, 98, 102–103, 105–106, 109–110, 116–119, 121–122, 124, 131–132, 172, 214, 222, 224, 255, 259, 261–262, 265, 271, 314, 320, 323, 337
prayer. *See* Prayer, Jesus
Resurrection, xv, 8, 29–30, 47–48, 95, 98, 103, 105, 113, 119, 121–127, 129, 131, 203, 205, 214, 216, 219, 225, 228, 255, 257–258, 261, 265, 277, 280, 294, 304, 308, 310, 389–390, 411, 423, 431

Son of God, xv, 8, 18, 20–21, 47–48, 58, 86–87, 89, 95–96, 113, 116, 130, 156, 161, 207–208, 224, 226, 239, 249, 293, 299, 334, 336, 366, 410, 415, 425, 432, 441

John (Apostle and Evangelist), St., 30, 33, 98, 246, 258, 441

John XXIII, St., 162, 166

John Bosco, St., 407

John of Damascus, 409

John Paul II, St., xvii, 41, 63, 68, 104, 154, 156, 167, 186, 200, 229, 267–268, 284, 290, 345–346, 367, 379, 401, 407, 438, 442

John the Baptist, St., 49, 93–94, 121, 130, 223–224, 260, 288, 366

John Vianney, St., 401, 407, 429

Josemaria Escriva, St., xvii, 129, 158, 229, 268, 435, 438

Joseph, St., 88–93, 117, 121, 267, 279, 314, 318, 334, 367, 411, 432

Joy, xii, xiv, 27, 31, 42, 77, 89–90, 94, 97, 103, 108, 119, 125, 135, 137, 204, 213–214, 228, 230, 239, 242–243, 249, 266, 273, 276, 284, 287, 289, 291, 293, 304, 314, 316, 319–320, 325, 338, 362, 373, 381, 384–385, 396, 404, 417, 419, 435, 438, 441

Judgment
- Last, 323–325
- Particular, 304, 309–321, 324

Just war, 70, 173–177

Justice, 3, 18, 27, 33, 43–45, 55, 59–60, 63–64, 85, 112, 118, 120, 161–162, 164, 166, 175–176, 186–188, 191, 193–198, 200, 202, 230–231, 248, 272, 303–304, 315, 374, 412. *See also* Social justice

Justin Martyr, St., 262

K

Kenosis, 116–117

L

Last Supper, 21, 105–109, 126, 131, 133, 135, 205, 258–259, 261–262, 265, 275, 388–390

Lay faithful, ix, xiv, xvi, 10, 147–148, 201–202, 229, 231, 263, 271, 283, 306, 391–392, 397, 407, 419, 440–441

Life
- culture of, 177–187, 194
- right to, 76, 167, 173, 177, 179, 184, 192–193, 240

Liturgy. *See* Eucharist

Lord's Prayer, 265, 416–418, 421, 426, 431

Love
- God's revealed by Christ, xv, 57–58, 102, 112, 120, 293
- human vocation, 353
- in marriage. *See* Marriage, sign of God's love
- Law of, 56–60, 66, 107, 109, 142, 144, 168, 172, 187, 196, 243

Lumen Gentium, 33, 59, 140, 145, 147, 153, 202, 205, 229, 230, 255, 391–392, 419, 430

Lust, 43–45, 57, 59, 86, 285, 291, 300, 305, 331–333, 342–344, 349–350, 434

M

Magic. *See* Occult

Maria Goretti, St., xvii, 136–138, 425

Marriage
- basic cell of society, 159
- between a man and a woman, 42, 44, 327, 328, 330, 333, 335, 341, 346–347, 352–355, 378, 387
- chastity within. *See* Chastity

covenant. *See* Covenant, marriage
faithful, 345, 362, 374
family and, 161, 329, 332, 334, 347, 365–385
image of Christ and his Church, 358, 398
lifelong, 212, 327–337, 348, 356, 359, 362, 372, 374–377, 440
procreative, 328, 372–373, 378, 380–381
unitive, 328, 372–373, 376, 378, 380, 382
See also Matrimony

Mary, Blessed Virgin
faith. *See* Faith, of Mary
fiat, 395
full of grace. *See* Grace, full of
Immaculate Conception, 88, 235, 270, 278–279, 310
model for all Christians, 278, 395
Mother of all Christians, 88, 156, 278, 344
Mother of Jesus, 21, 29, 88, 92, 94, 100, 130, 134, 156, 278–280, 344, 395, 415, 425, 437
Mother of the Church, 155–156
Queen of Heaven and Earth, 278–279
Theotokos, 100
"yes." *See* Mary, *fiat*

Mary, mother of James, 123

Mary Magdalene, 123–124

Mass
obligation to attend Sunday, 29–30, 68, 277–281, 283
Holy Days and, 29, 278–279, 283
See also Eucharist; Last Supper; Sunday

Masturbation, 347, 350–352, 382

Matthew, St., 288

Matrimony (Sacrament)
effects, 360–363
matter and form, 357
ordinary minister, 356–358
recipient, 356–358
rite, 356, 360
Scripture and, 354
See also Marriage

Maximillian Kolbe, St., 136, 138

Messiah. *See* Jesus Christ, Messiah

Modesty
in dress, 342–344
virtue, 135, 137, 344

Monica, St., 424

Moral act, 50, 56, 63–83, 242, 349, 351

Moral deliberation, 69–71

Moral law
freedom and, 52, 59, 81
justice and, 64–66
objective, xii, 3, 63, 234, 242
reason and, 6, 68, 78
Revelation and, 7, 49, 53, 55, 80, 86
universal, 6, 63

Moses, 7, 15–17, 29, 55, 85, 86, 98, 105, 107, 221, 221–222, 255–256, 258, 332, 335, 337, 368, 388, 403, 417

Mother Teresa. *See* Teresa of Calcutta

N

Name
God's (revealed to Moses), 16–18
Jesus', 18, 134, 215, 294–295, 387, 391, 401, 403, 422, 432

Natural law
available to reason, 54, 65
revealed, 54–55, 66

New Evangelization. *See* Evangelization

Nicolas Steno, Bl., 253

O

Object. *See* Moral deliberation

Occult, 27–28

One (mark of the Church). *See* Church, One

Original Sin. *See* Fall, Original Sin
Our Father. See Lord's Prayer

P

Padre Pio. *See* Pio of Pietrelcina
Papal infallibility, 10, 146
Passions
- Fall and, 42–43, 45, 50–51
- self-control and, 51–52
- sin and, 6

Paul, St. (Apostle), 150, 242, 279
Paul VI, St., 196, 317, 382
Penance (act), 95, 290, 296–297, 299, 301, 303–304, 344, 351, 407
Penance and Reconciliation (Sacrament)
- conditions, 270, 298–304
- development, 296–298
- effects, xii, 79, 81, 210, 270, 295, 304–306, 323
- healing and, 213, 286, 288, 325
- matter and form, 298–299
- need for a priest, 293–296
- ordinary minister, 209, 294–295, 400
- recipient (penitent), 295–296, 300–301
- rite, 299
- Scripture and, 293

Pentecost, 21, 127–128, 131, 134–135, 241–242, 245–246, 280
- Church and. *See* Church, Pentecost and

Persons of the Trinity, xv, 13, 15–33, 94, 98–99, 128, 149, 160, 206, 226–227, 346, 378, 410, 422. *See also* Father; Holy Spirit; Jesus Christ, Son of God
Peter, St., 29, 82–83, 98, 123, 126–127, 134, 141, 145–146, 152, 242, 246, 260, 279, 289, 438
Pharisee, 111–112, 126, 282, 289, 335, 412, 423
Pio of Pietrelcina, St., 407
Plato, xii, 54, 99
Pontius Pilate, 113–115, 118, 122, 224
Pornography, 77, 157–158, 339, 347, 350–352
Prayer
- challenges to, 432–435
- expressions of, 426–230
- for the dead, 143, 317–318
- forms of, 422–426, 433
- Jesus', 390, 410–417. *See also* Jesus, Agony in the Garden
- *Lord's. See Lord's Prayer*
- perfect. *See* Eucharist, perfect prayer

Presbyterate. *See* Priest
Priest / presbyterate
- *in persona Christi capitis*, 107, 263, 294, 394–395, 404–406
- ministerial, 391–393, 405
- ordained by Christ, 399–401
- Scripture and. *See* Last Supper

Priesthood
- common, 215, 250, 388, 391–392
- ministerial. *See* Priest, ministerial

Private property, 162–163, 190–191, 193–194, 196
Prodigal Son, 291–293, 296, 301, 319, 418, 423
Purgatory, 122, 143, 299, 309, 312, 315–318, 320. *See also* Prayer, for the dead

R

Racism, 63, 70, 162, 172, 185, 195, 201
Real Presence. *See* Eucharist, Real Presence
Reason (human)
- ability to know God, 19
- effects of sin. *See* Fall, effects
- faith and. *See* Faith, reason and

moral law and. *See* Moral law, reason and
natural law and. *See* Natural law, available to reason
Relativism (moral), 75–76, 440–441
Restitution, 120, 192, 303, 315
Resurrection. *See* Jesus Christ, Resurrection
Revelation
fullness in Christ, 19, 66, 133, 151
God's self-disclosure (Divine), ix, 2, 6–11, 13, 20, 23, 29, 55–56. *See also* Name, God's
supernatural, 31, 64
natural, 16, 38, 54
necessity, 28
Rosary
(prayer), x, 217, 318, 385, 431
mysteries of. *See* "Thematic Index" (p. 445)

S

Sacrament
divine institution, 205–206, 211, 216
matter and form, 207–209
ordered toward human nature, 216–218
See "Thematic Index" (p. 446) for individual Sacraments
Sacramental, 217–218. *See also* Rosary
Sacramental Seal, 238, 242, 296
Sacred Deposit. *See* Tradition
Sacrilege, 28, 301
Saint. *See* Communion, of Saints
Satan. *See* Devil
Scripture (Sacred)
canon, 8, 12
infallibility, 9, 35
senses of (literal and spiritual), 10–11, 35
Tradition and, 12–13
Seal of Confession. *See* Sacramental Seal
Self-control. *See* Passions, self-control and
Sexism, 162, 172, 201
Sin
culpability, 67–69, 71–74, 117, 169, 180–181, 236, 292, 301, 315, 351
gravity, 18, 30, 50–51, 56, 70–73, 77, 79, 117, 126, 165, 168–169, 171, 174–175, 180–182, 190, 197–198, 215, 269, 274, 280, 287, 293, 296–297, 300–302, 315, 318, 320, 352, 374, 379
loss of sense, 73–77
mortal, 50–51, 72, 270, 274, 293–294, 297, 301, 304, 315
Original. *See* Fall, Original Sin and
reality of, 49, 73, 75
venial, 50, 72, 274, 293, 298, 300, 305
Slander, 187, 189
Social justice, 162, 198
Social media, 188–189
Solidarity, 197–201
Son of God. *See* Jesus Christ
Stem-cell research, 183–184, 383
Subsidiarity, 162, 166
Sunday
fulfillment of the Sabbath, 30, 256–257
obligation to attend Mass, 29–30, 68, 257, 277–281
rest, 281–283
Superstition, 27, 29, 218, 387
Surrogate parent, 382

T

Ten Commandments, *See* Commandments, Ten
Teresa of Avila, St., 25, 324, 395, 416, 426, 428
Teresa of Calcutta, St., 276, 438
Theology of the body, 345–347, 352

Therese of Lisieux, St., 147, 395
Thomas, St. (Apostle), 123
Thomas Aquinas, St., 2, 49, 54–55, 65, 70, 117, 160, 191–193, 267, 416
Thomas More, St., 250
Tradition (Sacred), 8, 10–13, 18, 88, 206, 225, 226, 257, 323, 430
  Scripture and. *See* Scripture, Tradition and
Transgender. *See* Gender identity
Transubstantiation. *See* Eucharist, Real Presence
Trinity. *See* Father; Holy Spirit; Jesus Christ, Son of God; Persons of the Trinity
Truth, 8, 64, 79, 154, 190, 390, 439, 442

U

Unity (mark of the Church). *See* Church, One
Universal destination of goods, 193–194, 196

W

Will (human), 5, 40, 51–54, 65, 68, 144, 274, 291, 310, 318
Word (of God), ix–x, 7, 9–10, 12–13, 22–24, 64, 86, 95, 101–104, 120, 215, 229–230, 239, 262–263, 269, 278, 281, 284, 312, 375, 388, 392–393, 403, 410, 428, 437
Worship
  of God (adoration), xii, 27, 30, 115, 216, 255, 267–268, 271–272, 281, 335, 418, 422, 430. *See also* Eucharist, Adoration
  proper, 27, 29, 63

Y

Yahweh (YHWH). *See* Name, God's